THE DRAGONS AND THE SNAKES

David Kilcullen is a professor in the School of Humanities and Social Sciences of the University of New South Wales and a professor of practice in global security at Arizona State University. A former soldier and diplomat, he served as a counterinsurgency advisor during the wars in Iraq and Afghanistan. Dr Kilcullen is also the author of the highly acclaimed *The Accidental Guerrilla, Out of the Mountains,* and *Blood Year.*

THE DRAGONS
AND THE SNAKES
HOW THE REST
LEARNED TO FIGHT
THE WEST

DAVID KILCULLEN

SCRIBE

Melbourne • London

Scribe Publications
18–20 Edward St, Brunswick, Victoria 3056, Australia

Published by Scribe 2020

This edition published by arrangement with C. Hurst and Co.
(Publishers) Ltd., London. All rights reserved.

Printed and bound in Australia by Griffin Press, part of Ovato

Scribe Publications is committed to the sustainable use of natural
resources and the use of paper products made responsibly from
those resources.

9781925849158 (paperback edition)
9781925938272 (e-book)

A catalogue record for this book is available from the National Library
of Australia

scribepublications.com.au

CONTENTS

Introduction 1

Note on Terminology 7

1 The Dragon and the Snakes 9

2 Adaptive Enemies 38

3 Woolsey's Snakes 66

4 Liminal Warfare 115

5 Conceptual Envelopment 167

6 Ebb Tide of the West 216

Epilogue: A Better Peace? 251

Acknowledgments 257

Notes 263

Index 307

Introduction

I
t was mid-2012, as I was wrapping up *Out of the Mountains*, the book on future urban conflict that I finished later that year, when I began seriously researching the issues that underpin this book—the return of great-power military confrontation, the convergence of state and nonstate adversaries on remarkably similar operating methods despite their radically different points of origin, and the notion that something in the environment created by Western military dominance since the Cold War might be driving that convergent evolution.

Already clear was the growing influence (and increasingly sophisticated methodology) of competitive or actively hostile nation-states that were exploiting our exclusive focus on terrorism, seeking to fill the geopolitical, economic, and security vacuum we had left as we became bogged down in the wars of occupation in Iraq and Afghanistan.

The signs were everywhere if one cared to look: the Chinese-constructed container terminal on Colombia's Pacific coast, as well as Chinese military advisers and hardware appearing across Africa and in Sri Lanka's fight against the Tamil Tigers; the Russian air cargo companies dominating licit and illicit transport operations in the Horn of Africa; Russian private military contractors appearing in Syria to support Bashar al-Assad's regime; Russia's decision to reopen its signals intelligence station at Lourdes, Cuba, directly targeting the United States; the Iranian and North Korean advisers and military operators in Venezuela; the competition for influence among Turkey, Saudi Arabia, and Iran (and their Gulf allies) in the Horn of Africa and across North Africa—all of these were signs that, as we had doubled down on the costly fight against terrorism, other risks and competitors were growing apace.

To be sure, the signs were not as clear in 2012 as they are now. China's first aircraft carrier, the *Liaoning*, had yet to put to sea, and Beijing's island-building efforts across the collection of rocks, shoals, and atolls that it claims in the disputed South China Sea were just beginning, while the Chinese garrisons, radar jammers, anti-aircraft systems, and anti-ship missiles that now dot the area had still not yet been deployed. Russia had invaded and occupied Georgian territory, launched cyberattacks against Estonia, and promoted a frozen conflict between Azerbaijan and Armenia. But the seizure of Crimea and Moscow's barely covert invasion of Ukraine were still in the future, as was the shooting down of Malaysian Airlines Flight MH17 by a Russian anti-aircraft missile and Russia's return as a key player in the Middle East via its overt military intervention in Syria.

Iran had yet to expand its footprint in Syria and Yemen, its operations in Iraq remained clandestine though dangerous, and its nuclear program (suspended in 2003) was the subject of ongoing, secret negotiations with the Obama administration in the lead-up to the Joint Comprehensive Plan of Action, the Iranian nuclear deal, which became public in 2015. North Korea's new leader, Kim Jong-un, had yet to show his ruthless mettle, being regarded by many observers as young, callow, and likely to remain under the thumb of powerful generals and older relatives (many of whom he later killed). And while the Arab Spring was in full retreat by mid-2012, the

Benghazi attack had yet to hammer home the failure of the Libya intervention. And the rise of Islamic State was still a niche concern for Iraq watchers who struggled to gain attention or traction from a US administration that considered the Iraq War done and dusted the moment we withdrew, as if leaving the conflict equated to ending it.

By early 2013, I was researching and writing, conceptualizing the new strategic environment through the lens of James Woolsey's testimony exactly two decades earlier, in 1993, in which he had talked of the West slaying a large dragon (the Soviet Union) only to find itself facing a bewildering variety of snakes in the post–Cold War environment. By the end of 2013—particularly after Moscow's diplomatic victory in resolving the crisis created by the Eastern Ghouta nerve agent attack in Syria and Washington's failure to enforce its own redline over Assad's use of chemical weapons—it seemed clear that the dragon, in the form of Putin's Russia, was back. We were dealing with both state and nonstate adversaries, at the same time and in many of the same places.

But it seemed equally clear that, in the intervening twenty years, the dragons (including China) had been watching and learning, figuring out how to fight like the snakes that had so bedeviled us since the Cold War, and particularly since 2003. While keeping a wary eye on Iraq, and as our field teams continued to support humanitarian and stability efforts in Syria and Afghanistan, my research team and I were increasingly focused on developments in Russian and Chinese asymmetric and unconventional warfare, which appeared as capable adjuncts to these countries' military modernization and expansive political and economic programs. But then all of us were forced into a massive detour.

The breakout of Islamic State across Iraq and Syria in the spring and summer of 2014 was not just a huge setback for the United States and western countries seeking to stabilize Iraq. Nor was it merely a massive embarrassment for a US president who had described ISIS as a "junior varsity" team just months earlier and talked of the receding tide of war only days before ISIS tanks captured Iraq's second-largest city, Mosul, in June 2014. It also showed that—just as the dragons had been learning from the snakes over the past decade or more—nonstate actors were copying state techniques and deploying levels of technology and lethality previously restricted to governments.

My book *Blood Year* (published in 2016) chronicled the rise of ISIS, but it came out too early to track the group's eventual, albeit partial demise in 2017–18, as its core pseudo-state "caliphate" in Iraq and Syria lost control of the territory and population it had seized in its initial wave of success, eventually to be extinguished as a territorial entity in March 2019. Its worldwide international network survived—and continues to inspire and direct attacks—while a dozen ISIS-aligned groups ("provinces," *wilayat*) remain active from Afghanistan to Nigeria and from Libya to the Philippines. But even as I traveled across the region, spoke with numerous sources from Iraq, Syria, and North Africa, and finished *Blood Year*, I kept returning to the main ideas of the earlier book on convergent evolution, the way in which unlike actors confronting a similar environment can come to resemble each other. And to be sure, ISIS provides a striking example of one of these ideas—the increasing adoption by nonstate actors of statelike tactics, techniques, and technologies.

ISIS thought of itself as a state, levying taxes, establishing civilian governance structures, selling electricity and water, and trading oil on the international market. It fought like a state, adopting conventional tactics borrowed from nation-state adversaries or derived from the large portion of its leaders trained in Soviet tactics under Saddam Hussein. It acquired tanks, artillery, at least a couple of working aircraft, rockets, and mortars, and sought to seize and hold cities and control populations using remarkably conventional means. Its strategy—which amounted to seizing and holding territory, then expanding that territory through conventional military conquest supported by guerrillas, terrorist cells, and subversion efforts in its enemies' hinterland—was entirely statelike. The group's horrific atrocities and its mastery of social media tended to distract from its utterly statelike strategic approach. And though ISIS was eventually defeated as a territorial entity—in part because of its insistence on conventional warfare and on continuing to hold cities and control populations rather than melting away, as a traditional nonstate actor might have done—it came terrifyingly close to success.

If ISIS represented one-half of the equation, the other major developments of 2014–15—Russia's seizure of Crimea, its use of guerrillas and proxies in combination with conventional armored battlegroups to invade Ukraine, the shooting down of MH17, and direct military intervention in Syria—illustrated the other. For, clearly, Russian efforts were not solely conventional or statelike; on the contrary, just as ISIS borrowed techniques, organizations, and equipment from nation-states, Russia proved increasingly adept at drawing from the playbook of nonstate actors. Sponsorship of militias and guerrilla groups (both in the physical world and via cyber militias and botnets online), the promotion of coups and separatist movements, the application of agitation and propaganda to destabilize adversaries, the manipulation of migration, the assassination of political opponents, the weaponization of energy supplies, and election interference all showed Russia's willingness to adopt the techniques of nonstate actors while pursuing nation-state objectives. The election of Donald Trump in the United States, Britain's vote to leave the European Union, Catalonian separatism in Spain, an attempted coup in Montenegro, and ongoing attacks on Russia's neighbors in the Baltic and Caucasus regions all showed signs of increasingly active Russian political and information warfare. At the same time, the unveiling of a series of advanced new weapon systems and a newfound swagger in international affairs showed that Russia was back to stay.

Meanwhile in the Pacific, South Asia, Latin America, and Africa, China's military, commercial, and industrial expansionism was demonstrating that other nation-states could play a similar game, drawing from a nonconventional playbook in order to achieve traditional, conventional goals. China's trade practices, industrial and economic espionage, political interference, and military modernization showed the country's aspirations to attain global great-power status, its mercantilist ambitions, and its ability to fill the vacuum left by Western loss of credibility and tunnel vision on terrorism after 2001. Again, we saw a nation-state drawing on a combination of conventional and nonstate means (as well as innovative approaches like the building of island fortresses in the South China Sea and the use of commercial loans to acquire ports and naval bases) in order to achieve its goals. And Iran and North Korea—both nation-states that had benefited from our distraction after 9/11 to advance nuclear programs supported by unconventional warfare, cyberwarfare, and terrorism—were also applying creative combinations of conventional and nonconventional means.

This book is the result of my efforts—both before the detour of 2014 and with renewed vigor since 2016—to make sense of what is happening in the global security environment as great-power and nation-state competition returns, the dominant global position of Western powers (more or less a given after the end of the Cold War) erodes, and warfare assumes new forms that combine old tools and techniques in new ways. It is also the result—tentative and partial—of an attempt to combine knowledge from the fields of military innovation and geopolitical analysis with those of evolutionary science and anthropology to explain both how, and why, this is happening. Ultimately, it is also an effort to confront the ways in which our own behavior since 9/11 has brought the dragons back and consider what we can do to deal with both dragons and snakes into the future. These efforts seem more relevant now than ever.

If there is one takeaway from the chapters that follow, it is that the military model pioneered by US forces in the 1991 Gulf War—the high-tech, high-precision, high-cost suite of networked systems that won the Gulf War so quickly and brought Western powers such unprecedented battlefield dominance in the quarter century since then—is no longer working. Our enemies have figured out how to render it irrelevant, have caught up or overtaken us in critical technologies, or have expanded their concept of war beyond the narrow boundaries within which our traditional approach can be brought to bear. They have adapted, and unless we too adapt our decline is only a matter of time.

Denver, Colorado
April 2019

Note on Terminology

Throughout this book, I use the capitalized term "Western" or "the West" to describe a particular military methodology, along with the group of countries whose warfighting style is characterized by that methodology. In essence, it is an approach to war that emphasizes battlefield dominance, achieved through high-tech precision engagement, networked communications, and pervasive intelligence, surveillance, and reconnaissance (ISR). It is characterized by an obsessive drive to minimize casualties, a reluctance to think about the long-term consequences of war, a narrow focus on combat, and a lack of emphasis on war termination—the set of activities needed in order to translate battlefield success into enduring and favorable political outcomes.

The West, as I use the term in this book, is thus both a military and a geopolitical concept: it means the loose collection of countries, most of which are allied or aligned with the United States, that fight using methods pioneered and perfected by the United States and that often collaborate in coalitions or international institutions. This is not the same as European civilization—countries that apply Western military means include non-European nations such as Japan, South Korea, and Taiwan, for example—and this book is mainly about military, not cultural or political, matters.

Still, we should not forget that the modern world (for good or ill) was largely built by nation-states in that group, applying Western military methods. Indeed, the world we live in, with the growth of trade, the stamping out of slavery, the creation of global institutions for conflict prevention and dispute resolution, and the spread of free enterprise, human rights, and democracy, depends—to a far greater extent than some might wish or imagine—on two continuous centuries of British and then American global naval supremacy. Today's Western-led world order, then, relies to a great extent on the efficacy of Western military methods. And if this book is right, that efficacy is fading.

1

The Dragon and the Snakes

S hortly before 10 a.m. on a windy, freezing Tuesday morning in February 1993, James Woolsey seated himself at the long oak witness table in room 216 of the Hart Senate Office Building, on Constitution Avenue in Washington, DC.[1]

Woolsey was a Cold War insider—a Democrat by party affiliation and a lawyer by training, he had been under secretary of the navy in 1977–79 during the administration of President Jimmy Carter, represented the United States in nuclear disarmament talks with the Soviet Union, and served as general counsel to the Senate Armed Services Committee at the height of the Vietnam War. In 1989–91, in the closing months of the Cold War, he had served in Vienna as US ambassador to the negotiation on Conventional Armed Forces in Europe, which established limits on conventional (i.e., non-nuclear) weapons in Europe and mandated the destruction of excess weaponry. Now he was appearing before the Senate Select

elligence, seeking confirmation as newly inaugurated
on's director of central intelligence—chief of CIA and,
of the vast US intelligence bureaucracy.

r, Woolsey would succeed Robert Gates, a future secretary of ut to take up his appointment, he would first have to convince the committee—including a future secretary of state, Senator John
Kerry, who had been extremely critical of US covert operations and intelligence activities abroad—that he had what it took to lead the intelligence
community into a new era.

The Cold War had ended fourteen months earlier, in December 1991,
with the formal dissolution of the Soviet Union. But the United States
already found itself committed to a messy intervention in Somalia,
experiencing "mission creep" toward the battle that would kill eighteen
Americans and thousands of Somalis within months of Woolsey's testimony and be immortalized in Mark Bowden's book *Black Hawk Down*.[2] In
Europe, Washington and its NATO allies were facing the bloody breakup
of Yugoslavia and dealing with an emerging power vacuum in post-Soviet
space. In the Middle East, US aircrews were operating no-fly zones around
the clock over northern and southern Iraq, and US troops were conducting
a humanitarian operation in Iraqi Kurdistan while dealing with a huge
range of threats in other regions.

In the course of his long (and ultimately successful) confirmation
hearing, Woolsey made a defining statement on the era to come. "In many
ways," he said, "today's threats are harder to observe and understand than
the one that was once presented by the USSR":

> The proliferation of weapons of mass destruction and ballistic
> missiles to carry them; ethnic and national hatreds that can metas-
> tasize across large portions of the globe; the international narcotics
> trade; terrorism; the dangers inherent in the West's dependence on
> Mid-East oil; new economic and environmental challenges—these
> and a number of other important threats to our security and our
> interests present intelligence problems that are extraordinary in
> their complexity and difficulty. And these challenges, if unmet, can

decidedly affect our daily lives for the worse. Our two surrounding oceans don't isolate us anymore. Yes, we have slain a large dragon, but we live now in a jungle filled with a bewildering variety of poisonous snakes. And in many ways the dragon was easier to keep track of.[3]

All the challenges of the 1990s—the proliferation of weapons of mass destruction (WMD), the rise of transnational terrorism, narcotics trafficking, organized crime, environmental and energy risks, ethno-sectarian conflict—are stated or implied in Woolsey's list of snakes, a catalog of threats that came to define the first two decades of the post–Cold War world. Indeed, his prediction so accurately described the following twenty years that it's no exaggeration to say that we lived, then, in a Woolseyan security environment, where threats emanated mostly from weak or failing states and from nonstate actors (snakes) rather than from capable state adversaries (dragons).

For two decades after Woolsey's testimony, great-power confrontation and state-on-state conflict (issues that were front and center during the Cold War) retreated, while day-to-day military operations and the strategic attention of policymakers focused on a greatly expanded range of nonstate or intrastate conflicts. The first decade of that Woolseyan era—from Woolsey's Senate testimony in February 1993 until the US-led invasion of Iraq almost exactly ten years later, in March 2003—was defined by chaos across a swath of post-Soviet space in Europe, the fracturing of nation-states in Africa and Asia, and a series of far-flung peacekeeping and humanitarian interventions.

I came of age in that world, as a young infantry officer in the Australian Army. My generation—those of us who enlisted or graduated from Western military academies just as the Cold War was ending—served throughout the 1990s in a series of chaotic, ambiguous operations in places such as Cambodia, Bosnia, Rwanda, Somalia, Cyprus, Haiti, Kosovo, East Timor, and Sierra Leone. Skills necessitated by high-intensity war—urban combat, armored warfare, air-to-air combat, anti-submarine warfare, air defense, contested logistics, national mobilization or defense against weapons of mass destruction—atrophied in many major armed forces. Some countries ended Cold War–era conscription, while others stood down their border security forces or did away with elite mobile formations. High-tech weapon systems were canceled by bureaucrats or politicians looking for a "peace dividend." For professional soldiers, training for state-on-state conflict was something we dutifully tried to squeeze in around our real day jobs, which increasingly consisted of peacekeeping, counterinsurgency, humanitarian reconstruction, counterterrorism, and military advisory missions.

To be sure, these missions often involved high threat levels (even, occasionally, intense combat, as in Mogadishu), but they generally lacked clear enemies against whom traditional military power could be brought to bear. In 1993, US secretary of state Madeleine Albright famously asked General Colin Powell, then chairman of the Joint Chiefs of Staff, "What's the point of having this superb military that you're always talking about, if we can't use it?"[4] In the same vein, a 1992 book on Australian defense strategy was titled *Threats without Enemies*, while in Europe the French theorists Loup Francart and Jean-Jacques Patry characterized military operations of that era as *contre-guerre*, "counter-war"—where the phenomenon of war itself (not a particular armed adversary) was the enemy and the fundamental goal was to end the conflict, not to win it.[5]

In the second decade of the Woolseyan era, from March 2003 onward, as the ill-judged invasion of Iraq slid rapidly from a triumphal three-week blitzkrieg to a messy reconstruction mission, then into a horrifically violent insurgency, the United States and allied countries focused their resources and attention almost entirely on combating terrorism. Those of us who had cut our teeth in the peacekeeping and stabilization operations of the 1990s made the sudden transition to large-scale counterinsurgency in Afghanistan and Iraq, and smaller-scale irregular or unconventional warfare missions in Somalia, the Philippines, and numerous other African and Asian countries, as part of a global war on terrorism (GWOT).

Our peers in the intelligence community likewise found themselves increasingly engaging in lethal combat operations, as CIA and other agencies became warfighting organizations in their own right, allegedly (according to a series of published accounts by agency insiders) launching their own drone strikes, fielding shadowy armies of thousands of local fighters led and trained by paramilitary operations officers, and leading Counter-Terrorism Pursuit Teams (CTPTs) on raids that were increasingly hard to distinguish from straight-up military operations.[6]

The wars in Iraq and Afghanistan were much more lethal than anything we'd done in the 1990s, but the difference was one of degree, not kind: like the missions of the 1990s, our post-9/11 campaigns dealt with a multiplicity of nonstate threats and sought primarily to end conflicts and stabilize local environments so that we could leave rather than conquer and occupy. To extend Woolsey's analogy, from 1993 we focused on snakes rather than dragons, but from 2001—intensely so after 2003—we narrowed our gaze to just one snake (terrorism) and one subset of terrorism (Salafi jihadism, the variant of Islamic extremism exemplified by Osama bin Laden) as we sought to "cut the head off the snake"—to repurpose bin Laden's own phrase—by killing or capturing Al Qaeda leaders.[7]

A series of strategy documents in this period (foremost among them the 2002 *National Security Strategy of the United States*) read as if the sole organizing principle of national security and foreign policy would henceforth be countering terrorism.[8] "Terrorists are organized to penetrate open societies and to turn the power of modern technologies against us," the 2002 strategy argued, claiming that "the gravest danger our Nation faces lies at the crossroads of radicalism and technology":

> To defeat this threat, we must make use of every tool in our arsenal—military power, better homeland defenses, law enforcement, intelligence, and vigorous efforts to cut off terrorist financing. The war against terrorists of global reach is a global enterprise of uncertain duration. America will help nations that need our assistance in combating terror. And America will hold to account nations that are compromised by terror, including those who harbor terrorists—because the allies of terror are the enemies of civilization. The United States and countries cooperating with us must not allow the terrorists to develop new home bases. Together, we will seek to deny them sanctuary at every turn.[9]

One problem with this formulation was the idea of terrorism as a single, unified opponent—one that could stand in for a traditional state-based adversary and be considered to have an overarching intent and objectives. Nobody, of course, believed that Salafi terrorism was monolithic—the tendency of jihadist groups to splinter, turn on one another, and engage in bloody internecine conflict over the most hair-splittingly banal doctrinal differences was well understood.[10] Likewise, other varieties of terrorists—Shi'a groups such as Hezbollah sponsored by Iran, narcoterrorists such as the FARC in Colombia, and European separatist groups such as the Irish Republican Army and the Basque ETA—had little in common with jihadism. But the need to apply military decision-making processes, designed for the dragon during the Cold War, to the post-9/11 snakes, led by default to two-sided adversarial planning: as the *National Security Strategy* conceptualized the environment, there was something called "terrorism" and its allies on one side, with "civilization" and its allies on the other. This in turn led to the notion of terrorists being organized, structured, and motivated by long-term strategic goals that were equivalent, though diametrically opposed, to ours. This planning construct, always artificial, proved increasingly hard to sustain over time.

Far from being organized and focused, the enemies we fought in Iraq and Afghanistan turned out to be fractured into a perplexing multiplicity of competing groups. Rather than a single worldwide conspiratorial network guided by the invisible hand of Osama and his henchmen, as the threat evolved after 9/11 terrorism proved a much more diffuse and variegated phenomenon, an agile and adaptive threat complex capable of rapidly morphing into an almost infinite variety of forms. As I discuss in Chapter 2, some of this adaptation was driven by conscious learning, as jihadist groups gained experience fighting us, but much of it was an unconscious, blind, organic process of natural selection operating at both the individual and group levels, as selective pressure created by the GWOT killed off weak, stupid, or unlucky individuals and groups, while those that exhibited strongly adaptive traits prospered and grew, surviving to pass their ideological and tactical DNA on to the next generation. A process of convergent evolution emerged (again, discussed in Chapter 2) where multiple simultaneous mutations in the terrorist threat prompted responses from many independent counterterrorist actors, which in turn reshaped the environment, drove the next evolutionary cycle, and spawned the next generation of terrorist actors and techniques. This was a multilateral, emergent, systemic process that looked much more like an ecological system than like any traditional military opponent.

By 2019, with the emergence, temporary triumph, and ultimate collapse of Islamic State's pseudo-nation-state "caliphate" in Iraq and Syria, Salafi jihadism had become little more than a cast of mind, a branding device, or a repertoire of common techniques—increasingly defined by methodology rather than ideology. It was an ecosystem of loosely related networks, fluid organizational structures, and temporary, shifting alliances of convenience among ad hoc cells and self-radicalized or remotely radicalized individuals. The "jihadist tendency" (to borrow a European political term) was promoted more through violent memes than via any formal doctrine or organizational entity. This made the notion of treating terrorism—even "terrorists of global reach"—as a single strategic adversary, an entity equivalent in planning terms to a state opponent, something of a logical dead end.

More problematic was our post-9/11 tendency to enshrine terrorism at the apex of the threat pyramid, with transnational jihadism taking the place of world communism, the greater Middle East becoming the new central front, and Al Qaeda and its extended networks assuming the role of the new main enemy in a replay of the Cold War. Terrorism was certainly a grave danger. But was it "the gravest," as the 2002 *National Security Strategy* claimed? Likewise, countering it was—and certainly still is—a necessary endeavor. But strategy is about choices, prioritizing a range of necessary endeavors and grave dangers, of balancing, resourcing, and sequencing multiple tasks, all of which are important.

Treating the complete defeat of terrorism as the single non-negotiable goal of what the 2002 strategy called a "global enterprise of uncertain duration" and the effort to "hold to account nations that are compromised by terror" ran the risk of indulging an obsessive prioritization of one particular nonstate threat to the exclusion of a vastly wider (and cumulatively more dangerous) array of challenges and national security interests. Thus, far from being a break with the 1990s, Western strategy after 9/11 took the post–Cold War focus on nonstate threats to its logical extreme. No state actor or conventional threat was available, so we devoted our superb military (in Albright's phrase) to counterterrorism.

And we ran with it, hard. The 2002 *National Security Strategy's* legislative counterpart was the 2001 *Authorization for the Use of Military Force* (AUMF), which authorized the president "to use all necessary and appropriate force against those nations, organizations, or persons he determines planned, authorized, committed, or aided the terrorist attacks that occurred on September 11, 2001, or harbored such organizations or persons."[11] Nineteen years later, this 275-word resolution, passed by Congress only seven days after 9/11, following an extraordinarily brief debate—and with only two abstentions in the Senate and a single "nay" vote in the House of Representatives—remains the sole legal basis for an ongoing, worldwide, functionally unlimited campaign, a "forever war" against an ever-expanding collection of mutating groups most of which did not even exist on 9/11 and some of which—notably Islamic State—are active *enemies* of the groups the 2001 AUMF was designed to combat.[12]

In this period, in pursuance of our strategy and the 2001 AUMF, we deployed whatever we had at hand—including (with the sole exception of nuclear weapons) our complete range of exquisite and expensive high-end air, land, and maritime capabilities designed for state adversaries—against low-end, mostly land-based, nonstate actors. In 2004, Donald Rumsfeld, then secretary of defense, dismissed troops bound for Iraq who requested extra armored protection for their vehicles, saying, "You go to war with the army you have, not the army you might want."[13] He had apparently forgotten that the US government had started the Iraq War on its own initiative, at a time of its choosing, and so should have had ample opportunity to prepare "the army it might want"—if only political leaders had listened to the professionals who predicted the coming chaos. (One such professional, a friend in Iraq, responded philosophically, "Oh, well, you go to war with the politicians you have.")

The result was that hugely expensive capabilities, designed for high-intensity conflict against sophisticated state adversaries, were thrown into unequal combat against vastly poorer, less advanced (but stealthier and harder to find) enemies. And under the special circumstances of irregular warfare in Iraq and Afghanistan, these awesome weapons proved less effective than their exorbitant price tags might have suggested. In Iraq, Abrams tanks worth nine million dollars apiece were disabled by improvised explosive devices that cost, at most, thirty bucks to make.[14] In Afghanistan, in two separate incidents almost a decade apart, Chinook helicopters costing forty million dollars, carrying superbly (and very expensively) trained special operators, were shot out of the sky with rocket-propelled grenades (RPGs) worth a hundred dollars each and wielded by illiterate hill tribesmen.[15] Apart from the horrific loss of human life—rightly our main concern— even merely in resource terms this was little short of military malpractice.

Exacerbating this asymmetry of cost—what Rudyard Kipling, writing in 1886 of colonial wars fought in nearby terrain, called "arithmetic on the frontier"—we threw increasingly higher-end capabilities at increasingly greater unit cost and in growing numbers into the fray.[16] Between 2001 and 2016, for example, the US Navy, Air Force, and Marines flew the wings off a fleet of warplanes designed for air-to-air combat, air superiority, and strike missions, in high-tempo air campaigns against irregular terrorist and guerrilla fighters who lacked air forces or significant anti-air defenses. By 2016, the cost of the post-9/11 wars, counting veterans' expenditure but not including refurbishment of capabilities like these combat aircraft, was estimated at US$4.79 trillion.[17] And in 2017, when we needed these same capabilities in the face of Russian adventurism and North Korean aggression, some elements of the arsenal were all but worn out.

But what of the dragons—the peer and near-peer state threats that had dominated our threat perception during the Cold War? Although we will begin (in the next two chapters) by examining the snakes and their evolution after 9/11, this book is mostly about the dragons. It's about how state adversaries learned to fight the West by watching us struggle after 9/11, recovered from their eclipse after the Cold War, and transformed (and are continuing to transform) the global threat environment in the process.

State adversaries exploited the explosion of new, mostly Western-designed consumer technologies around the turn of this century, took advantage of our tunnel vision on terrorism, and blindsided us with new subversive, hybrid, and clandestine techniques of war. Those technologies and techniques eventually found their way back to terrorists and insurgents, creating boomerang effects that blurred traditional distinctions between domestic and international space, crime and conflict, peace and war, policing and military operations, and reality and "fake news." Western exhaustion and dysfunction, after two decades of the "global enterprise of uncertain duration," contributed to the bandwidth challenge we face today, and will face in the future. But before we get to that, we need to remind ourselves of the historical context—particularly, of developments during the decade between the end of the Cold War and 9/11.

DRAGONS TO SNAKES

Already by the late 1980s, it was clear that rather than one dragon, the conventional threat involved two greater and two lesser state adversaries, two big and two little dragons: Russia and China, on the one hand, and Iran and North Korea, on the other. Our preoccupation with weak states and nonstate threats gave these state adversaries (which I discuss in Chapters 4 and 5) breathing space to grow and—most important—the opportunity to watch and learn from our struggles. In particular, after 2003, as we struggled in Iraq and Afghanistan, the dragons designed new capabilities to sidestep our strengths while exploiting the weaknesses that became increasingly evident as each campaign progressed.

Two years before Woolsey's testimony, the hundred-hour ground campaign of the 1991 Gulf War had shown everyone how not to fight the West—in the open, conventionally arrayed, using force-on-force tactics, seeking decisive outcomes on the battlefield through orthodox maneuver. The so-called highway of death (where coalition warplanes destroyed up to two thousand Iraqi vehicles fleeing along Highway 80 near al-Jahra, west of Kuwait City, on 26 February 1991, and in the process incinerated thousands of Iraqi troops and a still-disputed number of civilians in a matter of minutes) had shown what the outcome would be.[18]

Less than twenty-four hours later, with the smoke still rising over al-Jahra, the Battle of 73 Easting—where a future national security adviser, then-captain H. R. McMaster, with nine Abrams tanks destroyed forty-four Iraqi armored vehicles and thirty trucks in twenty-three minutes with no losses whatsoever—showed that what was true in the air was equally so on the ground, as the Tawakalna Division, pride of Saddam's Republican Guard, was annihilated.[19] The combination of sophisticated air power, advanced armor, precision targeting, Global Positioning Systems (GPS), and the integration of air, land, and sea capabilities into a networked system-of-systems had given the United States unprecedented battlefield dominance within one narrowly defined conventional form of warfare. The rapid, humiliating disintegration of Saddam's forces during the long-delayed rematch, in 2003, only underscored that lesson.

But by contrast, from the 2003 invasion onward, our ineffectual struggles to stabilize Iraq and Afghanistan showed our adversaries exactly how to fight us—using a dynamic swarm of self-synchronized small groups, with lightly equipped, fast-moving irregular forces that operated in the shadows, staying below the detection threshold of our intelligence, surveillance, and reconnaissance (ISR) platforms, avoiding our major combat forces whenever possible, targeting the vulnerable populations and infrastructure we needed to protect, and attacking or subverting our (often unreliable) local partners.[20] By taking the long view, avoiding our strongest units and most capable combat assets, and targeting the weakest links in our system (usually civilian agencies, indigenous police, local government officials, and public opinion at home), our opponents in these wars of occupation managed to evolve a form of protracted resistance warfare that enabled them to survive while running out the clock, waiting until our publics lost patience, our partners lost ground, and our politicians pulled out.

To borrow a term from US defense policy, our adversaries had adopted a suite of "offset strategies" to sidestep our conventional power.[21] To me and to others who served in Iraq and Afghanistan during this period, these guerrilla enemies—who always seemed to skip around the corner just before we arrived, committing attacks (mostly on civilians) before disappearing into thin air—deserved the name Russian troops gave them during their own Afghan war: *dukhi*, "ghosts."

The *dukhi* employed asymmetric and irregular warfare techniques—ambushes, hit-and-run attacks, terrorism against soft targets, manipulation of populations and information—designed to avoid presenting us with actionable targets, and thereby rendering our superior size and firepower meaningless. But while we were struggling to deal with these nonstate offset strategies, state adversaries were busy developing offset strategies of their own.

These included weapons of mass destruction (nuclear, biological, and chemical weapons) designed to deter us from attacking them, along with disruptive technologies (laser systems, cyberweapons, thermobaric explosives, distributed command-and-control tools) that also aimed to render conventional forces irrelevant. Entire new classes of weapons—miniaturized non-nuclear electromagnetic pulse (EMP) devices that could knock out all electronic systems within a specific distance, advanced chemical weapons with fearsome lethality and novel mechanisms of action, ballistic missiles that could target ships on the move at sea, and hypersonic missiles that could evade advanced air defenses—were all in the works. While we were preoccupied with post–Cold War chaos in the 1990s and bogged down in the war on terrorism after 2001—beating the bushes to find the snakes—the dragons were watching and learning.

The most important of these dragons was the Russian Federation (whose adaptation I examine in detail in Chapter 4). As Woolsey told me in 2015 (and as CIA documents from the period, later declassified, confirm), he and other leaders of Western intelligence services were by no means complacent about the possibility of threats emerging from Russia during this period.[22] Still, for much of the 1990s, the Russians were absorbed in their own immense internal challenges of economic restructuring and rapid privatization, dealing with state weakness and the political and human fallout from the collapse of the Soviet Union and the economic "shock therapy" that followed.[23] The rise of the oligarchs, the descent of Russian society into a cesspool of gangsterism and corruption, the dissolution of the Soviet-era social compact, and the evaporation of economic certainty for millions of people in Russia and across the whole former Soviet empire seemed to be unfortunate internal issues for Russia. They looked like inherent "problems of post-Communism," to quote the title of an influential academic journal on the subject, rather than things that we in the West had inflicted on the Russians and that were storing up resentment which would later break into open confrontation.

Most consequentially, the geopolitical whiplash suffered by twenty-five million Soviet citizens who, in the words of future Russian president Vladimir Putin, "went to bed in one country and awoke in different ones" seemed like a manageable concern compared with the wave of revolutions and civil wars that remade eastern Europe, the Balkans, and the Baltic during the 1990s.[24] Likewise, the flood of former Soviet weaponry into Africa, Asia, and the Middle East, with whole Russian units leaving the service with their vehicles, weapons, aircraft, and equipment, and setting up shop as commercial traffickers (a process admirably chronicled in Matt Potter's *Outlaws Inc.*), was interpreted as just one more aspect of post-Soviet chaos rather than a portent of future conflict.[25]

Thus, at one level, Western leaders of the time saw the collapse of the Soviet Union as the inevitable outcome of Moscow's defeat in the Cold War. But as Woolsey told me and as others have written, for much of the 1990s it also seemed as if Russia and the West (defined by the expanding NATO alliance and centered on the United States) could be partners. It seemed as though Russia was becoming a "normal country"—normal, that is, by the standards of capitalist democracies, the victors of the Cold War, which increasingly equated their own institutions with universal norms.[26]

In this period Boris Yeltsin, Russia's first democratically elected president, developed a privately friendly (albeit often publicly contentious) relationship with President Bill Clinton, who saw the Russian leader's survival as inseparable from Russia's transition to democracy.[27] This subjective sense of partnership and shared destiny persisted to the end of Yeltsin's term, despite objective signs of an emerging geostrategic competition in eastern Europe and the Balkans. These were clearest in Moscow's support for Serbian leader Slobodan Milosevic during the brutal Balkan wars and during NATO's campaign to stop Serbian-sponsored ethnic cleansing in

Kosovo. The competition escalated in spectacular fashion during the "race for Pristina" in June 1999, when a Russian armored column sprinted into Kosovo to seize Pristina airport ahead of NATO airborne troops, provoking a tense months-long standoff.[28] Kosovo not only highlighted the enduring nature of competition between Russia and the West, but also triggered alarm in the Kremlin about NATO's advanced conventional capabilities, spurring Russian moves to rearm and modernize, and prompting a new doctrine emphasizing limited nuclear strikes to defeat a conventional enemy.[29]

Even so, Yeltsin's successor, Vladimir Putin, has claimed that at the start of his tenure in 2000 he proposed to President Clinton that Russia join NATO.[30] Clinton seems to have thought well of the new Russian president, while Putin developed a particularly close relationship with Italy's Silvio Berlusconi and an even closer relationship with former German chancellor Gerhard Schröder.[31] In 2001, the British prime minister Tony Blair originated the idea of a NATO-Russia Council to allow Putin's representatives to discuss security issues with NATO leaders before key decisions were taken, a move that British foreign secretary Jack Straw described as the "'funeral of the Cold War'. He added: 'With this, Russia comes out of the cold as a partner, ally and friend of NATO.'"[32]

Likewise, President George W. Bush sought constructive engagement to move beyond residual Cold War tensions, famously declaring at a press conference after his first meeting with Putin, in Slovenia in June 2001, that "I looked the man in the eye. I found him very straightforward and trustworthy—I was able to get a sense of his soul."[33] By May 2008, the Bush administration had proposed a US-Russia nuclear cooperation pact, a move opposed by a skeptical Congress and one that looked appropriately naive only eleven weeks later, when Russian tanks rolled into Georgia in the first seizure by force of one European state's territory by another since the Second World War.[34]

Despite the tensions triggered by the Georgia invasion, and not to be outdone in naïveté, the incoming Obama administration tried again a few months later. In February 2009, I sat in a crowded ballroom listening as Vice President Joseph Biden told the Munich Security Conference, an annual gathering of national security leaders, that the United States wanted to "press the reset button" and seek ways to make Russia a part of the solution to a range of security challenges.[35] A month later, meeting in Geneva, the incoming secretary of state, Hillary Clinton, presented Russian foreign minister Sergey Lavrov with an actual red plastic button. Lavrov agreed to put the gimmick on his desk, though only after politely pointing out that it was mislabeled with the Russian word for "overcharge," not "reset."[36]

President Obama and President Putin established a joint US-Russia Bilateral Presidential Commission with the goal of "strengthen[ing] and expand[ing] cooperation between the United States and Russia," including security cooperation, whereby "U.S. and Russian armed forces conducted numerous joint exercises, consultations, and exchanges" together.[37] Under this program, in 2012 Russian special operators received training from US special operations forces.[38] When the Russian Federation later established a new special operations command, known as KSSO, it drew directly on lessons from the United States and looked extraordinarily similar to the elite US Joint Special Operations Command (JSOC), on which it was patterned.[39] Chuck Hagel, President Obama's defense secretary, met with Russian defense minister Sergey Shoygu on 9 August 2013 and "stated that the Department of Defense is determined to overcome impediments to deeper cooperation by concluding necessary enabling agreements that will allow for improved information sharing, exchanges, joint exercises, and training."[40]

During this period, Russian observers attended NATO exercises, and there were Russian liaison officers at supreme headquarters in Belgium. Russian officers participated in some NATO training courses—between 2009 and 2013 there were Russian students in the classes I taught at the NATO defense college in Rome, for example, while Russians attended seminars at the US-funded George C. Marshall Center for European Security Studies in Germany. At least in the minds of some politicians, the era of great-power competition with Russia seemed firmly consigned to history. In a 2012 presidential debate, then-president Barack Obama mocked Republican candidate Mitt Romney for labeling Russia a geopolitical threat:

A few months ago, when you were asked what's the biggest geopolitical threat facing America, you said Russia, not Al Qaida; you said Russia. And the 1980s, they're now calling to ask for their foreign policy back because, you know, the Cold War's been over for 20 years. But Governor, when it comes to our foreign policy, you seem to want to import the foreign policies of the 1980s, just like the social policies of the 1950s and the economic policies of the 1920s.[41]

All these attempts—the effort to look into Putin's soul, NATO-Russia security cooperation, the reset button, President Obama's 1980s foreign policy quip (which provoked much hearty laughter at the time)—seem quaintly complacent now. They also underline the fact that, whatever the objective threat posed to Russia by Western interests and NATO expansion after the Cold War, in subjective terms European and American leaders throughout this period wanted to make a "normal" partner country of Russia, albeit always defining normality and partnership on their own terms. In effect, what Western leaders meant by normality was that Russians should accede to a unipolar, US-led international system, an unequal partnership where the price of prosperity was political subordination, a permanent second-tier status that many Russians (who remained intensely and justifiably proud of their civilization and heritage, whatever their reduced geopolitical circumstances after 1991) proved increasingly unwilling to accept.

Something similar happened in the case of China. When Woolsey testified in 1993, the People's Republic was certainly not the basket case that post-Soviet Russia had already become, but China's economy then was less than one-twentieth of its size today, and its military capabilities were far less developed.[42] Conventional wisdom among Western analysts was that the Chinese Communist Party's four-man ruling council—China's de facto cabinet—was focused almost entirely on economic and industrial development, seeking to pacify a restive population and cement the party's political position by trading economic liberalization and increased prosperity for continued Communist control.

China's Cold War conflicts, in Korea in 1950–53, with India in 1962, and with Vietnam in 1979, had been primarily land wars. By the 1990s,

Chinese forces—including the People's Liberation Army (PLA) and internal security agencies such as the newly created People's Armed Police, the Ministry of State Security, the Ministry of Public Security, and the local People's Security Bureaus—were large but burdened by antiquated technology, and many Western analysts saw them as bloated, inward-looking bureaucracies, consumed with managing internal dissent in the aftermath of the June 1989 Tiananmen Square massacre of democracy protesters. The very proliferation of internal security agencies, it was thought, showed where the country's focus lay, while the PLA had little capacity for or interest in regional or global power projection.

In fact, however, the 1991 Gulf War had profoundly influenced Chinese strategists' views of future war. Combined with the collapse of the Soviet Union at the end of that same year, the seemingly effortless defeat of Saddam Hussein's large, Soviet-style army by a numerically smaller but technologically much more advanced Western force had spooked Chinese planners, showing them the primacy of precision over mass. The unprecedentedly low American casualties and the almost unbelievable speed of the Iraqi collapse prompted debate within the Military Commission in Beijing and intense discussion in the war colleges. Chinese analysts were well aware that Iraqi forces had relied on a strategy of mass—using quantity to offset technological inferiority, much as China had done in Korea, India, and Vietnam—and had failed utterly.

At the same time, Chinese technical intelligence officers, who had examined Iraqi tanks and aircraft captured by Iran during the Iran-Iraq War, were well aware that Saddam's military technology outclassed their own. The two inescapable conclusions were, first, that China was at risk of attack by external aggressors now that the end of the Cold War had rendered it the sole remaining major Communist power and, second, that the PLA would be immensely outgunned in a future conflict. Chinese military thinkers began focusing on a dual-track strategy of peaceful economic and political engagement with the West (seeking to postpone or entirely avoid any possible conflict) while simultaneously accelerating their development of new military capabilities that emphasized quality over quantity.

Beyond hardware, Chinese military analysts looking at the lessons of 1991 emphasized the need to move from a land-centric view of conflict to one that encompassed joint (air, land, and sea) operations, and therefore increased the relative importance of air and naval forces in both strategic and capability terms. They also emphasized the lessons for information technology offered by the US "system of systems" during the Gulf War. Chinese military planners began to focus on the "informationalization" of the PLA, bringing it into the modern digital era and renewing their emphasis on political warfare, along with its key subcomponents—known to Chinese planners as the "three warfares"—of psychological warfare, public opinion warfare, and legal warfare or "lawfare."[43]

The historian Arthur Waldron, one of a handful of American analysts who worried at the time about Chinese military power, recounts that as the Cold War ended, "specialists on the People's Liberation Army began to hold informal, privately funded gatherings . . . I was among the first participants and remember well how, whenever I suggested that Chinese history indicated an overriding concern with military power, I was met with the most excruciatingly patient of explanations that my concerns had no foundation. China's military was obsolete. She sought to modernize it a bit and reach a threshold of minimal deterrence. But beyond that her government's primary concern was to raise living standards and the welfare of the population. We and our friends had nothing to fear, provided of course we did not somehow 'provoke' China, 'forcing' her to react by seeking military capabilities she would otherwise not have wanted."[44]

Through the 1990s—during that period of the Woolseyan security environment—Chinese leaders pursued their twin-track policy of "peaceful rise," which sought to avoid antagonizing potential rivals and emphasized economic integration with the globalizing economy, but simultaneously regarded other powers with suspicion and pursued multipolarity rather than accede to a US-dominated unipolar world.[45] Chinese leaders focused on economic integration with the global economy while simultaneously pursuing military modernization and vigorously defending China's national security interests and socialist ideology against Western encroachment.[46]

Through the second half of the 1990s, economic growth and global integration continued at the forefront of China's political posture. The return of Hong Kong in 1997 and Macau in 1999 were portrayed (and widely perceived) as the righting of colonial-era wrongs by a peaceful, primarily commercial nation, placing the country on a path to becoming, if not necessarily a "normal" democracy as Western leaders still hoped of Russia, then at least an integrated member of the Western-led international rules-based order. China's accession to the World Trade Organization in December 2001 underlined this process of "normalization" and was seen by analysts as representative of a Chinese embrace of globalization—with implied political as well as economic integration with the global (i.e., the Western-led) system.[47]

But in parallel, Chinese strategists sought capable military hardware—improved power projection platforms such as ships, submarines, aircraft, and advanced weapons systems—that would allow them to build a military that could deliver what Chinese leaders considered the country's rightful natural position: that of a global great power, which by definition meant sea, air, space, nuclear, and cyber capabilities, as well as more capable land forces. By the mid-2000s, through a combination of indigenous technological development, judicious purchases of dual-use and overtly military capabilities from abroad, technical and industrial intelligence gathering, and, increasingly, cyberespionage and reverse engineering, China's military had acquired an impressive array of new capabilities. Advanced fighter aircraft, stealthy drones, submarines, amphibious ships, and air and maritime platforms capable of long-range power projection emerged in the Chinese arsenal. Anti-access and area denial (A2/AD) systems such as anti-ship cruise missiles, long- and intermediate-range ballistic missiles, improved nuclear weapons, anti-satellite weapons, and space warfare systems also appeared. Chinese land forces went through a thorough modernization program, shrinking in size while improving in firepower, mobility, readiness, and morale, while special operations forces, cyberwarfare, intelligence agencies, and coast guard capabilities all grew dramatically. China's foreign policy increasingly sought to position Beijing at the center of world affairs while building a long-term pathway to global great-power status by expanding its influence in the Pacific and Indian Ocean basins and across Africa, South Asia, and Latin America.

If Russia and China, as global powers whose actions shaped thes Cold War, could be considered "big dragons," then Iran and North Korea might be considered "lesser dragons"—states that concerned policymakers during and after the Cold War, but primarily as regional players and so-called rogue states, asymmetric actors who bucked the Western-led international order and engaged in the export of terrorism, weapons pro-liferation, sponsorship of armed and criminal networks, and other nefar-ious activities.

Iran in the early 1990s was recovering from the devastating social and economic consequences of the Iran-Iraq War, which had killed more than 200,000 Iranians, wounded 400,000, and cost Iran US$500 million (more than a billion dollars in today's money, in a country whose gross domestic product was then only around $2,200 per capita). The war severely dam-aged several Iranian cities and destroyed critical infrastructure, including the oil industry and Iran's nascent nuclear power capability (initiated under the shah). Driven by animosity toward Tehran dating back to the 1979 Islamic Revolution and the ordeal of American hostages kidnapped when the US Embassy in Tehran was overrun, Washington had quietly supported Saddam Hussein during the conflict, though Henry Kissinger's alleged quip, "It's a pity they can't both lose," encapsulated American ambivalence toward the struggle between two deeply oppressive authoritarian regimes.[48]

When Saddam moved against Kuwait in August 1990 and the United States rapidly routed his military in early 1991, Iran's official position was one of neutrality—though many in Tehran viewed Saddam's defeat with a certain schadenfreude. But as the Gulf War ended, the regional situation was deeply unfavorable for Iran. American garrisons were now established in Qatar and Saudi Arabia; the United States had much greater influence in the region, and it was building close relationships with the United Arab Emirates, Saudi Arabia, and the other Gulf Arab states. A US air and mari-time presence now sat right on Iran's borders, at sea in the Arabian Gulf and in the air over northern and southern Iraq.

Saddam Hussein's regime was still intact and in control, however, and his 1991 Scud missile strikes on Israel and Saudi Arabia (as well as the discovery of his nuclear and chemical/biological weapons programs) highlighted the ongoing risk to Iran from Iraq's weapons programs, as well as the potential for a future nuclear Iraq. From 1993, America's "dual containment" strategy kept both Iran and Iraq under pressure by means of sanctions, embargoes, the occasional use of force (primarily against Iraq), and restrictions on international trade and finance.

Given these circumstances—a hostile external environment, the risk of a nuclear-armed regional rival in Iraq, and limited resources to rebuild their badly damaged conventional military—leaders in Tehran adopted a two-track approach: continuing and deepening the regime's investment in its nuclear weapons program while further building its capacity for asymmetric operations against Western interests, not only in its own region but worldwide. As the historian Joseph Kostiner points out, Iran's reasons for adopting its asymmetric strategy were grounded in an assessment similar to that of the Chinese leaders after 1991 or the Russians after 1999, namely that confronting the United States conventionally was simply not feasible. Iranian leaders understood they could not fight the United States directly—they had just "witnessed the U.S. demolish Iraqi forces that had [themselves] beaten Iran into submission [only] three years earlier."[49] But at the same time, they also "realized the U.S. had specific limits on its ability and willingness to use military force . . . Iran's strategy was asymmetric because it would attack the U.S. consistently but at levels that would not trigger the U.S. to engage in a direct military response against Iran. The method of these attacks could be diplomatic, propaganda, financial subversion, or support for terrorist proxies."[50] The goal was to inflict enough pain to push the United States out of the Arabian Gulf, without prompting direct retaliation.[51]

Iranian strategists were therefore some of the first to pursue what we might call a "liminal strategy" in relation to Western conventional power, seeking to ride the edge, doing just enough to frustrate the United States and further their own interests but not enough to trigger an outright military response. The same strategy, as we will see in Chapter 4, was later perfected by Russia. In addition to this approach—and alongside a set of methods that would nowadays be described as "hybrid warfare"—Iran's other response to its conventional military inferiority was the pursuit of its own nuclear weapons.

Mohammed Reza Pahlavi, the last shah of Iran, had initiated an atomic energy program during the 1950s in partnership with the United States under the Eisenhower administration's Atoms for Peace program.[52] By the time of his overthrow in 1979, Iran's first nuclear energy reactor, located at Bushehr on the northern shore of the Arabian Gulf, had been partially completed with German assistance. Ayatollah Ruhollah Khomeini, on seizing control of the country during the Islamic Revolution of February 1979, was initially uninterested in the nuclear program and made moves to close it, but the Iran-Iraq War quickly changed his thinking: after the war, "Ayatollah Mohammed Beheshti and Ayatollah Akbar Hashemi Rafsanjani, Khomeini's two top lieutenants, urged [him] to develop nuclear weapons. Aided by Ali Khamenei, they formed an 'inner nuclear sanctum' . . . which argued that a bomb would have prevented Iraq from invading," thereby avoiding the war altogether.[53] Beyond deterring Iraq, these leaders (and key figures in the Revolutionary Guard) argued that a nuclear umbrella would deter American retaliation for Iranian-sponsored terrorism in the region.

Combined with the belief that Saddam was continuing his pursuit of nuclear weapons and that Israel already possessed such a capability, Iranian leaders seem to have secretly restarted their nuclear and missile programs in the early 1990s. As the Swiss Iranian analyst Shahram Chubin noted in 2001, the goals of the program were to deter other states' nuclear programs (Iraq, Pakistan), deter intervention by external states (Israel or the United States), compensate for deficiencies in Iran's conventional capabilities, and serve as a diplomatic tool (for intimidation, for status enhancement, or to compensate for domestic weakness).[54]

As the 1990s progressed, although Iran's air force and its conventional ground army lagged, Iranian naval capability grew as the Revolutionary Guards fielded a growing fleet of fast, agile small attack craft that threatened shipping in the Arabian Gulf and disrupted the flow of trade and oil through the globally critical Straits of Hormuz, becoming a serious concern for Western strategists. Iranian-sponsored terrorism, including attacks by Iran's proxies, Hamas and Hezbollah, and the covert operations of the Guards' special operations component, the Quds Force, worried intelligence officers in the CIA and strategists in Israel, Iraq, Saudi Arabia, and the United Arab Emirates. Iran developed its fleet of reconnaissance drones (originally fielded as artillery spotters during the Iran-Iraq War) into armed and increasingly capable platforms—and allegedly provided them to Hezbollah, which used them to overfly Israel. As a result of these developments, in combination with Iran's funding and training of terrorists around the region, a small but influential group of defense intellectuals in Washington (the group, later known as neoconservatives, that was ultimately to be accused of driving the United States into the invasion of Iraq) saw Iran's terrorism sponsorship and its accelerating nuclear and missile programs as an existential threat to Israel, and pushed for action against Tehran as a top US priority.

Still, under the comparatively moderate leadership of reformist president Mohammad Khatami in the late 1990s and with a generally pro-Western population, Iran too seemed capable of "normalizing"—liberalizing politically and economically and becoming a somewhat integrated member of the global system, while acceding (in practice if not in theory) to the same US-led international order that politicians like Bill Clinton and Tony Blair hoped could accommodate Russia and China. President Khatami's proposed "dialogue among civilizations" (a response to Samuel Huntington's "clash of civilizations" thesis) and his approach of engagement with international institutions reduced the perception of threat from Iran in the immediate pre-9/11 period—even though the Islamic Republic's nuclear and hybrid warfare programs were proceeding apace behind the scenes.[55]

Unlike Iran, nobody in the early 1990s seriously expected North Korea's regime to liberalize, normalize, or integrate in any meaningful way with the post-Soviet global system; on the contrary, many fully expected it to collapse. As a protégé of Stalin, the country's founding leader Kim Il-sung had initially been Russian-oriented, but after Chinese assistance saved the regime during the Korean War, North Korea had perfected the art of swinging between Soviet and Chinese poles of influence, playing its patrons off against each other for influence and profit. By the end of the Cold War, North Korea's economy was dependent on Soviet aid (especially oil) and was overshadowed by economic growth and industrialization in the democratic South, while its population was smaller, weaker, less healthy, and less fertile than South Korea's. The Soviet breakup in 1991—and with it, the near-immediate cessation of Russian assistance—threw North Korea into crisis. Given its internal issues, it seemed to be the proverbial "hermit kingdom," its regime posing little threat except to its own population.

To be sure, the Korean War was officially still on, despite the 1953 armistice, and throughout the Cold War North Korea targeted South Korea and Japan with espionage, sabotage, and subversion, carried out criminal activities and kidnappings, launched covert operations, built up its forces along the Demilitarized Zone (DMZ) in the center of the Korean Peninsula, and inserted raiders by aircraft, submarine, and small boat.[56] Pyongyang's policy of "all-fortressization" turned the North into an armed camp, while the doctrines of *juche* (self-reliance, a form of nationalistic socialism with Kim's leadership central to the Korean people's progress) and *songun* (the military-first policy, with the Korean People's Army taking first place among all institutions of society) made North Korea less a traditional communist state than an absolute monarchy whose despot was propped up—and held hostage—by a praetorian guard.[57] As early as 1980, Kim Il-sung designated his son, Kim Jong-il, as his successor, and dozens of Kim's relatives and in-laws held key military and state positions. By 1993, as the elder Kim's health failed, North Korea looked like a hereditary dynastic state centered on the Kim family.

Given its weakness after 1991, the most dangerous thing the Kim regime therefore seemed likely to do was to collapse, triggering a humanitarian catastrophe and sending refugees flooding into China and across the DMZ into South Korea. In other words, the peninsula was a perfect illustration of Woolsey's "snakes": a place where weak states, faltering regimes, and post-Communist chaos posed humanitarian and stabilization challenges rather than serving as an active theater of war with a capable state adversary presenting a direct threat.

But Woolsey also warned, in the same set of hearings in February 1993, of the risk of nuclear proliferation and the spread of missile technology from North Korea.[58] He called it correctly: just three weeks later, in mid-March 1993, Pyongyang announced its intention to leave the Nuclear Non-Proliferation Treaty (NPT). That May, it launched a Nodong-1 medium-range ballistic missile (MRBM) into the Sea of Japan, the first test of a system that later proved capable of carrying chemical, nuclear, or conventional warheads almost a thousand miles.[59] And by the end of 1993, reports emerged of North Korean plans to sell up to three hundred Scud-C missiles to Iran as part of a broader exchange of military technology in return for oil, which North Korea desperately needed, having lost its Soviet supplier.[60]

North Korea had possessed a nuclear program since the 1960s, ostensibly for power generation, which made sense given the country's oil shortage.[61] At the same time, Kim sought atomic weapons to ensure his regime's survival, which also made perfect sense given that the United States had threatened a nuclear attack on the North in 1951 and placed nuclear weapons on the peninsula in January 1958, keeping them there throughout the Cold War.[62] In reaction to American positioning of nuclear artillery and rockets in South Korea, Kim sought atomic weapons from the Soviets in 1962 but was rebuffed, since the Kremlin under Khrushchev doubted the wisdom of sharing such technology with the volatile regime in Pyongyang. Instead, the Soviets helped build a plutonium reactor at Yongbyon, sixty miles north of Pyongyang, from which the North Koreans began harvesting small amounts of plutonium in the 1970s. They expanded production in the 1980s, began exploiting domestic uranium deposits, and allegedly sought capabilities to produce weapons-grade uranium.[63]

The Korean People's Army (KPA) quickly adapted to the presence of US nuclear weapons in South Korea: they built up extremely capable conventional artillery and rocket forces able to reach South Korea's capital, Seoul; deployed troops right onto the DMZ in a "hugging" strategy designed to deter US use of nuclear weapons by positioning forces so close to the border that any US nuclear strike would create fallout in the South; dug an extensive network of tunnels and underground bunkers; and enacted "all-fortressization" to limit the impact of an attack.[64] Along with their growing stockpile of fissile material, they acquired missile technology—including short- and medium-range Frog and Scud missiles—from Soviet-bloc states and quickly began improving the designs.[65] And having entered into the NPT in 1985 (thereby promising not to build a bomb and to open all nuclear sites to international inspectors), North Korea had already missed several inspection deadlines by the time the Berlin Wall fell.

Understanding North Korea's drive for nuclear weapons involves appreciating the basis for the regime's genuine, and not unreasonable, fear. Though the United States withdrew all nuclear weapons from South Korea at the end of 1991, the combination of US military presence in the South, active training between American forces and the Republic of Korea (ROK), and South Korea's economic, industrial, and population growth created intense threat perception in Pyongyang.[66] The decision of Kim Jong-il (de facto ruler since the 1980s, though he did not formally inherit his father's mantle until the old man died in July 1994) to leave the NPT, trade missile technology for oil from Iran, and seek nuclear expertise and technology from Pakistan is thus entirely understandable: North Korea desperately needed oil, food, and cash, and exchanging missile technology for critical commodities was one way to acquire them.

An active nuclear program was also a way to increase the perception that North Korea was too dangerous to attack, thereby warding off perceived aggression from the South and keeping America at bay.[67] The impression of a volatile leader—on a hair trigger, heedlessly pursuing risky strategies—also had a deterrent effect on North Korea's enemies, who worried Kim might do something crazy if provoked. As a variant of the Nixon "madman theory," North Korea's pursuit of nuclear weapons through the 1990s and 2000s brought a string of concessions from the international community, as Pyongyang played off the United States, China, and the United Nations against each other in an updated version of its Cold War strategy of swinging between Moscow and Beijing.[68]

Kim Jong-il's 1993 gambit worked. By 1994, the Clinton administration had put in place the Agreed Framework, whereby North Korea undertook to freeze its existing program, shut down its plutonium reactors, and remain in the NPT, in return for fuel oil and two light-water reactors (considered more proliferation-resistant) from the United States. Pyongyang got oil and the promise of nuclear assistance from the United States, while continuing to develop advanced missile technology and covertly acquire expertise and technology for weapons-grade uranium enrichment from Pakistan.[69] By 2002, it was clear that North Korea was circumventing the Agreed Framework, and President Bush included the country in the "Axis of Evil" in his January 2002 State of the Union address. The deal finally died in January 2003, when North Korea reiterated its decision to withdraw from the NPT after a confrontation with US officials over its uranium-refining centrifuge program.[70]

Like many things after 2003, US attempts to pressure North Korea to give up its nuclear ambitions took a back seat to the crisis in Iraq. At the same time, watching Washington threaten Pyongyang, then overthrow Saddam for allegedly possessing weapons programs (but not actual nuclear weapons), then bog down in Iraq, Kim's regime presumably concluded it had no time to waste in acquiring nuclear weapons itself, so that if the United States ever extricated itself from Iraq it would be too late to move on North Korea.

In 2005, the North Korean government announced it had acquired nuclear weapons for self-defense and withdrew from six-party talks with the international community; in October 2006, the country conducted its first nuclear test.[71] After Libya's Muammar Gaddafi gave up his WMD programs under Western pressure—only to succumb, in 2011, to a popular uprising supported by Western air power—the incoming North Korean leader, Kim Jong-un (who took over on his father's death in December 2011), undoubtedly appreciative of the wisdom of his father and grandfather in acquiring such a powerful deterrent, accelerated the program. By September 2017, North Korea had detonated a hydrogen bomb capable of being fitted to an intercontinental ballistic missile (ICBM); by November, it had tested such an ICBM—the Hwasong-15, capable of carrying a nuclear warhead to any target in the United States, including Washington, DC; and in his New Year's speech in January 2018, Kim Jong-un announced that his country's nuclear capability was complete.[72] He concluded that "thanks to this deterrent, the US would not dare to ignite a war 'against me and our country.' "[73] The snake of 1993 was well on the way to becoming a dragon.

AFTER WOOLSEY

Obviously enough, given all these developments, the Woolseyan era is over. Today, we face both dragons and snakes, at the same time and in many of the same places. The dragons—the state-based threats—include a newly aggressive Russia, an increasingly assertive China, an Iranian regime that may or may not be pursuing nuclear weapons but is certainly consolidating its control from the western border of Afghanistan all the way to the Golan Heights while spearheading a global confrontation with Sunni Islam, and a North Korean hereditary dictatorship, now in its third generation under Kim Jong-un, that combines internal repression, external adventurism, and nuclear brinkmanship. All of these are pursuing liminal strategies—riding the edge of detection in order to achieve political and military goals without triggering a response.

Meanwhile, the snakes (nonstate actors and threats from state collapse) are just as strong. From Ukraine and the Baltic states to Niger and Somalia, from state collapse in Libya to Islamic State in Iraq and Syria, from economic collapse in Venezuela and insurgency in Colombia to civil war in Yemen, from major urban battles with insurgents who fight like states in Iraq, Syria, and the Philippines to terrorist attacks in Belgium, France, Germany, Australia, Canada, and the United Kingdom, we face an environment where state and nonstate threats combine in new ways and in unfamiliar configurations.

This book, then, is about what our enemies have learned in the quarter century since Woolsey's testimony—how the dragons learned from the snakes, how the snakes copied the dragons, how the rest learned to fight the West—and about what we in turn must learn if we hope to succeed in the new environment we now face.

Map 1 Europe on the Eve of the Soviet Collapse

Adaptive Enemies

The guy is barefoot, skinny, in his late teens or early twenties. He wears striped tracksuit pants, a *shemagh* scarf around his waist, and a gray T-shirt. He has a neat military-style crewcut, but his face is rimed with dirty stubble. Kneeling fully exposed in the very center of the street, he aims an RPG and is immediately hit by seven rounds from a machine gun out of sight to the left. He drops the unfired rocket launcher, sits upright for an instant, startled, then takes another burst and flops flat on his back, left arm almost severed, the rear of his skull shot away, brain matter seeping red, then black onto the hot tarmac. His companions howl, too shocked to shout their *Allahu Akbar*. The total time of the engagement, from the moment the guerrilla aims the rocket until he is lying dead in the street, is 2.6 seconds, roughly one-tenth the time it takes the average person to read this paragraph.

One of my tasks early in the Iraq War, when I worked in Australian Army Headquarters, was to track the developing insurgency and identify evolving guerrilla tactics, organizations, and weapons so that we could adapt to the changing threat. The video clip that I just described—shot by a Spanish news crew during street fighting in Baghdad—was one of hundreds of videos, photographs, documents, and intercepts I had to review, scanning for patterns of enemy evolution.[1]

My boss at the time was Brigadier Justin Kelly, head of the Australian Army's future warfare branch, who later served as a senior operations officer in Iraq, becoming known as one of the most perceptive coalition leaders of the war. After I had watched this clip about a dozen times with the video slowed to one-tenth speed, I felt a presence and glanced around to see him looking over my shoulder.

"Run it again, normal speed."

Shots, howls, somber Spanish voice-over.

"Run it again . . .

"Dave, that howling you hear—that's the sound of an adaptive enemy adapting."

I watched the clip one last time, shaking my head. *We're killing the stupid ones*, I thought. *Nobody who saw this guy get wasted will ever make that mistake again. Next time they'll be smarter, and the harder we kill them, the faster they'll improve.*

This chapter is about adaptive, nonstate enemies—the terrorists, insurgents, and militias whom I have dubbed, following Woolsey, the "snakes"—and it examines *how* adaptive enemies learn, while the next chapter examines *what* nonstate enemies have learned since Woolsey's testimony in early 1993.

This topic—the manner in which adaptive enemies learn, or what we might call "mechanisms of evolution in irregular warfare"—is somewhat theoretical. But it matters because, if we can figure out the process by which adversaries evolve (and if we realize that our own actions create, in part, the selective pressure that drives their evolution), then it may be possible to alter the environment, drive their adaptation along different pathways, and thereby reduce the threat. The processes I outline in this chapter hold true not only for nonstate adversaries but for states as well, and so they are worth examining in detail.

MECHANISMS OF EVOLUTION IN IRREGULAR WARFARE

The video I just described is one of many examples of what we used to call "Combat Darwinism" in Iraq and Afghanistan. It was the subject of much gallows humor in both places, since of course the selective pressure of combat applied to us as much as to the enemy. But is there more to it than mere metaphor, the trivial observation that the strong and lucky survive while the weak and unlucky die? The reality seems both more complicated and more interesting than that.

It's a truism that militaries adapt, and combat in particular imparts instantaneous, uniquely indelible lessons that affect not only individuals but also organizations, tactics, weapons, targets, and a host of norms and institutions that shape every aspect of how a military force operates. "Adaptation" is used in a technical sense here to designate any new trait (an organizational structure, process, technique, weapon, or behavioral pattern) that enables an entity to better survive and reproduce itself; it is also the process of change, in response to environmental pressure, that gives rise to new traits.[2]

Vast numbers of small adaptations can add up to astoundingly rapid and far-reaching change in wartime, especially compared with the slow-moving, top-down processes of peacetime change. As the military theorist Stephen Rosen points out, innovation during peacetime is fundamentally different from adaptation in war: whereas peacetime innovation is driven by perceptions of change in the external environment, as well as conceptual hypotheses about the new technologies, organizations, and tactics needed to prevail in future conflict, wartime adaptation is a direct response to enemy action.[3] As a result, military organizations—whether state-based militaries or nonstate armed groups—tend to engage in steady, self-generated, conceptually driven innovation for long periods in peacetime before undergoing sudden, rapid, combat-driven "growth spurts" of wartime adaptation. Combat losses—deaths and injuries—are inseparable from these wartime adaptation spurts.

Several of the instructors who taught me and my classmates fieldcraft, weapons, and tactics when I was an officer cadet at Australia's Royal Military

College, Duntroon, in the 1980s had served as professional soldiers in Malaya, Borneo, and Vietnam—some doing multiple tours in all three campaigns. One of their frequent sayings was that "doctrine is written in blood." Every lesson is a life, they would say; someone suffered for every insight: the soldier dies, but the army lives and learns.

Of course, this is true only up to a point. Casualties at a certain level definitely drive doctrinal change, but there's a bell curve: too high a loss rate (too many killed and wounded in too short a time frame) can create pressure so intense that the organization itself perishes. Likewise, too low a loss rate can generate insufficient pressure to spur innovation, so that the organization stagnates, stalling its adaptation. In the middle is a band of selective pressure that makes the organization better over time, as it responds to a loss rate intense enough to be survivable only if it adapts, but not so intense as to destroy it. In this middle part of the bell curve, the improving effect—or what scholars of evolution would call the "fitness effect"—of selective pressure is at its greatest. We might think of this bell curve effect as akin to the spectrum from stagnation to eustress to distress in a physical organism—too little stress leads to stagnation, too much to damage (or distress), while eustress ("good stress") in the middle band helps make an organism stronger.[4]

We could also consider it a variation of the "selection-destruction cycle" advanced by the military sociologist Roger Beaumont in his seminal 1974 study of military elites.[5] As Beaumont points out, one defining feature of specialized elite forces (mountain troops, rangers, special forces, elite light infantry, aircrew, submariners, and so on) is that they tend to select from the best available personnel—choosing fitter, more intelligent recruits with better leadership skills, initiative, and endurance than ordinary units do.[6] They may even (as in Australian, British, and American special operations forces) recruit primarily from existing members of high-readiness units who themselves are already highly trained and subject to rigorous selection. But as Beaumont shows in a comprehensive study of twentieth-century elites, such forces also tend to have higher loss rates—they operate at the upper end of the stress bell curve. They are thrown into dangerous or demanding missions, experience higher than usual rates of death and wounding, and so erode more quickly than the general mass of the force.[7]

This selection-destruction cycle means that a force with too high a proportion of elites—an army with too many special forces units, a navy that diverts too many of its most aggressive junior commanders into the submarine arm, or an air force (like that of imperial Japan) with aircrew standards that prove unsustainable over a long war—can actually damage its adaptive potential. Such a force experiences a brain drain, where individuals who would have been leaders in regular units (and would likely have survived to spread their knowledge to others) are instead segregated into subgroups where, even if they survive, their talents are lost to the wider force. Meanwhile, major combat formations can cease to be much more than feeders for specialized units, providing the recruiting base for elite forces that increasingly usurp normal combat roles, exacerbating both the brain drain and the selection-destruction cycle that Beaumont describes.

More broadly, when we consider the idea that "doctrine is written in blood," it's worth remembering that the most important doctrine is actually not the formal kind found in military manuals, but rather the experiential, organic knowledge that percolates through groups of humans in battle and assumes folkloric status. I'm going borrow a term from evolutionary anthropology here, to call this kind of informal doctrinal development "social learning"—and to suggest that social learning, along with natural selection, artificial selection, and institutional adaptation, is one of the four key dynamics that we can observe when watching how adaptive enemies adapt.

Social Learning

The British historian Timothy R. Moreman, in his 1998 study of frontier warfare in the mountainous borderland of Britain's Indian empire, described a process of local, bottom-up adaptation, with officers and noncommissioned officers gathering, sharing, and gradually codifying insights observed over hundreds of combat engagements, in dozens of campaigns and small wars. A wide variety of military forces participated in these campaigns, including British Army regiments on short-term tours, resident

Indian Army units who spent years on campaign, specialized frontier scouts and irregulars who recruited from the local area, Gurkha regiments from Nepal, tribal levies, and others. Over time, certain units, leaders, and ethnic groups were recognized for above-average combat performance, and their methods were imitated by others. Because of the wide variation in unit types, there were many different approaches, some of which worked well while others failed, and this created a sort of continuous natural experiment in frontier warfare, a living laboratory of combat.

Units that performed well in a given engagement became models for others to emulate, and techniques that were pioneered in one campaign were refined during multiple subsequent operations. Successful adaptations to the environment were replicated through informal discussion, gossip, professional literature, and debate. They spread through the force via debriefings, transfer of individuals among units, exchange of training cadres from experienced outgoing units to green newcomers, and publication of training notes. Conversely, units that did badly were often literally wiped out—either in a physical sense, through annihilation by a pitiless enemy, or organizationally, by being broken up and disbanded following failures.

This created strong selective pressure: while units and individuals who failed were culled, those who did better in combat not only survived but developed greater reputational capital, making their techniques more likely to be imitated by their peers and successors and thus to be reproduced across multiple generations of troops on the frontier, thereby allowing these techniques to spread and solidify into authoritative lore. The army as an institution absorbed this lore and gradually formalized it into field manuals, which themselves were subject to active, ongoing debate and revision among those engaged in later operations.[8]

Moreman's discussion of the evolution of frontier warfare in this small-scale and tightly knit (though very diverse) warrior society is a pretty good description of social learning, a process that scientists have identified in creatures as diverse as rats, pigeons, chimpanzees, and octopuses but that is especially well developed in humans.[9] Both individual learning and social learning play a role in adaptation: humans learn not solely through reinforcement of behaviors acquired in response to individual stimuli (as many animals do), but also through a social (that is, a group-based) cognitive process.[10] Individual learning involves trial and error, observation, and deduction, and it generates novel behaviors.[11] By contrast, social learning occurs through interaction with other humans, involves imitation and copying, and helps spread those behaviors among individuals within a group.[12] As both individual learning and social learning happen on a local scale, different groups innovate differently.[13]

In effect, people learn not just by observation and imitation, but also through knowledge transfer within and among groups, which then develop and replicate variations in behavior, which in turn congeal into culture. Quirky or innovative behaviors arise (much like mutations in genetic code) through individual trial and error, and some prove to be beneficial. Beneficial behaviors—those that confer a survival (or "fitness") advantage—are replicated more widely than behaviors that offer no advantage or are harmful, and groups that adopt these beneficial behaviors outcompete others over time, eventually occupying a dominant place within a population.[14] They propagate their tactical DNA, as it were.

Reputation and gossip (as described by Moreman in the frontier warfare example) are other key elements of the explanation and are important for human social learning: "only in humans is reputation used for communicating behaviors that are good or bad for the group,"[15] while gossip performs the valuable evolutionary function of punishing "free-riders" (individuals who benefit from group membership while failing to contribute).[16] Likewise, while other species engage in social learning, cumulative culture—the accretion of behaviors into a comprehensive set of universal norms and institutions such as language, warfare, marriage, and religion—seems to be peculiarly human.[17]

The material and institutional cultures of militarily dominant groups such as the ancient Romans, the Prussian Army of Frederick the Great, and the modern US military are also copied by others, often with no understanding of the reasons for particular behaviors. This contributes to the spread of once-beneficial behaviors, even past the point of real-world relevance.[18] Trends in military fashion—including the copying of clothing or equipment of high-status allies or enemies and the propagation of certain styles of dress or grooming (the Roman military belt, the hussar's fur hat, the rifleman's green jacket, the aviator's silk scarf, the mountaineer's beret) among larger military forces—are the subject of a whole field of study, as is the way military fashion of one era becomes civilian fashion in the next (think of "operator" beards, *shemagh* scarfs, camouflage prints, and chunky plastic watches in the United States, Britain, and Australia today, or Red Guard uniforms and Mao suits in China during the Cultural Revolution).[19] Clearly, fashion—which, in ethnographic terms, is just one prominent example of status-driven emulation—is an important transmission pathway for socially acquired knowledge as it is disseminated from high-status to lower-status military groups and then to wider societies, as is the deliberate imitation of well-understood beneficial behaviors within peer groups.

These factors partly explain two issues that scientists have long debated regarding the applicability of evolutionary theory beyond individual genes: "group selection," or the mechanism by which groups, rather than individual organisms or genes, evolve; and the apparent "heritability of acquired characteristics" (something that is not expected in classical evolutionary theory but seems to occur in human groups via cumulative cultural evolution over multiple generations). I should be clear that both these ideas are controversial among scientists, and there is an ongoing debate about group selection in particular.[20]

Back on the gritty streets where actual combatants do battle, opportunities for observational learning (watching another insurgent get his brains blown out after making the mistake of kneeling in the open, for example) are myriad. At the same time, gossip and rumor, the making and sharing (in traditional warrior societies and modern military units alike) of epic sagas about heroic or victorious acts, as well as mentoring by respected teachers and leaders all help propagate lessons beyond those individuals directly involved in any particular incident, thus replicating behaviors that a group of warriors, as a social organism, collectively perceives as beneficial. Given that groups of warriors are, in effect, tribal hierarchies where older, more competent, and experienced fighters have higher social status, the reputation of elders—like our Duntroon instructors—significantly enhances the replicability of their behaviors.

For example, one of the most influential documents cited by Moreman is General Sir Andrew Skeen's 1932 classic, *Passing It On: Short Talks on Tribal Fighting on the North-West Frontier of India*, which was to have a substantial influence on the way soldiers in India conceived of the terrain, the adversary, and the nature of the war in which they were engaged. In his preface, Skeen directs his advice toward junior light infantry officers (i.e., younger members of his own subtribe in the complex regimental society of the army in India) and links it to oral tradition passed down on the authority of his elders.[21]

There is a subtle but significant distinction, though, between the tribally mediated social learning that Moreman and Skeen describe (or the jungle lore our mentors channeled at Duntroon) and the learning those guerrillas experienced in the Baghdad streets, watching their comrade getting killed. For whereas professional militaries tend to learn consciously, deliberately adapting their behavior within one combat generation (say, within a single operational tour or campaign or, in Skeen's case, within the professional lifetime of a single career infantry officer), fragmented terrorist and guerrilla groups may learn in a different way, through a blind process of variation, destruction, and replication (sometimes expressed in shorthand as "blind variation and selective retention," or BVSR)[22] over multiple successive generations, something much more closely akin to natural selection.

Natural Selection in Irregular Warfare

It's worth noting that even a small unit (say, a rifle company) within a professional military force is far larger than the average guerrilla band. Even in mass insurgencies numbering millions of people, actual guerrilla warfare takes place within small, geographically separated groups of a few dozen people at most. For example, the United Nations estimated in 2014 that during most winter campaign seasons in Afghanistan, the average group size of Taliban fighters was only seven to twelve individuals, growing to a maximum of thirty to fifty during the winter of 2013–14.[23] (These bands could, of course, cooperate among themselves to generate hundreds of fighters for specific battles—but this was relatively rare, at least during that phase of the war, and often required months of careful guerrilla diplomacy by insurgent leaders.)[24] Likewise, the largest Iraqi guerrilla attacks, as the insurgency went through its growth spurt in 2005, were conducted by groups of forty to fifty, while most were mounted by far smaller groups, even as the overall number of guerrillas approached twenty thousand.[25]

Guerrillas themselves are just the tip of an insurgent iceberg, the tiny minority—2 to 3 percent at most—of the people engaged in an uprising who actually carry weapons openly and operate above the "detection threshold" at which an adversary becomes aware of them. They are the "relatively small visible element . . . organized to perform overt armed military and paramilitary operations using guerrilla tactics."[26] Urban environments, which I have described elsewhere as a "disaggregated battlespace," break such guerrilla groups up even further, forcing them to take part in a large number of dispersed, small engagements rather than a few big ones.[27] Sticking with our theme of evolutionary anthropology, regular military units are like mini-states of relatively high conformity and structural complexity, whereas guerrilla groups resemble mobile hunter-gatherer bands— they exhibit a high degree of cohesion within bands, but loose coordination (at best) outside the immediate *comitatus*, the family-like fighting group bonded by kin-like (or often actual kinship) relationships among members of a warrior band.

As anthropologists have observed, most mobile hunter-gatherers live in bands of fifteen to fifty people, interacting with relatives in about six to ten nearby bands. These so-called maximum bands gather only occasionally for feasts or ceremonies (or perhaps for a maximal effort in a major harvest or hunt).[28] In the same way, the size of guerrilla groups tends to hover around twenty to forty fighters, with semi-autonomous combat groups banding together with nearby groups to cooperate for specific purposes, then dispersing. Underground movements in resistance warfare, or urban militias and terrorist networks, can be even more fragmented, adopting a cell-based structure where individuals know only the members of their own three- to four-person group, and perhaps not even that many.[29] In complex mass insurgencies, military-style organizations (such as the Main Force guerrillas and North Vietnamese Army in Vietnam and the FARC-EP in

Colombia) can exist at one level, while at another—that of the underground, such as the Viet Cong Infrastructure in Vietnam and the *Partido Comunista Clandestino* in Colombia—a clandestine resistance warfare cell structure prevails.

Moreover, as with hunter-gatherers, geographical separation among guerrilla bands creates an effect that scientists call "reproductive isolation," in which each local group develops independently, evolving its own language, norms, materials, technologies, and way of doing things (i.e., its own culture). This distinctive military culture is propagated over multiple generations, as new members join and older members die, defect, or retire and as the group fissions (splits off copies of itself) to propagate new groups.

The British anthropologist Robin Dunbar (originator of "Dunbar's Number," the idea that the human brain-to-body-size ratio imposes a cognitive upper limit of around 150 people in any individual's social network)[30] also offers insight into optimal military unit size, observing that human groups tend to grow to around 150 before fissioning into smaller groups, which then grow again to roughly the same number before themselves splitting. Dunbar points out that human groups have "a distinctive layered structure with successive cumulative layer sizes of 15, 50, 150, 500 and 1500"[31] and that this structure, which reappears in hunter-gatherer societies, offline and online social networks, campsites, kibbutzim, nomad bands, and subsistence villages, also seems to recur throughout history in military groups. This suggests that human organizations tend to fragment at distinct sizes, and Dunbar points out that "the question arises as to whether there are natural 'sweet spots' at which communities are likely to be more successful (i.e. survive longer without fissioning) because they map better onto natural grouping patterns and their underpinning psychology."[32]

Our examination of selective pressure on the battlefield suggests that guerrilla group size, in particular, evolves toward smaller bands (15 and 50) for survival under normal circumstances, with larger aggregations of 150 and 500 coalescing for critical events (e.g., for major attacks or to defend a key leader or sanctuary area), before dispersing again to survive. It may therefore be that a guerrilla band of 15 is optimal for survival on dispersed operations, whereas concentrating forces by aggregating ten to thirty such bands (generating a temporary coalition of 150 to 500 fighters) confers survival (i.e., fitness) advantages in the attack.

As well as operating in small groups, guerrillas mostly conduct small battles. As in the 2.6-second engagement I described earlier, most combat takes place in a matter of moments, up to a few minutes at most, and even large battles (say, the two battles of Fallujah in 2004, the battle of Mosul in 2016, and that of Raqqa in 2017) involve not one big sustained fight between large units, but many small fleeting ones among lots of tiny groups. Of course, just as guerrillas can concentrate into "maximum bands" for specific operations, combat groups and small teams can conduct collaborative engagements, and some fights can develop into battles that last hours or days, but these too are relatively rare. In most urban fighting or terrorist action, combat action lasting more than one hour is the exception.

Group isolation tends to produce huge *variation* among guerrilla groups, even within a single theater of operations. As already discussed, guerrilla bands (along with the underground cells and auxiliary networks that support them) are under *selective pressure* from an environment that instantly and lethally punishes maladaptive behavior. Finally, kinship and social ties among members of different groups, horizontal transfer of members, cross-pollination of ideas, lifeboat effects (where remnants from destroyed groups survive by rallying to other groups, bringing with them new adaptive traits), and connectivity (increased access to cellphones, the internet, secure messaging, and social media) create means of *replication* whereby beneficial behaviors can be passed from one group to others.

As it turns out, these three factors—variation, selective pressure, and replication—are the building blocks of the evolutionary process known as "natural selection." To quote the population ecologist and military theorist Dominic Johnson:

> Darwinian [i.e., natural] selection weeds out poor performers and
> propagates good performers, thus leading to a cumulative increase
> in effective adaptations over time . . . as long as three conditions are
> in place: variation, selection, and replication. Applied to asymmetric
> warfare, Darwinian selection predicts that, counter-intuitively,

stronger sides may suffer a disadvantage across all three conditions: (1) *Variation*—weaker sides are often composed of a larger diversity of combatants, representing a larger trait-pool and a potentially higher rate of "mutation" (innovation); (2) *Selection*— stronger sides apply a greater selection pressure on weaker sides than the other way around, resulting in faster adaptation by the weaker side; (3) *Replication*—weaker sides are exposed to combat for longer (fighting on the same home territory for years at a time), promoting experience and learning, while stronger sides rotate soldiers on short combat tours to different regions.[33]

Thinking back to Beaumont, we could add that these same factors, which Johnson argues make irregular forces more adaptive, also confer a fitness advantage by protecting guerrilla groups from the selection-destruction cycle. Rather than being siphoned off into separate, elite organizations where their talents are lost to the group and their chances of death or injury are higher (the effects of the selection-destruction cycle on conventional troops), for guerrilla elites—the best-performing members of a given band or combat group—the natural pathway is to rise to the top of their small group and then stay there. There they acquire social and reputational capital through good combat performance, and the resulting prestige helps replicate their successful approaches, keeping the fitness benefits within the group and helping its general chances of survival and success.

At the other end of the performance spectrum, and as the Iraqi video clip demonstrates, selection pressure—generated by enemy action through thousands of diffuse combat engagements—kills off individuals who lack certain advantageous traits. Others—better organized, more appropriately equipped, smarter, or simply luckier—survive to pass on their tactical DNA vertically (to the next generation) or horizontally (by an exchange of ideas or people with other concurrently existing groups). Because of variation and reproductive isolation among groups, a variety of tactical approaches emerge, some of which prove beneficial ("adaptive") while others are mal-adaptive, leading to the demise of individuals, and ultimately groups, who adopt them.

Over time, through this natural experiment in irregular warfare, strongly adaptive traits come to predominate within a population of guerrillas, maladapted individuals are culled, and those who are particularly well suited to the environment rise to greater organizational or reputational influence, where they replicate their traits by promoting and encouraging others like themselves, propagandizing their successes, or training their juniors. The overall population thus improves in fitness relative to the environment. Thus, whereas professional armies consciously adapt, guerrilla groups may unconsciously morph through processes of blind variation and selective retention, shaped by the pitiless evolutionary mathematics of combat. Despite its unconscious nature, this process can create quite sophisticated structures: to quote the late Rafe Sagarin, "The simple process of individual organisms trying to survive and reproduce ends up producing networked ecosystems that are unpredictable, complex, resilient and beautiful."[34]

I am not sure I would describe terrorist and insurgent groups as "beautiful," even in the limited sense of being beautifully adapted to the ecological niche they happen to occupy in a broader conflict ecosystem. Natural selection—at least in this context—seems to produce as many false starts, blind alleys, and monstrous mutations as it does brilliant successes. Groups can also evolve toward isolated peaks in what scientists call a "fitness landscape"—the operating environment composed of the sum total of all potential trait combinations they may exhibit in response to the selective pressures acting on them. They can achieve temporary adaptive success, only to discover the environment shifting around them, to find themselves marooned and vulnerable.[35] (This happens more often than one might expect in war, where the threat environment is extremely dynamic, so that characteristics that confer adaptive benefits in one phase of a conflict can become massive liabilities when the situation changes.) Still, if Johnson and Sagarin are right about the applicability of natural selection to insurgent and terrorist groups, then the nonstandardization, organizational diversity, and small-unit autonomy of these groups may create ideal conditions for adaptive adversaries to evolve, as Johnson points out, faster than we do.

Adversaries clearly also adapt more rapidly the more effectively we target them. In insurgent theaters, a "survival of the fittest" dynamic emerges.

Because multiple groups compete for control over population and terrain, adaptability in changing circumstances is at a premium.[36] As a result, the most dangerous groups may not be the strongest, but rather the most adaptable, the best able to leverage an asymmetric advantage—and hence the most survivable. This kind of insurgent adaptation creates a shelf life for any particular countermeasure against guerrillas. Indeed, the more effective a tactic is, the quicker it becomes obsolete, because the more pressure it puts on the guerrilla group to adapt.[37]

Although I have been writing since 2003 about the relevance of biological and ecological systems thinking to the evolution of insurgent and terrorist groups, I have always been wary of applying biological metaphors to military enemies, mostly on moral and political grounds. Dehumanizing adversaries (describing them as insects, bacteria, bacilli, viruses, or metastasizing cancers) is a staple of political propaganda on all sides, and it can lead to horrific cruelties and atrocities, while not necessarily helping us understand our enemies any better. It's absolutely essential to remember that the enemy is a human being, not just for ethical reasons but because of individual human agency, which always adds an "X factor" to any generic behavioral insight.

But in this case, the biological systems metaphor (as we've seen in the Indian frontier warfare example) applies to ourselves as much as to our irregular adversaries, so that far from dehumanizing them it actually demonstrates how similar their condition is to our own. At the same time, there is an argument that this is not actually a metaphor at all, but rather a concrete, computationally valid observation of how adversaries evolve. And if the same ideas apply to us too—if we are not outside the system looking in, clean in our lab coats peering into the petri dish, but rather organisms in the same ecosystem—then in some sense we are just another species in the combat food chain.

Among atomized, factionalized guerrillas, militias, street gangs, or terrorist cells—the building blocks of the nonstate armed groups that Woolsey labeled "snakes"—every time someone is killed, an operation fails, or an enemy develops countermeasures for some previously successful technique, selective pressure drives adaptive change. Groups fission and split, push out replicas of themselves, die or disappear, and exchange information and people. The result is an evolutionary dynamism, an irresistible drive for continuous change, that is unconscious, self-shaping, and organic: virtually a pure analogue of natural selection. But natural selection and social learning are not the only factors here—a third key factor is artificial selection.

Artificial Selection

One of the best-known originators of an early version of currently accepted theories of evolution was, of course, the nineteenth-century naturalist Charles Darwin. Along with natural selection, Darwin wrote about what he called "artificial selection"—the breeding of populations for desired traits. The power of artificial selection to morph physiological and behavioral traits to a virtually unlimited degree is readily apparent if we simply consider that all 339 officially recognized dog breeds in the world today probably descend from a single population of gray wolves, with only about fifty-one breeding females, that was domesticated by early humans somewhere in Asia about 17,000 years ago.[38] This is extremely recent in human history, given that our species has been around for 270,000 years or so. From that single point of origin, the diversity of dog breeds has exploded, not through natural selection but through deliberate action by breeders. In *The Origin of Species*, Darwin used dogs—along with sheep, pigeons, and other domesticated animals and plants—to demonstrate how changes in every aspect of an organism can be effected, in remarkably short periods, by humans applying selective breeding.[39]

But Darwin distinguished two kinds of artificial selection. The first he called "methodical selection," whereby a breeder consciously attempts to modify a plant or animal population by selecting for specific traits; the breeder has some definite aim in mind and the knowledge that exaggerating traits over multiple generations will cause the breed to diverge from its original form. The second he called "unconscious selection," whereby a farmer or gardener, weeding out inferior specimens and breeding the best, may (with no intent to change the breed, but simply by seeking to maintain the available stock) end up creating remarkably different sub-breeds, or new ones altogether. This second kind of artificial selection is particularly relevant to evolution in irregular warfare.[40]

If unconscious artificial selection by breeders trying to improve or maintain a species can cause massive change, the flip side is that attempts to eradicate organisms (say, disease-causing bacteria) can accidentally drive evolutionary changes that result in organisms that are fitter (i.e., better able to cope with selective pressure) than before. Here, the desire to destroy can generate as much improvement as selective breeding—and with equally little intention. Antibiotic-resistant bacteria are the classic case.[41]

Yet another way of thinking about artificial selection in warfare is based on what population ecologists call "predation models," in which predators and prey coevolve through a series of codependent cycles of population growth and collapse.[42] Growth in a given prey species creates more food for predators, whose population expands as they consume the prey, but then collapses once the number of predators can no longer be sustained by the surviving prey.[43] The prey species, relieved of selective pressure from the predator (whose population has now dropped owing to the lack of food supply), then recovers, creating more food for the now smaller number of surviving predators, whose population then expands once more, and the cycle begins anew.[44] A more sophisticated version of this model, taking selection effects into account, suggests that as each cycle runs, survivors of the preceding population collapse (within both predator and prey species) are selected for specific adaptive traits—and therefore over a number of cycles the two species can coevolve and experience significant "drift" from their original forms.

The basic predator-prey model produces a sequence of peaks and troughs in the population of both predators and prey, with predator peaks lagging behind those of prey (since an increase in prey drives the next growth cycle for predators, while a collapse in the prey population triggers the next fall in predator numbers). Adding multiple competing species into the mix, accounting for environmental carrying capacity (which imposes limits on population growth even in the absence of predators), and considering species that consume more than one type of food create the basis for the complex food webs, interdependent coevolutionary processes, and ecological niches that define ecosystems. Accounting for changes in an ecosystem's carrying capacity and for selection effects—where predators kill the weak, slow, or unlucky members of a prey species, and thereby improve it (by prompting evolutionary change in its makeup)—further explains evolution within a conflict ecosystem in a way that is directly applicable to irregular warfare. These notions of artificial selection and predator-prey dynamics might sound excessively theoretical, so let me give three practical military examples to illustrate them: the evolution of the Pakistani Taliban under a decade of US drone strikes, the effect of Israeli targeted killings on Palestinian terrorists, and the impact of US surges and withdrawals on the population of Iraqi insurgents.

Pakistan began attacking tribal militias in 2002 in the Tirah Valley—part of the Upper Khyber Agency in what was then known as the Federally Administered Tribal Areas (FATA)—in response to US pressure to target Al Qaeda remnants who had escaped into Pakistan after the Battle of Tora Bora in late 2001.[45] Local tribes at this time were poorly armed and organized, the Pakistani Taliban did not yet exist, and the skill level of first-generation guerrilla leaders such as Nek Muhammad Wazir (the local insurgent chief in the Tirah Valley) was average at best. Despite his inexperience, Nek Muhammad managed to fight the Pakistani army to a draw and gained status through what the tribes saw as a successful peace negotiation in 2004.[46] He was killed in June that year, allegedly in an American drone strike, and replaced by Beitullah Mehsud. Beitullah was more experienced than Nek Muhammad, came from a more influential subtribe, and achieved higher status than his predecessor by defeating the army in multiple engagements and representing the tribes in successful truce talks.[47]

Beitullah unified the loose confederation of five tribal militias, which Nek Muhammad had led, into a united Pakistani Taliban (Tehrik-e Taliban Pakistan, TTP), gained official recognition from the Afghan Taliban, and conducted attacks all over Pakistan, including, according to one theory, the assassination of presidential candidate Benazir Bhutto in 2007.[48] In other words, killing Nek Muhammad (though clearly intended to damage or destroy tribal militias in the FATA) instead improved their performance, generated greater unity, and helped drive the emergence of a new and fitter entity, TTP.

Beitullah, in his turn, was killed in another alleged US drone strike in August 2009 and replaced by his deputy and kinsman, the young and aggressive Hakimullah Mehsud. Hakimullah had been known for a series of successful raids as a junior commander, winning prestige with midlevel field commanders. He was appointed unanimously by the TTP leadership council, giving him greater political support than Beitullah, who had been plagued by internal rivalries. Moreover, whereas Nek Muhammad started as leader at the very outset of the campaign (and therefore, by definition, with no prior combat experience against the Pakistani army), and Beitullah began his term with twenty-three months of experience (July 2002 to June 2004), Hakimullah had amassed more than seven years (March 2002 to August 2009) campaigning against the Pakistani military before becoming leader, making him more experienced, though younger and more aggressive than his two predecessors.

Reflecting Hakimullah's greater aggression, experience, and political capital, under his leadership TTP expanded outside Pakistan to attack more ambitious targets, among other things launching a deadly suicide bombing against the CIA base at Camp Chapman in Khost, Afghanistan, in December 2009, attacking the US Consulate in Peshawar in April 2010, and claiming an attempted bombing in New York's Times Square in May 2010.[49] Hakimullah, in his turn, was killed in yet another alleged US drone strike in November 2013. One outcome of the leadership struggle that followed his death was the emergence of an Islamic State *wilayat*, or province, in Afghanistan and Pakistan—a faction founded by a TTP splinter group, now a major player in the ongoing violence in Afghanistan.

In other words, through selective pressure on its leaders, over an eleven-year period between 2002 and 2013, alleged US drone strikes helped turn a loose collection of local tribal militias, with no real goal other than to be left alone, into a unified, transnational terrorist group affiliated with other extremist organizations and directly targeting (even operating inside) the United States. Darwin's notion of improvement by unconscious artificial selection applies directly here, as does the bell curve I mentioned earlier: by picking off leaders roughly every five years, thereby causing three generations of leadership turnover, the alleged US strikes generated enough selective pressure to create the TTP and then make it fitter through adaptation, but not enough to destroy it.

Less intense pressure (say, leaving the tribes alone in 2002 or using lower-key intelligence and policing approaches or political engagement rather than a full-scale military invasion of the FATA) may have kept selective pressure low enough to keep the group stagnant or to enable the natural centrifugal tendency of the tribes' fractious family-based social organization (what anthropologists call their "segmentary lineage structure") to reassert itself, rather than the coalescing effect of outside threat. Conversely, more intensive targeting—killing leaders every five weeks, for instance, rather than every five years—might have created intense enough pressure to collapse the group by posing an adaptation challenge that it simply lacked the agility to meet in time.

Ronen Bergman's history of Israel's targeted killing program, *Rise and Kill First*, offers an instance of a counterterrorism force attempting to do just that. It also provides a second practical example of military artificial selection. Through a series of increasingly sophisticated targeted killings and network disruptions, Israeli intelligence in the 1990s had seriously damaged Palestinian terrorist groups such as Hamas. By 2002, the Israelis "were able to stop more than 80 percent of attacks before they turned deadly. The targeted killings were clearly saving lives. But there was a disturbing trend in the data, too: the number of attempted attacks was increasing."[50] Rather than being degraded, the threat network was growing. "But it also raised a fear that, over time, the terrorist groups would learn from each individual defeat and would adapt and get smarter and tougher, leading to a potentially endless escalation in a potentially endless war".[51]

Bergman points out that, though Israeli intelligence agencies successfully adapted to the evolving terrorist threat—which, arguably, selective pressure from their own operations had helped improve—their tactical success fed an addiction to covert operations on the part of Israel's political leaders. Israeli politicians came to believe that "covert operations could be a strategic and not just a tactical tool—that they could be used in place of real diplomacy to end the geographic, ethnic, religious, and national disputes in which Israel is mired."[52] Bergman concludes that Israel's targeted killing program represents "a long string of impressive tactical successes, but also disastrous strategic failures."[53]

There was also a clear pattern of predator-prey coevolution. As Avraham Shalom, head of Israel's internal intelligence agency, Shin Bet, from 1980 to 1986, put it in a 2013 documentary film, "As soon as we stopped dealing with [political negotiations over] the Palestinian state and started dealing with terrorism, terror became more sophisticated, and so did we. Suddenly we had a lot of work in Gaza and the West Bank, and overseas too. So we forgot about the Palestinian issue . . . How many people were caught? How many informers were there? How many attacks were prevented, how many weren't? The picture was always rosy, but it was point-specific: there was no strategy, only tactics."[54] Of course, as our own experience in the war on terrorism indicates, this is far from unique to Israel—indeed, it seems to be an almost mathematically certain result of the selection effects (artificial and natural) generated by targeting irregular "snakes."

At the macro level, the predator-prey effect is well illustrated by the relationship between coalition troop numbers and insurgent strength in Iraq. Of course, counterinsurgent forces don't literally eat guerrillas, so unlike natural and artificial selection the predator-prey effect is an analogy. But it's a powerful one: before March 2003, obviously enough, there were neither coalition soldiers nor anti-coalition insurgents in Iraq. The initial invasion brought roughly 150,000 American and 23,000 coalition troops into the country. Within weeks, the Iraqi regime had collapsed, but by midyear an insurgency was developing, growing to more than 50,000 fighters (across dozens of different Sunni and Shi'a factions) by late 2005. This prompted an insurgent population explosion in 2006 (the most violent period of the war), which in turn triggered a massive expansion in the counterinsurgent population in 2007 (the so-called surge of US forces, along with the Sunni tribal Awakening, the Sons of Iraq, and the growth of the Iraqi military and police). In the terms of a simple predator-prey model, the growth in prey population in 2005–2006 drove (after a time lag) an expansion in predator numbers in 2007.

The spike in predators (counterinsurgents, Iraqi government and Kurdish forces, "turned" Sunni militias, and tribes joining the Awakening) in 2007 led to a population collapse of prey (Sunni insurgents). By 2008, nine months after the onset of the surge, the active insurgent population had crashed, as indicated by the number of incidents, which had dropped by 96 percent. This prey-population collapse drove (again, after a time lag) a corresponding reduction in predator numbers, as US and coalition troops withdrew in 2009–11, the Sons of Iraq were disbanded, and Iraqi police took over from the military in most cities.

By 2012, this reduction of selection pressure (i.e., predation) on the guerrilla remnant had enabled a recovery—and the insurgent survivors of the 2008 population collapse, like drug-resistant bacteria, had been selected for characteristics that made them better fighters in the post-drawdown environment of 2012. This (literal) new breed of insurgents—members of Islamic State, as distinct from the old Sunni insurgency—was, in effect, a new species. Its members thought differently, fought differently, were organized along different lines, and were led by hard-bitten survivors of the massive purge of 2007–2009, with all the experience that entailed—and with the social capital and military-elder status to replicate their traits in the new organizations they spawned.

By 2013, insurgent numbers were rising once again. In 2014, Islamic State seized one-third of Iraq's territory and several of its major cities, and this in turn prompted a resurgence of predator (counterinsurgent) numbers, which by late 2017 had triggered another insurgent population collapse. Again, though, counterinsurgents from 2014 onward were survivors of the surge and drawdown, and had adapted through that cycle, so that their methods, composition, and means of "predation" were different and better. A much larger proportion this time around was composed of Shi'a communitarian militias (the Popular Mobilization Forces) rather than Sunni Sons of Iraq; a larger subgroup of their mentors and advisers consisted of Iranian Quds Force members; and so on. Today, of course, the Islamic State group is once again a fraction of its former size, has lost control of territory and population, and has dropped back a stage, into dispersed guerrilla operations. Triumphalist politicians (notably President Trump) have celebrated its demise and responded by planning to draw down US forces in the region. Suffice it to say, the predator-prey model suggests that any such celebration is wildly premature.

If this sounds simplistic, that's because it is: a guerrilla conflict like that in Iraq, with multiple competing armed actors, looks much more like a food web or ecosystem—where prey species in one scenario are predators in another, populations both prey on and are preyed upon by others, resource competition in an environment with limited carrying capacity can lead to one population outcompeting another, and apex predators can suffer population collapse for multiple reasons—rather than just a simple binary model. Predation against one "species" can also reduce competition for space and resources, creating an ecological niche for another: the classic example of this occurred in eastern Afghanistan, where US efforts in 2006–12 decimated the Taliban in key districts of Kunar, Nuristan, and Nangarhar Provinces, only to create a vacuum that was quickly filled by Al Qaeda as American forces withdrew in 2014.[55]

And there is vastly more to guerrilla conflict than mere ecological modeling, of course—notably, as mentioned, human agency, the cooperative innovation and adaptive ingenuity that individuals and groups apply to problems of survival. Nonstate armed groups are not just blindly evolving, nor are they simply engaging in bottom-up social learning or responding to natural and artificial selection. Rather, like their regular military opponents, they are also engaging in conscious adaptation, in ways that mimic (and in some ways exceed) our own. Institutional adaptation, then, is the final mechanism of evolution for adaptive enemies in irregular warfare.

Institutional Adaptation

"Check *this* out." My analyst handed me the printout with a smirk. It was 2011, we were working on an Afghanistan project, and he was holding a transcript from CIA's Open Source Center (OSC). The center collects, translates, and posts foreign-language media—including, nowadays, social media and internet chatter from jihadist forums.[56] All such material is, by definition, unclassified and publicly available—including this document, posted on an internet forum called "Ansar al-Mujahidin," which had been around since 2008 and reliably reflected Al Qaeda and affiliate messaging. Undated, but written sometime before 1 May 2011, it was an after-action review analyzing the defeat of Al Qaeda in Iraq in 2007 and offering lessons for groups in Afghanistan. Its author's nom de guerre—Shinkai al-Najdi—strongly suggested an Arab-Afghan connection: it combined a Saudi regional name (al-Najdi, reflecting a connection to Saudi Arabia's central, religiously conservative plateau) with that of an Afghan district, Shinkai, part of Zabul Province, which had recently seen heavy fighting and was just to the northeast of where my research team was operating.[57] The reason for my analyst's reaction was that the document referred to me as "Petraeus's Australian mercenary, Kilcullen."[58] We had a good laugh— enemy comments are always more interesting than those of allies. But then I read the document in detail.

It was a thorough and revealing assessment of the Iraq surge from Al Qaeda's point of view, offering an analysis of recent US leadership changes at CIA and the Pentagon, an assessment of the counterinsurgency strategy being implemented in Iraq and its main points of danger for the insurgents, plus an evaluation of Sunni insurgent infighting and the emergence of the Awakening Councils (which al-Najdi regarded as "the last straw, which made the people abandon the mujahidin").[59] The document rated the additional thirty thousand US troops deployed during the surge as less important than the new counterinsurgency techniques, which themselves came into their own only when combined with the tribal uprisings of the Awakening. It considered tactics and technology, including special forces raids, the use of concrete barriers in Baghdad, and the way that MRAPs (mine-resistant ambush-protected vehicles) reduced the effectiveness of roadside bombs.[60] In short, it was the kind of comprehensive, concrete assessment you would expect to see from the lessons-learned organization of any professional military force.

As the existence of this after-action review indicates, along with social learning, natural selection, and artificial selection, nonstate armed groups engage in conscious adaptation to their environment through lessons-learned processes, reviews like this one, and continuous deliberate development of new capabilities. Just as regular armed forces do, non-state groups gather observations, codify these into lessons, develop new approaches, which are then debated online and in a professional literature, and then implement revised organizations, weapon systems, and tactical approaches to try to get ahead of the adaptation curve. The 2011 document I was reading was one of dozens of similar assessments, commentaries in chat rooms, articles on discussion forums, and other efforts to learn, adapt, and disseminate improved techniques.

Islamic State's online magazines—*Dabiq* and *Rumiyah*—published how-to articles and tactical commentary on their own operations and those of others (including our own). Some were intended as propaganda, but many were straight lessons-learned or teaching tools, with articles on how to conduct an ambush, build a pressure-cooker bomb, launch a vehicle-based ramming attack, or operate an underground cell. Al Qaeda, with its original Arabic magazine, *al-Battar*, its English-language *Inspire*, and a series of training films from its As-Sahab media arm, focused even more on propagating such techniques—some of which were gleaned from observations of what worked in specific operations, while others seem to have been pioneered by specialized tactical concept development teams. Individual operatives with skills in, say, sniping or bomb-making built reputations within the professional literature of these groups, and their techniques became the jihadist equivalent of "doctrine." Indeed, over time, specific techniques or the presence of characteristic components or methods became markers for us, indicating involvement with particular groups or instruction by specific mentors. Training camps taught these techniques, and generations of terrorists and insurgents learned them over the internet or during face-to-face training sessions.

Professional militaries use unwieldy acronyms such as DOTMLPFI (doctrine, organization, training, materiel, leadership and education, personnel, facilities, and interoperability) to capture the categories of activity within which they seek to adapt. As Williamson Murray and Barry Watts point out in a seminal study of military innovation, even though technological development facilitates new ways of fighting, technologies themselves are the least important element of innovation.[61] As well as allowing time for new technologies to mature, military forces have to develop new organizational structures and command-and-control (C2) systems in order to make use of them, and they must combine newly fielded weapons with new tactics, concepts, and doctrine. As Murray and Watts point out, in many well-known cases of military innovation, there was also "nothing inevitable about the outcomes; much of the more successful innovation that occurred was the result of ad hoc improvisation."[62] While different military organizations conceive of innovation differently, it's clear that nonstate actors follow similar adaptation pathways.

To some extent (as pointed out earlier by Dominic Johnson) the fact that irregular and asymmetric actors are so prone to local variation, lack unified organization and equipment, and employ nonstandardized weapons and tactics simply creates more opportunities for lessons learned, while the proliferation of social media and internet communication (not just the open internet, but also the dark web, secure messaging, video sharing, and other tools) has given a dramatic boost to this process in the past decade or so.

In the year 2000, for example, when Osama bin Laden was planning the 9/11 attacks from his base in eastern Afghanistan, that country—like much of the developing world at the time—had no cellphone network, no internet, and extremely limited access to news and international communications. Since then, Wi-Fi, mobile phones, and satellite television have proliferated, particularly in developing countries, while smartphones have transformed the options for nonstate actors in terms of communication, finances, and information gathering.

It's worth remembering that virtually the entire connectivity explosion happened after 9/11. Since 2001, we have seen the BlackBerry (whose first email-capable version appeared in 2002), Facebook in 2004, YouTube in 2005, and Twitter in 2006 (which between them generated social media), the iPhone and Android smartphones (in 2007 and 2008, respectively), and applications including WhatsApp (2009), Instagram (2010), Snapchat (2011), and Telegram—the messaging app of choice for Islamic State—in 2013. Nonstate armed groups can now plan, reconnoiter, radicalize, recruit, pass targeting information, mount cyberattacks, and track their operations, all online via smartphones. And just as professional soldiers like me, back in

2003—reviewing films, after-action reviews, and signals intercepts—had been tasked to get a grip on how the enemy was changing, that enemy has been doing exactly the same thing to us.

I will discuss the specifics of what that enemy learned and how it has been applied in the next chapter, but for now it's enough to recognize that, as well as experiencing natural and artificial selection and engaging in bottom-up social learning, nonstate groups are also conscious learning organizations that observe their environment keenly, learn from their own experience and that of others, and seek to adapt their institutions, by which I mean not just organizational structures, but social institutions in the sense of stable and complex behavior patterns that help organize roles and activities within a group, to improve survivability and success.[63]

Stephen Rosen's notion, mentioned earlier—that military innovation in peacetime is driven by observed changes in the external environment, whereas wartime adaptation is driven by direct exposure to enemy action—is highly relevant here. The fragmentation of nonstate groups across multiple irregular conflicts means that, while one group is engaged in conflict-driven adaptation, others can be sitting back, observing, and developing new approaches in the same way that professional militaries innovate in peacetime.[64]

It also means that, just as professional militaries do, nonstate groups tend to enter each cycle of conflict-driven evolution with the set of adaptations they developed as a result of the previous "growth spurt." Some of these so-called pre-adaptations turn out to be advantageous, whereas others are neutral or negative. The other key point—which we will examine in subsequent chapters—is that not only have groups engaged in internal and intergroup learning and adaptation, but over the past nineteen years of the war on terrorism (and the post–Cold War period of the 1990s that preceded it) state and nonstate actors have learned from each other, so that today many of the most effective techniques used by nonstate armed groups draw on ideas or technologies acquired from states, while many successful state strategies are copied from nonstate groups. The snakes have learned to fight like dragons, and the dragons now fight like snakes.

With this understanding of *how* such groups learn and evolve, we can now look at *what* nonstate armed groups have learned, at the specific set of adaptations that have occurred among key nonstate armed groups, since Woolsey first described them as snakes in 1993.

3

Woolsey's Snakes

Since Woolsey's testimony in 1993, the terrorists, militias, and other nonstate armed actors he called "snakes" have continuously evolved, adapting to a changing threat picture, the spread of conflict into new domains such as cyberspace, the urbanization of war, the connectivity explosion, and a host of transformative technologies. These changes have enabled a democratization of lethality—putting into the hands of nonstate groups and hyper-empowered individuals a suite of lethal capabilities that was (until recently) the preserve of nation-states. In the preceding chapter, we looked at *how* adaptive enemies learn; this chapter examines *what* the snakes have learned.

In Chapter 2, I used the term "fitness landscape" to describe the combat environment within which adaptation occurs, along with the relative advantages that various combinations of traits confer on the armed actors who are trying to survive in it. This is a slight twist on an idea, originating in evolutionary genetics during the 1930s and refined by complex systems theorists since the 1980s, concerning the relationship between trait combinations, on the one hand, and adaptive success, on the other, within a given environment.[1] A fitness landscape maps all the potential combinations of characteristics for a given organism in that environment, so that any point on the landscape represents a particular combination. The more adaptive (i.e., the more conducive to survival and success) a given combination turns out to be, the higher its elevation as plotted on the fitness landscape, making altitude a metaphor for fitness. Selection pathways—the journeys toward greater fitness undertaken by evolving actors in the landscape—can thus be visualized as routes that climb upward to higher (more survivable) elevations, or fitness peaks.[2] There may be multiple peaks in a landscape—several distinct combinations that each offer significant advantages for a specific set of selective pressures. On rare occasions there may be a single peak only, representing a fitness terrain with just one optimal configuration. In other cases there are a great number of fitness peaks, so that the landscape (when plotted on a graph) looks like a hilly mountain range and is known as a rough or "rugged" fitness landscape.

Computer scientists and designers borrowed the notion of fitness landscapes from biologists to help them think about adaptation, innovation, and optimization strategies.[3] In this book, I use the term in a more generic sense: to describe the sum total of adaptive pressures acting on individuals and groups in a given environment, which in turn results in variable outcomes depending on the combination of characteristics they possess. In effect, a given environment—defined by a certain set of selective pressures—will punish certain behaviors and traits, while rewarding others. Actors in that environment, subjected to those pressures, will therefore evolve toward one or more fitness peaks in the landscape.

The landscape metaphor breaks down a bit in practice, because—in many environments, but particularly in war—the landscape is not static, but dynamic: by changing the pressures on actors in the environment, it is possible to shift the fitness peaks in the landscape, forcing actors to adapt or die. The implication is that, if we can map the pressures acting on our adversaries (and understand that our own actions contribute to the fitness landscape within which they operate), then we might be able to shift those pressures, alter the landscape, and leave them marooned and vulnerable. The next section therefore attempts to map the main pressures in the current fitness landscape for our adversaries.

THE FITNESS LANDSCAPE FOR ADVERSARIES

Over the quarter century since the end of the Cold War, the operating environment has become dramatically more crowded, cluttered, urbanized, coastal, and connected. Beside the long-standing megatrends of population growth, urbanization, littoralization, and connectivity, globalization has shaped the operating environment for states and nonstate adversaries alike.[4] In particular, the connectivity explosion has massively expanded the ability of state and nonstate actors to conduct remote warfare, letting them mobilize distant capabilities to lethal and nonlethal effect. Drone warfare by states is one example; remote radicalization and the weaponization of diaspora networks and social media are the flip side, as practiced by nonstate groups.

Increasingly, however—as we will see in the next two chapters—states are borrowing nonstate techniques and applying them in their own ways as an adjunct to (or replacement for) conventional military operations, and nonstate groups likewise are borrowing from states. The operating environment was largely created by Western democracies, the victors of the Cold War, after 1991, and it defines the fitness landscape within which adaptive threat actors evolve. So it's worth beginning the discussion of their evolution with a brief review of that landscape's key features and the forms of selection pressure it generates.

Air Supremacy, but with Severe Limitations

The first defining feature of the post–Cold War conflict environment is Western air supremacy, albeit a supremacy that has become increasingly constrained over time, through restrictive, self-imposed rules of engagement and partnerships with less than capable ground forces. This means that adversaries must deal with the constant threat of airborne surveillance and lethal strikes from the air—but provided they possess certain characteristics, that threat is eminently survivable.

The last American ground troops killed in an enemy airstrike were Private First Class Herbert Tucker and Corporal William R. Walsh, who died on the island of Cho-do in a raid by low-tech, fabric-and-plywood Po-2 biplanes from North Korea on the night of 15 April 1953, in the closing months of the Korean War.[5] Not a single American ground soldier or Marine has been killed by an enemy aircraft in any subsequent conflict, meaning that as a practical matter, American land forces have experienced an unbroken run of friendly air superiority for more than sixty-five years.

Still, during the Cold War, nobody thought to take this for granted. On the contrary: measures such as dispersal, stealth, night action, exploitation of battlefield obscuration (e.g., dust, fog, or smoke), ground-based air defense, and countersurveillance capabilities were fundamental to Western ground operations, while air and maritime forces were trained for air-to-air combat, seeking to gain and maintain air superiority over the battle area.

But after 1991—and especially since 9/11, in campaigns against insurgent and terrorist enemies who until recently lacked any serious air capability—allied ground commanders understandably came to take friendly control of the airspace as a given. This cozy assumption is now clearly out of date, as indicated by the US Army's recent scramble to update its long-neglected Short-Range Air Defense capabilities in the face of increased threat from states operating advanced attack aircraft and nonstate actors with weaponized drones.[6]

For their part, air forces throughout the Cold War fully expected a contested combat environment in which an adversary would field lethal air-to-air capabilities, deploy effective ground-based air defenses, and possess strike assets that could attack friendly ground forces and achieve air superiority at the decisive point, if not enduring theaterwide air supremacy.[7] Air-to-air combat (as distinct from enemy air-to-ground strikes) did take place after Korea, notably in Vietnam, where one estimate suggests that up to 249 US aircraft were shot down by enemy planes.[8] After the Cold War, however, as Warsaw Pact air forces collapsed, Western air superiority became largely uncontested, and "the U.S. . . . enjoyed a prolonged period of unchallenged military dominance in space."[9] As a result, an entire generation of Western ground troops and aircrew grew up facing nonstate enemies who struggled to defend against airstrikes, interfere with our control of air and space, or seriously threaten our aircraft.

Counterintuitively, though, over the same period (through peacekeeping operations in the 1990s and counterinsurgency campaigns after 2001) and despite an increased use of precision munitions, the ability of US and allied air forces to apply heavy airborne firepower actually diminished, while ground forces increasingly lacked the capacity to force adversaries to expose themselves to air strikes. We went from a Cold War environment where highly professional ground and air forces trained for a contested air environment to one where air forces lacked a serious threat but ground forces were small, constrained by restrictive rules of engagement, or tethered to local partners of limited effectiveness.

For example, over the forty-three days of the Gulf War air campaign in 1991 (which, as described in Chapter 1, was the conflict that showed adversaries how *not* to fight us), the number of strike sorties—round trips by a single aircraft carrying one or more strike weapons—averaged roughly a thousand per day. There were thousands of missile strikes as well, and coalition aircraft flew three hundred to five hundred additional sorties per day in order to maintain air superiority.[10] During that campaign, the largest number of strike sorties in a day was around three thousand, concentrated in the relatively small area of Kuwait and a portion of southern and western Iraq, an area of only about 35,000 square kilometers.[11] By the 2001 invasion of Afghanistan, over a seventy-six-day air campaign, the daily average of strike sorties had fallen to eighty-six, and the largest number in one day was only about two hundred, across the far larger area (roughly 184,000 square kilometers) of Afghanistan.[12] By 2014–17 the average number of strike sorties against Islamic State (across the whole of Syria and Iraq, or about 620,000 square kilometers) was only fifty-six per day.[13] To be sure, many more of those strikes involved precision weapons, and there were heavier bombs and missiles available. It's also worth noting that raw strike sorties alone do not measure the effectiveness of an air campaign or fully capture its intensity—though they do offer a useful benchmark. Likewise, in this context we are less interested in the overall effectiveness of any given campaign than in the particular types of selective pressure it imposes on enemy forces.

Still, these data suggest that, for adversaries able to disperse and hide, the danger posed by Western air assets diminished considerably between 1991 and 2001, and even more so by 2014. From 28 strike sorties per day per thousand square kilometers in 1991 to 0.46 in 2001, to 0.09 by 2014, intensity fell an order of magnitude from each campaign to the next.[14] Again, noting that intensity doesn't equal effectiveness, far fewer strikes over a much larger area translated into less "airpower pressure" on any given adversary force in any one location. This in turn meant that Western-led air campaigns—with the exception of those supported by Western ground troops—became increasingly survivable for enemies able to disperse or disappear against the human and physical background.

In evolutionary terms, the fitness landscape favored actors who combined characteristics such as stealth, dispersion, and modularity, especially small semiautonomous bands that presented fewer and smaller targets for attack. It also rewarded autonomy (the ability to operate without orders and therefore avoid communications that might be detected by enemy sensors) and the ability to blend into the background, which we could call "adaptive coloration." In urban environments in particular—and the battlefield, as we have seen, is increasingly urban—it rewarded the ability to "infest" urban terrain (the Israeli military's term for disappearing into and maneuvering wholly inside buildings and underground or internal passages).[15] Entities with these characteristics tended to be more survivable under air attack. Conversely, the environment punished size, overtness, anything that generated a sustained contrast against the human or physical background, large troop concentrations, active communications, and hierarchical organizations.

Perhaps counterintuitively, effective air campaigns in fact rely heavily on capable ground forces, who play a crucial role in forcing enemies to concentrate (which ground troops must do to survive attack from another ground force), flushing them out of cover, or baiting them to draw them into the open, thereby creating targets that can be seen and struck from the air. Conversely, dispersing to avoid air attack makes ground troops vulnerable to another land force, so that the presence of air forces helps ground units attack larger, more capable enemies, who cannot concentrate against them lest they be destroyed from the air. Recognizing this, modern tacticians try to create what they call a "combined arms" effect, catching adversaries on the horns of a dilemma in which, to defend against one arm (ground forces), they must expose themselves to another (air power) and vice versa.

Indeed, joint maneuver is all about creating this dilemma for the enemy, for example by using "Joint Air Attack Teams," which force an enemy to bunch up and present a target for air strikes, missiles, or artillery.[16] But if land forces lack numbers (as in much of the war on terrorism since 2001, when there have never been enough ground troops to go around) or quality (as in Iraq and Afghanistan after Western troops withdrew or in many parts of Africa and Asia today) enemies can disperse and hide, since ground troops pose insufficient threat to make them concentrate. Lack of capable ground forces creates survival opportunities for adversaries, given the diminished weight of airborne firepower, which in turn is driven by a second key feature: increasingly tight legal and political constraints.

Tightening Self-Imposed Legal and Political Constraints

The reason for the reduced weight of effective airborne firepower between 1991 and 2017 was not lack of capability or technology. Nor was it a shortage of aircraft and munitions (though almost twenty years of sustained campaigning in Iraq and Afghanistan have certainly taken their toll on aircrew and airframes, while distorting both ground and air forces' understanding of close air support).[17] Rather, it involved two other factors: the massive expansion in the size of operational areas (so that, as we have seen, airpower was spread much more thinly than in the past) and the imposition of ever more restrictive legal and political constraints. These took the form of rules of engagement, caveats (whereby nations in a coalition create carve-outs that limit what their contingents can do), and increasingly restrictive international norms. This is the second key feature of the fitness landscape for adversaries.

During the Cold War, NATO fully expected to fight the Soviets in the populated urban terrain of central and western Europe. Not only would military targets be intermixed with civilian populations (exposing civilians to harm, and property to collateral damage) but everyone expected to fight in a battlespace poisoned by nerve gas while facing extremely heavy conventional firepower, as well as nuclear and possibly biological weapons. The expected speed of maneuver (Soviet forces planned to reach the Rhine within forty-eight hours and the English Channel within seventy-two hours of the outbreak of conflict)[18] meant that roads would be choked with refugees and injured or dying civilians for whom military forces could do little. In a superpower nuclear exchange, targeting cities with weapons of mass destruction was also par for the course. In training films of the era, legal and humanitarian requirements to protect the civil population and their property were clearly spelled out, but few commanders truly expected to be able to protect civilians once the war began.[19] In popular culture—pulp-fiction books like James Rouch's *Zone* novels of the 1980s, telemovies like *The Day After* (1983) and *Threads* (1984), and Tom Clancy's 1986 technothriller *Red Storm Rising*—large-scale civilian death and destruction were more or less taken for granted.[20]

In the 1991 Gulf War, executed by late–Cold War militaries a few months before the Soviet collapse and mostly fought across open terrain, rules of engagement were extraordinarily robust, imposing few restraints beyond the formal laws of war.[21] The combination of capable air and ground forces created the combined arms dilemma that destroyed Saddam's forces. The "highway of death" was one example, where ground threats forced Iraqi units to withdraw, bunch up, and create a target for aircraft.

US commanders at the time commented that lack of political interference—and politicians' willingness to let troops do what had to be done—were a welcome change from what many had seen as political tinkering in Vietnam and micromanagement during the deployment to Beirut in 1983.[22] Not that there were no restrictions—there certainly were, and they were generally obeyed (among them, a no-target list and restraints on weapons use in built-up areas)[23]—but these conformed to norms of state-on-state war and the laws of armed conflict, with few extra self-imposed restraints.

After 1991, however, with the collapse of the Soviet Union and the shift to lower-intensity peacekeeping and humanitarian operations, Western forces began to adopt increasingly restrictive self-imposed rules of engagement. Protecting civilians and preventing property damage became paramount, while killing or capturing adversaries became less central, in "counterwar" operations where conflict itself was the enemy. After 9/11, troops trained in the 1990s peacekeeping era deployed to Afghanistan and Iraq, bringing the same focus on prevention of civilian casualties and property damage. The view even emerged—bizarrely, to many combat troops—that minimizing damage to the enemy (not just to innocent bystanders and civilian property) was or should be mandatory.

As the defense analyst Colin Kahl noted in 2006, the result of this shift in norms—at least in Iraq—was a sharp drop in civilian casualties compared with previous conflicts and better compliance with humanitarian and legal requirements than at any time in history.[24] He noted the use of "no-strike lists" to prevent attacks on schools, mosques, hospitals, and other civilian installations; Collateral Damage Estimation Methodology (CDEM) software to minimize property damage and injury to bystanders; reluctance to use artillery (especially in cities); reliance on precision air weapons; and graduated use of force against targets showing hostile intent.[25] Overall, he concluded, rules of engagement had "grown much more restrictive since the beginning of the counterinsurgency period."[26] Of course, in counterinsurgency there are definitely times when violence has to be minimized in order to achieve a larger objective, and it should go without saying that reducing civilian casualties and property damage is absolutely a good thing, in ethical and political terms. Still, what concerns us here is not the moral excellence or political prudence of this approach, but rather its impact on enemy evolution.

That impact further selected for enemies with the ability to hide within the civilian population or urbanized terrain, "hug" protected populations or sites, manipulate an adversary into disproportionate strikes, and exploit errors or overreactions by leveraging a media or diplomatic backlash when they did occur. Thus, the environment encouraged the emergence of adversaries with media manipulation and political warfare skills. Enemies with these abilities could exploit our mistakes, including operator error by ground or air forces and targeting errors by intelligence analysts, when they inevitably occurred. This reflected a third feature of the fitness landscape after 1993: the increasing ability of intelligence agencies to collect electronic emissions of all kinds, but the decreasing ability of analysts to keep up with that collection.

Omnipresent Surveillance, Overwhelmed Analysts

Despite budget cuts at the end of the Cold War—and after a period of flux in the early 1990s while they figured out how to reorient from the Soviet target toward new threats—Western intelligence agencies experienced a massive increase in collection capacity after 1993. The ability to gather an enormous volume of data of all kinds, using an ever-increasing variety of assets (ground-, air-, and space-based) across an exploding array of sources and in ever-expanding geographical space and cyberspace, was truly transformative.

The 1993 Battle of Mogadishu, perceived within the US Congress as an intelligence failure, led to the 1994 Aspin-Brown inquiry.[27] This commission recommended, among other things, a reorientation of US intelligence effort toward the "snakes" Woolsey had described a few months before the battle. As if channeling Woolsey, the commission's report listed counterterrorism, counternarcotics, countering WMD proliferation, and dealing with international organized crime as key intelligence missions.[28] It also emphasized the need for improved resourcing (in terms of money, materiel, and personnel) to retool intelligence systems for the 1990s and beyond.

In the same time frame of the mid-1990s, handheld electronics—cellphones, GPS devices, personal digital assistants, laptop computers—became increasingly common and capable in the civilian market, while their size and cost plummeted. Mobile phones—which were still, in the early 1990s, roughly the size and weight of a house brick—had been around since the 1970s but began to spread widely in the late 1980s after the introduction of pioneering cellular telephone networks in Australia and Finland. The IBM Simon, the first rudimentary smartphone, was unveiled at a trade show in late 1992.[29] Cellular networks improved rapidly through the 1990s as cell towers proliferated, mobile technologies advanced, and miniaturized components shrank cellphone handsets. The real explosion in connectivity, however, began around the year 2000 and kicked into high gear after the invention of the iPhone in 2006. All of this massively increased the volume of communications available for intelligence agencies to collect. The combination of renewed funding and focus on intelligence, the enormous increase in traffic volume, and the fact that nonstate adversaries (with limited access to encryption or security countermeasures, and therefore relatively accessible communications) were now the dominant target, made signals intelligence (SIGINT) collection increasingly important.

The National Security Agency (NSA, responsible for signals intelligence in the United States) "drastically re-engineered its SIGINT collection network beginning in the early 1990s. By the late 1990s, NSA's SIGINT collection system had become smaller but more capable and flexible than the old Cold War architecture."[30] By the year 2000, it comprised satellites, large listening posts, clandestine sensors in embassies, and ship-based, airborne, and submarine reconnaissance platforms. The new generation of intelligence satellites gave NSA increasingly comprehensive coverage of an ever-widening range of emissions by the early twenty-first century.[31] NSA and its partners in the "five eyes" intelligence community sought to suck up all communications, of every kind, everywhere, all the time.

The 9/11 attacks and the resulting belief that intelligence agencies needed to connect the dots to prevent future attacks brought an even greater expansion of collection after 2001. The 2004 showdown over Stellar Wind—an NSA program involving the collection of content and metadata from telephone and internet communications of American citizens—as well as the 2013 leaks by the NSA defector Edward Snowden and a string of revelations by the radical transparency group Wikileaks demonstrated that intelligence agencies could now apply their massive collection capacity to "gather a haystack so [they] can search for needles."[32]

But even as collection capacity expanded, analytical capacity lagged. As late as 2009, in Afghanistan, despite "literally terabytes of classified and unclassified data" being collected, analysts lacked the capacity to keep up with collection, hampering their ability to understand terrorist networks or comprehend the wider environment.[33] As the Israeli intelligence officer Hannan Gefen wrote in 2014, this outpacing of analysis by collection created a real dilemma:

> How do you deal with undefined entities, devoid of a permanent structure, constantly-changing and unpredictable? How do you cope with a massive amount of communication traffic that keeps growing at an alarming rate? How do you connect all of the communication appearances of an objective that can pop up in a telephone conversation, an SMS message, Skype communication, electronic mail and so forth? Finally, how do you differentiate between communication traffic you can monitor and invasion of privacy? In all of these situations, the data had not existed in the context of the "old world" of intelligence gathering. The solution, as far as [SIGINT agencies] were concerned, was . . . long-term collection and storage of all of the communication traffic you could lay your hands on, with no filtration.[34]

This feature of the fitness landscape—pervasive surveillance, limited analysis—selected for adversaries with a cyber or electronic version of the same adaptive coloration they were applying in the physical and social realms. The more an entity could blend into the background, hide in the clutter of giant volumes of electronic traffic, and avoid attracting SIGINT analysts' attention, the more survivable it would be. Such a group could avoid triggering an operational response, even while under constant surveillance. Knowing that their communications were almost certainly being monitored and their data collected and stored, adversaries could nevertheless calculate that the chances of any human ever actually looking at those data were manageably small. The very explosion of connectivity that made intelligence collection possible became itself the cover within which these adversaries could hide while enabling propaganda and command-and-control techniques that exploited mass communication and social media.

Proliferation of Consumer Smart Systems

A fourth, closely related feature of the environment was the spread of smart, handheld consumer electronic systems. Not only did the new technologies have the communications potential and social impact of smartphones, they put precision hardware into the hands of individuals and nonstate groups around the world, giving them access to advanced systems previously available only to governments.

The military application was not long in coming—indeed, in many ways it was there from the start: Global Positioning System (GPS) satellites, so central to virtually every aspect of modern life worldwide, are a constellation of US military space platforms, while Google Earth, originally known as "Keyhole Viewer" in a coy reference to the special security system for US spy satellites, was created with CIA funding in 2001 before being acquired by Google in 2004.[35] By 2011, Google Earth had been downloaded a billion times and was running on laptops, iPads, Android and iOS smartphones, and a host of other devices around the globe.[36] By 2017, there were more than five billion global navigation system satellite (GNSS) devices worldwide, and that number was expected to grow to eight billion by 2020.[37]

The US government announced that GPS had reached its initial operational capability on 8 December 1993—making satellite navigation yet another feature of the modern world, which, though it sometimes seems to have been around forever, in fact dates to that same seminal year of Woolsey's testimony.[38] When GPS was first introduced, civilians could not use the full military-grade version of it; only a degraded-accuracy version was available. In May 2000, the US government stopped degrading civilian GPS and, in September 2007, announced that future GPS satellites would no longer have the ability to do so.[39] In effect, bipartisan decisions by the Clinton and Bush administrations made military-grade precision available to everyone on the planet at US government expense: the strapline of the official GPS webpage currently reads "GPS: A Global Public Service brought to you by the U.S. Government."[40]

This was not pure altruism: the more devices out there, the more easily intelligence services could track movement, creating a whole new category of data to collect and expanding the new disciplines of GEOINT (geospatial intelligence) and MOVINT (movement intelligence) through tracking GNSS devices—now, of course, including all smartphones and wearable technologies, as well as an increasing number of GPS-enabled vehicles and other devices. Still, combined with the public availability of military-grade GPS after 2000, the massive proliferation of satellite navigation devices—literally one for every human being on the planet by 2020—created opportunities for nonstate actors to achieve levels of precision well beyond those available to most developing-world militaries, and even some advanced forces. The application has been increasingly obvious in recent conflicts.

During the Libyan and Syrian uprisings of 2011, rebels used Skype, Google Earth, and GPS-enabled smartphones (then in relatively short supply) to support their operations. A photo from the period shows Syrian rebels using the compass app from an Android cellphone to determine where to point a homemade multibarrel rocket launcher. This is not particularly innovative—a magnetic compass would, of course, be thrown off by such a large chunk of metal, so it makes sense to use an electronic one while keeping the rest of the traditional firing system unchanged. But within a few years, technology and connectivity had advanced to the point where guerrillas could construct an entire smartphone-based precision firing system for mortars and rockets.

By 2014, mortar teams in Aleppo could use their iPad or smartphone's GPS (which told them their mortar's precise location) along with its compass app to determine the azimuth for a given target, then refer to firing tables downloaded over an internet browser, or use a ballistic computing app (also on the phone) to determine the correct elevation and propellant charge for a particular range. They could then set that elevation using the smartphone's inclinometer and fire their first ranging shot. A remote observer—on the scene or, more likely, located elsewhere but in contact via phone or secure messaging app with someone able to see the target—would place a pin in Google Earth to mark the fall of shot. This pin could be made to appear on the version of Google Earth running on the mortar team's smartphone, and they could immediately launch multiple rounds to destroy the target after just one ranging round. For comparison, this fire-control system lets nonstate armed groups attain a level of precision equal to, or better than, what most state-based military forces can achieve. And the fire-control system that enables that precision sits on a cellphone—a far lighter, cheaper, more discreet, and less bulky platform than used by conventional forces.

By 2016, Ukrainian artillery officers using the venerable D-30 122mm howitzer (a Soviet-era artillery piece in widespread use across the former Warsaw Pact nations) had created a similar system using Android smartphones—which, like the mortar app, relied on knowing the phone's, and therefore the gun's, location with a high degree of accuracy—enabling them to deploy in dispersed and camouflaged positions while converging and timing their fire to ensure that multiple rounds from dispersed gun positions arrived on target simultaneously. Thus, in the space of six years, individuals repurposing consumer smart systems had gone from simply using civilian tools in a combat setting (Libya, 2011), to developing precision-fire systems better than many militaries (Syria, 2014), to engaging in integrated cyberkinetic combat in ways conventional militaries are yet to do (Ukraine, 2017).

Hobby drones offered similar opportunities to repurpose consumer technology and combine it with existing military hardware to generate something new and better than most states had. From a standing start around 2007, autonomous air vehicles—powered by the same suite of technologies driving development in smartphones—exploded in numbers and improved exponentially in quality. Every smartphone improvement drove a related advance in drone technology: as the tech reporter Dave Hambling observed in 2015, "A drone is simply a smartphone with wings, and the wings are the cheap part."[41] Much as with piloted aircraft a century ago, the military use of drones rapidly evolved under the adaptive pressure of wartime, morphing from reconnaissance to air-to-ground attack, then air-to-air combat, and increasing in capability and range. By 2015, "kamikaze drones" carrying explosives were targeting troops and installations; by 2016, Islamic State had fielded quadcopters that could drop grenades and then return to base to rearm like miniature bombers; by 2017, purpose-designed bomblets were being dropped by larger fixed-wing drones in Syria and Iraq, and by 2018, swarm attacks with multiple drones had occurred in Syria.[42]

A report late in 2018 by the US National Academy of Sciences noted that modern hobby drones increasingly operated without radio, using automated target recognition and tracking, GPS chips, obstacle avoidance, and other software that made them relatively invulnerable to jamming—and hence much more survivable.[43] By 2025, the same report predicted, commercially available capabilities would enable nonstate adversaries to field coordinated groups, swarms, and collaborative networks involving tens to hundreds of weaponized, miniaturized drones.[44]

This feature of the fitness landscape favored adversaries who engaged in technological "hugging" of Western systems, using capabilities (Google Earth, smartphones, hobby drones, iPads, GPS) that advanced military forces also relied on, and thereby making it extremely difficult for governments to shut these systems down without also hampering their own operations. By piggybacking on the same systems that advanced militaries were using, nonstate adversaries improved their survivability, and via the selective processes discussed in the preceding chapter, groups that successfully did this proliferated and their techniques were replicated by others, while those who failed to adopt these techniques died out.

The kinds of adversaries who could successfully apply this strategy tended, by definition, to have access to connectivity (which, since cellphone reception is better in cities, meant they were generally urban) and to the technical and mechanical skills needed to hack hardware, repurpose consumer technologies, or integrate military hardware into improvised systems. They also usually had some familiarity with computer coding, electronic systems, and software hacking—again, implying an urban population and a degree of technical education. Thus, the urbanization of the battlefield in the twenty-first century favored such groups, even as their emergence also accelerated the already existing tendency for combat to take place in cities and among urban populations.

Adaptive Traits of Nonstate Groups

To summarize, today's fitness landscape—created by background changes like urbanization, globalization, and connectivity, and further shaped by Western countries' own actions after the end of the Cold War—reflects a set of selection pressures that forced armed actors to adapt. It incorporates (in its current configuration) a series of "fitness peaks," as described earlier—combinations of traits that confer a survival advantage on actors with the following characteristics:

- *Stealth*—the ability to blend into the physical, social, and informational background, adopting "adaptive coloration" to disappear when threatened
- *Dispersion*—the ability to move and fight dispersed, either without having to concentrate at all (using connectivity and remote-warfare tools) or concentrating for specific operations to overwhelm a weaker enemy, before dispersing again
- *Modularity*—the ability to operate in small bands, employing combat groups that can survive the destruction of other groups and self-healing networks that can regenerate new combat groups if necessary
- *Autonomy*—the ability to operate for long periods without orders or communications, thereby reducing the electronic signature of the group and improving its survivability
- *Hiding in electronic plain sight*—the ability to hide within gigantic volumes of electronic traffic, adopting low-profile behaviors to avoid attracting analysts' attention or triggering an operational response, even while accepting the reality of pervasive surveillance
- *"Hugging"*—the ability to get close to protected populations or sites or to piggyback onto systems (GPS, Google Earth, smartphones, the internet) that opponents cannot disable without harming themselves

- *Media manipulation*—the ability to goad, provoke, or trick an adversary into inflicting disproportionate civilian casualties or property damage, and then exploit such errors through a manipulated media backlash
- *Political warfare*—the ability to manipulate and mobilize supporters through mass communication, social networks, weaponized diasporas, and online networks, using protest movements and agents of influence to undermine an opponent's operations, unity, and legitimacy
- *Technology and connectivity hacking*—the ability to rapidly repurpose consumer systems, use civilian devices in combat settings, and develop precision or collaborative-engagement systems that are better than those available to state opponents (using both hardware and software skills)

Each of these was an adaptive response to a particular kind of pressure generated by the environment—and actors who developed these traits (or combinations of them) improved their survivability and thereby climbed toward peaks in the fitness landscape. Each of these evolutionary pathways is also evident in the way nonstate actors have adapted over the past twenty-five years.

ADAPTATION TRENDS IN IRREGULAR WARFARE: THE EVOLVING SNAKES

When those of us who served in Iraq or Afghanistan think of evolution among nonstate armed groups, we tend to think mostly about Al Qaeda. This is understandable, of course, but there are other models of irregular warfare, and what we think we know about Al Qaeda has to be informed by an understanding of those other approaches and how they too have evolved in response to the pressures just described. So in this section, while initially covering Al Qaeda, I will also discuss three other models, each of which illustrates something unique. These are Islamic State, the Syrian Al Qaeda affiliate HTS (Hayat Tahrir al-Sham), and the Lebanese group Hezbollah. Al Qaeda is the place to start, though, because of its centrality in Western strategy since 2001.

Al Qaeda at Thirty

The first known meeting of the group that became Al Qaeda (AQ) took place in the Pakistani frontier city of Peshawar on 11 August 1988.[45] This meeting brought together Osama bin Laden, Ayman al-Zawahiri, and other key ideologues.[46] Around this time the AQ founders met Mohammed Salah al-Din Zaidan ("Saif al-Adel"), a former Egyptian Army officer trained in explosives and unconventional warfare. Saif al-Adel later became AQ's star military trainer among other things, allegedly advising the Somali militias who fought at the October 1993 Black Hawk Down battle in Mogadishu, which would make that battle, eight months after Woolsey's 1993 testimony, the first time AQ engaged in direct combat against Americans.[47] That means AQ was thirty years old by 2018—and if the Mogadishu claim is true, as well as adding yet another significant event to the seminal year of 1993, it would mean that the group has been fighting us a full quarter century. Thirty years is an entire generation in human terms, but because of rapid turnover in Al Qaeda's personnel, with many individuals killed, captured, or leaving the group since 2001, it equates to three or more generations of organic evolution, group and individual adaptation, and cross-pollination of adaptive characteristics within AQ.

Back in its pre-9/11 incarnation, Osama bin Laden, Zawahiri, and the other founders saw AQ primarily as a transnational base from which would grow a global insurgency. AQ saw itself less as a terrorist group than as a revolutionary vanguard for a broader mass movement.[48] The concept of a jihadist vanguard that seeks to spark, shape, and enable a larger mass movement was first advanced by Sayyid Qutb in 1964, in his influential work *Milestones*, acknowledged by early AQ leaders as one of the strongest inspirations for their thinking.[49] Qutbism has been described as an "Islamo-fascist" ideology, but the debt of Islamist ideologues to early communist theorists is actually deeper than any fascist connection.[50]

Indeed, Qutb could just as easily be described as "Islamo-Leninist." As early as 1902, Vladimir Lenin had described the Communist Party as the "vanguard of the proletariat," arguing for an elite professional cadre of experienced revolutionaries who would guide and rally the inchoate revolutionary masses.[51] Qutb's argument almost exactly replicates Lenin's idea of sixty years earlier. And this notion—of an elite cadre pulling the people along with them—is precisely what shaped AQ leaders' sense of their own role. Through funding, propaganda support, access to training facilities and manuals, as well as the deployment of advisers from a central cadre, they sought to sponsor local guerrillas and insurgents. The goal was to aggregate the effects of multiple local groups into a unified whole, inspire the global Muslim *ummah* to mass revolt, and thereby force the United States out of the Middle East, causing apostate regimes in North Africa and the Arabian Peninsula—the group's "near enemy"—to collapse for lack of American support.

In the early 1990s, through advisers like Saif al-Adel, training materials, funding, technical advice, and equipment, AQ supported Somali, Kenyan, and other African groups, as well as networks in Yemen, Saudi Arabia, the Levant (Syria and Lebanon), and other parts of the Middle East. After moving in the early 1990s to Sudan, where they operated under the protection of the Islamist leader Hassan al-Turabi, the group was forced back to Afghanistan in 1996, where its headquarters remained—housed in a network of urban safe houses and rural camps and training facilities—until 2001.

In its Afghan base, AQ built a large, complex, and hierarchical organizational and financial structure, and began to sponsor attacks against US interests, initially outside the United States, beginning with the East African embassy bombings in 1998 and the attack on the warship USS *Cole* in 2000. This reflected an evolution in AQ leaders' thinking, based on experience since 1988, away from the "near enemy" (apostate regimes in the region) toward the "far enemy," the United States. As Osama bin Laden put it during a planning session, "We have to cut the head off the snake."[52] In Stephen Rosen's terms—discussed in Chapter 2—AQ leaders were engaging in the kinds of concept-driven, self-generated innovations we expect of military forces in peacetime. But this was soon to change.

The 9/11 attacks were designed to fit the new strategy of forcing the far enemy to withdraw support from local regimes. They were transformational not just for the United States and its allies—who were finally forced to confront the reality of a transnational insurgency that could strike directly at the heart of Western global financial, political, and military power—but for the evolution of AQ itself.[53]

The 9/11 attacks were (and remain) the most ambitious terrorist operation ever launched, taking years to plan and costing the group five hundred thousand US dollars. They also had by far the largest impact, killing 2,976 people and maiming thousands more (not counting those who died from the aftereffects of the attacks) and costing the US economy $500 billion in direct financial impact. Adding the cost of the war on terrorism (including the wars in Iraq and Afghanistan), homeland security spending, and the costs of follow-on conflicts, a mid-2018 study found that spending "totaled $2.8 trillion during fiscal years 2002 through 2017."[54] Most important, the 9/11 attacks kicked off a cycle of conflicts that are with us still and show no sign of ending anytime soon.

But as well as reordering the global strategic landscape, the 9/11 attacks transformed the fitness landscape for Al Qaeda—indeed, the response they provoked came close to destroying the group. By mid-December 2001, only twelve weeks after the attacks, AQ's Afghan base had ceased to exist, its Taliban host regime had been overthrown, its leadership had been scattered, thousands of its fighters had been killed or captured, and Osama bin Laden and his key followers were pinned down in the mountains of Tora Bora, just across the Afghan-Pakistan border from the Tirah Valley. Bin Laden had written his last will and testament, and was intercepted in a radio transmission apologizing to his followers as they hunkered down under bombardment, expecting imminent death or capture.[55] Key lieutenants— notably Saif el-Adel, who had opposed 9/11 because he expected precisely the response that occurred—had broken with bin Laden, while leaders and family members of senior AQ personnel had fled into Iran, where they were promptly interned.[56]

AQ's survival in late 2001 came about largely through luck and the inability of Western airpower to find and finish key leaders, scattered in the Tora Bora hills, due to the lack of a capable partner ground force. A band of Afghan militia under a local warlord failed to close the AQ remnant's escape route into Pakistan, and there were simply too few US and Australian special operators on the ground to do the job themselves—an early example of two features of the environment (thinly spread airpower and shortage of effective ground forces) that were to become more obvious as time went on.[57]

It was also, not for the last time, an instance of naive overconfidence among US leaders, epitomized by the decision of Secretary of Defense Donald Rumsfeld and General Tommy Franks, head of United States Central Command, even as the battle at Tora Bora was still raging in December 2001, to pull assets away from the fight and redirect planning efforts toward war against Iraq.[58] Osama bin Laden lived to fight another day, ultimately surviving almost another full decade, until May 2011. And as AQ recovered from its near-death experience in 2002, the survivors embodied a set of adaptations to the changed fitness landscape, even as the organization itself adopted a wartime evolution model in which its approach coevolved with enemy actions and responded directly to combat pressure.

Al Qaeda's first major wartime adaptation was decentralization. As noted, AQ before 9/11 was hierarchical and centralized, with committees, installations, training facilities and camps, and a large overt base area in eastern Afghanistan. By 2002, this was gone, and with the guts torn out of the central structure, the organization's affiliates—in Yemen, Indonesia, East Africa, and Saudi Arabia—became more influential. Core AQ leaders in Pakistan spent several years reestablishing themselves, regrouping and rebuilding, even as first-generation leaders including Khalid Sheikh Mohammed (the planner of 9/11) were captured, while others (like Abu Hafs al-Masri, AQ's military chief) were killed.

In its second generation, as AQ recovered, its core group reemerged more as a propaganda hub and a center for guidance and targeting direction than as an operational organization. AQ central was a vanguard in ideological and conceptual terms, not a combat cadre. Instead, the leading operational role was assumed by regional affiliates (AQ "franchises") rather than the core. Merely by continuing to exist in Pakistan, surviving as a symbol of defiance and issuing periodic propaganda statements, bin Laden and Zawahiri acted as an inspirational rallying point that helped aggregate the effects of a global insurgency which was increasingly decentralized in its tactical execution.

Indeed, core AQ at this time operated very much like the governments in exile of European countries under Nazi occupation during the Second World War: as a source of political coordination and legitimacy for resistance groups, as an inspiration offering hope for victory, and as a source of information, intelligence, and operational resources for underground movements in enemy-occupied territory. Like the governments in exile, AQ central ran espionage and propaganda networks, partnered with potential allies, negotiated (often acrimoniously) with host governments, and periodically sent advisers, trainers, and covert operators to assist its affiliate movements—and just as in the Second World War, those resistance movements increasingly saw themselves as having distinct identities and different interests than their sponsors.

Further, just as during the 1940s better-armed and -organized Communist movements (in France, Yugoslavia, Greece, Poland, and elsewhere) attempted to crowd out resistance groups who remained loyal to the exiled regimes, new movements—notably Al Qaeda in Iraq (AQI), particularly in its later incarnation as the Islamic State of Iraq and al-Sham (ISIS)—arose to challenge AQ's authority in zones of Western occupation (Iraq and Afghanistan). But we are getting ahead of ourselves: in the immediate post-9/11 period the most noticeable change, beyond AQ's tactical decentralization, was the rise of guerrilla terrorism.[59]

The 9/11 attacks were an instance of "expeditionary terrorism," in which a terrorist organization recruits, trains, and equips a team in one country, then infiltrates that team into another to assault a predetermined target. In the aftermath, as both AQ and Western governments adapted to the new environment, a pattern of wartime coevolution emerged. Governments and businesses spent billions on border surveillance, airport security, and international information sharing, specifically to prevent another attack. AQ responded with new methods, which in turn shaped Western responses and drove new cycles of evolutionary adaptation on AQ's part, in an accelerating—and increasingly codependent—manner.

Guerrilla terrorism emerged as a means of sidestepping the international travel security measures put in place after 9/11, in one of the first instances of coevolution between threat and defender. An early example was the London 7/7 bombing of 7 July 2005, where, rather than send in nineteen people covertly, AQ brought one man out openly. Mohammed Sidique Khan traveled openly, on his own passport, to Pakistan's tribal areas for training, then returned to the UK, again openly, where he recruited a four-man team inside Britain's international border but outside London—three out of four attackers came from Leeds in the north of England. The team trained, rehearsed, prepared rucksack bombs, conducted a final reconnaissance, and then traveled to London, where they blew up three Tube trains and a double-decker bus. At low cost, AQ had employed guerrilla techniques to invalidate enhanced international security, pioneering an evolved form of operations in direct response to post-9/11 pressure.

A second adaptation began to appear within a few years of the 7/7 bombing, namely the urban siege. The technique itself was not new, but the size and complexity of modern cities, and the interdependent systems they rely on, made siege approaches increasingly effective. A bombing like that in London, even a spectacular attack like 9/11, was over quickly—the 7/7 attack lasted just over an hour, while the elapsed time between the impact of the first and last planes on 9/11 was fifty-one minutes. By contrast, in Mumbai in November 2008, ten Lashkar e-Tayyiba operatives seized two hotels and a Jewish center, sparking intense combat that lasted sixty hours and massively disrupted the city, and al-Shabaab's attack on Nairobi's Westgate Mall in September 2013 triggered an urban siege of a hundred hours.[60] Both sieges generated sustained global publicity, inflicted billions in costs on their targets, and paralyzed huge urban areas.

In the same time frame, we began to see a proliferation of home-grown terrorists targeting Western societies. But these were not really home-grown: rather, they represented what might be called "remote radicalization," the third major evolution during this middle period of AQ's development. Remote radicalization exploited the connectivity explosion of the preceding fifteen years—the massive expansion in smartphones, internet penetration, social media, and precision tools discussed earlier.

Connectivity made it possible for remote actors to use unconventional warfare techniques to mobilize people in distant locations without ever meeting them. Anwar al-Awlaki, notably, inspired the Fort Hood shooting in 2009, the 2007 London bombers, and a series of other attacks, and Samir ibn Zafar Khan wielded influence as editor of AQ's *Inspire* magazine. Awlaki and Khan were killed in the same drone strike, allegedly carried out by CIA at President Obama's direction, in northern Yemen on 30 September 2011.[61] The forms of remote-control unconventional warfare pioneered by men like Awlaki and Khan (and later refined by ISIS) were mirrored by the extraterritoriality of drone warfare, itself a form of remote engagement, and both adaptations undermined traditional geographical and legal boundaries around concepts like speech versus violence, war zones versus safe zones, and citizenship versus nationality.

If someone could remotely operationalize and direct guerrilla groups, acting as a sort of virtual Jedburgh—an advisor providing operational, training and targeting support to a local guerrilla force—over the internet while launching attacks without physical contact, then the distinction between speech and action was blurred. Indeed, riding these edges (a characteristic known as liminality, which we will discuss in detail later) was exactly the point of the new techniques, which evolved spontaneously in response to the post-9/11 threat environment and the possibilities of technology.

The rise of remote radicalization enabled a fourth evolutionary response: leaderless resistance. In a leaderless resistance system, symbolic figures (sometimes anonymous, sometimes acting openly but without detectable links to the movement) issue guidelines for action, which self-recruited independent groups and individuals then act upon without coordination or direct communication. Coded language is sometimes used for public statements, allowing specific messages to be passed, but a hallmark of the technique is the lack of any paper trail or communications link between an overt, legal group that gives general direction only and a much larger ad hoc cloud of illegal actors. Leaders stay within the bounds of legality, while adherents conduct extralegal activities in the shadows.

Leaderless resistance, like other forms of liminal maneuver, reduces risk for the resister, since there is nothing to compromise—no hierarchical structure, no communications system, no secret plan, no formal organization. It thus enables the dispersion, stealth, and adaptive coloration discussed earlier as responses to a threat environment with pervasive surveillance but overwhelmed analysts or to one in which an adversary has operational superiority but suffers under tight self-imposed legal and political constraints. Unsurprisingly, this technique—originally invented to counter US law enforcement efforts against white supremacist groups in the 1980s—was picked up by others irrespective of ideology, given that it was an ideal evolutionary response to the changed threat environment after 2001.[62]

Al Qaeda on 9/11, as we have seen, was the antithesis of leaderless resistance: it had twenty-five thousand members organized in a tight hierarchical structure and sought to preserve itself by maintaining the secrecy of its clandestine cells outside Afghanistan, not by eliminating the need for the network itself. For that reason, once 9/11 triggered the war on terrorism, AQ's structure proved highly vulnerable to direct action—the drones and special operations raids that enabled CIA and the military to kill or capture individuals and disrupt operational networks.

AQ was also vulnerable to surveillance of communications, interdiction of finances and supplies, provocation and entrapment, and intelligence penetration by human sources or electronic means. As a result, with AQ's vanguard damaged and its global leadership challenged after 2011 by competitors like ISIS, individuals and groups in the wider AQ allied movement evolved toward an advanced version of leaderless resistance, exploiting social media, the dark web, and broadcast journalism to motivate, train, and direct loosely affiliated movements.

A Cycle of Catastrophic Success

The history of AQ is well known, so there is no need to cover it in more detail; as this brief history of the group's evolution suggests, the organization's three decades represent multiple generations of adaptation by an entity that has been continuously evolving from the outset. AQ's adaptation is far from random; indeed, its evolutionary pathway in the 1980s and 1990s

closely tracked Stephen Rosen's notion of concept-led peacetime innovation, changing after 9/11 into wartime threat-driven coevolution in response to enemy action. More broadly, AQ shows a clear cyclical pattern
that we might call "catastrophic success."[63] After 2001, what had been a
relatively static fitness landscape for AQ since its foundation in 1988 suddenly became enormously dynamic as the United States reacted to 9/11.
AQ repeatedly achieved spectacular victories, but in each case the reaction
to these successes transformed its fitness landscape so fundamentally that
they were followed by near destruction, then evolution and recovery.[64]

The group's first and hugest success, clearly, was 9/11. But that success
was catastrophic for AQ, because the backlash it provoked almost killed
the group. This was a clear example of a predator effect, as discussed in the
preceding chapter—a growth in AQ's size and activity, culminating in 9/11,
triggered a massive response that brought a population crash in Afghanistan,
followed shortly thereafter by a local reduction in predator numbers as US
forces turned away to Iraq, thereby reducing pressure on the AQ remnant
and allowing it to recover. The group survived the first of its near-death
experiences, to undergo an evolutionary shift as bin Laden, Zawahiri, and
the surviving leaders escaped to Pakistan, where they reestablished the network. But the surviving cells of this remnant were different from those of
pre-9/11 AQ: the new AQ was much more decentralized, a loose global
movement rather than a centrally directed hierarchy. The core in Pakistan
played the role of government in exile and acted as vanguard and ideological beacon to the broader movement. Self-recruited, self-motivated
individuals mounted attacks in AQ's name, and affiliates came to dominate
the next evolutionary cycle.

Jemaah Islamiyah, AQ's Southeast Asian affiliate, carried out the
Bali bombings of 2002 and 2005, along with multiple other attacks in
Indonesia; al-Shabaab emerged in Somalia in 2006 and soon sowed cells
across East Africa. Anwar al-Awlaki and Samir Khan were linked to the
powerful AQ affiliate in Yemen, with ambitions to attack Europe, Australia,
and the United States. The self-selected team under Mohammed Sidique
Khan, trained by AQ in Pakistan but operating on its own initiative,
launched the London 7/7 bombings. Affiliates in Pakistan assaulted the

Indian parliament and mounted a deadly raid on Mumbai. But it was a cell of Moroccan immigrants in Europe who mounted the most strategically decisive attack of this period—the 2004 Madrid train bombing, which killed 193 people, wounded two thousand, brought down the Spanish government, and knocked the country out of the "coalition of the willing" in Iraq. And it was also in Iraq that the most powerful Al Qaeda affiliate—the group led by the Jordanian Abu Musab al-Zarqawi, known as Al Qaeda in Iraq (AQI)—achieved the movement's next catastrophic success, on the back of the US-led invasion.

Zarqawi, Baghdadi, and the Islamic Pseudo-State

Immediately before 9/11, Zarqawi was running a training camp in the western Afghan city of Herat.[65] His camp was crushed and his small group scattered during the American-led invasion in late 2001. Zarqawi himself was wounded in the chest and fled into Iran, where he received medical treatment. By mid-2002, at the latest, he was in Iraq. Expecting, like many others (though not apparently Saddam Hussein himself), the imminent overthrow of the Iraqi regime following a US invasion, Zarqawi began setting up underground cells, creating auxiliary networks, and laying down weapons caches in preparation for an anti-occupation war of resistance.[66]

By August 2003, five months after Saddam's fall, AQI had established itself as the leading jihadist faction in the Iraqi resistance, at the top of the evolving insurgent food chain, through a series of horrific, spectacular attacks. By 2005, an insurgency was in full swing. By the time Zarqawi was killed in June 2006, AQI was by far the deadliest and most ideologically extreme of the Al Qaeda affiliates worldwide as well as increasingly independent of the Al Qaeda core, and its anti-Shi'a attacks, in line with the sectarian goals Zarqawi had pursued all along, had succeeded—through the February 2006 Samarra bombing—in transforming Iraq from a resistance war into a sectarian bloodbath. But again, this success was catastrophic, in that it brought such a severe pushback that the organization suffered a near-total collapse. The 2007 surge, a massive US troop reinforcement and strategic shift that occurred in direct response to AQI's success of 2006, almost destroyed it.

As I noted in the preceding chapter, the mechanism that best explains this rapid growth and sudden collapse of AQI may be a variant of the predator effect, whereby AQI's success in 2006 fundamentally altered the dynamic fitness environment in which the group operated, drawing a massive response from the United States, which in turn triggered a collapse in the AQI population in terms of both numbers and incidents. This AQI collapse, again in line with what we know of predator effects, was then followed by a subsequent drop in the population and activity level of US forces stationed in Iraq—allowing the AQI remnant, transformed by its near-death experience (which culled maladaptive individuals and cells while enabling fitter ones to survive and proliferate) to recover after 2011.

After this second near-death experience, as it progressed through successive phases of transformation and recovery, AQI was eclipsed by other Al Qaeda affiliates in different regions, while core Al Qaeda leaders in Pakistan and Yemen promoted the even more diffuse "leaderless jihad." At the same time, the survivors of AQI's collapse—including its new leader after April 2010, Abubakr al-Baghdadi, and its regional commander for the Mosul area, Syrian-born Mohammed al-Jolani—sought to learn the lessons from their defeat.

The two men drew starkly different conclusions from their experience, as became clear in 2011 when the Arab Spring, the death of bin Laden, and civil wars in Libya, Yemen, and Syria brought the next wave of evolutionary transformation. This provoked a great schism between Baghdadi's faction, now officially separated from Al Qaeda and styling itself the "Islamic State of Iraq and al-Sham" (ISIS), and the broader Al Qaeda network, including Jolani's group, now fighting the Assad regime in Syria as the "Victory Front," Jabhat an-Nusrah. Both groups had emerged from the original Al Qaeda base, but—like Stalinists and Trotskyists or rival drug cartels in Colombia—were now separate networks with dramatically different approaches.

Baghdadi's movement doubled down on sectarian hatred and adopted a strategy of advertising its ferocity and extreme barbarity as a way to cow local populations and bolster recruiting worldwide, drawing in individuals inspired by the purity of the group's uncompromising ideology or excited by its extreme violence. Islamic State quickly grew to many thousands of fighters. It built up conventional military capabilities like tanks, artillery, and rockets, organizing itself as a statelike entity and seeking to mount an open, conventional war of conquest rather than a guerrilla or terrorist campaign. This approach triggered the next cycle of catastrophic success and near collapse.

The speed, ferocity, and success of the ISIS advance in mid-2014 pushed the group to the pinnacle of the world jihadist movement, overshadowed Al Qaeda (now a bitter enemy), and thrust Baghdadi and his movement into the spotlight. By 2015 Islamic State controlled more than a dozen cities across Iraq and Syria, a population roughly the size of Singapore's, and revenue sources that generated more than a million dollars a day to fund the building of Baghdadi's self-declared caliphate. Its success brought a massive influx of recruits from all over the globe, including up to forty thousand foreign fighters who traveled to Syria to join the group, along with many families or individual women and children. At its peak, ISIS was far bigger, more sophisticated, and more militarily capable than Al Qaeda had been in its pre-9/11 heyday—indeed, Baghdadi's "caliphate" came the closest any jihadist terrorist group has ever come to establishing an actual, physical state.

Yet, once again, success carried the seeds of destruction: politically, because of the backlash it generated against the group's ferocious ideology, and militarily, because by operating at scale, in the open, with tanks and large combat units, seeking to seize and hold cities, Islamic State shifted the conflict from guerrilla warfare and terrorism (where the United States and its allies struggled) to exactly the conventional forms of open warfare where Western forces excelled. Abandoning the shadowy liminal world of guerrilla warfare, Islamic State fighters stood, fought, and died—in Ramadi, Tikrit, Mosul, Raqqa, Marawi, Baghouz, and elsewhere—as their caliphate was crushed and their civil structure dispersed. Islamic State today is far from gone, though it is much less visible than it was in its state-building stage: the weight of evidence suggests it is simply going through its latest cycle of evolutionary transformation, having dropped back from overt conventional warfare into guerrilla mode, entering yet another recovery and rebuilding phase.

A Better Breed of Jihadist?

Baghdadi's nemesis, Mohammed al-Jolani's faction—the former Jabhat an-Nusrah, which in January 2017 rebranded itself as Hayat Tahrir al-Sham (HTS)—was for a time one of the most impressive and capable terrorist groups on the planet. From mid-2015 onward, HTS controlled a significant part of the northwestern Syrian province of Idlib, including the second provincial capital (after Aleppo) to be seized from the regime and the last remaining corner of Syrian territory controlled by jihadist rebels. In consolidating its grip over this area, HTS practiced a combination of governance, political alliance-building, economic development, and military activity that set it apart from Baghdadi's group and made it unique among AQ affiliates.

Where Baghdadi emphasized sectarian hatred and dialed up the public display of brutality through a series of increasingly horrific execution videos, the softspoken Jolani opted instead—at least at the level of overt propaganda—for a popular front strategy. He offered to cooperate with other groups, sought alliances, and branded HTS as a moderate, rational version of jihadism. His public speeches and interviews emphasized the need to oppose Syrian dictator Bashar al-Assad and work with other Syrians rather than pursue apocalyptic global jihad, Baghdadi-style. On one occasion his group held a public debate in a town in Syria with rival factions who disputed its interpretation of Islamic law, an event that left my analysts—who had watched AQI and then ISIS ruthlessly massacre hundreds for hair-splittingly minor disagreements, only to see HTS (and former AQI leader Jolani) calmly sitting down to talk—scratching their heads.

Yet beneath its more moderate image, HTS had all the military capability of Islamic State (or of AQ before 9/11) while possessing much of the political savvy and talent for social and political work of Shi'a groups like Hezbollah (discussed later). Indeed, given Jolani's Syrian origin (hence his likely familiarity with Hezbollah) and the presence of Hezbollah-like Shi'a groups in Iraq during HTS's formative period, it's possible that HTS represents an example of horizontal evolutionary transfer—cross-pollination of characteristics from one group to another (in this case, an enemy). From 2016 through 2019, HTS achieved a measure of public support in areas it controlled and maintained the ability (though not necessarily the intent) to strike abroad—into Turkey, Europe, or farther afield—if desired. In many ways HTS therefore represented the most mature and capable iteration of the original AQ concept that had been pioneered a generation earlier by Osama bin Laden. The staying power and survivability of HTS seemed strong, even as its success triggered an increasingly intense response.

As of 2019, there does exist the possibility—albeit a very slim one—that like the Soviet Union in the late 1920s (when Stalin abandoned Trotsky's notion of global permanent revolution for a doctrine of "socialism in one country" that emphasized Russia's national interests) and the Islamic Republic of Iran in the 1980s (when the mullahs maintained their theoretical commitment to world revolution while increasingly acting like traditional Persian rulers), HTS might settle into something like an "Islamic Emirate of Idlib." Left unmolested, it might evolve into a state among states within the international system, though clearly one that other governments would seek to contain.

If anyone could pull off such a transformation, it would be Jolani and his fellow HTS leaders. But of course, the key lesson governments drew from 9/11—that allowing a jihadist group to control territory, administer population, and develop economic resources (in other words, to become a state or statelike entity) inevitably entails the unacceptable risk of a global terrorist threat emanating from that territory—meant that no government, democratic or otherwise, was likely to tolerate that outcome. Until a group like HTS (or its successors) formally swears off global jihad and demonstrates by its behavior that it poses no external threat, governments are virtually certain to maintain military activity (and therefore a high degree of evolutionary pressure) against it.

Failing the unlikely outcome of HTS renouncing global jihad, we can expect that sooner or later Baghdadi's faction of Islamic State will recover from its current eclipse, though if its evolutionary history is any guide it will look different next time around. We can expect a sustained, persistent threat in Western countries from small ad hoc cells and self-recruited individuals inspired by ISIS ideology. Australia, New Zealand, Europe, North America, and Russia will remain targets, as will Israel, India, other South Asian countries such as Bangladesh, Myanmar, and Sri Lanka, and to some extent China. While Western military interventions continue—albeit with fewer troops—in Africa, Afghanistan, and Iraq, and civil wars rage in Syria, Yemen, and Libya, the forever war against terrorism will drag on and continue to spread. The war's spread is most noticeable in the shift from the first decade after 9/11—when Western countries bore the brunt of the effort—to the period since 2011, when Russia, Iran, and Hezbollah increasingly joined the fight.

As we have seen, AQ arose from a specific set of background conditions in the Middle East. These included the collapse of the Ottoman Empire in 1918, the fall of the Ottoman Caliphate in 1924, domination by European powers under League of Nations mandates in the 1920s and 1930s, the failure of secular Nasserist and Arab Socialist visions of a greater Arab region in the 1950s and 1960s, the disruptive emergence of Israel in the heart of that region in 1948 and its defeat of Arab powers in 1956, 1967, and 1973, and what Sunni extremists saw as the betrayal of Islamic integrity by Egyptian, Jordanian, and Saudi rulers partnering with the infidel West. The notion of "apostate regimes" and the near-enemy/far-enemy construct that shaped AQ's outlook trace their origins to this environment. The specific form that AQ took, however, was driven by the experiences of its founding group in opposing apostate regimes in their home countries and then in the anti-Soviet jihad in Afghanistan, its initial period of peacetime, concept-driven innovation, and its wartime evolution under lethally intense pressure after 2001.

Likewise, the transformation of AQ after 9/11 and Zarqawi's experiences in Jordan, Afghanistan, and Iraq spurred the emergence of AQI, but its evolution was then driven by the cyclical logic of catastrophic success and coevolution under wartime conditions in Iraq. AQI's evolution under pre-dation in Iraq spawned two very different successors—HTS under Jolani and ISIS under Baghdadi—each of which arose from founding cells within AQI in Syria, through wartime adaptation in a lethally competitive fitness landscape. This, in some ways, was a form of speciation, with different species of terrorists emerging to fit different ecological niches and pursuing different adaptive strategies in a conflict ecosystem. To use the fitness landscape metaphor, each of the two groups had evolved toward a separate fitness peak in a rugged landscape.

But the clearest example of a militant group emerging through direct wartime adaptation in a conflict ecosystem is probably Hezbollah—and given its very different origins from those of the Sunni groups just discussed, as well as the divergent trajectory of its evolution, the Lebanese Shi'a group is worth discussing in detail.

The Evolution of Hezbollah

Lebanon has an enormously complex political ecology. It is also, by the way, an incredibly beautiful country. With its parallel mountain ranges, fertile central valley, and urbanized coastal strip, its unevenly distributed water, forest, and arable land, and its topographically fragmented hinterland, this tiny country of only about 4,000 square miles has a highly compartmented geography.[67] Over millennia, more than a dozen groups have settled in a mosaic of adjacent enclaves across this complex terrain, competing for physical and demographic living space and political power. While almost all Lebanese are ethnically Arab, they are divided by religion: Shi'a, Sunni, Druze, Maronite, Orthodox, and Catholic sects were only the largest among seventeen confessional communities in a population of just 2.6 million in 1982, the year of Hezbollah's founding.

Lebanon's geopolitical position as a strategic crossroads and Mediterranean trading hub connecting Europe, Asia Minor, Africa, and Arabia—and more recently, as a "frontline state" bordering Israel and Syria—has driven a dynamic and violent history of conflict and conquest, refuge and rebellion. The pull of trade, the entrepôt role of levantine coastal cities, and a series of wars and crises during the nineteenth and twentieth centuries generated a Lebanese diaspora with considerable influence as a middleman minority in places as far-flung as Argentina, Australia, Brazil, Canada, Ghana, Paraguay, Senegal, Sweden, and the United States.[68]

All these factors generated enormous adaptive pressure on Lebanon's social and ethno-religious entities, coevolving through economic, political, and military competition as they jockeyed for local advantage. In this environment, group identity has always been crucial for community and individual success—often even for survival. Over time, allegiances of place, kinship, and patronage increasingly merged with religious loyalty, so that sectarian affiliation became both synonymous with group identity and virtually impossible to escape.[69]

Under four centuries of loose Ottoman rule, from 1516 to 1918, Lebanon's Turkish viceroys outsourced local day-to-day control to urban Sunni elites, who in turn governed the hinterland through tribal and community elders. On the empire's margins, Ottoman sultans enforced their rule indirectly, through often-brutal Druze and Kurdish irregular militias.[70] After the fall of the Ottomans in 1918, Lebanon was governed by France under a League of Nations mandate from 1920 to 1943 and dominated by a de facto alliance of Sunni Muslims and Maronite Christians who monopolized the political and economic institutions of the central state, while local fiefdoms maintained relative autonomy through patron-client relationships with urban elites, as under the Ottomans.[71] After independence, this arrangement was codified in the National Pact, which, despite its surface stability, institutionalized a permanent Shi'a underclass.

Living in the southern third of Lebanon, in the slums and poverty-stricken suburbs on Beirut's southern outskirts, and in the northern part of Lebanon's central Beqaa Valley, Lebanese Shi'a were politically underrepresented for the size of their population, economically and socially marginalized, and structurally sidelined by their confessional rivals through the National Pact. This, along with rising demographic pressure as the Shi'a birth rate far outpaced those of other groups after 1945, generated massive resentment among Lebanon's Shi'a population and led to calls to restructure the country's political and social order.

Shi'a militancy, in turn, provoked a backlash from other groups and—when the state proved unable or unwilling to protect the Shi'a—spurred the creation of communitarian militias. After the Arab-Israeli War of 1948, Lebanon's southern Shi'a were further inundated by a flood of refugees from Palestine and, when the Palestinian Liberation Organization (PLO) was expelled from Jordan to Lebanon in 1971, were increasingly exposed to cross-border conflict between Israeli troops and PLO *fedayeen*.

Responding to all this, in 1974 the Lebanese Iranian Shi'a cleric Musa al-Sadr organized Harakat al-Mahrumin, the "Movement of the Deprived," which focused on community organizing and political mobilization among the Shi'a, promoted self-help efforts, including the building of schools and clinics, and pushed for greater Shi'a inclusion in the Lebanese power structure. While strongly sectarian, Sadr's movement emphasized welfare and justice—calling for a sociopolitical revolution as well as a religious awakening. (Iraq veterans may recognize here an ideology—opposition to foreigners, local elites, and non-Shi'a alike, along with a joining of religious militancy with populist economics and social justice activism—similar to that of Musa al-Sadr's distant relative Muqtada al-Sadr and his Jaysh al-Mahdi.)

Thus, Hezbollah evolved in a context of religiously defined identity politics, social and political inequality, refusal of cozy elites to adapt to changing demographic reality, and concept-led innovation—including radicalization and militarization—by increasingly militant marginalized groups. This pattern of peacetime innovation switched into wartime coevolution mode as the 1975 civil war, triggered by conflict between Maronite Christian militias and Palestinian *fedayeen*, spread to the whole of Lebanese society and sucked in regional players like Israel and Syria, as well as the United Nations and global powers like the United States and France. Sadr's movement created the Lebanese Resistance Regiments, Afwaj al Muqawamah al-Lubnaniya (known by their acronym, Amal, meaning "hope" in Arabic), which rapidly evolved beyond its founder's ideas under pressure of war.

When Sadr disappeared under suspicious circumstances in August 1978 during a visit to Libya, Amal allied with Lebanon's Syrian-backed government, then led by the Maronite politician Elias Sarkis. Many younger, more militant Amal members—including Hassan Nasrallah, later to become the leader of Hezbollah—were disaffected by the organization's secular turn, and groups began fissioning from Amal to become early recruits for Hezbollah. A year later, when Iran's Islamic Revolution brought down the shah and energized Shi'a communities worldwide, Iranian notions of religious militancy, clerical government, and liberation from oppression resonated strongly in Lebanon. This environment—of internal competition, external destabilization, and the radicalizing influences of the PLO and the Iranian revolution—was galvanized when the Israelis invaded in June 1982.

Israel had hoped its invasion would push the PLO back from the border, knock Lebanon out of Syria's orbit, and foster a regime in Beirut that could collaborate with Israel to control both religious militants and secular Palestinian fighters. Instead it triggered the formation of Hezbollah. As Israeli prime minister Ehud Barak remarked in 2006, "When we entered Lebanon there was no Hezbollah. We were accepted with perfumed rice and flowers by the Shia in the south. It was our presence there that created Hezbollah."[72] Hezbollah secretary-general Hassan Nasrallah commented that had Israel not invaded, "I do not know whether something called Hezbollah would have been born. I doubt it."[73]

The Israeli invasion's impact fell disproportionately on the southern Shi'a, destroying scores of villages, killing thousands of civilians, laying waste to farmland and crops, and displacing almost five hundred thousand southerners to the Beirut outskirts. The war legitimized the newly created Hezbollah—founded in mid-1982 at Ba'albek in the Beqaa Valley with Iranian funding, weapons, and advisers, though not publicly announced until 1985—as a vehicle to resist the invaders, their Lebanese collaborators, and international peacekeepers alike.[74] Israel's initial offensive, which reached as far north as West Beirut, quickly settled into a bruising occupation by the Israeli Defense Force (IDF), its ally the South Lebanon Army (SLA), and a series of smaller secular and Christian militias. Israel withdrew in 1986 to a "security zone," where destruction, displacement, and detention—up to half the males in the area were allegedly detained, at one time or another, in the IDF-run Ansar prison camp—further radicalized southern Shi'a.[75]

From its ragtag beginnings, Hezbollah quickly evolved, gaining credibility as one of the foremost guerrilla groups opposing the occupation and rising to prominence through a series of tactical successes against the Israelis and the SLA. These successes encouraged imitators and rallied recruits, helping Hezbollah's methods proliferate and expanding its base. From the outset, Hezbollah was much more than a guerrilla movement, though: it reflected its Sadrist social-justice origins, combining military operations against the Israelis and the SLA with a series of social and political programs—everything from clinics and schools to reconstruction services, employment support, and food aid—for populations in its control. The combination of coercive (military and enforcement) capabilities with administrative and persuasive tools helped Hezbollah crowd out competitors like Amal and the secular militias. These tools became particularly important after May 1988, when Hezbollah fought a full-scale internecine war with Amal.[76]

By the late 1980s, Hezbollah was a highly structured and multifaceted organization. It was divided into military and political wings with "political and administrative councils, military and security organs, and specific service subunits including a social unit, a health unit, an education unit, an information unit," cadres for community and labor organizing, "an external relations unit, a finance unit, and an engagement and coordination unit."[77] Its executive comprised a seven-man Shura Council elected by a Central Committee, itself in turn elected and composed of two hundred members serving three-year terms. It also had a Politburo and a Parliamentary Council, reminiscent of Lebanese leftist political parties. Most leaders were clerics (with Iranian representatives acting as advisers and arbiters), but lay cadres with specialist skills also played key roles. A Jihad Council—including advisers from Iran's Revolutionary Guards—decided strategic questions while leaving most tactical decisions to the movement's military wing.[78]

This combination gave Hezbollah a spectrum of coercive, administrative, and persuasive tools that made it both resilient and highly capable, a sort of do-it-yourself Shi'a para-state established in opposition to both the discredited government and the despised invaders.[79] Hezbollah offered social and economic support, suppressed crime, reconstructed houses damaged or destroyed by Israeli action, and provided governance services to the entire population in its areas, not just the Shi'a, helping expand its appeal and consolidate its control. This gave Hezbollah a loyal following in the vast southern slums of Beirut, in the Beqaa Valley, in a dense network of hilltop villages across southern Lebanon, and crucially, among non-Shi'a inhabitants of these regions as well as its own sectarian group.

In hindsight we can identify several phases in Hezbollah's evolution. In its first decade, from mid-1982 until the death of its secretary-general, Abbas al-Moussawi, in February 1992, the organization showed a classic wartime coevolution pattern—responding through a series of tit-for-tat adaptations and counteradaptions to actions by the IDF and SLA. Combat in the southern security zone was intense enough to generate a selection effect, but not so intense that it seriously damaged the group or impeded its growth. This period forged the group's military wing and gave it a distinctly decentralized, small-unit character.

Several early Hezbollah tactics—including suicide bombings, kidnapping of Westerners, attacks on high-profile installations such as Western embassies and military bases—came to define the group's popular image outside Lebanon.[80] The most spectacular was the massive October 1983 truck bombing of the Multinational Force (MNF) barracks outside Beirut, which killed 241 American and 58 French peacekeepers, along with six local civilians, as well as the two bombers.[81] Israeli and American analysts later blamed Hezbollah, Syria, and Iran, but the name used by the attackers was "Islamic Jihad Organization," and Hezbollah has repeatedly denied responsibility (while accepting the prestige generated by the political outcome of the attack, namely that MNF was driven out of Lebanon).[82] The peacekeepers' withdrawal, several months after the bombing, imbued it with strategic significance similar to that of the Madrid attack two decades later, and the ambiguity of its authorship prevented decisive retaliation, helping Hezbollah avoid the catastrophic success cycle of AQ and ISIS.[83] In this sense it was an early, if probably unintentional, example of liminal maneuver.

The demonstration effect of these spectacular attacks (that is, their impact on other armed groups' perception of what was possible) was huge, and they immediately spawned imitators, but in fact Hezbollah quickly evolved away from these techniques after the civil war ended in 1991. Also, such methods were already being superseded by classic small-unit guerrilla tactics after the peacekeepers left in 1984 and the Israelis withdrew in 1986 to their security zone. As Shana Marshall points out in her study of Hezbollah, despite the group's reputation for perpetrating suicide bombings based on these early, high-profile attacks, "the vast majority (81 percent) of suicide attacks during the Israeli occupation (1982–86) were carried out by Christians or affiliates of secular or leftist parties, and only twelve of Hizbollah's attacks involved the intentional death of a party operative."[84] By the mid-1980s, the real action was the guerrilla fight in the south.

In the hill country of southern Lebanon—the crucible in which Hezbollah's distinct combat characteristics evolved—villages cluster on hilltops surrounded by crops and woodland, with abandoned villages and farms offering concealment for small groups only. This terrain punishes large, overt concentrations of troops—as in the Iranian-style human-wave attacks that Hezbollah initially mounted against SLA bases but that it abandoned after heavy losses.[85] Large groups perished to little effect, since they were immediately seen and smacked by Israeli warplanes or struck by artillery placed safely in depth and controlled from a forward network of Israeli hilltop observation posts.

This is light infantry country, difficult for tanks and armored vehicles—indeed, vehicles of any kind—while dismounted forces, moving dispersed with a mix of light weapons and heavier mortars, machine guns, and rockets, could exploit the terrain to maneuver. Snipers, mortars, and improvised explosive devices (IEDs) were critical here. Hezbollah quickly evolved away from its early wave tactics toward dismounted, dispersed operations, flattening its command-and-control structure and making more use of autonomous combat groups.[86] Likewise, Israeli SIGINT in the security zone was good enough to intercept and locate radio emissions produced by detailed planning and coordination, but since Hezbollah combat groups were operating on their home turf they could conduct that activity "off the air" as long as they learned to operate with a high degree of small-team autonomy, which they soon did.[87]

Along with its tactical evolution on the ground and the political maturation of its noncombat elements into an effective system of competitive control, Hezbollah began to exploit the global Lebanese diaspora as a source of money, recruits, and intelligence, a channel for propaganda messaging, and—in a series of overseas operations in Spain, Argentina, and elsewhere—a venue for external actions to raise its profile and punish its enemies. Unlike AQ, however (which sought, as we've seen, to impose itself from the top down as a vanguard for local guerrilla groups worldwide), Hezbollah's global reach grew organically, from the bottom up, through its ability to exploit the preexisting diaspora and tap into resources and support from overseas Lebanese as well as its Iranian mentors.

In the second period, from 1992 to 2000, Hezbollah responded to the end of the Lebanese Civil War in 1991 by doubling down on its southern insurgency against Israel but simultaneously entering Lebanese politics, participating in parliamentary processes while enhancing its counterstate and repairing relationships with Amal and the Lebanese and Syrian armies.[88] Simultaneously, it developed political warfare capabilities that it used to win credibility as a Lebanese political party while consolidating local support and further mobilizing the diaspora.[89] The genius of Hassan Nasrallah, who succeeded Abbas al-Moussawi as Hezbollah secretary-general after Moussawi was killed in February 1992, played a key role in this transition, yet another example of the positive effect of artificial selection through targeted killing that we noted in the preceding chapter.

On the military front, Hezbollah began building an arsenal of rockets and artillery capable of striking across the border into Israel—initially, just a local evolutionary response to the need to suppress IDF artillery positions in depth, but later a strategic evolution in its own right—and put its increasingly sophisticated capabilities to more explicitly political ends. As other groups disarmed after 1991, Hezbollah used its continued resistance against Israel in the south as a pretext to retain its weaponry, becoming the most powerful military player in Lebanon.

Reflecting its growing capacity for political warfare, Hezbollah chose its targets for political effect, then amplified these effects through social networks and propaganda on the group's radio stations, via its television channel, through diaspora networks, and online. Attacks targeted IDF reservists, killing or kidnapping individual soldiers to demoralize Israel's population at home, and sought to undermine IDF confidence in the SLA and thereby force Israel to spend more money and lives to maintain its occupation.[90] Hezbollah targeted the families of SLA members and taunted the SLA as "sandbags" in reference to Israel's habit of holding its troops back in well-protected bases while hiding behind a screen of more vulnerable SLA.[91]

While Hezbollah's strategy of attrition remained constant through this period, its tactics continuously evolved, again in the classic wartime pattern of coevolution. As Iver Gabrielsen has noted, this evolution happened rapidly, in tit-for-tat fashion: when Israel and the SLA employed fixed outposts, Hezbollah launched frontal assaults. When Israel reinforced the outposts in response, Hezbollah switched to mortar and rocket fire. When Israeli forces again changed their tactics, getting out on the ground and employing more mobile forces to reduce the impact of mortars and rockets, Hezbollah responded with ambushes and IEDs and acquired advanced missile systems.[92] Likewise, "when the IDF employed sniffer dogs to discover wire-triggered bombs, Hezbollah answered by hiding IEDs inside fibreglass rocks and used radio control to set off the bombs. The IDF responded by sweeping radio frequencies from listening posts at Mount Hermon. Hezbollah then switched to using cell phone receivers to trigger the IEDs. The IDF answered by jamming cell-phone signals, while Hezbollah responded by using infra-red beams to set off the IEDs . . . At the end of February 1999, Hezbollah enjoyed the biggest success of their IED campaign, killing the top Israeli commander in Lebanon, Erez Gerstein," with a powerful IED of the same type, known as an explosively formed penetrator, that later proved so deadly in Iraq.[93] When Israel finally withdrew in May 2000, the SLA quickly disintegrated and Hezbollah took the credit while expanding its political and social influence in Lebanon and the diaspora.

The next decade—from Israel's withdrawal until the outbreak of the Syrian Civil War in 2011—saw Hezbollah evolve from a Lebanese guerrilla resistance movement against Israeli occupation to a regional actor with an increasingly powerful arsenal, combining conventional and irregular methods in pursuit of statelike goals. It also took on a role as regional protector of the Palestinians, especially after the Second Intifada began in September 2000. Hezbollah struck northern Israel with increasingly capable rockets and missile systems, operated inside and outside Lebanon, and after the 2006 July War with Israel, expanded its already significant political influence within the Lebanese state.

In the six years between Israel's withdrawal and the July War, Hezbollah's focus shifted from guerrilla operations in the now-abandoned security zone to political warfare and a conventional military buildup. Thus, in the aftermath of Israel's pullback, selective pressure in the south diminished for a time. A string of retaliatory engagements kept the conflict going at a low level of intensity, as Hezbollah contested Israeli control of the Sheb'aa farms astride Lebanese and Israeli territory near the Golan Heights, generating much political capital but few casualties. Hezbollah's internet penetration and political warfare capabilities improved significantly also: the organization's central internet bureau released video games in 2003, and again in 2007, that rewarded players for killing Israelis, glamorized the resistance, demonized Israel, and attracted recruits, while al-Manar television began broadcasting worldwide. All this made perfect sense, since the purpose of preserving the conflict, for Hezbollah, was primarily political and internal: maintaining its resistance credentials as a means of exerting continued influence in Lebanese politics even after their original raison d'être (Israeli presence in the south) had evaporated.

Hezbollah's tactics further evolved in this period, with heavier and longer-range rocket attacks into Israel, enhanced surveillance and reconnaissance activity, and a string of cross-border operations, including raids on Israeli strongpoints and kidnapping of IDF soldiers.[94] Iran (and to a lesser extent Syria) played a key role in funding these efforts, but as before specific military decisions were left to Hezbollah itself. Israel responded with artillery and air strikes into Lebanon, but since Hezbollah no longer presented obvious military targets, these focused on industrial infrastructure or on Syrian installations.[95] In the 2006 July War—triggered by the kidnapping of two IDF soldiers from a border patrol—Hezbollah operated as a conventional force, launching more than four thousand rockets into Israel and conducting a sophisticated positional defense against IDF ground assault.[96]

During the opening moves of the July War, Hezbollah's largely successful defense in the south forced Israel to launch an increasingly costly series of ground offensives, while broadening its focus to the rest of Lebanon. The resulting Israeli air campaign, which engaged targets across the entire country while heavily damaging the area south of Beirut, caused widespread property damage and casualties. It created resentment, which Hezbollah then exploited, through its political warfare, reconstruction, and social-services capabilities, to increase local influence and expand its presence in the Lebanese parliament.[97] Hezbollah's propaganda tools operated around the clock, spreading imagery that harmed Israel's global reputation, mobilized the diaspora (which Hezbollah increasingly treated as a virtual strategic hinterland), and helped generate international pressure for a ceasefire. The war's ultimate result was to cement Hezbollah as a permanent fixture of the Lebanese state, enhance its status relative to all other armed groups in the country, and make the organization (and its Iranian backers) the leading regional opponents of Israel.[98]

But Hezbollah's evolution—from a local guerrilla group resisting Israel inside Lebanon to a regional and global player projecting power well outside Lebanon's borders—came fully into its own in 2012, as it responded to the Syrian Civil War. By that year Bashar al-Assad's regime was under pressure from an array of secular rebels and Sunni terrorist groups, and Iran and Hezbollah rallied to support it.

Initially, Hezbollah's response was defensive, reacting to Syrian rebel and ISIS advances into northeastern Lebanon and the spillover of violence into the Qalamoun region on the Lebanese-Syrian border. Hezbollah forces moved into the northeast in a late-2012 counteroffensive to push ISIS out of Lebanon, but then continued on into western Syria, fighting alongside the Assad regime against both secular rebels and Sunni jihadists. Hezbollah also operated against Lebanese groups that supported the rebels, fighting secular and Sunni factions in the Lebanese towns of Tripoli and Sidon in 2012–13. On 25 May 2013, facing criticism from a range of leaders inside Lebanon (including former senior Hezbollah figures), Nasrallah formally announced Hezbollah's entry into the war inside Syria.[99] He deployed an expeditionary force—in Hezbollah's first-ever large-scale conventional deployment outside Lebanon—to support Assad in the battle for Aleppo.

By 2015, as Assad's regime slid toward collapse under pressure from several successful rebel offensives in multiple parts of the country, Hezbollah, with Russia and Iran, formed a rescue package of troops, advisers, money, and equipment that ultimately restored the regime's fortunes and helped it regain control of almost all of Syria's territory.[100] Later, Hezbollah played a critical role in the recapture of Aleppo, in the regime's central Syria offensive, the retaking of Daraa, and other operations. From being a subordinate and often disrespected player during Syria's long game to control Lebanon and destabilize Israel—notably under Bashar al-Assad's father, Hafez, in the 1980s and 1990s—Hezbollah was seen as "winning the war in Syria."[101] It operates, as of 2019, as a regional power broker, dealing with Damascus on far more equal terms than in the past and provoking fears of a coming clash with Israel.[102]

Hezbollah fielded fully capable conventional expeditionary forces in the Syrian conflict, with armored vehicles, heavy artillery and rockets, large-scale combat formations, a fleet of weaponized drones, a well-organized logistic and personnel system, and a formidable intelligence, surveillance, and reconnaissance capability.[103] Besides these combat forces, Hezbollah helped Assad establish the Jaysh al-Sha'abi, or Popular Forces, a pro-regime militia designed for rear-area security but increasingly drawn into direct combat as the war escalated. In many parts of Syria, the Popular Forces now form a parallel governance structure much more capable than the formal state, much like the Popular Mobilization Forces in Iraq.[104] Thus, quite apart from the military evolution that its history of transformation implies, Hezbollah's political evolution is truly remarkable.

DIFFERENT EVOLUTIONARY PATHWAYS, DIFFERENT OUTCOMES

Why was Hezbollah's evolution so different from the cycles of catastrophic success, near death, transformation, and rebirth of other "snakes" discussed in this chapter? Clearly, internal factors and external circumstances both played a role.

Internally, as we have seen, Hezbollah arose within a complex internal political ecology of sectarian competition and communitarian identity politics that marginalized Lebanese Shi'a and prompted sustained calls for restructuring based on demographic and economic realities. As such, Hezbollah's evolution was pushed from behind by real environmental pressures rather than—as in the AQ or ISIS "vanguard"—pulled along by a small, self-consciously elite group of outsiders.

Political and social organizing among the Shi'a in the 1970s progressed naturally to the formation of Sadr's Harakat al-Mahrumin, which in turn— when subjected to militarized pushback from other groups—led organically to the formation of militias and the emergence of Amal. When civil war broke out in 1975, Amal radicalized and grew to a size where (as Robin Dunbar, the anthropologist whose study of group size we examined in the preceding chapter, might say) it naturally began to fission. External factors—in particular, the Iranian revolution, PLO presence in southern Lebanon, and, most notably, Israel's 1982 invasion—accelerated the fissioning of groups from Amal and helped transform them, through Iranian sponsorship and money, into Hezbollah's founding cadre.

The nascent organization coevolved with its adversaries in a classic wartime pattern from the outset, forged in the civil war and in the harsh operating environment of the south—a tiny, intense combat ecosystem that punished very specific behaviors and rewarded others, becoming in effect a combat laboratory or guerrilla university from which Hezbollah's distinct style emerged. At the same time, Hezbollah's Sadrist roots in the sociopolitical justice movement among southern Shi'a continued to push its evolution from behind, even as Israeli actions and Hezbollah counteractions in the security zone generated a set of pull factors. Under these twin pressures, the organization rapidly outgrew its Iranian mentors, abandoned their costly human-wave tactics, and developed its own distinct operational methods.

In each case, however, military developments followed and consolidated political and social steps that the movement had already taken with the support of its mass base. This sequencing is important: building upward from underlying social trends, through a mass popular movement, to a political organization with an increasingly developed parallel state or counterstate, the group first developed an underground network, then formed an auxiliary support system, and only then created combat units. These in turn started out small and irregular, becoming increasingly capable and conventional over time. This organic development, with the resilience generated through Hezbollah's full-spectrum system of competitive control, made its evolution much less cyclical than that of ISIS or AQ.

In addition to these internal factors, Hezbollah's relatively recent acquisition of conventional capabilities was largely a side effect of external circumstances. The most obviously transformative of these was the 1982 Israeli invasion, which created the group and guided its early evolution. The next was the 2006 July War, which cemented Hezbollah's position inside Lebanon and marked its arrival as a hybrid actor possessing both conventional and irregular capabilities while simultaneously running its own parastate within Lebanon. Finally, the war in Syria—especially after Hezbollah's direct intervention in May 2013 and up to the present—took it from a local Lebanese group to a powerful regional player. Although its evolution followed a different (and ultimately more successful) pathway than did that of AQ, ISIS, or HTS, it's worth noting that Hezbollah was responding to the same set of environmental conditions as they were—patchy air superiority, pervasive signals intelligence but overwhelmed analysts, increasingly restrictive self-imposed constraints, and so on. Despite no evidence of collusion with, or copying from, other groups (though clearly with some degree of cross-pollination in the case of Jolani's AQ offshoot, HTS), Hezbollah seems to have independently hit on a remarkably similar set of techniques.

I have suggested, in this chapter and the preceding one, that much of this can be ascribed to natural and artificial selection effects arising from our own actions (and those of allies like Israel). But it is equally clear that conscious innovation and, in particular, the techniques of liminal maneuver that allowed Hezbollah to avoid the catastrophic overreaching seen in other groups also played a key role. And this is true not just of nonstate actors, as the next chapter will show; for the real master of that technique—and the next adversary we will look at—is Russia.

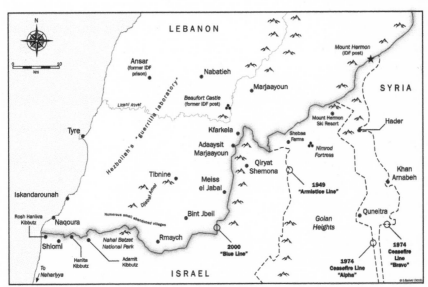

Map 2 Hezbollah's Guerrilla Laboratory in Southern Lebanon

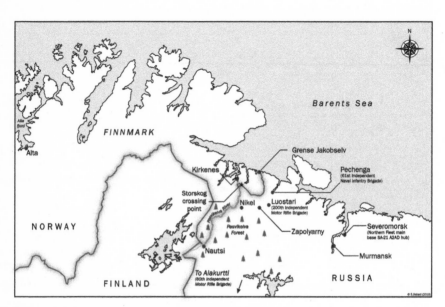

Map 3 The Norwegian-Russian Border

4

Liminal Warfare

5:45 p.m., 18 September 2016, Norwegian-Russian border

My escort—call him "Corporal J"—guns the Polaris quad bike as we ride along a wooden track over the forest floor, slung rifle banging on his back.[1] The day is draining away: afternoon sun glows on the escarpment to our left, but we are in shadow now, working north along the cliff base through cold, waterlogged birch forest. The track is barely wide enough for the motorcycle's knobby all-terrain tires, which periodically slip off into the black mud. A second Polaris bike follows with survival gear and another armed escort. We are 220 miles above the Arctic Circle and roughly 25 feet from Russia.

I'm with a specialized unit that patrols Norway's northeastern border, on the second day of a journey along the frontier—by bike through the forest and boat along the Pasvikelva River, which divides Finnmark County in

Norway from Pechengsky District in Russia's Murmansk Oblast. Autumn comes early at this latitude: we still have thirty minutes of daylight, but the temperature is plummeting and a northeasterly wind is picking up. It's blowing straight from the Barents Sea, just over the horizon beyond the Kola Peninsula.

The creek to our right is the frontier. It's a few feet wide, easily forded, and marked with tall wooden stakes—yellow with black tops on the Norwegian side, striped red and green on the Russian. To our left, a few yards back, the Norwegians have erected a wire-mesh fence, not much of an obstacle for humans, mostly to control wildlife and meet the requirement for a border-security barrier, imposed by the European Union on Norway (which is not an EU member) as a condition for joining the EU's free trade area and visa-free Schengen agreement. We are skirting the edge of Europe—inside the frontier by a few feet, but outside the wire. Little is visible among the birches and firs on the Russian bank, but this is deceptive: towers, minefields, and barbed-wire entanglements are arrayed in depth through the forest, forming a complex obstacle belt patrolled by border troops of FSB, Russia's federal security service, successor to the Soviet KGB.

In the twilight we scan a topographic map as the wind stirs the treetops. Days before, and miles from the border, I had seen a map of the Russian side with its "false frontiers"—barriers laid out to funnel defectors into dead ends, corral border-crossers in bends of the river, or fool fugitives into thinking they have crossed when they're actually still in Russia, their movements observed from towers and tracked by automated cameras. From the map, it's clear that Russia's defenses are oriented inward: unlike Norway's border, constructed to keep things out, the Soviet-built system is still designed to keep people in—even now, three decades after the fall of Communism.

During the Cold War, Norway maintained a brigade—a military formation of several thousand troops—in this region. British, Dutch, and American marines also regularly rotated through Norway to practice mountain and arctic warfare and demonstrate NATO's ability to reinforce its northern flank at speed. But the Norwegian brigade stood down as NATO refocused in the 1990s. By 2017, Russian aggression in the Baltic and Arctic, the arrest of several Russians inside Norway for espionage, and Russia's invasion of Ukraine had prompted Oslo to reinforce the border, while the British Royal Marines and United States Marine Corps resumed rotations to northern Norway in 2018.[2] Still, Russia today has more than ten times as many troops as Norway in the frontier zone at any one time.

Three Russian brigades, with thousands of soldiers and hundreds of vehicles, sit behind the FSB border screen—the 61st Independent Naval Infantry (i.e., marine amphibious) Brigade near Pechenga in the north by the Barents coast, the mechanized 200th Independent Motor Rifle Brigade a few miles south at Luostari, and a specialized Arctic Brigade, the 80th Independent Motor Rifle Brigade, at Alakurtti on the Kola Peninsula, closer to the Finnish border but still within easy striking distance of Norway. Along with these major units, for the last three years running, VDV (Vozdushno-Desantnye Voyska, Air-Landing Troops), the elite airborne forces considered a separate branch of Russia's military, have conducted airdrops into the Arctic, demonstrating their capacity to rapidly reinforce the region, and there are several Special-Purpose Forces (Spetsnaz) detachments in the area, with missions ranging from counterterrorism to long-range reconnaissance and sabotage.

Surface ships, submarines, warplanes, and Spetsnaz of Russia's Northern Fleet are also based nearby, along with missile systems and a truly astonishing array of cyber, electronic attack, radio jamming, and eavesdropping equipment. Several of Russia's growing fleet of nuclear-powered icebreakers—the country has ten of these specialized vessels with a much larger variant currently under construction—are based in Murmansk. And sitting over all of this is a powerful air defense umbrella provided by S-400 surface-to-air missiles (known to NATO as SA-21 "Growlers" and roughly equivalent to the US Patriot) at Severomorsk, generating what planners call an anti-access and area denial (A2/AD) "bubble" that reaches well into Norway.

Close to the border, bridging materials are stockpiled for a rapid river crossing into Norway—in one spot, looking across the border, I saw decking stacked under a tarpaulin just on the Russian side, close beside the supports of a bridge built by the Wehrmacht and abandoned when the Germans withdrew in 1944. Russian units periodically run mock assaults, launching in formation toward the frontier, then peeling off before they reach it. Back in Oslo, as I was leaving for the north, an analyst told me that each of these Russian brigades, during the recent exercise cycle, had fired the entire Norwegian Army's annual allocation of ammunition.

The sweat is freezing on us now, and we're starting to shiver; we need to get moving again before darkness comes down. This late in the season, the ground is flooded several inches deep as the permafrost, a few feet down, traps meltwater on the surface and turns woodland into swamp. In a few weeks the place will be frozen solid and smooth as concrete, so that T-80 tanks from the Russian bases could race into Alta, Finnmark's main town and the most northerly major city in the world. An analyst later told me that, if reinforced by naval infantry penetrating Alta fjord, covered by S-400s and supported by VDV air drops and Spetsnaz diversionary operations, Russian mechanized forces could probably capture Norway's northernmost region in about a day, cutting it off from the rest of the country and presenting Norway (and NATO) with the invidious choice of either launching a counterattack—with dangerous implications for escalating conflict—or negotiating with an adversary who would now be holding a major bargaining chip.

A couple of weeks after my return from the north, the RAND Corporation published the results of a wargame examining a similar scenario for the Baltic: a rapid assault to seize key locations in a single sudden move—known as a coup de main—followed by political-diplomatic bargaining from a position of strength. The RAND analysts found that "across multiple games . . . the longest it has taken Russian forces to reach the outskirts of the Estonian and/or Latvian capitals of Tallinn and Riga, respectively, is 60 hours."[3] Why Russia would want to do that, of course, is a different question.

An hour later I am drinking hot chocolate at the Storskog frontier checkpoint, thawing out as I chat with its commander. Recent events here show why Moscow might never need to mount such an attack and why, even if it did, Russia would probably use a blend of nonconventional means to win during what military planners call the "shaping" phase—before the first tank ever crossed the frontier—so that the T-80s might never roll at all.

This, in turn, offers a clue as to how Russia, Woolsey's original dragon, has evolved into a new and far more challenging adversary over the past quarter century.

As I will show in this chapter, Russia has well and truly recovered from the eclipse Woolsey described in 1993. In confronting a landscape of NATO expansion, unipolar military and economic dominance by the United States, Western encroachment into what Moscow calls its "near abroad," and interference in its internal affairs, Russia since the Cold War—but especially since 2008—has evolved toward a form of maneuver I call "liminal warfare."

The term "liminal" comes from the Latin word for a threshold and is used in anthropology to describe the ambiguity experienced by people or societies transitioning between two states of being.[4] Things that are in limbo, transitioning, or on the periphery, that have ambiguous political, legal, and psychological status—or whose very existence is debated—are liminal. Liminal geographies recognize thresholds not as sharp lines but as transitional zones, while in warfare guerrillas, militias, terrorists, and resistance movements are all liminal actors, as are refugees and diasporas. Thresholds that seem sharply delineated from a distance (say, the Russo-Norwegian border) turn out to be fuzzy and ambiguous up close—and as we will see, a lot happens inside those blurred lines.

Liminal warfare exploits this character of ambiguity, operating in the blur, or as some Western military organizations put it, the "gray zone."[5] As a form of maneuver, it is neither fully overt nor truly clandestine; rather, it rides the edge, surfing the threshold of detectability, sometimes subliminal (literally "below the threshold" of perception), at other times breaking fully into the open to seize an advantage or consolidate gains before adversaries can react. Likewise, the approach exploits undefined or legally ambiguous spaces and categories—using these as cover for action without retaliation.

Like the other evolutionary developments discussed in this book, Russia's embrace of liminal warfare is best understood as a reaction to Western dominance, since the Cold War, of a narrowly defined form of symmetrical, force-on-force conflict. It is an adaptive response to this dominance, shaped by an environment of pervasive electronic surveillance, a social media landscape that makes true clandestine or deniable covert operations increasingly hard to pull off, and tightening political and legal constraints on democratic governments, which need time and proof before they act. As such, liminal warfare is a survival mechanism for a power that lacks the capacity to compete directly with the West and faces a limited window of opportunity to carve out tradespace for its future interests while rebuilding its conventional capabilities.

SYRIANS IN THE ARCTIC

On the Russo-Norwegian border, a classic liminal space, not everyone is a fan of the government, some 1,200 road-miles to the south in Oslo. During the Second World War, hundreds from this region fled to the Soviet Union to train with the Russians, then joined partisan (i.e., guerrilla) groups operating in northern Norway that were controlled by NKVD, the predecessor of KGB.[6] Arguably, these Norwegians may have been just as patriotic as the resisters who sabotaged German occupation in Oslo or destroyed the heavy-water plant at Vemork (a raid by Norwegians with Britain's Special Operations Executive, SOE, that disrupted the Nazi atomic bomb program and was celebrated in the 1965 film *Heroes of Telemark*). Yet in the context of the Cold War, the Russian-sponsored partisans were treated very differently than the allied Free Norwegian Forces. Far from being lionized as heroes, until the 1990s Soviet-sponsored Norwegian partisans were denied recognition for their wartime service, and they and their families were regarded with suspicion by a government facing Soviet aggression.[7] To this day, Norwegian border patrols sometimes encounter obscene gestures or scowls from this group or its descendants.[8]

There may be eight to ten officers from Russian military intelligence (GRU, now known as GU, the Main Intelligence Directorate of the Russian General Staff) operating on the Norwegian side of the border at any one time, collecting intelligence, conducting reconnaissance, and preparing guerrilla cells and sabotage networks to be activated in the event of conflict.[9] By definition, this kind of activity, known in the business as "operational preparation of the environment" (OPE), is virtually impossible to prove. And of course, even if the estimate is accurate, it would not mean that members of local communities are disloyal, though such stereotypes linger, especially among Russian speakers in northern Norway.[10] Rather, it simply suggests that the border, like any frontier, is a complex, liminal space with multiple actors, many simultaneous overlapping activities, and plenty of cover (including human cover) for things best kept quiet.

In fact, most border activity is legal, friendly, cooperative, and commercial. There are cross-border social, community, and artistic events, a range of person-to-person contacts, and strong traditional trading relationships. Russians regularly drive to Norway to buy consumer goods (especially diapers, which it seems neither the Soviet nor post-Soviet Russian economies have ever managed to produce efficiently), sell handicrafts in local markets, or catch flights from Kirkenes airport.[11] For their part, Norwegians go to Russia for gasoline and alcohol, both overpriced in Norway. (In 2017, a bottle of vodka costing 300 Norwegian kroner, about 35 US dollars, could be had for the equivalent of kr.112 in Russia, and filling the tank of a typical passenger car in Norway cost kr.825 compared with kr.302 in Russia).[12] Russian rules make it illegal to cross the border on foot, and Norwegian law penalizes drivers carrying passengers without passports. But, it turns out, both sides allow cyclists—creating a loophole for border crossing by bike.

That legal loophole in border regulations became operationally important for a few weeks in the summer of 2015, when more than fifty-five hundred Syrian, Afghan, and Iraqi refugees cycled from the Russian factory town of Nikel, crossed the border, then abandoned their bicycles at Storskog and sought asylum.[13] A year later, a few weeks before my visit, another group tried the same thing. It was not just Norway: all along Russia's European border, Middle Eastern refugees made the same dash. The following spring, the Baltic states of Estonia, Latvia, and Lithuania cooperated to build enhanced fencing on their borders with Russia to thwart similar incursions.[14] Finland experienced a rush of crossings into its Lapland region the same winter.[15]

A few months after this, in Helsinki, a Finnish security service officer told me that while it was clear the migrants had help from organized crime—some mafia groups acknowledged selling "package deals" of minibus rides and bicycles to asylum-seekers arriving at Murmansk airport—there was almost certainly government involvement. For one thing, she noted, crossings spiked along the entire length of Russia's Scandinavian and Baltic frontier in the same week, as if someone had turned on a tap, which would be hard to explain by pinpointing the refugee social-media grapevine alone. For another, Norway (whose relations with Russia are frostier than Finland's) was hit first, after imposing sanctions on Russia for its not so covert invasion of Ukraine, and the Baltic states followed. Finland—whose links with Russia have historically been at least as complex as Norway's—was initially spared but suffered an influx after criticizing Moscow's seizure of Crimea. My own observation in the frontier zone suggests it would be highly unlikely for so many border-crossers to thwart a Russian border system designed to keep people in rather than out, all in the same few weeks—even as eyewitnesses claim to have seen FSB guards helping asylum-seekers cross the border.[16] As my Finnish contact commented, "This didn't just happen: these people had professional help."[17]

Clearly, beyond the humanitarian challenge of dealing with a flood of refugees in the Arctic, the hardship experienced by the asylum-seekers themselves, the bureaucratic burden of processing their applications, and the social and financial costs of integrating new arrivals into welfare systems, there were obvious benefits for the Russians in testing European borders. For one, it allowed FSB and GRU to evaluate how quickly frontier forces could respond to incidents and to understand their surge capacity. As we will see later, understanding an adversary's reaction parameters (especially decision time) is a critical element of liminal warfare. For another, an influx of refugees from terrorism-affected countries provided material for Russian information campaigns stoking dissent over European refugee policy, which were ramped up in the months that followed.[18] And inserting intelligence assets under the cover of a flow of refugees allowed intelligence officers to understand border systems from the inside.

For this and a host of other Russian-sponsored activity along the edges of Europe there is reasonably strong evidence, but—and this is the critical point—little in the way of actual proof. Everything is ambiguous, unproven, and in some sense unprovable. Border-crossers are classic examples of liminal actors, and Russia's ability to exploit them is itself debatable: some observers are convinced of Russian government involvement in incursions and violations of European sovereignty, while others, seeing the same evidence, doubt there is much more here than coincidence.

Likewise, there is strong circumstantial evidence of Russian government attempts to influence Britain's Brexit referendum and the US presidential election in 2016, the Catalonian vote for independence from Spain in 2017, German federal elections and US midterms in 2018, Montenegro's entry into NATO in 2018, and the rise of Far Right (and Far Left) parties from Greece and Hungary to Austria, Sweden, and France.[19] By definition, prosecutorial indictments, such as those against alleged GRU-sponsored hackers in the American case, are allegations, not findings of guilt—and to the extent that these indictments target officials whose extradition Moscow would never approve, there is no chance those allegations will ever be tested in court.[20]

The Mueller Report, released in April 2019, painted a deeply unflattering picture of President Trump's petulant response to the investigation of his campaign and gave details of efforts by two GRU cyberwarfare and information warfare units to influence the 2016 election, as well as the role of WikiLeaks as a conduit for illegally obtained material. But the report's conclusions, too, were sufficiently ambiguous that partisans on both sides of US politics claimed vindication.[21] The report also left key questions unanswered—for example, the origin of the so-called Steele Dossier (a classically GRU-style *kompromat* operation) and whether it was fed to US intelligence agencies and political opponents of candidate Trump by GRU or some intermediary as a provocation to destabilize American politics. On this issue, too, the report (and Russian interference generally) became a Rorschach test: observers' prior assumptions and personal biases explained their conclusions more than the evidence itself. This sort of nonfalsifiable reality distortion field is a classic characteristic of liminality—whether you see a phenomenon, and how you interpret the data, depend mostly on who you are.

Likewise, the intelligence community's assessment (released by outgoing Obama administration officials three days before President Trump's inauguration in January 2017) that "Russian President Vladimir Putin ordered an influence campaign in 2016 aimed at the US presidential election . . . to undermine public faith in the US democratic process, denigrate Secretary Clinton, and harm her electability and potential presidency" and that "Putin and the Russian Government developed a clear preference for President-elect Trump"[22] is an aggregation of analytic judgments based on partial (and continuously changing) evidence, reflecting probability rather than proof. This is not to disagree with the assessment—I happen to agree with it, on the merits—but merely to point out what any analyst knows, namely that an intelligence assessment is just that: an assessment. Indeed, Annex B of the document noted that judgments within it "are not intended to imply that we have proof that shows something to be a fact. Assessments are based on collected information, which is often incomplete or fragmentary, as well as logic, argumentation, and precedents."[23]

I just noted the ambiguity inherent in certain parts of the Mueller Report and related indictments; the ambiguity here involves *attribution* of responsibility rather than *detection* of activity: analysts may believe certain activities occurred but cannot necessarily prove the Russian government was responsible for them. Vladimir Putin's June 2017 comment that it was "theoretically possible" that election hacking emanated from Russia, but attributing it to "patriotically minded" Russians "making their own contribution," exploits this ambiguity.[24] Likewise, the best assessment of the US intelligence community, as of April 2019, suggests that there were multiple parallel hacking and influence activities, some involving Russian government employees and some using "volunteers," and that dissemination of compromising material was filtered through a diffuse set of independent actors, some of whom were witting participants in a Russian disinformation operation, while others were unwitting (or so politically partisan as to accept on face value materials that should have triggered suspicions).[25] And as President Trump's reaction to the intelligence assessment and Putin's comments illustrates, the prime targets of ambiguity are political decision-makers rather than military commanders or intelligence analysts—a point we will return to later.

Likewise, GRU involvement in the poisoning of former Russian VDV and GRU officer Sergei Skripal and his daughter Yulia in March 2018, like FSB's alleged role in the radiation poisoning of former FSB officer Alexander Litvinenko in November 2006, has been strongly asserted by British courts and police, yet contemptuously denied by Russia. Some observers have suggested that the attackers may have been working for the Russian mafia in Spain rather than the government in Moscow: Skripal was allegedly cooperating with Spanish intelligence to uncover Russian mob activity at the time of the attack, and Litvinenko had also helped Spanish law enforcement agencies fighting organized crime.[26] To paraphrase Putin, it's therefore "theoretically possible" that moonlighting intelligence operators, linked to the mafia, committed these attacks on their own initiative without Moscow's approval or knowledge. Possible does not mean probable—in fact, such a scenario is highly implausible and is contradicted by other evidence—but the ambiguity is sufficient for a political denial in an environment of fake news and partisan media. Indeed, fostering a fragmented, polarized political and media environment can become a military objective in its own right, since it increases the scope for maneuver by widening the zone of ambiguity.

Even stronger is the evidence for allegations that Russian forces gave Ukrainian separatists the Buk-4M anti-aircraft missile that they used to shoot down Malaysian Airlines flight MH-17 in July 2014, as well for the role of Russian naval infantry and Spetsnaz in seizing the Crimean peninsula that February and March.[27] But a lack of irrefutable proof—and brazen denials by leaders in Moscow—make such events and actors liminal (rather than either overt or truly covert) and partly explain why they brought little military, as distinct from political and economic, blowback for Russia.

The Arctic frontier is just one of several borderlands where Russia has been exploiting this ambiguity, surfing the edge of confrontation with the West, conducting a campaign of competition across multiple geographies, technologies, and categories of activity that stops, for the most part, short of war—but periodically crosses the threshold into ambiguous forms of conflict. The Middle East and the Baltic are other areas, as are cyberspace, energy markets, the electrical grid, space and missile systems, agitation and propaganda, and political warfare against NATO and in Europe, Latin America, and parts of Africa. More broadly, Russia's liminal activity reflects an evolution that has fully emerged only in the past five years but which, looking back, has been present since the Cold War. To trace its development, and thus understand how we got here, we need to go back a bit—to one of the most controversial episodes in the history of Russian-Western relations, which took place exactly three years before Woolsey's testimony.

RUSSIA AFTER THE COLD WAR

In February 1990, amid a diplomatic frenzy following the collapse of Communism in East Germany, West German chancellor Helmut Kohl met Soviet premier Mikhail Gorbachev in Moscow and secured a key concession: Gorbachev told Kohl that he would agree to a unified Germany joining NATO in return for a commitment that NATO would not expand beyond Germany's eastern border.[28] By removing the threat of NATO encroachment into Soviet space, Kohl—and at least nine other NATO leaders who gave similar assurances in that crucial spring of 1990—reduced the risk of conflict, which had spiked as Moscow's control over its eastern European satellites collapsed. The classic formulation was offered by US secretary of state James Baker, who assured Gorbachev on 9 February 1990 that NATO "would not shift one inch eastward from its present position."[29]

The two years from the fall of the Berlin Wall in November 1989 until the final Soviet breakup of December 1991 were a time of immense danger—a transitional period that was in some ways the riskiest of the entire Cold War. The cascading collapse of Soviet control in Europe undermined the stable deterrent balance that had existed between the superpowers, disrupted the central front between NATO and the Warsaw Pact, and created a real risk of conventional or even nuclear war. Chaotic power dynamics within the dying Soviet Union, culminating in a coup attempt against Gorbachev in August 1991, underscored the risk that hardliners might seize control and plunge into conflict to preserve their power.[30] Given these dangers, it's not hard to imagine—or justify—Western leaders saying whatever they had to in order to stop the Soviet collapse from spiraling out of control.

Their assurances (documented in diplomatic cables and cabinet minutes that were declassified in 2017) almost certainly helped end the Cold War peacefully.[31]

But they also prompted a perception in Moscow—and, arguably, in the mind of Vladimir Putin, then a thirty-six-year-old KGB officer in the East German city of Dresden—that Russia had been tricked into standing down, betrayed by empty reassurances that NATO then blithely ignored. Once Russia's withdrawal created a power vacuum in Europe, the Western allies proved only too ready to fill it, expanding NATO to the very doorstep of a diminished Russia.

There is, to this day, a lot of debate about what was said during these conversations on the brink of Soviet collapse. In some ways, it matters little whether what Gorbachev (and, after him, Boris Yeltsin) believe they heard was what Western leaders meant to say.[32] In fact, the archival documents seem pretty clear on this point: Russia's peaceful pullback does appear to have been premised on promises that NATO would not expand to fill the gap—assurances that soon proved hollow. Whether NATO leaders lied (as many Russians remain convinced) or were merely misunderstood (as Western politicians of the period maintain), the fact is that, by the time Russia realized NATO did intend to expand, it was too late for Gorbachev, Yeltsin, or anyone else to do much about it.

All this still rankles Russians—and so it should. Indeed, it's impossible to understand Russia's evolution since the Cold War without first acknowledging the impetus for that evolution: the intense adaptive pressure on Russia after the Soviet collapse, the fitness landscape of unipolar American dominance (both discussed in Chapter 1), and the way these factors shaped Russian military adaptation. The fact is that Russians have every justification for feeling humiliated by what happened in the 1990s, that they suffered hugely after the Soviet collapse, and that the Russian Federation, like any other country, has a right to pursue its sovereign interests. Of course, this doesn't excuse Russia's behavior in places like Syria, the Baltic, and Ukraine or make Russia any less dangerous as an adversary. Neither does empathy imply approval: Russia has a right to pursue its interests, but so do Western powers; when those interests clash there will be conflict, and that conflict will occasionally rise to the level of war. But the competition (both competition short of war and confrontation leading occasionally to active conflict) among the great powers today is dramatically different than it was during the Cold War, largely because of what happened to Russia in the 1990s. So to understand how the Russians evolved toward liminal warfare, we need to put ourselves in their shoes.

Consider the 1990s from the Russian point of view. On the basis of assurances from NATO, the Soviets withdrew an enormously potent military force, the Group of Soviet Forces Germany (GSFG), which, with 338,000 troops, was assessed by CIA as the most powerful conventional combat unit on the Continent.[33] They permitted the peaceful reunification of Germany—entailing the loss of a pivotal client state, the German Democratic Republic, without which the Warsaw Pact's posture in Europe was unsustainable—then stood by while Poland, Czechoslovakia, Hungary, Bulgaria, and Romania threw out pro-Soviet regimes in 1989–90. The Warsaw Pact collapsed in January 1991, and the Soviet Union lost the Baltic states in August that year when Estonia, Latvia, and Lithuania unilaterally declared independence, marooning the enclave of Kaliningrad, the former East Prussian Königsberg, seized by the Soviets in 1945. (Today, Kaliningrad looks like an aggressive bridgehead into NATO—it's the headquarters for the Russian Baltic fleet and a major military base with nuclear-capable missiles targeting Germany and an air defense umbrella covering the entire Baltic region. But at the time, it was merely the far-western edge of a continuous swath of Soviet territory stretching all the way to Vladivostok on the Sea of Japan.) Then on 21 December 1991, leaders of twelve Soviet republics met and agreed to dissolve the USSR. Attempts to form a continuing confederation, the Commonwealth of Independent States, foundered, and the Soviet Union was gone.

RUSSIA IN DEFEAT

In the aftermath of that collapse, Western businesspeople and advisers descended on Moscow to preside over the deeply damaging "shock therapy" (implemented by the Harvard economist Jeffrey Sachs and a team of Western experts) and a widely condemned privatization scheme involving the selloff of state assets to well-connected insiders, canny bidders (including Westerners like the American investor Bill Browder), and corrupt officials who made immense personal fortunes off the collapse of Russia's economy and the misery of its people.[34] In the view of many Russians, the combination of shock therapy and privatization created a mafia state dominated by scavenging and extraordinarily violent oligarchs whose only claim to fame was being in the right place, at the right time, with the right (often Western) connections.

The consequences were widespread, and dire: in the 1990s, life expectancy fell eight years for Russian men and two for Russian women, productive capacity dropped 8 percent per year from 1989 to 2001, capital flight averaged $1.5 billion a month, and the number of people living in poverty across the former Soviet Union rose from 14 million in 1989 to 147 million in 1998.[35] Mafia murders skyrocketed, with hundreds killed as rival gangs and competing oligarchs fought for control of lucrative, newly privatized industries and booming illicit business.[36] It was a social, humanitarian, and economic catastrophe unprecedented in peacetime. The Cold War never went hot in Europe, leading some to suggest that it was "not an actual war."[37] But losing it was a real defeat for Russia, with consequences akin to those suffered by Germany in the 1920s. At the peak of shock therapy and privatization, in 1992–94, Russia's GDP fell by half while mortality rose so dramatically that "demographers did not believe the figures. The toll from murder, suicide, heart attacks, and accidents gave Russia the death rate of a country at war."[38]

From his apogee as a democracy icon facing down the 1991 coup attempt, Boris Yeltsin, seen by many Russians as the architect of post-Soviet misery, had sunk to an approval rating of 5.6 percent by 1995.[39] As Bill Browder put it in his 2015 memoir, Red Notice, "Instead of 150 million Russians sharing the spoils of mass privatization, Russia wound up with twenty-two oligarchs owning 39 percent of the economy and everyone else living in poverty. To make ends meet, professors had to become taxi drivers, nurses became prostitutes, and art museums sold paintings right off their walls. Nearly every Russian was cowed and humiliated, and they hated Yeltsin for it."[40]

Adding insult to injury, Western governments then meddled in Russia's electoral process, intervening to ensure Yeltsin's reelection in 1996 despite his deep unpopularity with almost every segment of Russian society. The Clinton administration pushed for a $10.2 billion emergency loan to Russia from the International Monetary Fund, which Yeltsin promptly (and illegally) diverted to campaign spending against his rival, the Communist Gennady Zyuganov.[41] A team of US political operatives moved to Moscow, set up a war room in the President Hotel across the river from the Kremlin, and provided policy input and political advice to Yeltsin's campaign in an effort to sway the election—something they acknowledged on their return.[42] This was a bipartisan effort: the advisers came from the Republican Party but coordinated with President Clinton, a Democrat, to determine what comments and actions from Washington could most help Yeltsin.

Again, one could argue that this was done with the best of intentions, since Yeltsin—for all his flaws—was still seen as Russia's best hope for democracy, and Zyuganov's election might have meant a relapse into Cold War confrontation. But whatever its motives, US support meant that Yeltsin's dirty tricks and diversion of funds from Russia's central bank to his campaign were seen as US "black operations," and instances of corruption, drunkenness, mismanagement, and incompetence in Yeltsin's second term (of which there were plenty) were also blamed on the West. This perceived meddling, which far exceeded in directness (though not severity) any recent Russian interference in the United States or Europe, also set a precedent for similar behavior by Moscow.[43]

MILITARY EVOLUTION IN POST–COLD WAR RUSSIA

Russia's military, once the largest in the world with 3.4 million troops, was in free fall during this period. After the dismemberment of the Soviet armed forces and their distribution among the successor states, the Russian Federation was left with a large, unaffordable, and inefficient rump military establishment, ill-suited to its new circumstances. As the analyst Mikhail

Barabanov points out, the enormous Soviet structure was hollow. The "bulk of the Army consisted of reduced-strength units (manned to 50 percent of their full wartime strength) and skeleton-strength units (manned from 10 to 20 percent). Of 132 combined-services divisions [in the army in 1991], only 20 were manned and equipped to 70 percent of their full wartime strength... of the 3.4 million people who served in the Soviet Armed Forces in 1991, almost 1.2 million were storage depot personnel" maintaining vast stockpiles of weapons and equipment (often obsolete) needed for mobilization for major war, the main focus of the Soviet military.[44]

Not only did the armed forces inherit all these problems, their position after 1991 was ill-suited to the new geography and security challenges of post-Soviet Russia, with key strategic assets and elements of the defense industrial base now located in other countries and with formerly interior districts that were held by low-readiness units (such as the North Caucasus and Moscow military districts) transformed into border regions.[45] Yeltsin's priorities understandably lay elsewhere, given the huge challenges Russia faced, and thus the armed forces shrank rapidly, budgets were slashed, and even those funds that were allocated often disappeared or remained unspent. In 1996, for example, the budget execution shortfall (i.e., the difference between what the government allocated to defense and what was actually spent) was twenty-five billion rubles, while the average officer was owed ten thousand rubles in back pay; by 1997 the shortfall had risen to thirty-four billion, soldiers were moonlighting in other jobs, and some units had to pick mushrooms for food.[46] Funding fell even further following the 1998 global financial crisis.[47] Huge numbers of soldiers were dismissed, left unemployed on the streets during one of the worst crises in Russian history.

This loss of skilled, experienced personnel—particularly officers and noncommissioned officers—caused a drastic drop in effectiveness, highlighted during the first Chechen War in 1994–96, when poorly trained Russian troops were surrounded and slaughtered by Chechen guerrillas (many of whom had previously served in the Soviet Army).[48] Both Ukraine and Russia claimed the former Soviet Black Sea Fleet in an acrimonious dispute that dragged on for five years, from 1992 to 1997.[49] Yevgeny

Shaposhnikov (the last Soviet defense minister and first commander of post-Soviet Russian forces) was accused of selling off naval assets behind Ukraine's back and encouraging defections.[50]

Shaposhnikov also engaged in his own, unique privatization program, issuing "a command granting the right to anyone of battalion-commander rank or higher to dispose of 'surplus property' belonging to the air force. They could dispose of it in exchange for payment . . . and to suitable buyers."[51] In effect, this was an open invitation to plunder state assets. Whole warehouses, squadrons of aircraft, stockpiles of ammunition and uniforms, and "anything else that wasn't nailed down" disappeared in "an orgy of privateering and black-market arms sales the likes of which had never before been seen in peacetime."[52] Urgent steps had to be taken to secure the Soviet nuclear arsenal—components of which were in Belarus, Kazakhstan, and Ukraine as well as Russia—leading to a major dispute with Ukraine and fears of "loose nukes," the proliferation of nuclear materials and weapons systems from former Soviet sources. Likewise, a flood of former Soviet weaponry spread to the Balkans, Africa, and the Middle East. If anything, Russia during this period served as the perfect illustration of Woolsey's argument that the main threat came not from strong state adversaries but from failing states and nonstate actors.

NATO EXPANSION

Yugoslavia was the most prominent of these failing states, and it was in the Balkans that Western powers began flexing their military muscle in regions Russia considered its turf. Again, from the Western standpoint the intervention in Bosnia (from February 1992 under UN auspices, then under NATO from 1994) was a peacekeeping mission to prevent genocide and contain chaos that could have destabilized all of Europe. The same was true of NATO's bombing of Yugoslavia and intervention in Kosovo in 1999, seen in the West as robust humanitarian interventions to halt the ethnic cleansing of Kosovo's Albanian Muslim population. In this narrative, the United States intervened late, altruistically, and reluctantly, at the urging of the UN and its European allies, to stave off humanitarian disaster. In the official Western view, the US bombing of China's embassy in Belgrade in May 1999 (discussed in detail in the next chapter) was a tragic accident, and the fact that MPRI—a private military company led by former American generals—provided crucial support to Croatia's 1995 invasion of the Krajina was not a case of government-backed American mercenaries helping dismantle a state that Russia considered part of its orbit, but simply a commercial firm pursuing free enterprise.[53] Needless to say, this is not how things looked from Moscow or from St. Petersburg (where Putin was now managing external affairs in the mayor's office).[54]

As the war intensified in Yugoslavia, NATO was expanding. And far from following Baker's "not one inch eastward" formula, its expansion drove directly into the Russian borderlands. As early as 1991, NATO established the North Atlantic Cooperation Council, "a forum for consultations between NATO members, East European states and former Soviet republics."[55] Created the day before the Soviet Union collapsed and a few months after the Warsaw Pact was dissolved, the council offered an alternative affiliation to former Soviet satellites and republics (such as the Baltic states), drawing them into the Western orbit. Two years later, as operations in Bosnia ramped up, NATO's Partnerships for Peace program was established to create a mechanism for these states to form an association with the alliance.[56] The Baltic countries—frightened by Russia's evident unwillingness to accept their sovereignty—began creating a joint military unit (BALTBAT, the Baltic Battalion) in August 1994, assembled its troops and equipment for joint training in February 1995, and deployed it to Bosnia under NATO command, with British and Danish advisers in 1996.[57] In 1999, the Czech Republic, Poland, and Hungary became the first former Warsaw Pact states to join NATO, "taking the alliance's borders some 400 miles towards Russia," and in November 2002, Lithuania, Estonia, Latvia, Bulgaria, Romania, Slovakia, and Slovenia were formally invited to join.[58]

Again, it's difficult to overstate how threatening this appeared from Moscow's standpoint. Perhaps more than most countries, Russia is defined—one might almost say haunted—by its history.[59] In the years after 1945, Russia—scarred by four invasions from the west in less than 150 years (Napoleon in 1812; the British, French, and Ottomans in the

Crimea in 1854; imperial Germany and Austria-Hungary in 1914; and Hitler in 1941)—had built a buffer of client states along its borders. As George Kennan observed in his "long telegram" of February 1946, this was not so much an ideologically driven Soviet strategy as a Russian response to realities that would have existed with or without Stalin.[60] As the respected Russia watcher Keir Giles points out, Moscow's practice of controlling, subverting, and destabilizing its neighbors is based on a perception that "equates depth of territory held with security gained" and a "permanent and persistent belief throughout history that Russia's land borders present a critical vulnerability and that in order to protect itself, Russia must exert control far beyond them"—independent of the ideology of any particular ruler in the Kremlin.[61] As Giles points out, Russians are only half joking when they say that the only secure Russian border is one with a Russian soldier standing on *both* sides of it.[62]

The Russian geopolitical theorist Aleksander Dugin makes the same point more expansively, arguing that "the territory of contemporary Russia, earlier the Soviet Union (USSR), and still earlier the Russian Empire, is the Heartland; it is the land-based (telluric) core of the entire Eurasian continent."[63] Dugin (whose work is also discussed in the next chapter) is a colorful character: leaving his academic post as a neo-Eurasianist philosopher, he took up arms in his mid-fifties to fight as a volunteer in Ukraine on behalf of pro-Russian separatist groups and is allegedly close to Colonel Igor Strelkov, the Russian veteran and alleged GRU Spetsnaz officer who led separatist militias and served as the "Minister of Defense of the Donetsk People's Republic."[64]

Dugin claims that its geopolitical position makes Russia, or whatever entity occupies the current territory of the Russian Federation, the dominant power of what geopolitical theorists call the "world-island" (the single contiguous landmass comprising all of Europe, Asia, and Africa) and a natural adversary to sea-based powers reliant on oceanic trade, formerly led by Great Britain and currently by the United States.[65] He argues that its size and land-based character render Russia naturally statist and authoritarian (due to the need to control an immense internal space, diverse populations, vast resources, and vulnerable land borders), while sea-based powers tend to be capitalist due to their dependence on trade, as well as internally liberal since they can rely on secure oceanic borders (and historically do not need standing armies). Also, according to Dugin, whichever state controls the world-island is by definition one of the great powers, perhaps the greatest, so that Russia's drive for such status is both natural and right. Dugin's influence on contemporary Russian politics is disputed and his geographic determinism (like that of many geopolitical theorists) is contested; still, his perspective is close to that of Vladimir Putin's political party and reflects one key strand of Russian thinking since the Cold War.

But it was not just a matter of geopolitics. Many Russians had (and have) a profound spiritual and emotional commitment to the "Russian World"— a civilizational space that is partly geographical but more deeply defined by shared Russian language and culture, Orthodox religion, kinship, and ethnicity.[66] Russians see themselves as protectors, defenders, and natural leaders of a region covering not only their country but also the Balkans, Ukraine—the historical point of origin for Russian civilization—and other Slavic countries, parts of the Middle East and Central Asia, anywhere Orthodox Christianity is practiced or Russian is spoken, and even places in Alaska and the Japanese archipelago where indigenous peoples have ties to Siberia. And after the Soviet collapse, with ethnic-Russian minorities marooned all over the Baltic states, eastern Europe, and the former Soviet republics of the Caucasus and Central Asia, the inability of Mother Russia to spread her protective wings over this expansive, self-declared cultural *votchina* (patrimony) was agonizing.[67] Discrimination against ethnic Russians—particularly in the Baltic states and Georgia after 1991—was keenly felt (and completely understandable, of course, given these countries' history of invasion and oppression by Russia).[68]

ADAPTATION UNDER PRESSURE

It is a harsh reality that most successful military adaptation is driven by defeat. Examples abound, from Prussia's reforms after its loss to Napoleon in 1806[69] to the British Army's modernization following colonial catastrophes in the 1870s,[70] the British invention of tank warfare in 1916 in the wake of a string of bloody setbacks on the western front,[71] the German development of *Blitzkrieg* in response to defeat in 1918,[72] Australia's transformation from desert to jungle warfare after defeats by the Japanese in 1942,[73] and the creation of US Special Operations Command (SOCOM) after the Desert One disaster of 1980.[74] I could list a dozen more examples, but the point is obvious: leaders rarely rack their brains to discover explanations for their *success*, which they tend simply to ascribe to their own raw, naked tactical brilliance or inspired leadership. Rather it is the shock of *defeat* that prompts painful introspection, innovation, and the search for future victory. At one level, this is just an organizational way of framing the evolutionary argument we have been exploring in previous chapters. Russia was no exception: arguably it was defeat in the Cold War, the pain of post-Soviet suffering, and the drive to recover lost greatness that created the strongest impetus for adaptation.

And the pervasive chaos and confusion of Russia at this time may have enhanced the adaptive effect. As discussed in Chapter 1, Dominic Johnson, in his work on Darwinian selection in warfare, points out that weaker sides often include a larger diversity of combatants, giving them greater adaptive potential.[75] Stronger sides apply "more selection pressure on weaker sides than the other way around, resulting in faster adaptation by the weaker side," while "weaker sides are exposed to combat for longer (fighting on the same home territory for years at a time), promoting experience and learning."[76] While Johnson focuses on nonstate groups, his point applies equally to Russian forces after the Cold War, which as we have seen had suffered a major defeat, were under significant adaptive pressure in the 1990s, and had large variations among units in terms of composition, structure, and weapons.[77]

By the time Vladimir Putin came to power in 2000, Russian forces had also been exposed to combat on their home territory for a lengthy period, having conducted a continuous series of internal wars against separatists, terrorists, and breakaway regions for almost a decade, as well as external campaigns to influence neighboring states. They thus had significant experience on which to build. Likewise, prompted by its abysmal early performance in Chechnya, the Russian Army had adapted, developing specialized units, upgrading equipment, and introducing new tactics for urban and irregular warfare in time for the second Chechen campaign.[78] Failures flowing from the hollow mobilization structure inherited from the Soviets prompted leaders to develop what they called "constant combat readiness units"—battalion-sized groups drawn from lower-readiness divisional and brigade structures but maintained at permanently higher levels of personnel, training, and equipment, enabling rapid deployment for crisis or conflict. Each brigade or division would cobble together people and equipment to create one fully resourced battalion group and would then be responsible for sustaining it on operations, rotating troops from their base area through the operational theater, and cannibalizing assets to keep the deployed subelement going. These constant readiness units eventually evolved into the battalion tactical groups (BTGs), the building blocks for later Russian interventions in Georgia, Ukraine, and Syria.[79]

This adaptation was one response to selective pressure from the wars in the Caucasus and on the frontiers. But it was an outlier against a generally negative background: the Russian defense industry had been battered by privatization, corruption, and lack of investment, and Russia's naval, air, and nuclear capabilities were in a parlous state, as tragically underlined only four months into President Putin's first term by the loss of the nuclear submarine *Kursk*, with its entire 118-man crew, during an exercise in the Barents Sea in August 2000—a disaster compounded by Moscow's unwillingness to accept British and Norwegian offers to help rescue twenty-three sailors, who subsequently died trapped inside the stricken submarine.[80] Likewise, Russia in the 1990s simply lacked the money to modernize a nuclear arsenal that was already reaching the end of its service life when the Soviet Union collapsed—and that shrank by a factor of 4 to 4.5 during the next decade.[81]

Though little-known when appointed by Yeltsin as his successor on New Year's Eve 1999—after leaving St. Petersburg he had been a bureaucrat in Moscow, then the classic intelligence "gray man" as head of FSB, before serving as a competent technocratic prime minister during Yeltsin's last months as president—Vladimir Putin set out to restore Russia's honor, rescue the country from humiliation, and reassert its dominance: first in the near abroad, then across the Russian World, and eventually beyond it. His initial approach was to buy time while putting in place a program of political, economic, and military rebuilding. The program had three military strands—nuclear, conventional, and asymmetric.

On the nuclear front, Russia first sought to expand its options at the lower, "tactical" end of the scale, creating low-yield weapons that could be used for fighting wars rather than merely deterring them. A CIA intelligence memorandum of August 2000 (declassified in 2005) noted that Russian strategists since the 1990s had argued for the development of "subkiloton nuclear weapons with minimal long-term contamination" as an "'asymmetric response' to US superiority in conventional weapons."[82] Under Putin, Russia increased its investment in these weapons, which had yields as low as the equivalent of 300 tons of TNT, were relatively clean in terms of radioactive fallout, and were designed to destroy military targets on the battlefield (as distinct from strategic weapons, with yields in the millions of tons and limited accuracy, designed to kill whole cities). Recognizing their lack of conventional capability—and threatened by NATO's encroachment into their sphere of influence—Russian strategists compensated by developing nuclear weapons that could be used in conventional conflict as a form of gigantic artillery, without triggering a full-scale nuclear exchange.

One notion—perhaps reflecting NATO intelligence perceptions more than Moscow's own view—was that such weapons might let Russia "escalate to de-escalate," using nuclear strikes against military targets early in a conflict in order to end it quickly.[83] The idea was that by, say, sinking a US aircraft carrier strike group at sea or destroying incoming NATO reinforcements before they could reach Europe, Russia could remove an enemy's ability to fight conventionally while inflicting minimal collateral damage, killing few or no civilians, and avoiding an attack on the American homeland. Moscow could then negotiate from a position of strength to end the conflict or contain escalation.[84] Such a strike, it was thought, might be attractive for Russian strategists confronting superior NATO conventional forces, who might believe it entailed little risk of a global thermonuclear exchange, since it would be irrational for Western leaders to kill millions of their own civilians by starting a worldwide war in retaliation for a localized hit on a purely military target. Thus, low-yield nuclear weapons could become usable even in limited war, offsetting Russia's conventional weakness and blurring the distinction between nuclear and non-nuclear conflict.[85]

Russia watchers disagree as to whether any such doctrine ever formally existed.[86] Still, the idea is consistent with the coup de main concept that I described earlier in relation to northern Norway and the Baltic—a surprise stroke to present an enemy with a fait accompli, enabling political leaders to then negotiate from a position of strength. It is also consistent with Russia's approach to the war in Georgia (discussed in detail later), its use of high-end missile systems in Syria, and the scenario used for a major military exercise, *Zapad-17*, in 2017.[87] The *Vostok-18* maneuvers, a year later, embodied elements of a similar approach while also creating an opportunity for Chinese forces, which participated in Russia's largest-ever exercise, to learn from Russia's experience.[88]

More broadly, this discussion points to a real difference in how Russian, as compared with Western, strategists view nuclear missiles: not as militarily unusable superweapons whose primary purpose is deterrence, but as part of an integrated tactical repertoire for limited war. Russian theorists have long believed in what they call "interchangeability of fires and forces"— the notion that a given number of troops on the battlefield equal a certain amount of massed firepower, so that weight of fire (nuclear, non-nuclear, electronic, or cyber) can counterbalance lack of physical mass.[89] The principles of mass, simultaneity, depth, and isolation that infuse the Soviet theory of deep operations (and employ this idea of interchangeability) remain influential in today's Russian military—and also, ironically, in the US Army and other NATO forces.[90]

At the same time, nuclear weapons (tactical or strategic) are status symbols. They confer great-power status on their owners, admit them to an exclusive global club, and facilitate saber rattling to intimidate or destabilize adversaries short of war—a use to which President Putin, like previous Russian leaders, regularly puts them in a sort of nuclear gunboat diplomacy.[91] By right of its strategic nuclear arsenal alone, if for no other reason, Russia could still claim global great-power status even at the nadir of its post-Soviet collapse. For this reason, Moscow moved to modernize its strategic rocket forces as well. A CIA estimate of worldwide missile developments in December 2001 suggested Russia had a long way to go, arguing that "force structure decisions resulting from resource problems, program development failures, weapon system aging, the dissolution of the Soviet Union, and arms control treaties have resulted in a steep decline in Russian strategic nuclear forces over the last 10 years."[92] But in the decade after that assessment, up until 2011, Russia invested heavily in strategic nuclear modernization, research and development for nuclear warheads, and advanced missile systems—and by 2017–18 was testing new missiles and warhead designs in its military exercises.[93] New "doomsday weapons" announced by President Putin in early 2018, including a nuclear-powered cruise missile with theoretically unlimited range, a hypersonic missile allegedly capable of defeating most modern missile defense systems, and a large underwater drone known as "Status-6" that could carry a massive 100-megaton thermonuclear warhead to wipe out any coastal city, served a similar saber-rattling function during times of tension.[94] They also, not incidentally, served as shiny objects to distract Western intelligence analysts in an area (strategic nuclear weapons) where Western countries were then obligated to continue spending money, soaking up attention and resources even as Russia's true transformation took place in the realms of asymmetric and conventional warfare.

In the conventional realm, Russian forces were working to upgrade their capability, initially with limited success. Despite several attempts to reform the armed forces in the late 1990s and early 2000s, drawing on lessons from Chechnya, Russia was caught between the demands of its operating environment (which created adaptive pressure for a small, professional, mobile, high-tech, light- or medium-weight force) and its economic situation, which made such a force unaffordable and forced Moscow to rely instead on a large, low-quality mass-mobilization base of conscripts. It was also torn between the grand-strategic imperative of maintaining an army fit to fight NATO as proof of Russia's great-power status and the near-term need for forces fit for counterinsurgency, counterterrorism, internal security, and peace enforcement in Russia and the near abroad. This situation remained largely unchanged—despite the demands of a second Chechen war in

1998–2004, anti-terrorist operations in the Caucasus, the emergence of the BTGs as a workaround for hollowness, and a program in 2003–2005 that sought to professionalize permanent-readiness units—until the pivotal year of 2008 and the Five-Day War in Georgia.

THE FIVE-DAY WAR

The Republic of Georgia, ruled by Russia until 1917, was (after a brief period of independence following the revolution) forcibly incorporated into the Soviet Union in 1921 as the Georgian Soviet Socialist Republic (SSR).[95] Georgia's significance stems from its location in Transcaucasia—the isthmus that connects Turkey and Iran with Russia and separates the strategically crucial Black Sea from the oil-rich Caspian basin. The country controls key mountain passes through the Caucasus, giving it a chokehold on Russia's southward access. Georgia's geopolitical importance (alongside its role as a buffer between Russia and the Muslim east, and as a transit route for oil from Azerbaijan, Iran, and Turkey into Europe) prompted the Bolsheviks to seize the country soon after the Russian Revolution, securing their southern approaches much as they sought to stabilize their western flank by controlling Ukraine and annexing Estonia, Latvia, and Lithuania.[96] The fact that Soviet dictator Josef Stalin, infamous NKVD chief Lavrentiy Beria, Politburo member Sergo Ordzhonikidze, and foreign minister Eduard Shevardnadze were all Georgians further emphasized Moscow's tight grip on the Georgian SSR.

But that same grip caused Georgians—like many in the Baltic SSRs—to resent Soviet Russo-centrism, prompting a powerful surge of nationalist sentiment as the Soviet Union unraveled in the late 1980s. Georgia declared independence on 9 April 1991, the first Soviet state to do so outside the Baltic region. In response Russia backed two ethnic-separatist enclaves in Georgia: Abkhazia in the northwest and South Ossetia in the north. In part, Russia was protecting what Boris Yeltsin called "compatriots abroad," cut off by the fall of Communism.[97] In part, this was traditional Russian frontier-craft, stoking separatism to sap Georgia's unity and create a pretext for interference in its affairs. Too weak to control Georgia during its post-Soviet eclipse, Moscow saw its security interests served by destabilization and subversion of its neighbor's sovereignty—an approach that, as we saw earlier, Russian regimes have consistently applied in border zones.[98]

After conflict erupted in 1991 between the Georgian government and South Ossetian separatists, Russia imposed a ceasefire and deployed peacekeepers in June 1992. A similar conflict in Abkhazia in 1992–93 enabled Russia to carve out another enclave, leading to continual confrontation and low-grade violence, with periodic flare-ups in 1998 and 2001. This was an early example of a post-Soviet "frozen conflict," in which Russia promoted its goals by perpetuating rather than winning the confrontation and which the British international relations scholar Neil MacFarlane defined as a "conflict where there are no active large-scale hostilities (although there may be smaller-scale violence), there is a durable mutually agreed ceasefire, but efforts to achieve a political settlement or peace are unsuccessful."[99] By 2003, when the Rose Revolution brought the pro-European, pro-American government of Mikheil Saakashvili to power in Tbilisi, Georgia's capital, Moscow had established a de facto protectorate over the enclaves.

Saakashvili's new democratic government threatened the status quo, sending troops to support the United States in Afghanistan, orienting Georgia's economy toward Europe and the United States, and pushing to reintegrate Abkhazia and South Ossetia. In 2006, facing down threats from Moscow, Georgia's parliament voted to seek NATO membership. This potential encroachment of NATO into its southeastern backyard, even as the alliance expanded in eastern Europe and the Baltic on Russia's western frontier, represented an incipient encirclement that was absolutely unacceptable to Moscow.

Thus, from early 2007, according to US diplomatic cables later leaked and published in the *Guardian*, Russia ramped up efforts to draw the enclaves closer and destabilize Georgia while staying below the threshold of open conflict: it offered Russian passports to inhabitants of South Ossetia and Abkhazia (thereby creating a body of Russian citizens over whom Moscow could now claim a responsibility to protect), gave anti-air and ground attack missiles to separatist militias, launched mortar and rocket attacks into Georgian-controlled regions, conducted disinformation to discredit Saakashvili, and attempted to assassinate at least one politician, among a host of other liminal operations.[100] Russian spokespeople likened South Ossetia to Kosovo, which NATO had forcibly removed from Yugoslavia, citing the same "responsibility to protect" that Russia now claimed for the Georgian enclaves.[101] FSB advisers provided political support to South Ossetian and Abkhazian separatist leaders, and GRU officers trained and equipped their militias.[102]

If this was meant to deter Georgia from joining NATO, it backfired badly: in a referendum held in January 2008 in reaction to Russia's activity, Georgians overwhelmingly voted to join the alliance.[103] In April, as Putin prepared to swap jobs with Prime Minister Dmitri Medvedev (who would become president, while Putin played the part of prime minister for four years to abide by Russia's rules on term limits), he attended NATO's summit in Bucharest. Putin warned Western leaders that "their plan to expand eastwards to Ukraine and Georgia 'didn't contribute to trust and predictability in our relations [and] would be taken in Russia as a direct threat to the security of our country'. NATO statements that this was not directed against Russia were not enough."[104] Leaders in Bucharest may or may not have taken the hint, but in some ways it was too late: events in Georgia were rapidly moving toward war.

Just after dark on the evening of 7 August 2008, Georgian forces initiated rocket and artillery strikes against separatist positions in South Ossetia; the following morning they invaded the enclave. Saakashvili's government was responding to months of mortar attacks and shootings from the enclaves into Georgian-controlled territory, which had been escalating all year. The last straw came on 1 August when, as sniping further increased from South Ossetia, militia fighters used an improvised explosive device to destroy a Georgian police truck near Tskhinvali, the separatist capital. Coming on top of the wave of covert operations (known in Russia as "active measures") since 2007, Georgia had finally had enough, and moved to restore Georgia's territorial integrity and "unfreeze" the conflict around the enclaves.[105] Provoking Georgia to launch a first strike may have been a goal of Russian shaping operations all along: according to the same US diplomatic cable of August 2007, "one Kremlin aim [is] to remove Saakashvili [but] the variety and extent of the active measures suggests the deeper goal is turning Georgia from its Euro-Atlantic orientation back into the Russian fold" and to "provoke the Georgian leadership into a rash reaction that separates Georgia further from the west."[106]

The same day that Georgian forces entered South Ossetia, Russian troops—ten thousand of whom were already in Russia's nearby North Caucasus region, having just completed a major exercise, *Kavkaz-2008*, that included rehearsals for just such an operation—began mobilizing to move into South Ossetia. After negotiating the chokepoint of the Roki tunnel—a 2.3-mile-long highway tunnel that sits at an altitude of 6,600 feet in the Caucasus mountains and is the only road route into South Ossetia from Russia—they fanned out, ran into advancing Georgian forces around the southern edge of Tskhinvali, threw the offensive back, and then continued into Georgian-controlled territory.[107] This was a rapid, combined-arms maneuver involving nineteen thousand troops, with an advance on two fronts using armored columns, airstrikes, heavy artillery, and rocket bombardment, Spetsnaz operating in depth, and warships of the Black Sea Fleet blockading Georgia's principal port, Poti.[108] Five days after their intervention, a column of tanks and motor-rifle troops from Russia's Fifty-Eighth Army, accompanied by BTGs from other formations, seized the critical provincial capital of Gori, only 50 miles west of Tbilisi, while Russian troops supported by militia advanced from Abkhazia. Russian aircraft struck Tbilisi, VDV airborne troops occupied Poti, sealing Georgia off from external support, and a motor-rifle regiment advanced to within 30 miles of Georgia's second city, Kutaisi.[109] By 12 August, EU-sponsored ceasefire talks were underway. Russia, by rapidly seizing territory and infrastructure (the port, road, and rail junctions) early in the conflict, capturing Gori and quickly threatening Tbilisi, had created a strong bargaining position, which the new president, Dmitri Medvedev, then used to good effect in the negotiations, trading territory gained at the outset of the war for enduring political advantage. It was a classic (albeit non-nuclear) case of escalating to de-escalate.

Beyond the physical, Russia's war in Georgia involved a new virtual maneuver space: the domain of cyberwarfare and information warfare. There had been Russian-sponsored cyberattacks before—notably against Estonia in April 2007, following a dispute over a Soviet-era war memorial in Tallinn, in which Russia-based hackers used many of the same techniques they later employed in Georgia. But the Georgian campaign was one of the first cases where cyber activity seems to have been coordinated with, and conducted in direct support of, kinetic combat operations, something we might call "cyberkinetic" or "info-kinetic" maneuver.[110] Here too, much of the most important action occurred before the first tank rolled, during the shaping phase, and was conducted by liminal actors—"an army of patriotic citizen hackers" and self-recruited "cyber-privateers" acting on their own initiative within guidelines set by the state.[111]

Attacks against Georgian websites and servers began around 20 July, as *Kavkaz-2008* ended and a full ten days before the escalation of separatist actions that provoked Georgia's move against the enclaves; they included distributed denial-of-service (DDOS) attacks that overloaded Georgian sites and servers, as well as hacks that defaced websites with propaganda messages or intermittently took down traffic.[112] The attackers harnessed a botnet comprising thousands of zombie computers, some in the United States. DDOS attacks targeted President Saakashvili's website, media, communications and transportation sites, and government departments, including the National Bank of Georgia, and spread rapidly once the fighting kicked off on 7 August.[113] Two Russian websites offered DDOS software to anyone wanting to attack Georgia, and Russian telecom firms routed Georgian traffic through their servers even as much of the country's internet infrastructure was crippled.

Attribution rather than detection was the problem. Researchers quickly linked the activity to a Russian organized crime group in St. Petersburg, and "in the run-up to the start of the war over the weekend [they] watched as botnets were 'staged' in preparation for the attack, and then activated shortly before Russian air strikes began on Saturday [9 August]."[114] A 2018 assessment concluded that "fifty-four news, government, and financial websites were defaced or denied, with the average denial of service lasting two hours and fifteen minutes and the longest lasting six hours. Thirty-five percent of Georgia's internet networks suffered decreased functionality during the attacks, with the highest levels of online activity coinciding with the Russian invasion of South Ossetia on August 8, 9, and 10. Even the National Bank of Georgia had to suspend all electronic services from August 8 to August 19. While there is strong political and circumstantial evidence that the attacks were encouraged by the Russian state, definitive technical attribution—and thus definitive legal culpability—have remained elusive."[115] Indeed, attribution remains such a tricky—and often contentious—issue that the respected cyberthreat intelligence analyst Jeffrey Carr has described many recent attribution efforts (which have been heavy on interpretation and light on actual evidence) as "faith-based attribution."[116]

This inability to pin responsibility on the Russian government, even after more than a decade of subsequent investigation, highlights one key advantage of using liminal actors (in this case, a self-synchronized, self-recruited cyber militia) for deniable—though not really covert or clandestine—operations. Likewise, cyber-maneuver in the Georgian campaign involved ambiguous activity that could have been considered crime, war, or just patriotic fervor, depending on the observer's bias. The attacks had little impact on the battlefield. But "by impeding the Georgian government's ability to react, respond, and communicate, the cyberattacks created the time and space for Russia to shape the international narrative in the critical early days of the conflict"—a point we will revisit shortly.

At the political-strategic level, Russia undoubtedly won the Five-Day War: Georgia agreed to a ceasefire on 14 August, leaving the two enclaves firmly and permanently under Russian control. Russia established permanent military, air, and naval bases on Georgian territory, and—most important—any idea of Georgia joining NATO was shelved. At the operational level, Russian forces showed marked improvement over their performance in Chechnya, conducting rapid combined-arms maneuver, coordinating infantry with armor and artillery, launching GRU Spetsnaz deep operations, and performing littoral maneuver using naval forces, among them major surface combatants, a submarine, and amphibious forces, including a large landing assault ship.[117] Their use of deception, their complex scheme of maneuver employing two simultaneous assaults from Abkhazia and South Ossetia, which prevented Georgian forces from concentrating against either thrust, the seizure of Poti by coup de main, and the coordination of VDV with ground and naval assets were equally impressive.[118] A higher proportion of precision munitions was used by aircraft and artillery than in previous conflicts, avoiding the wholesale urban destruction and carpet bombing seen in Chechnya (cluster bombs used in the towns of Gori and Rusi did kill civilians, but Russia's response was simply to deny outright that this ever happened).[119]

But at the tactical level, real weaknesses were apparent. The Russian Air Force lost several warplanes, including a Tu-22 strategic bomber and at least three Su-25 ground-attack aircraft, despite Georgia's lack of an integrated air defense system.[120] The commanding general of the Fifty-Eighth Army, Lieutenant General Anatoly Khrulyov, was wounded when his column ran into a Georgian ambush outside Tskhinvali due to poor reconnaissance, and Russian troops suffered losses as they exited the Roki tunnel through inadequate air-ground coordination.[121] In a strikingly critical report published three weeks after the ceasefire by RIA Novosti (then Russia's official international news agency), correspondent Nikita Petrov listed a string of failures. These included slow mobilization by the Fifty-Eighth Army; poor reconnaissance leading to an inability to locate Georgian artillery, rocket, and tank positions; a lack of UAVs that forced Russia to overfly Georgian air defenses with piloted aircraft, some of which were then shot down; obsolete aviation systems, including navigation and targeting suites, radar sights, beyond-line-of-sight missiles, scarcity of precision munitions, poor maintenance, and aircrew proficiency; failure of electronic warfare assets to jam Georgian systems; lack of night sights for tanks and missing armor components, leading to loss of vehicles and crews; lack of tank support combat vehicles for mountain and urban warfare; absence of attack helicopter support for armored columns; and lack of an integrated command-and-control system.[122] Some of Petrov's criticisms were unfair—older armored vehicles did predominate, but upgraded tanks were seen, while ground troops used newer equipment and applied tactical lessons from Chechnya, and despite problems with air and artillery support there were effective precision strikes, with relatively little collateral damage (by Russian standards), on towns and a key oil pipeline.[123]

A more measured critique, published a year later by the Swedish analysts Carolina Pallin and Fredrik Westerlund, noted "an evolution [from] Soviet strategy towards contemporary Western warfare"[124] and suggested that while the Georgian campaign offered "undisputable signs that Russian military capability has improved considerably compared with the 1990s, the record has made military analysts raise concerns about the future of Russia's military."[125] They too pointed to obsolete equipment, breakdowns in command-and-control and ground-air cooperation, poor electronic warfare, and lack of precision weapons, and observed that "in conventional military technology Russia is lagging behind the West in some of the key areas."[126] Not discussed in the open literature at the time, the conflict's cyber maneuver aspects also came in for criticism behind the scenes. Discussion within the Russian military focused on "poor performance in the information domain as evidence of the need for 'Information Troops' within the Russian armed forces who were capable of conducting full-spectrum information operations."[127] This led to the development of specialized troops capable not only of cyberwarfare and electronic warfare, but of network engineering and disruption, fielding fiber-optic engineers as well as electromagnetic pulse (EMP) weapons.[128]

I noted earlier that much military adaptation is prompted by the pain of defeat. But for such adaptation to occur, a force must first recognize that it has in fact been defeated. Organizations that manage to convince themselves of their own success despite evidence to the contrary are unlikely to adapt; conversely those who see themselves as failing—or experiencing a near miss—may, despite overall success, evolve as a result. This was the case for Russia after Georgia: neither Medvedev nor Putin was happy with the armed forces' performance, and Defense Minister Anatoly Serdyukov, an outsider brought in as a bureaucratic and financial reformer in February 2007, initiated a major modernization program (the "New Look") in response.

The New Look has been described as "the most radical military reform since the creation of the Red Army following the 1917 Bolshevik

Revolution," a "stark departure from the approaches used over the past century," and the cause of "significant improvements to the Russian Army's fighting ability and battle readiness" in Crimea, Ukraine, and Syria.[129] The reform sought to address key shortfalls identified during the Five-Day War, campaigns in the Caucasus, and other conflicts since 1991. At its heart was a new strategic direction from the Kremlin: almost twenty years after the fall of the Soviet Union, Russian forces finally resolved the contradiction between their Soviet-era structure and their post–Cold War environment, and optimized for local conflicts in former Soviet territories.[130] (Another way of putting this would be to say that the organization had finally adapted to the change in a dynamic fitness landscape.) The role of deterring, and if necessary fighting, NATO was now to reside with nuclear forces, while Russia's conventional military would focus on short-notice, limited wars in places like Chechnya, Georgia, and other former Soviet states (including Ukraine and the Baltic).

The reforms—enacted between October 2008 and December 2012—involved shrinking the armed forces, trimming the officer corps, centralizing training, merging headquarters and reducing the number of military districts to streamline command, civilianizing and commercializing logistics, and bringing all units to permanent-readiness status while restructuring reserves, retaining private soldiers as conscripts on compulsory service, but creating professional long-service NCO and officer career streams.[131] The New Look disbanded hollow units, centered the army on newly designed brigades rather than the old divisional/regimental structure, reorganized the air force and Air Defense Service around airbases and aerospace defense commands, restructured the navy, and created a Cyber Command and Special Operations Command.[132]

By 2013, many of the shortfalls identified in Georgia had been addressed, the conventional and nuclear instruments that Putin (now president again) would use in subsequent campaigns were in place, and asymmetric assets were developing fast. These included tame hackers, cyber militias, relationships with organized crime networks, manipulation of migration as discussed in the Norway example, propaganda tools, alliances with what Lenin called "useful idiots" (including political extremists, separatist groups, and perhaps even those involved in presidential campaigns) in the West, the development of extensive intelligence networks, and putting in place the capability for "active measures"—up to and including assassination and sabotage. Russia's wartime evolution in Chechnya and the Caucasus, plus the peacetime innovation of the New Look after Georgia, formed the basis for Russia's resurgence, and so it's worth exploring the theory that underpinned it.

THE THEORY OF LIMINAL WARFARE

I should start this section by apologizing for adding yet another term to the burgeoning lexicon for recent Russian operations.[133] Many others are in use, including "hybrid warfare,"[134] "asymmetric warfare,"[135] "non-linear warfare,"[136] "new-generation warfare,"[137] "gray zone operations,"[138] and the "Gerasimov doctrine" (named for Valeriy Gerasimov, deputy defense minister and chief of the Russian General Staff).[139] Each is useful, emphasizing certain aspects of the adaptive process we are witnessing. So why inflict yet another? Mainly to emphasize yet another aspect—the liminal, or threshold-manipulation, element—in Russian practice since the New Look, which has arguably been present in Russian thinking at least since Soviet times.

Russia's ability to ride the edge, operating right on the detection threshold—taking sufficiently few and ambiguous actions to achieve core political objectives, but not enough to trigger a military reaction—is an example of what I earlier called "liminal maneuver" and described as an adaptive response to an environment in which Russia faces adversaries that are extremely well-armed conventionally but extremely constrained politically. Liminal phenomena (as the name suggests) sit astride a sensory or perceptual threshold. Actions that are barely perceptible, ride the edge of observability, or oscillate in and out of detectability can be considered liminal operations, and a style of warfare that optimizes such operations is liminal maneuver.

This style is ideally suited for weaker players like Russia, adapting in a fitness landscape where adversaries have greater hard military power but are constrained by tighter political and legal limits, and where news and so-cial media are pervasive enough to make clandestine (or deniable covert) action extremely hard to pull off, yet where these same media are simulta-neously vulnerable to "fake news" or signature manipulation that can create enough ambiguity for determined leaders to get away with murder. In other words, this approach is well adapted to the environment that Russia and others have faced since 1993, as described in Chapter 2.

The detection threshold here is not fixed. Rather, it is defined by intel-ligence, surveillance, and reconnaissance (ISR) capabilities, and thus it changes depending on the type, size, and signature of an enemy's actions, as well as the quality and coverage of ISR available. Where we have poor ISR and the enemy operates with a low profile, taking occasional actions in small groups, the detection threshold may be very high, so that an adver-sary can get away with a lot before we realize what is going on. Where ISR coverage is better or the enemy operates at higher signature or tempo and in larger groups, that threshold may drop dramatically, so that very few ad-versary actions remain undetected.

The Liminal Maneuver Space

The detection threshold thus represents a movable boundary between clan-destine and covert operations, on the one hand, and overt action, on the other. In Figure 4.1, I have drawn the activity around these thresholds as a pyramid or triangle. This is because overt combat is a tiny component of conflict, the tip of the iceberg, whereas the vast majority of the action takes place below the waterline, well away from violent contact with an enemy. Some militaries—for example, the Australian and British—distinguish competitive action below the threshold of warfare (which the Australians term "contest") from direct combat (designated "conflict"). The United States talks of "competition short of armed conflict."[140] Even within war it-self, only a tiny proportion—as few as 3 percent of individuals in a typical guerrilla movement, for example—participate in combat.[141] Similarly, con-ventional armies (taking the US Army since 1941 as a guide) average only about 32.5 percent of troops in combat roles. Of these combat troops, far

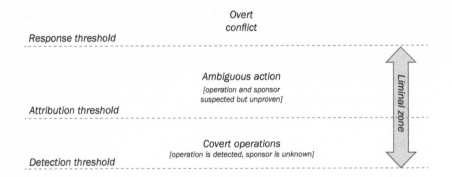

Figure 4.1. Liminal Warfare

fewer (7 to 10 percent of the total force) are deployed, an even smaller proportion of those deployed troops are in combat at a given moment, and of these only 20 to 80 percent actually fire their weapons, bringing the total of active combatants down to roughly the same tiny percentage as that for insurgents and militias.[142] In resistance warfare—particularly in urban guerrilla war or cyberkinetic operations of the kind described earlier—combatant numbers may be even lower.

But although the image of an iceberg (with its bulk mostly underwater) is useful, the notion of a waterline breaks down in practice, because the threshold between armed conflict and competition is not in fact a line, but rather a transitional space or liminal zone (arguably, this is also true of an actual waterline in the physical world).

As the diagram illustrates, the liminal zone begins at the *detection threshold*, where an adversary first perceives the existence of an operation. Below that threshold, activity is clandestine (the operation remains undetected), whereas above it, it is covert (the operation is detected, but the sponsor's identity remains unknown or plausibly deniable). I should note that I am following Commonwealth usage here—American doctrine draws the covert-clandestine distinction differently. Commonwealth terminology is more useful here, though, since it more clearly distinguishes the clandestine level, at which an adversary remains unaware of an operation's very existence, from the covert level, where the adversary detects the operation but cannot determine who is carrying it out. Some activities—espionage, some forms of cyberintrusion, political subversion, or the organizing of underground networks—can theoretically remain clandestine forever, whereas others (raiding, terrorism, sabotage, cross-border incursions) are virtually always eventually detected, even when the sponsor's identity remains hidden (making them *covert* rather than clandestine).

At some point, an adversary has enough data to attribute responsibility for a detected activity to a given sponsor. This is the *attribution threshold*, and above that threshold operations are no longer clandestine or covert. But they are not yet quite overt either: given the difficulty of attribution (particularly for cyberattacks, sabotage, or terrorist activity) and the politico-legal constraints that we explored in detail earlier, there is effectively another layer of transitional space—that of ambiguous activity, which sits above covert operations (i.e., above the attribution threshold) but below the *response threshold*, where an adversary has enough certainty and political support to respond and combat action becomes fully overt. The zone between detection and response thresholds thus creates a playspace within which liminal maneuver occurs. In effect, the theory of liminal warfare moves beyond a simple overt-clandestine dichotomy, recognizing that the zone of ambiguity between overt and clandestine activity creates a maneuver space in its own right, a place where liminal actors and their sponsors can operate in the gap between detection, attribution, and response.

Of critical importance, unlike the two lower thresholds, the response threshold is determined not by ISR capability but by decision-making capacity—making it a political and diplomatic threshold rather than a military or intelligence one. Democracies (like the United States and its Western allies) that are constrained by domestic and international opinion, international norms, and the rule of law, or alliances such as NATO that require consensus before initiating collective action, or countries with publicly stated response criteria (otherwise known as "redlines") tend to have high and predictable response thresholds, creating significant vulnerabilities for themselves while expanding the liminal warfare space for their adversaries. Even dramatic improvements in ISR capability, which push attribution and detection thresholds downward, only open greater space for liminal warfare if political response thresholds remain high.

Conversely, countries whose leaders act unpredictably, avoid public redlines, or respond promptly and unilaterally to threats (Israel being one obvious example and France another) can collapse this liminal space, denying adversaries maneuver room by lowering or obfuscating response thresholds, regardless of ISR capacity. In the most extreme case, states (such as Russia) whose leaders are willing to issue bald-faced denials of blatantly obvious action by their own forces or by actors they sponsor (the MH-17 shootdown, the Skripal and Litvinenko attacks, the Estonian and Georgian cyberattacks) can create a zone of "implausible deniability" where external political pressure loses impact, so that even if people believe Russia was responsible for a particular action, leaders in Moscow simply go on as if nothing had happened.

The fact that the response threshold is politically driven rather than capability-dependent emphasizes the reality that liminal warfare is a form of political warfare—the application of a combination of military and non-military means to achieve fundamentally political objectives. The explosion of connectivity and social media over the past two decades (discussed in Chapter 1) has changed the methods available, but the target of such warfare remains the same: the legitimacy, cohesion, and effectiveness of political institutions, leaders, and decision-making processes. Undermining such targets buys time, allowing operations to succeed before an adversary can respond. Understanding an enemy's political limits—the parameters of a likely reaction in terms of response time, range and nature of likely responses, and constraints on decision-makers—creates space for liminal maneuver. This is why, as mentioned earlier, Russian cyberoperations against Georgia were valuable despite having little battlefield impact and why manipulation of migration flows into Norway's north was a valuable activity for Russian intelligence.

It may also explain the thinking behind GRU's alleged attempt to disrupt the 2016 US election—as an attempt not to achieve a permanent effect, but rather to create a temporary window of opportunity in late 2016 and early 2017 when an incoming Hillary Clinton administration (which Russian planners, like virtually everyone else, including both presidential candidates, seem to have assumed would be the case) would be paralyzed by dissent and unable to interfere as Russia moved on a number of fronts. The period just after the election did indeed coincide with major Russian moves, including in those in Syria (where Russian-backed forces captured Syria's second city, Aleppo, in December 2016 and then launched the East Aleppo offensive, retaking a critical northern Syrian province in January 2017) and in Ukraine (where Russian and Ukrainian separatist forces launched the Avdiivka offensive in January 2017, triggering the most intense fighting since the beginning of the war in 2014). These moves succeeded spectacularly, and with zero opposition from the United States, in large part because of the intense disruption created by Russian-sponsored political warfare operations around the 2016 election.

In this reading, GRU operators aimed for a temporary political effect to create time and space for physical maneuver elsewhere, and—especially important—the effect of the operation would only have been enhanced by detection. Given that the whole point of the operation was to sow dissent, there was no need for it to be clandestine or covert in order to succeed—on the contrary, the existence of the operation had to become known, and Russian sponsorship had to be at least suspected, in order to generate the full disruptive effect of paranoia, suspicion, claim, and counterclaim, and the shadow of illegitimacy that has hung over the US administration ever since.[143]

This is relevant because, as discussed previously, in an era of pervasive surveillance and omnipresent media, there is no such thing as a permanently clandestine operation. Virtually all operations will eventually be compromised, and sooner or later, sponsor identities will out. But at the same time, the pervasiveness of social media and the contested nature of reality and truth (in an environment of partisan echo chambers and self-segregated social media bubbles) increase opportunities for deception, enabling actors to hide in plain sight, mimic others, exploit "fake news," or manipulate their physical and electronic signatures to increase ambiguity.

The Information Warfare Dimension

What has been described as Russia's "firehose of falsehood" information warfare model exploits this. As researchers Christopher Paul and Miriam Matthews point out, it represents "a remarkable evolution in Russia's approach to propaganda" since the war in Georgia, one that "is completely new and is driven by the characteristics of the contemporary information environment."[144] In fact, the method draws heavily on Soviet ideas originating in the 1960s (known as "reflexive control") in which operators seek to cause "targets to act in the interests of the propagandist without realizing they have done so."[145] Reflexive control is "a means of conveying to a partner or an opponent specially prepared information to incline him to voluntarily make the predetermined decision desired by the initiator of the action."[146] Actions may include transferring a particular framing of the situation to the target's mind, creating a goal for the target, and playing to what targets believe (or want) to be true in order to use their own responses to amplify the effect of an initial action.[147] The aim is not only to manipulate perception or to persuade an audience on a particular issue (as in traditional propaganda) but to influence opponents' entire framing of reality, distort their decision processes, and exploit their resulting actions. The Russian theorist S. A. Komov, writing in 1996 but building on Soviet ideas from the 1960s and earlier, described the components of reflexive control as "distraction, overload, paralysis, exhaustion, deception, division, pacification, deterrence, provocation, suggestion, and pressure, all with the intent of manipulation."[148] While the theory predates the twenty-first-century connectivity explosion, today's environment creates (as Paul and Matthews note) an array of new opportunities and tools to put it into practice.[149]

Any random five-minute segment on virtually any US cable news network since the 2016 election illustrates this process in action: the American news media have deepened, extended, and amplified the destabilizing effect of what was, at best, a modest Russian influence operation as described in the 2017 US intelligence assessment, the 2018 indictments of the Internet Research Agency and other Russian actors, and the Mueller report.[150] Cable news personalities have prattled on for literally thousands of hours about what they frame as a past Russian information operation from 2016—whereas, seen from Russia, the operation is ongoing and is now self-sustaining thanks to these same news personalities. This is classic reflexive control: the very commentariat that endlessly laments the operation has now itself *become* the operation.[151] What may have been intended initially as a limited shaping operation, seeking merely to create a three-month window of opportunity to keep the United States busy while Russia completed the Aleppo and Avdiivka offensives, has taken on a life of its own. GRU leaders, viewing the results from the "Aquarium"—their own version of a US media-style "glass-enclosed nerve center" at GRU's headquarters at Khodinka outside Moscow—must be surprised and gratified at the extraordinary return on their modest investment.

More broadly, the Russian model that Paul and Matthews describe is designed to simultaneously entertain, confuse, and overwhelm the audience.[152] To this end, it is "high-volume and multi-channel," deluging targets with an enormous number of messages through many channels simultaneously; it shows "a shameless willingness to disseminate partial truths or outright fictions" and thus "lacks commitment to objective reality"; it is "rapid, continuous, and repetitive" and it "lacks commitment to consistency."[153] This last characteristic puzzles some observers; but in an age of compartmented reality, extremely rapid news cycles, and fragmented discourse, a target's lack of long-term memory on the details of specific issues lets information operators float inconsistent messages with impunity. Not that this is a new feature of Russian information warfare: as George Orwell and Arthur Koestler both noted in the 1940s, rigid adherence to a constantly changing party line was a hallmark of Soviet propaganda.[154]

The Temporal Dimension

Beyond these signature-management and political-warfare elements, if all operations are *eventually* but not *immediately* compromised then there is also a temporal dimension to liminal maneuver: to achieve key goals, liminal actors and their sponsors do not need permanent deniability, just temporary ambiguity. Once an adversary's response threshold and reaction time are identified, operators can calculate the time window available—to achieve objectives before a response can occur, render that response ineffective, or prevent it altogether. As in a Hollywood heist movie, where the bad guys (knowing the cops' response time) start their stopwatches the moment they hit the bank vault, a good understanding of enemy reaction time—or, better, the ability to extend and disrupt it—can define the parameters for a successful strike operation.

In this context, reaction time has five components, each of which can be quantified by planners or affected by operators. These are shown in Figure 4.2, and they include *detection time* (the time it takes for ISR assets to detect the existence of an operation), *attribution time* (the time taken by analysts to identify the operation's perpetrators and sponsors), and *decision time* (the time needed to convince political leaders to act, decide what to do, and build public and international support for action). This is the longest component of reaction time, and it is both highly variable compared with other components and inherently political. Hence, this is the window in which political action—including reflexive control, political subversion, cyberattacks, and diplomatic negotiation—has its greatest effect. And that

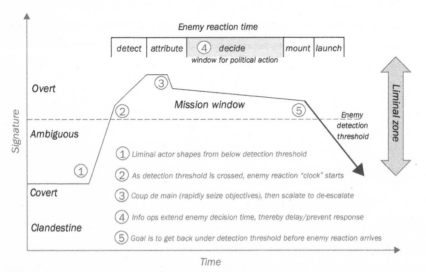

Figure 4.2. Sequence of a Liminal Warfare Operation

effect may be critical, since delaying a decision by twenty-four hours, or creating enough ambiguity that it takes an extra day to convince alliance partners to act, buys time to achieve goals while slowing, hampering, or preventing the enemy response.

Again, using alleged Russian US election hacking in 2016 as an example, an operation to destabilize US political processes, undermine institutions, and discredit leaders would not need to achieve permanent impact in order to be strategically valuable, nor would it matter which politician eventually emerged as president. Rather, such an operation would merely need to create a diversionary effect and thereby generate a window of opportunity for success in Syria, Ukraine, and elsewhere under cover of chaos in Washington. The last two components, *mounting time* and *launching time*, depend on military factors, including readiness, time to mobilize, deployment speed, and survivability of assets in-theater, and are harder for an external actor to influence because they tend to be hardware-dependent. Thus, of the five components, the first two (detect and attribute) are intelligence-related, the middle component (decide) is primarily political, and the last two (mount and launch) are mainly military.

The arrow on the diagram represents the signature (the external, detectable signal, which may be physical, electronic, virtual, or media-driven) generated by a liminal actor. As can be seen, the actor seeks to remain below the enemy's detection threshold up to the last possible moment, even while recognizing that omnipresent citizen media, surveillance systems, and news organizations will make truly covert or clandestine activity impossible. As a consequence, the goal in the shaping phase is ambiguity—obfuscating, confusing, or manipulating perceptions so as to create temporary doubt and confusion, make it harder for an adversary to attribute responsibility, and complicate opposing intelligence officers' tasks in convincing their political leaders to respond.

Once the detection threshold is breached, however, the clock is running, so the imperative immediately shifts from stealth to speed: when as much as possible has been achieved during the shaping phase, the goal is to secure any remaining objectives as rapidly as possible, regardless of stealth. Surprise, speed, and violence of action—principles of the assault that are familiar to any combat soldier—become paramount in this phase. As a consequence, the actor's signature spikes and stays high for at least the initial part of the operation, as in a classic *coup de main*, while critical objectives are seized.

As soon as these are secured, the liminal actor immediately seeks to reduce activity level and minimize signature (most important, reducing the perception of any threat toward a potential responder) while initiating political warfare and diplomatic action to delay the response as long as possible. This is a classic "escalate to de-escalate" approach, where even as the emphasis shifts to political action the operational element continues reducing its signature, attempting to get back below the detection threshold (or at least back into the zone of ambiguity) before the blow of an opponent's reaction can fall. The operation does not, of course, end here, even though its overt phase concludes—rather it continues as a shaping effort below the threshold.

The Primacy of Shaping Operations

This temporal aspect of liminal maneuver again underscores the primacy of OPE (operational preparation of the environment) or shaping operations. Ideally, in liminal warfare, actors on the ground (such as Ukrainian, Abkhazian, and South Ossetian militias, Syrian refugees in the Arctic, cyber militias and patriotic hackers in Estonia and Georgia, and WikiLeaks in the case of US election hacking) act as adjuncts to conventional shaping by combat forces (or strategic posturing using nuclear weapons) so that campaign objectives are achieved before the first airstrike goes in, the first assault troops hit their landing zones, or the first tank crosses the line of departure.

And ideally, if critical objectives can be achieved before conventional operations begin—if the purpose of combat becomes merely to consolidate gains already won by a liminal warfare (e.g., by a resistance movement, cyber militia, or subversion) campaign coordinated with political warfare and conventional shaping—then conventional combat operations are no longer decisive and may in fact never occur. If an enemy can be beaten before the first tank rolls, the tanks may never need to roll at all. Clearly, for a player lacking conventional combat capability, such as Russia (or indeed any other adversary of the West since 1993), that situation would be ideal. Likewise, if decisive shaping plus liminal activity can achieve goals without combat, the iceberg may never break the surface: competition and resistance warfare may remain permanently below the threshold of combat, engaging only in very limited, small-scale acts of violence, yet still achieving military goals.

THE "GERASIMOV DOCTRINE"

As admitted earlier, I made up the term "liminal warfare"; you will not find it in Russian writings. But I did not invent the concept, which is very much present in historical and contemporary Russian thinking. One well-known recent example is the writing of General of the Army Valeriy Gerasimov, who, as mentioned, is chief of the Russian General Staff and deputy defense minister.[155] In February 2013, just as the New Look reforms were being completed, he published an article on future war in *Military-Industrial Courier*.[156] In July 2014 (five months after the "little green men" mounted their Crimean *coup de main*), the Russia scholar Mark Galeotti published a translation, arguing that the article "represent[ed] the best and most authoritative statement yet of what we could . . . call the 'Gerasimov Doctrine'" and that it foreshadowed Russia's approach in Crimea and Ukraine.[157] Galeotti later regretted his choice of title, emphasizing that what Gerasimov offered was not a unified doctrine: it was more a description of how the Russian General Staff interprets contemporary *Western* methods of warfare than a depiction of Russia's own approach.[158] Still, as we will see, Gerasimov's ideas bear a striking resemblance to Russian practice since Georgia and the New Look; Gerasimov advanced similar ideas at a military conference in Moscow in May 2014, and given his influential position, his thoughts are worth considering.[159]

Gerasimov suggested that the color revolutions in Europe and the former Soviet Union, the uprisings of the Arab Spring, and Western operations in Iraq, Afghanistan, Libya, and Syria illustrate a new, emerging approach to achieving political-military goals.[160] He argued for "indirect and asymmetric methods" and a "roughly 4:1 ratio of nonmilitary and military measures," including economic sanctions, disruption of diplomatic ties, and political and diplomatic pressure.[161] In addition to his emphasis on indirect and asymmetric operations, Gerasimov contrasted traditional forms and methods (which he labeled, in a diagram, "the use of military forces") and new forms, which he called "the use of political, diplomatic, economic and other non-military measures in combination with the use of military forces."[162] As the military analyst Charles Bartles points out, one key aspect of Gerasimov's framing is that while the West considers these nonmilitary measures to be ways of *avoiding* war, Russia considers them *part of* war.[163] Gerasimov was thus offering a dramatically wider definition of warfare than the concept then current in US and allied thinking, which, as we have seen, involved an extraordinarily narrow notion of war as a conventional, force-on-force contest of arms among combat units on the battlefield.

Whereas the traditional approach saw military operations being initiated only after strategic deployment of forces, Gerasimov argued, new methods enabled a force to initiate military operations from its normal peacetime locations. Where old methods emphasized the frontal clash of large groupings of combat units, mostly ground troops, new forms of war involved mobile noncontact operations (i.e., stand-off strikes, such as missile attacks, and remote warfare, such as drone strikes) by joint forces. While traditional warfare emphasized destruction of personnel and weaponry, capturing of enemy defenses and seizure of territory, new approaches would rely on rapid destruction of critical civilian and military infrastructure in order to reduce an enemy's military-economic potential. Whereas traditional methods focused on land, air, and sea operations, future forms of conflict would involve warfare simultaneously in all physical environments and the information space, with the goal of achieving "simultaneous effects on line-units [i.e., combat forces] and enemy facilities throughout the entire breadth and depth of his territories."[164] New forms of war would make mass use of precision munitions, large-scale special operations forces, robotic systems, and "weapons based on new physical principles." And whereas traditional approaches involved strictly organized hierarchical command and control, the new approach would involve command and control of forces and assets in a unified information space, and would include the participation of a civil-military component in combat operations.[165]

It's worth pointing out, of course, that these last two points would be "new" only from the Russian perspective, since these have been features of the US and Western operating style since the Gulf War. From Russia's standpoint, it's also important to note that Gerasimov's article focused on future aspirations, not current capabilities. And as Galeotti noted, Gerasimov was ostensibly talking about Western rather than Russian methods. Still, in emphasizing Russia's need to evolve in response to observed Western adaptation, Gerasimov was—perhaps unconsciously—revealing that Russia had shifted from what Stephen Rosen called peacetime innovation (discussed in Chapter 2) toward wartime coevolution in response to the moves of an identified enemy. If Russia was already on a war footing, treating the United States as what military planners call a "pacing threat," an adversary against whom a force measures its capability—and if this was the case a full year before Crimea and just three months after President Obama had contemptuously dismissed the notion that Russia might be a threat—then this is revealing in itself.[166]

Gerasimov also emphasized the primacy of pre-conflict shaping, something we have noted in Russian practice since Georgia. He approvingly quoted the Soviet military theorist Georgii Isserson, who wrote that "war in general is not declared. It simply begins with already developed military forces. Mobilization and concentration are not part of the period after the onset of the state of war as was the case in 1914 but rather, unnoticed, proceed long before that."[167] This emphasis on pre-conflict shaping, the need to remain masked as long as possible, to rapidly seize objectives after unmasking, then quickly de-escalate and negotiate from a position of strength, was highlighted in another diagram in Gerasimov's article. This diagram (like Figure 4.2) depicted a progression from covert through potential, targeted, and direct military threats to overt military conflict, over a timeline running from covert origins of conflict through deepening contradictions, initial conflicting (i.e., shaping) actions, crisis reaction, localization of conflict, neutralization, and resolution. The diagram depicted a combination of military and nonmilitary measures to defeat an adversary prior to actual combat or, if combat did occur, rapidly secure objectives and then de-escalate while negotiating.[168] Thus, though the term appears nowhere in Gerasimov's writing (or in his conference presentation the following year), this is very clearly a depiction of what I have designated "liminal warfare."

HOW RUSSIA LEARNED TO FIGHT THE WEST

I have written elsewhere about Russia's interventions in Crimea and Ukraine in 2014, and then in Syria from 2015 onward. Clearly, each of these cases—along with Russian behavior in the Arctic, the Baltic, western and eastern Europe, Africa, and Latin America—is different, and each has its own governing logic that influences the selection of means employed. Just as clearly, however, there is a pattern here.

The combination of techniques and the history of adaptation that I have sketched in this chapter enable Russia to undermine its adversaries politically using military means, and militarily using political means. This combination—along with the undeniable genius of Vladimir Putin, who has played a very poor hand extremely well—has proved highly effective in bringing Russia, Woolsey's original dragon, back as a real threat. Yet whereas Russia began from a different starting point, employed different foundational concepts, and was of course a dramatically different type of entity than the nonstate actors discussed in the preceding chapter, one of the most striking things about Russia's evolution over the past twenty-five years is how similar its mode of warfare has become in response to similar selective pressures. And Russia is not the only state actor to have evolved since 1993 toward a strikingly similar approach: others include Iran and North Korea, discussed in some detail earlier, as well as the subject of the next chapter: China.

Map 4 The Russo-Georgian War

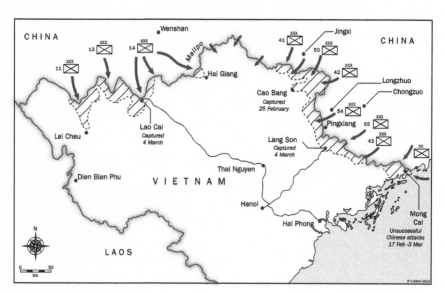

Map 5 The Sino-Vietnamese War

5

Conceptual Envelopment

7:15 p.m., 2 August 2016, Hotel del Coronado, California
I am sitting under a white fabric umbrella at the Sun Deck Bar of the Hotel del Coronado. It's a gorgeous Southern California evening; a warm murmur of conversation surrounds me as the sun sets through scattered clouds and the ice melts in my Manhattan. Opened in 1888, the Del is one of the world's grand hotels, a wooden building of unique and charming design, and an outstanding place for a beachfront drink after a long day's training. It also happens to be right in the center of one of the densest concentrations of naval power on the planet.

The sun is going down now behind Point Loma, home to the five *Los Angeles*–class nuclear-powered fast-attack submarines of Submarine Squadron 11, along with Space and Naval Warfare Systems Command (responsible for the US Navy's worldwide command-and-control networks) and Fleet Intelligence Command Pacific, the nerve center for US naval intelligence in the Pacific and Indian Oceans. To my right along the beach is Naval Air Station North Island, home of Carrier Strike Group 1 (CSG-1), centered on the nuclear-powered aircraft carrier USS *Carl Vinson*. To the left along Silver Strand, the strip of sand separating San Diego from the open Pacific, is Naval Amphibious Base Coronado, and just past it is Naval Special Warfare Command, home of the US Navy SEALs. Behind me in the main San Diego Naval Base is CSG-9, centered on the carrier USS *Theodore Roosevelt*. More bases, depots, and headquarters ring the harbor. Radio masts, rotating radar antennae, and satellite dishes abound. I can see five warships from where I sit, cocktail glass in hand. Seahawk helicopters and MV-22 Osprey tiltrotors are shuttling around the bay, and two fighter aircraft—they look like Navy F/A-18s to my infantry officer's eye—are coming in to land in the dusk.

What I can't see is the immense volume of military electronic traffic—radio and cellphone calls, microwave and satellite signals, Wi-Fi and sensor feeds, radar waves, GPS, navigation and timing signals—crisscrossing the bay. If you were to chart that traffic on a map, you would see a spider's web of emissions with the Hotel Del, its tall conical main building topped with the Stars and Stripes, close to the center. An observer or sensor in the upper part of that building could keep tabs, visually and electronically, on one of the largest naval facilities in the world, giving whoever owns the hotel a front-row seat on America's most important West Coast base. Whatever else it may be, the Del is a near-perfect listening post.

In March 2016, five months before I stayed there, Anbang Group, a Beijing-based diversified holding company, signed a deal to purchase the Hotel del Coronado for a rumored sum of US$1 billion. Anbang was privately held at the time but was later taken over by the Chinese government.[1] Its senior adviser was Chen Xiaolu, son of Marshall Chen Yi, a contemporary of Mao Zedong and a famous People's Liberation Army (PLA) commander who later became China's foreign minister. Chen, who died in early 2018, was himself a former PLA colonel and Red Guard who left the military in 1992, cashed in on his Communist connections, and built a business empire as one of China's first "princelings"—children of high party officials who parlayed political into economic power as the People's Republic introduced market reforms in the 1990s.[2] With Chen as its senior adviser, Anbang became one of the most politically connected firms in China.[3]

A third of a world away—fifteen hours' flying time from San Diego—Rosslea Hall Hotel sits at the base of a spit of land projecting into Gare Loch. Frequently fog-covered, this narrow northern inlet could not be more different from the sunlit splendor of Coronado. It is lightly populated (last time I checked, TripAdvisor rated Rosslea Hall "number 1 of 1 hotels" in the village of Rhu, population 1,970), is often bleakly windswept and bitterly cold, and connects to the Firth of Clyde, the complex coastal waterway west of Glasgow, Scotland's largest city and most important port. By all accounts Rosslea Hall is a pleasant place, with comfortable rooms, excellent food, and welcoming staff; presumably they also serve a decent Manhattan, though single malt is more the local style.

Just under four miles from the hotel, at the head of the sea-loch, lies Faslane, formally Her Majesty's Naval Base Clyde, home to Great Britain's entire fleet of four *Vanguard*-class missile submarines, the country's sole nuclear deterrent.[4] Almost from the moment they cast off, submarines in Gare Loch are in direct visual and electronic line of sight from Rosslea Hall. They must pass within 300 yards of the hotel, navigating the narrow channel between Rhu, on the eastern shore, and the industrial town of Rosneath, on the west. Once through the chokepoint it may still take the subs a couple of hours to reach the Atlantic, having revealed their time of departure, location, speed, and heading to any watcher on shore as they transit the bottleneck. Again, the area is packed with Royal Navy depots, Royal Marine Commando bases, and other installations, and the volume of electronic traffic is massive—much of it passing near Rosslea Hall, especially when submarines check in with naval surface units and their Royal Marine fast-boat escorts. So while different in almost every other respect from the Hotel Del, this too is a perfect listening post. It was purchased in early 2018 by a company with three owners, all Chinese nationals, which seems to have been formed solely for that purpose and has no other known properties or businesses.[5] Just under six months after creating the company and two months after purchasing the hotel, all three owners updated their nationality of record in company documents from "Chinese" to "Hong Konger."[6]

Now, I want to be crystal clear on this point: I do not intend to suggest, in any way, that anyone involved in the sale or purchase of either hotel had any connection to Chinese intelligence, witting or unwitting. Nor am I implying that any individual or firm had taken part in, or was planning to engage in, nefarious activity of any kind. There is no evidence for that whatsoever. In the case of Rosslea Hall, the Royal Bank of Scotland funded the deal, so one can only assume that the bank's officials (and the British government) did due diligence before signing off.[7] By contrast, in the case of the Hotel Del, Anbang's purchase was blocked in September 2016 after opposition from the Committee on Foreign Investment in the United States (CFIUS), a body chaired by the US Treasury that includes Homeland Security, the State and Defense Departments, and the National Security Council.[8] CFIUS based its objection on national security risks that it believed the purchase posed, allegedly in response to counterintelligence concerns raised by US Navy leadership. But the committee's deliberations are private and it has not yet released its report for 2016, so the specifics are not publicly known.[9]

Almost equidistant from Coronado and Faslane, the city of Darwin in Australia's northern territory has some of the most beautiful beaches anywhere. They are also rather risky, with rangers scanning for "salties" (the large, aggressive estuarine crocodiles that enliven any day on the water in northern Australia) and lethal jellyfish deterring swimmers during the wet season. This, too, is a major military base: bombed by the Japanese sixty-four times during the Second World War, Darwin was a logistic hub for Australia's war in New Guinea and for General Douglas MacArthur's Pacific campaign of 1942–45.[10] Recent Australian operations in East Timor, Papua New Guinea, and the Pacific Islands and across the country's maritime northern border have been supported from Darwin, as have Australian-US operations in the Pacific and the South China Sea. There is an important Australian Army garrison at Robertson Barracks (home to the 1st Brigade, one of Australia's most powerful combined arms combat formations, and to the attack helicopters of 1st Aviation Regiment). Royal Australian Air

Force Base Darwin often hosts USAF B-52 and B1-B bombers and F-22 fighters training with Australian aircraft, as well as joint terminal attack controllers who direct airstrikes on a nearby bombing range. The Darwin naval base, HMAS *Coonawarra*, is home to Australia's expanding fleet of offshore patrol vessels, and it hosts American and other allied warships. There is a commercial port serving the Indian Ocean, Southeast Asia, and the Pacific and, since 2012, a US Marine Air-Ground Task Force (MAGTF) comprising roughly twenty-five hundred ground troops, aircraft, and amphibious ships that rotates through Darwin every few months.[11] As part of a defense review in 2015, Australia announced a major upgrade to this already substantial presence, with plans to invest AUS$20 billion over the next two decades in Darwin's military infrastructure.[12] In the same year, China's Shandong Landbridge Group spent AUS$506 million to acquire a controlling stake in the Port of Darwin.

Like Anbang, Landbridge is privately held, but concerns about the purchase quickly emerged, in part because the company has ties to the Chinese military (it operates a "people's armed militia" that supports the PLA at its other major port in the northeastern Chinese city of Rizhao and hosts a two hundred–strong Communist Party branch headed by a former PLA officer), in part because the Northern Territory government did the deal directly with the Chinese company, but mostly because the federal government in Canberra allegedly did not discuss it with Washington, Australia's closest treaty ally.[13]

Of several US officials who raised the issue with me, none had any concern about Australia exercising its sovereign right to do whatever it wants with its own territory. Still, some said, they would have appreciated a heads-up, especially as the United States has invested heavily in upgrading some facilities in Darwin since the MAGTF began rotating through and since this is the southern anchor for a host of joint U.S.-Australian activities across the region. More broadly, not only is Darwin a listening post equal to or better than Coronado or Faslane, it's a piece of critical infrastructure—one that is now potentially subject to Chinese control.

Some of these criticisms seemed somewhat overblown at the time. China's money is as good as anyone else's, after all, and Darwin and San

Diego have respected Chinese communities and long-standing links with China (though, to my knowledge, Faslane does not). Many Chinese companies have ties to the PLA, since until the 1990s the military owned many commercial enterprises as a way of offsetting the defense budget.[14] And in a country that remains under tight Communist control, virtually every Chinese school, office, factory, and farm has its party branch— suggesting that neither Anbang nor Landbridge is unusual in this regard. Much more evidence would therefore be needed before it could be argued that anything was going on beyond simple commercial activity by one of the world's fastest-growing economies.

Likewise, the old slur of divided loyalty, where overseas Chinese have been accused of taking orders from Beijing, has an extremely ugly history in Australia, Southeast Asia, the Americas, and elsewhere. It seems paranoid to worry that Chinese port workers somehow threaten Darwin or that Chinese hoteliers compromise British or American naval power any more than, say, Russian oligarchs buying British football teams, Saudi sheikhs owning the Savoy Hotel, or American bankers in Belgravia compromising Britain's financial integrity. Still, there is a fact pattern here, and we should add a few more points to complete it.

China's investment in Darwin forms part of an overall plan—the "21st Century Maritime Silk Road," which includes Chinese-owned or -operated port facilities at Gwadar in Pakistan, at Kuantan, Melaka, Kedah, and Port Klang in Malaysia, and at Townsville (another major Australian military, naval, and air base) in Queensland.[15] It is part of a pattern in which the People's Republic, experiencing double-digit economic growth over the past twenty-five years, has sought to translate its enhanced economic power into increased diplomatic clout and military influence—at first in China's own region, but increasingly worldwide.

In Europe, for example, the state-owned enterprise China Ocean Shipping Company (COSCO) now controls the port of Piraeus, Greece's largest naval base and a hub for NATO operations in the Mediterranean, as well as for the US Navy's Sixth Fleet.[16] The same government-controlled firm recently took majority ownership of Europe's largest container terminal at Zeebrugge in Belgium and of the Spanish port operator Noatum

Port Holdings.[17] (This is a global trend: eight out of the world's top-ten container ports, as of 2016, were located in China, were majority-Chinese-owned, or had received heavy Chinese investment.)[18] In 2017, a consortium led by Gao Jingde, a member of the Chinese People's Political Consultative Conference (CPPCC, equivalent to China's upper house, though with advisory powers only), linked to the PLA and regarded as a Taiwan hawk, sought to build what would have been Scandinavia's largest harbor at Lysekil in southwestern Sweden, only to drop its plans after push-back from Stockholm on national security grounds.[19]

In Africa, Chinese construction companies have undertaken much of the urban development of Ethiopia's capital, Addis Ababa, home of the African Union and center of Africa's fastest-growing economy.[20] While doing field research in 2018 in Somaliland—the self-declared and internationally un-recognized (but democratic, functional, and well-governed) republic in the Horn of Africa—I staged through Addis several times, seeing exten-sive signs of Chinese enterprises constructing everything from highways, railways, and hotels to the city's international airport and telecommunica-tions networks.[21] Much of this is financed by China's Exim Bank, a state in-stitution charged with developing international markets for Chinese goods and services, which since 2012 has been the largest lender in Africa.[22] Somaliland, by the way, is one of the very few places in Africa with limited Chinese investment, since recognizing the republic would create a perilous precedent (in Beijing's view) for territories like Tibet and Taiwan.

Less than thirty minutes' drive from the Somaliland border, down a re-cently paved coastal highway, the US base at Camp Lemonnier, Djibouti, now shares the city with China's first overseas base, from which the PLA Navy (PLAN) sends warships into the Red Sea and Gulf of Aden, global arteries that carry at least 12 percent of world maritime trade.[23] The PLAN base sits next to Doraleh container terminal, a few miles west of the city, which the state-owned enterprise China Merchants Port Holdings has operated since Djibouti nationalized the terminal, allegedly bowing to ec-onomic pressure from Beijing despite a preexisting agreement with Dubai Ports World in 2018.[24] Chinese companies (including COSCO) are cur-rently building a railway from Addis Ababa to Djibouti as part of China's belt-and-road initiative.[25] China also uses the base as a support hub for its naval counterpiracy operations in the Gulf of Aden and to support roughly two thousand PLA troops deployed in peacekeeping missions across Africa, in such countries as the Democratic Republic of Congo, Liberia, Mali, Sudan, and South Sudan, among others.[26] Thus, Djibouti, a strategic outpost in the Horn of Africa—hosting American and allied counterterrorism forces ever since the US took over Camp Lemonnier (a former French Foreign Legion facility) after 9/11—now also hosts the United States' main geopolitical rival in Africa.

Roughly 6,000 nautical miles east of Djibouti, in the Central Pacific Ocean, in the US Commonwealth of the Northern Mariana Islands (CNMI), another Chinese company, Imperial Pacific, through its subsidiary Best Sunshine International, operates a lavish casino on the island of Saipan, servicing gambling syndicates—known as junkets—out of Shanghai, Hong Kong, and Macau. The casino funnels vast quantities of cash through CNMI, giving Imperial Pacific profound political and economic influence over an American territory halfway between the Philippines and Japan, and just 135 miles from the crucial US Naval and Marine base on Guam.[27] On Okinawa, near another key American base, the Japanese intelligence service claimed in December 2016 that China was working to co-opt the island's separatist movement, which seeks independence from Japan and opposes America's presence on the island.[28] China disputes Japan's sovereignty over the Ryukyu Archipelago, which includes Okinawa, stretches from Japan's southernmost main island, Kyushu, almost to Taiwan, and incorporates the Senkaku Islands, scene of a naval confrontation in 2016.[29] And in 2017, at Hambantota on Sri Lanka's south coast, a Chinese consortium with PLA links secured a ninety-nine-year lease on a harbor it had built for Sri Lanka's government, financing construction through a $435 million loan that Sri Lanka soon found itself unable to service, then doing a debt-for-equity swap to give China a 70 percent stake in the Indian Ocean port.[30]

You might ask, what does any of this have to do with warfare or with the adaptations we have been examining as evolutionary responses to US conventional military dominance? Much of China's activity is commercial, relating to Beijing's "One Belt, One Road" initiative that seeks to link Europe, Asia, and Africa through transport and trading infrastructure. China is a rising power with the world's second-largest economy, a mercantilist outlook, and a global role, and Chinese investment has to go somewhere: Why shouldn't it go to Europe, Africa, Australia, the Pacific, and the United States?

CONCEPTUAL ENVELOPMENT

In this chapter, I will argue that China's adaptive response to the external environment—the "fitness landscape," with its combinations of traits and pressures to adapt—created by US military dominance since the Cold War has involved not just military modernization, territorial expansion, cyberwarfare, and economic-technological competition. It has also involved a widening of the very definition of warfare, to the point where Western planners now risk what I will call "conceptual envelopment," a situation in which an adversary's conception of war becomes so much broader than our own that two dangerous things can happen. First, that adversary may be acting in ways it considers warlike, while we with our narrower notion of warfare remain blithely unaware of the fact, so that by the time we realize we are at war, we have already lost. Second, and what is even more dangerous, we can be taking actions that we define as normal peacetime competition, while a rival with a broader concept of conflict sees these as acts of war and responds accordingly. At worst, each of us may completely misunderstand the other's motivation, strategy, and outlook, risking lethal miscalculation.

Strategists distinguish *vertical escalation* (increasing intensity of action within a given location, category of competition, or environmental domain) from *horizontal escalation* (expanding the geography, categories, and scope of actions, with or without increasing intensity in any one location).[31] In this framework, the liminal warfare we saw Russia pursuing in the preceding chapter is a vertical maneuver, a form of brinkmanship that manipulates the intensity and detectability (the vertical "signature") of actions, seeking just enough intensity to achieve key goals but not enough to trigger a timely military response. By contrast, the Chinese approach we will explore in this chapter is a horizontal maneuver—posing a bandwidth challenge for a rival by expanding the spectrum of competition beyond that rival's capacity to cope, generating a multitude of simultaneous small challenges that hamper its ability to respond effectively to any one action, or perhaps even to conceptualize the overall situation as warlike at all.

In this case, the danger of conceptual envelopment is that, through miscalculation or misinterpretation, we might end up unintentionally going to war with China, sliding imperceptibly into confrontation or subconsciously losing a subliminal conflict we don't even realize we are fighting. Presumably, neither China nor the United States wants to wage war against the other. Quite apart from its massive human cost, such a conflict, even if it did not involve nuclear weapons, would destroy decades of progress toward prosperity in China, wreck the world economy, and erase Washington's global primacy (not least because the largest foreign holder of American national debt is China, at 1.12 trillion US dollars, or 28 percent of the total, as of December 2018).[32] Rather, the risk is that, in a variant on the traditional security dilemma—where countries behave in ways they themselves deem defensive but others interpret as offensive, prompting rivals to ramp up their actions until an unsought conflict occurs—conceptual envelopment could see one or both sides caught unaware by the escalatory impact of their own behavior. To understand the context of China's evolution and of the current pattern of conceptual envelopment, we need to go back a bit to explore the history of how we got here, as we did in the two preceding chapters.

THE CHINESE MILITARY IN THE 1980S AND 1990S

In 1992, as Colonel Chen Xiaolu (later Anbang's adviser on the Hotel Del deal) was retiring from the PLA to begin his business career, Chinese thinkers were engaged in an intense debate, seeking to make sense of what had just happened to Iraq. As mentioned in the first chapter, the Gulf War was a harsh wake-up call for China, especially since just two years before invading Kuwait, Saddam had beaten the Iranian military (which was partly Chinese-supported and -equipped) in the Iran-Iraq War.[33] If the Iraqis could defeat Chinese-equipped Iran, only to be themselves effortlessly crushed by the Americans, China was clearly at least two steps behind in adapting to the post–Cold War landscape of US military dominance.

China has not conducted a conventional land offensive since the 1979 Sino-Vietnamese War, and the modern Chinese navy has never fought a major maritime engagement (the last time Chinese warships battled a blue-water opponent was on 17 September 1894, at the Battle of the Yalu River, when the Imperial Japanese Navy defeated the Qing Dynasty's larger but less capable Beiyang Fleet).[34] The Battle of Yijiangshan in 1955, when a PLAN task force supported an amphibious assault on an offshore island eight miles from the mainland during the First Taiwan Strait Crisis, involved serious littoral maneuver and casualty-intensive ground combat against Taiwanese forces. It was the most complex combined-arms operation ever conducted by the PLA; but that was sixty-five years ago.[35] Since then, a January 1974 battle near the Paracel Islands, and a 1988 skirmish near Johnson South Reef in the Spratly Islands, which killed sixty-four Vietnamese, are the closest China has come to pitched naval battles in a generation.[36] As a result—unlike players described in previous chapters who evolved through their own experience of war—the Chinese military, especially when it comes to air and naval operations, tends to rely on what US analysts have called "lessons from other people's wars."[37]

The debate during the early 1990s was happening at a crucial time for China and the PLA. Like the death of Stalin in Russia in 1953, Mao Zedong's death in September 1976 was the beginning of the end of a massively disruptive period in China. Mao had transformed every aspect of Chinese society, but his doctrine of continuous revolution carried immense cost—from the coercive chaos of the Great Leap Forward in 1958–62 to the resulting famine that killed up to fifty-five million in 1959–61, to the Cultural Revolution of 1966–76, when fanatical teenage Red Guards (including a young Chen Xiaolu) victimized elders, teachers, and class enemies, killing perhaps another two to three million people while trashing the economy and unleashing chaos that destroyed intergenerational, social, and family cohesion.[38] After Mao's death and the arrest of his successors,

the ultra-Maoist Gang of Four, in 1976, Communist Party chairman Hua
Guofeng began to dismantle Mao's most destructive policies; Hua's successor, Deng Xiaoping, accelerated the reforms after 1978, and the party
repudiated key elements of Mao's legacy in 1981, declaring that the
Cultural Revolution had caused "the most severe setback and the heaviest
losses . . . since the founding of the People's Republic."[39]

Through the 1980s, Deng combined tight political control with increasing
economic freedom via market-based economic reforms.[40] Under Deng,
a respected former PLA commander who never held formal positions as
head of state, party, military, or government (yet effectively controlled all
four elements of the system), China moved away from Mao's centralized
personality cult toward collective responsibility through committees
guided by behind-the-scenes leaders.[41]

China's Military after Mao

The military under Mao had been optimized for large-scale, low-tech, protracted, and primarily rural "people's war," with secondary functions of internal security and nation-building. Having originated as a guerrilla force,
the PLA—like many other militaries, including the Israeli, Russian, and
American, which also began as rebel forces—inherited certain traits that
were well suited to its ancestral guerrilla environment but no longer appropriate once victory made it the standing army of a nation-state.

In common with many former guerrilla forces that later became national
armies, the PLA had also been used as an internal repressive force employed
by the Communist Party against the people to crush resistance and coerce
communities into compliance with Mao's often contradictory and unpop-
ular policies during the "campaign to suppress counterrevolutionaries," the
Great Leap Forward, and the Cultural Revolution.[42] Now the post-Mao
landscape imposed new selective pressures—in particular, the requirement for the PLA to support the Party's decision to refocus from politics
to economics, from class struggle to modernization.[43] Deng declared a
doctrine of limited, local war and "people's war under modern conditions"
that required a smaller, more professional PLA and the acquisition of more

modern technology, rather than the "guerrilla warfare with an emphasis on mass participation" that had marked the military under Mao.[44]

As June Teufel Dreyer points out, the "Maoist model of the military was characterized by multifunctionality, structural diffuseness, and politicization."[45] The PLA under Mao had a political role, and its leadership overlapped with that of the Party and (after 1949) the state. Since its founding, the PLA had been the army of the Communist Party—not, technically, that of the Chinese state. It thus made sense for soldiers to perform political, economic, and cultural tasks alongside military roles.[46] The PLA was also expected to be self-sustaining, providing its own food, clothing, and shelter so as to minimize its cost to the Party, a requirement that often soaked up effort in nonmilitary activity.[47]

During the Cultural Revolution, despite previous periods of professionalization, the PLA's development stalled and then went into reverse, as the "people's army" model became ideologically entrenched.[48] There is a further parallel with Russia here. Stalin's purges in the 1930s destroyed the flower of Soviet military talent, favoring politically timid military mediocrities: cautious officers who were well adapted to surviving their own government's lethal predations but who failed in the face of the even more lethal Nazi onslaught a few years later. Likewise, the expulsion of experienced but politically suspect cadres during the Cultural Revolution decimated the PLA's leadership, destroying much of the military's professionalism and purging many of the most combat-experienced and talented officers. Only under Deng, whose "Four Modernizations" included reforming and professionalizing the military, did the PLA again begin to specialize and modernize. Initially, also, the PLA was primarily a ground force, with little experience or expertise in maritime or air operations. That ground-centric approach was on display during China's first conflict under Deng's leadership, the Sino-Vietnamese war of February–March 1979.

A Painful Little War

Fought over mountainous jungle-covered terrain, along the 400-mile border between China and Vietnam, and in a series of northern Vietnamese cities, the Sino-Vietnamese War was limited in scope—PLA naval and air forces deployed in deterrent and support roles only, while a huge but poorly equipped force of 330,000 ground troops carried the entire combat burden during three weeks of intensive fighting in northern Vietnam.[49] There were no significant air or maritime combat engagements.[50] Employing human-wave tactics that seemed like a throwback to the Korean War, Chinese troops sought to overwhelm smaller but better-trained Vietnamese forces by sheer weight of numbers—an approach that not only underlined the PLA's lack of skill but also cost China at least 63,000 casualties.[51] It was as if the Cultural Revolution and its attendant self-inflicted turmoil had left the PLA stranded in the 1950s while the People's Army of Vietnam (PAVN)—benefiting from the selection effects of its recent war with the technologically advanced United States and from its extensive experience in ongoing regional conflicts in Cambodia and Laos—had forged ahead.[52]

Chinese objectives included destroying the defense system of northern Vietnam, ending border clashes—more than eleven hundred of which had occurred in 1978 alone, killing about three hundred Chinese troops and civilians—and relieving pressure on China's client, the genocidal Khmer Rouge regime in Cambodia.[53] The Khmer Rouge were under attack from Vietnam, whose forces captured their capital, Phnom Penh, on 7 January 1979.[54] The fall of Phnom Penh was the proximate cause of the conflict: in invading Vietnam, China sought to force PAVN commanders to withdraw troops from Cambodia in order to meet the threat from their north, thereby rescuing their Khmer Rouge allies.[55] Deng briefed his generals before the war started, emphasizing its limited, ground-based nature and his expectation that it would take only a few days to achieve these goals.

In the event, the war lasted three weeks, did not relieve sufficient pressure on the Khmer Rouge to prevent their defeat, and failed to trap and destroy the PAVN regular troops who were its main targets, though several towns—notably, the city of Lang Son, one of northern Vietnam's most important provincial capitals, just 80 miles from Hanoi, suffered severe damage.[56] The fall of Lang Son on 4 March offered a convenient excuse for Beijing to declare victory and leave. Though at the strategic level the war was painted as a Chinese victory, at the operational and tactical levels it brought harsh lessons for the PLA, some of whose veterans called the conflict a "painful little war."[57]

John Pike has argued that "no amount of strategic propaganda can cover the PLA's tactical failures of the Sino-Vietnam War. The campaign was racked by mistakes ranging from training and preparation to using Red Army meatgrinder tactics that the PLA had neither the training, the resources nor the experience to perform."[58] Lack of maps and compasses and poor navigational skills resulted in troops losing their way, throwing into chaos what had already become an overly complex, multipronged operation, with twenty-six separate axes of advance over rugged terrain.[59] Command and control were highly centralized and dependent on top-down direction. But the radio communications needed for this type of hierarchical C2 broke down due to poorly manufactured equipment and untrained operators: in one incident, an order by General Xu Shiyou, PLA commander in the eastern sector, directing the 67th Regiment to attack Lang Son, "somehow changed to a hold-and-defend order when it passed through the army and division headquarters. The regiment thus never joined the general attack on Lang Son."[60]

Likewise, logistics quickly collapsed, with some "units going without water for 24 to 48 hours after first contact" even in prewar training.[61] In combat, things were even worse: due to the bloody failure of their massed human-wave attacks in the early fighting, once the main battles developed, "company commanders would rather wait for tank and recoilless rifle support before taking on Vietnamese entrenched positions. The frontline units exhausted themselves, forcing a re-supply much earlier than planned."[62] The quality of weapons, ammunition, and equipment proved poor—though tactical employment, rather than equipment itself, was the key weakness, especially against an enemy like the PAVN, whose troops were similar to the Chinese in training and equipment, understood PLA tactics intimately, and could thus exploit every Chinese vulnerability.[63] The overall lesson was that the PLA was unready for "people's war under modern conditions." As a result, Chinese leaders identified several organizational, tactical, and technological deficiencies, and instituted a series of reforms in the years that followed.[64]

Learning from China's Last Major War

As Edward O'Dowd and John Corbett observe in their account of the lessons the Chinese took away from the conflict, the PLA published two sets of "lessons learned" from the war—a compilation of insights prepared in 1979 by the infantry school of Guangzhou Military Region (General Xu Shiyou's command) and a 1997 study by the PLA Academy of Military Sciences, China's highest-level military think tank.[65] The 1979 report identified problems such as poor infantry tactics; ineffective artillery fire control; lack of combat engineering capacity; inability to perform river crossings or detect and clear minefields; lack of uniforms, shoes, food, and water; and transport and supply failures across even a short (roughly 35-mile) resupply route.[66] It recommended more realistic exercises, including live-fire training; greater focus on technical and military subjects rather than political indoctrination; and matching training to the geography, climate, and anticipated combat conditions of likely areas of operations. To any professional soldier, this is a startlingly basic list of obvious points, and the fact that the Guangzhou instructors in 1979 saw these as reportable insights illustrates how far the PLA had fallen during the Cultural Revolution.[67] O'Dowd and Corbett quote a "writer in the *Liberation Army Daily* [who] noted in 1978 that 'military training was not strict, or at times . . . no training at all was given. Some soldiers had been in the armed forces for several years without ever touching a rifle and some cadres could not lead troops. The combat capabilities of the whole armed forces declined markedly.' "[68]

By 1997, eighteen years and several reform efforts after the war, the Academy of Military Sciences was emphasizing quite different lessons. The think tank highlighted lack of combat experience among commanders, low quality of combat troops (in physical and educational terms), ineffective tactics, and poor coordination. The 1997 study emphasized the need for more modern weapons and C2 systems, and blamed the Cultural Revolution, the Gang of Four, and the disgraced former PLA commander Lin Biao for the PLA's problems.[69] Thus, while covering some of the same basics as the 1979 study, the 1997 report revealed a PLA establishment that had lifted its sights in the intervening two decades and was now more technologically focused and engaged with the challenges of joint and combined-arms warfare under modern, high-technology conditions.

Reforms driven by these lessons and implemented slowly through the 1980s, then with increasing energy after the Gulf War, included improvements in infantry, artillery, and engineering equipment and tactics; motorization, enabling units to move about the battlefield in their own organic mobility assets; professionalization of logistics; and, most important, a shift from infantry-centric divisions and corps to "combined arms army groups" incorporating a balanced mix of all arms.[70] The Chinese officer corps in the 1990s became better educated, more specialized, and younger, while the PLA shrank, bloated Maoist-era structures were trimmed, and the military's average educational level increased significantly. In this regard China's problem in the 1990s was the opposite of Russia's, the key element of which, as we saw in the preceding chapter, was hollowness: the lack of personnel to fill billets in a structure with too many units and not enough people.

By contrast, the PLA was emerging from decades as a low-tech, mass land force with a nontrivial secondary role as a gigantic jobs program, where many soldiers never even handled a weapon, focusing instead on commercial, industrial, agricultural, or social tasks unconnected to warfighting. Refocusing from quantity to quality and increasing professionalism while reducing size became key goals. Reflecting this, the pace, scale, and complexity of PLA training exercises increased significantly through the 1980s and 1990s, with greater focus on combined-arms maneuver.[71] Formations were made more compact and maneuverable, while new types of troops—helicopter units, Western-style special operations forces, and rapid-reaction formations—emerged in the 1990s. The PLA also increasingly emphasized naval and air capabilities, attempting to break its historical ground-centric focus.

Reform after Tiananmen

This reflected, in part, the emphasis of Deng's successor, Jiang Zemin, who became president in 1993, on increased military budgets, improved weapons, and capabilities for the PLA to fight "limited wars under technologically-advanced conditions" and pursue what Jiang called a "revolution in military affairs with Chinese characteristics."[72] It also reflected PLA leaders' desire to professionalize for external operations, as a way of moving on from the return to repression that Deng had forced on them in 1989.

Deng's reforms had unlocked aspirations for prosperity and civil rights that could not easily be satisfied under tight Communist political control. Urbanization, industrialization, rural-to-urban migration (creating a "floating" peri-urban population of millions of temporary, unhoused, and unauthorized agricultural workers seeking jobs in China's cities), and withdrawal of party control over local administration created a series of stresses that came to a head in the spring and summer of 1989.[73] Deng (behind the scenes) and Li Peng (formally Chinese premier) declared martial law on 20 May 1989 and mobilized thirty PLA divisions from across the country. On the evening of 3 June, Deng ordered the PLA, over the protests of some commanders (and in opposition to Party general secretary Zhao Ziyang, who favored dialogue with the protesters), to suppress the democracy movement centered on Beijing's Tiananmen Square. Some units refused the order, but others obeyed, killing up to ten thousand civilians in what is known in the West as the "Tiananmen Square Massacre" and in China as the "June 4th Incident." Both are misnomers: the repression was extremely violent, involving tanks and heavy weapons, and vastly more than a mere "incident," but it was also not restricted to Tiananmen, with actions against protestors in more than four hundred cities across China.[74]

In the wake of the suppression, there was strong resentment within the PLA, and not just among units that had mutinied rather than massacre protesters. More generally, military leaders felt they had been made scapegoats for the Party's policy failures. As a result, the Party was forced to create an entire new armed service—the People's Armed Police—to take on the role of internal security and paramilitary suppression of dissent, relieving a resentful PLA of the requirement to do so.[75] Thousands of officers (especially younger, better-educated leaders who had risen during the reform-and-opening period of the 1980s) were prosecuted, purged, or forcibly retired in the early 1990s, a process that was still going on when Jiang Zemin succeeded Deng in 1993.[76] The protests underlined the failure of Deng's model to meet the Chinese people's desire for political freedoms to match their increasing prosperity, and their suppression discredited Deng while undermining public support for the PLA. Recruiting had already slipped as China's improved economy, urbanization, industrialization, and the replacement of communal farming with private agriculture made military service less attractive for young men in the countryside, traditionally the PLA's main recruiting base.[77]

Under Jiang Zemin and his successors, Hu Jintao and Xi Jinping, the notion, first advanced by Jiang, of a "revolution in military affairs with Chinese characteristics" and the associated conventional modernization—not only in the PLA's ground forces but also in the PLAN, PLA Air Force (PLAAF), and PLA Rocket Forces (PLARF, known until 2016 as the Second Artillery Corps)—has been the most prominent pathway for China's military evolution. It has been shaped in part by internal adaptation within the PLA, in part by massive changes in Chinese society over the past quarter century, and in part by shifts in the external environment. Along with the Gulf War, the US bombing of the Chinese Embassy in Belgrade in 1999 was a tipping point.

THE BELGRADE EMBASSY BOMBING

We have already discussed the impact on Russia of the Kosovo campaign and of NATO's air attacks against Serbia to halt the ethnic cleansing of Kosovar Albanians. From Russia's standpoint, in its willingness to use force in support of a newly discovered "responsibility to protect," the West treated Serbia's sovereignty as secondary to the wishes of Western powers, hubristically styling themselves the "international community" or "global public opinion," as if no other community of opinion existed.[78] These new norms were then unilaterally enforced by NATO, using airstrikes and ground troops, in retaliation for what Russia considered a legitimate government's treatment of its own population. Quite apart from the West's disregard for its own norms (notably, noninterference in the internal affairs of sovereign states and rejection of war as a means of resolving disputes), NATO's self-righteous arrogance—and its failure to consult Moscow—infuriated Russian leaders, whose anger deepened as the alliance went on to occupy Kosovo and eventually carve the province out of Serbia.[79]

None of this directly affected China until the night of 7 May 1999, when American B-2 stealth bombers dropped five bombs equipped with Joint Direct Attack Munition (JDAM) guidance packages—satellite-enabled systems that turn gravity bombs into precision weapons—on the Chinese Embassy compound in Serbia's capital, Belgrade, killing three journalists and injuring twenty other civilians.[80] The Chinese public reacted with outrage, as did officials in Beijing.[81] China saw itself as an innocent bystander in Belgrade, being a party neither to the Kosovo conflict nor to the international response. It also beggared belief in Beijing that the United States, with near-perfect ISR and mapping capability, a constellation of GPS satellites, and a functionally unlimited supply of precision weapons, could simply have made a mistake.

But this was exactly what US officials claimed, suggesting the strike had been intended for a nearby arms agency suspected of supporting Serbia's campaign in Kosovo but that the coordinates were confused with those of the Chinese diplomatic mission 500 yards down the street.[82] CIA director George Tenet later testified that the target had been chosen from a map by analysts at CIA headquarters in Langley, Virginia, that this was the only target so selected during the campaign, and that a mapping error was responsible for the mistake.[83] President Clinton attempted to apologize to Jiang Zemin a day after the bombing, and a delegation led by Under Secretary of State Tom Pickering traveled to Beijing, bringing documents and maps to substantiate Washington's side of the story.[84]

Chinese officials never accepted the US explanation, branding the bombing a "barbaric act and a gross violation of Chinese sovereignty" and regarding it, to this day, as deliberate.[85] Officials in Beijing blocked Chinese broadcasts of Clinton's apology for four days while mass protests erupted.[86] Some Western media supported the Chinese interpretation, with the Guardian claiming in October 1999 that NATO had deliberately targeted the embassy due to its role as a communications node enabling the Serbian government to keep functioning despite the alliance's attempt to knock out its telecommunications systems.[87] Persistent rumors, circulating soon after the bombing and repeated over many years in the media and in at least one academic study, allege the embassy was storing wreckage from an F-117A stealth aircraft shot down earlier in the campaign, suggesting the strike was planned to prevent PLA technical intelligence teams from studying the plane's stealth technology or sending its parts to China and explaining why this strike (and this one alone) was planned from Langley.[88]

Despite these outliers, the consensus at the time—and, remember, 1999 was high noon for the "end of history," when world media were overwhelmingly Western-dominated and NATO, the United Nations, and the United States could claim the moral high ground with near-effortless confidence in their own self-righteous exceptionalism—was that the United States was innocent of anything more than making a tragic mistake in a good cause, so that any outrage in China must either be insincere or manipulated by Communist propaganda.[89]

But as Peter Hays Gries showed at the time, the anger was far from fake. The bombing prompted "mass protests from Chinese across the globe . . . Chinese students in Europe and the United States demonstrated against what they called 'NATO Fascism'. The American consul's residence in Chengdu was firebombed. In Beijing Chinese students demanded revenge, chanting 'Blood for Blood!' Others threw bricks at US embassy buildings" while the PLA "looked on, and ambassador James Sasser and other American diplomats were trapped inside for days."[90] Gries's analysis, which draws on hundreds of letters to the editor of a major Chinese daily newspaper as a way of distinguishing spontaneous sentiment from state-sponsored protests, suggests that outrage in China over the Belgrade bombing was both heartfelt and indeed spontaneous.

Gries argued that this "prompted a shift in popular Chinese perceptions of America and of the world system. A Manichean, black-and-white view of Sino-American relations appears to have gained a wider currency in post-Belgrade China. Given that a similarly Manichean view of China may be emerging in the United States, these developments threaten to lock Chinese and American national identities into a dangerous state of negative interdependence, where every American gain is perceived as China's loss, and vice versa. The emergence of a zero-sum view of Sino-American relations on both sides of the Pacific would have grave implications for peace in the 21st century."[91]

Though the 9/11 attacks distracted many Americans, it's worth remembering that at the turn of the century, as George W. Bush's administration succeeded Bill Clinton's, tension with China was a cause of considerable concern. The April 2001 collision between a US Navy EP-3 signals intelligence aircraft and a PLAN J-8 fighter jet near Hainan in the South China Sea, which killed the Chinese Navy pilot, Lieutenant Commander Wang Wei, and forced the emergency landing and detention on Hainan of the EP-3 aircrew, was a crisis for the incoming administration and would have stood as a milestone in President Bush's first term had not 9/11 happened a few months later.[92] Looking back, almost twenty years later, it seems clear that Gries was right: the Belgrade bombing was indeed a tipping point, after which China and the United States increasingly framed their relations as zero-sum rivalry.

The "lessons of Belgrade" continued throughout the 2000s as a source of anger (and a driver of military modernization) for China, where as recently as 2017, researchers found that "the experience of being unable to respond to the U.S. military was deeply humiliating for the PLA and [Communist Party] . . . the PLA's 'vision of creating "assassin's mace" [or trump card] weapons that can "look far, shoot far, and shoot accurately" was driven by the 1999 embassy bombing.' "[93] This was happening even as competition with Beijing became a matter of secondary interest for Americans obsessing over the wars in Iraq and Afghanistan and for a US administration that framed almost every security issue through the lens of the war on terrorism. But something else is also worth noting—Gries's description of Sino-American relations as involving "both sides of the Pacific."

CHINA AS BOTH A MARITIME AND A CONTINENTAL POWER

This view of China as a Pacific power is a particularly American perception based on the obvious geographical fact that whereas the United States,

Mexico, and Canada dominate the eastern Pacific Rim north of the equator, China is by far the largest country on that immense ocean's western periphery. But for China—which, after all, considers itself the "middle kingdom" occupying a central position in the world system—it's not immediately clear that the country is mainly a Pacific power or, indeed, a maritime one at all. This is important for the PLA's evolution, since there are distinct differences between continental (i.e., land-power) strategies and maritime (oceanic) ones.[94]

As noted earlier, until the 1990s the PLA was largely a land force, reflecting a continental outlook that saw China as a power of the Eurasian heartland, with an army-centric view of military capability and a focus on threats from within its own landmass, including those from long-term rivals like India, Russia, and the Soviet client states of Vietnam and North Korea. With the notable exception of Japan, imperial China's traditional adversaries (from the Huns, Xianbei, and Mongols of the Central Asian steppes to the Turkic tribes and East-Iranian Jie of the far west) were land-based. Classical China's signature achievement was the Great Wall, a land-centric response to threats that were also entirely terrestrial. More recently, China's allies (Pakistan, Iran, Cambodia under the Khmer Rouge, and North Korea since the Cold War) have been located along China's landward periphery. To the extent that Communist China has had a seaward enemy, it was Taiwan after 1949, but for Chinese strategists (and, indeed, for the Chinese and Taiwanese people at large) Taiwan *is* China, and in any case actions against Taiwan—during multiple crises from the 1950s onward—were mostly coastal ("green"-water) rather than blue-water maritime operations.

But in the last two decades of the twentieth century, things began to change, with significant implications: If China is a continental power, its long-term adversaries would tend to be other land powers (Russia and India) with whom it would compete to control the Eurasian landmass. If, instead, the country is a maritime power, its ultimate rival would be the United States and its allies, including Australia, Japan, and other sea-based powers in the Western orbit. But China is both—and in fact, Chinese strategy shows significant subregional variation in both the continental and maritime domains.[95]

The Russian geopolitical theorist Aleksandr Dugin, whose ideas I referenced in the preceding chapter, lists China as an example of a land-based, traditional society.[96] But his distinction between *tellurocratic* ("land-ruling," continental, and in Dugin's view naturally authoritarian) powers dominating the Eurasian world-island and *thalassocratic* ("sea-ruling" maritime trading nations, which he sees as naturally capitalist and liberal) controlling the planet's oceanic periphery breaks down in China's case. Dugin is correct to the extent that China's government, for several hundred years after the return of the wide-ranging explorer Admiral Zheng He's seventh and last voyage in AD 1433, held an isolationist and mostly land-based view of itself.[97] But China has a long seafaring tradition, and its naval history is more complicated than this.

The Imperial *Haijin* edicts, the first of which actually predated Zheng He, did result in a two-hundred-year ban on maritime trade, the destruction of ships and ports, depopulation of coastal areas, isolationism, and a landward orientation under the Ming and, later, Qing Dynasties.[98] Still, as we have seen, China maintained naval fleets—albeit not very effective ones—under the Qing and conducted coastal and riverine operations throughout the eighteenth and nineteenth centuries. Chinese warships mounted blockades and naval expeditions against the British during the Opium Wars (1839–60), conducted riverine operations during the Tai Ping Rebellion of 1850–71, and launched a naval expedition to Formosa (Taiwan) against Japan in 1875; they also fought Russia, Japan, and Korea at sea.[99] Even with the *Haijin* edicts in force, Zheng He could still complete multiple imperially sponsored voyages of exploration. Scholars like Jack Goldstone and Ronald C. Po have argued that it is ahistorical to imagine China turning its back on the sea in the fifteenth century or at any time since: China is an Asian giant that has had both a continental and a maritime role, along with considerable global influence, through most of its history.[100] Indeed, China's "century of humiliation" after the Opium Wars and its land-centric conflicts under Mao can be seen as anomalies, while its more recent maritime reorientation is really a return to normality.

Dugin's notion that land powers are naturally authoritarian due to their need to control large populations and defend long land frontiers, while sea powers tend to be liberal and capitalist since they depend on commerce and can rely on oceans for protection, also makes limited sense in China's case. China has not only an enormous land area but also extensive oceanic claims. It has a land border of almost 14,000 miles, along with one of the largest surface areas and the largest population of any country on the planet, suggesting an authoritarian, centralizing tendency, according to Dugin. But the country also has a 9,000-mile coastline (the tenth-longest in the world) and depends heavily on maritime commerce, which would suggest an emphasis on trade, market economics, and a seaward orientation. Likewise, the militarily impenetrable Himalayas to China's south and the great Central Asian desert to its west offer a considerable measure of frontier security. The approach of Deng and subsequent leaders, pursuing a twin-track policy of political authoritarianism and economic liberalization, is thus arguably rational and appropriate for China's circumstances as both a continental and a maritime power.

China is not unique in this respect—India is another example of a gigantic country with both maritime and continental characteristics and an enduring tension between economic prosperity and political stability.[101] Russia would be another, except that much of its coastline (which, at 25,000 miles, is almost three times longer than China's) is in the Arctic and has historically been icebound. Climate change is, of course, altering this, so that Russia, India, and China may all turn out to be exceptions to Dugin's tellurocratic-thalassocratic distinction, rendering it meaningless in practical terms.

What is certainly true is that under Mao and in the initial reform period under Deng, Chinese forces were overwhelmingly land-based. In part, this reflected their guerrilla heritage, as we saw earlier—few insurgent forces possess planes or ships. In part, it reflected a lack of resources: naval and air assets are technology- and capital-intensive, requiring the kind of industrial base and educated, technically literate workforce that was largely lacking in China until the 1980s. And during Mao's repression, internal security (an almost entirely land-based endeavor) was the key PLA task.

But with market reforms bringing economic growth in the 1980s and 1990s, China became increasingly dependent on seaborne trade and on

imports of petroleum products and raw materials to power its industrialization and urbanization. And as industrialization progressed, manufactured
exports in turn became extremely important for Chinese prosperity, and
China's coastal cities boomed, in contrast to the country's inland areas,
contributing to littoralization (the tendency for populations, settlements,
and infrastructure to cluster on coastlines). By 2008, almost 85 percent
of China's international trade moved by sea, while by 2011 overseas trade
shaped 60 to 70 percent of the economy.[102] With littoral industrialization
and the reliance on maritime trade came the need to protect trade routes,
guarantee supply chains, and control sea lanes, which in turn implied the
need for a capable navy.

To be clear, Communist China had always fielded naval forces. Beyond
the Battle of Yijiangshan, the several Taiwan Strait crises from the 1950s
onward, and the skirmishes in the Paracels and Spratlys noted earlier, naval
operations—mostly in coastal waters—had been part of the PLA repertoire. But the early PLAN did not operate like a conventional navy; rather,
it adopted " 'guerrilla warfare at sea' and a naval version of People's War in
order to compensate for its disadvantages in modern capital ships during
the sporadic, long-running naval combat with Taiwan. [This included] secret movement of torpedo boats by hiding them from radar behind larger
commercial ships; precisely choreographed swarming and 'cutting up' tactics by many smaller gunboats and torpedo boats against larger but fewer
Taiwan Navy warships; carefully prepared ambushes at sea; and repeated
nighttime engagements."[103] But a modern maritime power seeking to secure global interests needed a conventional navy.

Thus, given China's increasing oceanic orientation and dependence on
the sea, Beijing began building up the PLAN as soon as it became finan-
cially feasible to do so, from the early 1990s. In its 2015 military strategy, the
Chinese government explained this buildup by reference to the country's
changing economic and strategic circumstances, noting that the "traditional
mentality that land outweighs sea must be abandoned . . . It is necessary for
China to develop a modern maritime military force structure commensurate with its national security and development interests, [to] safeguard its
national sovereignty and maritime rights and interests, protect the security

of strategic [sea lines of communication] and overseas interests, and participate in international maritime cooperation, so as to provide strategic support for building itself into a maritime power."[104]

But the Third Taiwan Strait Crisis, in 1995–96 (discussed later), the Belgrade embassy bombing in 1999, and the zero-sum rivalry that followed meant that both the United States and China began to see this buildup in threatening terms, as a Chinese challenge to US global primacy rather than simply as a natural consequence of China's growing prosperity and integration with the world economy. American analysts saw PLAN modernization as an effort to contest the US Navy's control of seaspace, "the first such challenge the U.S. Navy has faced since the end of the Cold War."[105] China's naval capabilities—along with its island-building program in the South China Sea and its developing anti-access and area-denial (A2/AD) and anti-ship ballistic missile programs—were seen in Washington as part of a broader threat to the "long-standing status of the United States as the leading military power in the Western Pacific."[106]

MODERNIZATION AFTER THE 1996 TAIWAN CRISIS

China's naval buildup began slowly, in the late 1980s, with the design of new classes of warships (principally frigates, submarines, and destroyers) for the PLAN. After 1991, following the shock of the Gulf War, naval modernization spending picked up, as did shipbuilding and the development of naval weapons, including torpedoes, missiles, mines, and naval aviation. But the most significant shock for the Chinese navy was the Third Taiwan Strait Crisis, during which, in March 1996, the US Navy sailed a full carrier strike group (CSG-5, USS *Nimitz*) and an amphibious task group based on the helicopter assault ship USS *Belleau Wood* between Taiwan and the mainland, defying PLAN and PLARF naval and missile threats. The United States also positioned another carrier strike group (CSG-7, USS *Independence*) nearby, in the largest show of force by the US Navy in the Pacific since the Vietnam War.[107]

As I have noted, militaries evolve through setbacks rather than successes, and leaders in Beijing certainly saw the 1995–96 crisis as a setback, in that the PLAN had failed to achieve the political goal set for it by the Party—coercing Taiwan to prevent pro-independence moves—while also failing militarily, being brushed aside by the *Nimitz* and *Independence* strike groups and the amphibious forces on *Belleau Wood*.[108] Likewise, as described in previous chapters, peacetime innovation tends to be concept-led and capability-based, whereas in wartime adversaries coevolve in tandem with their primary enemy, often coming to resemble that enemy over time. China's buildup after 1996, and particularly after the 1999 embassy bombing and the 2001 Hainan incident, showed a shift from a peacetime pattern—driven primarily by China's littoralization and increasing maritime orientation—to a wartime one where the PLAN began to mirror and evolve toward its "pacing threat" (or benchmark adversary), the US Navy. This is another way of framing Gries's notion of "negative interdependence," with China evolving to copy or compete with the United States, even as Washington became so focused on terrorism after 9/11 (and on extricating itself from its self-inflicted quagmire in Iraq after 2003) that few resources could be freed up to face the Chinese challenge.

Twenty years later, in 2016, Cortez Cooper noted that the 1995–96 crisis and the embassy bombing forced China's leadership to confront the fact that there was little they could do to stop the United States from coming to Taiwan's assistance. This showed Chinese strategists "that they were dealing with a new way of war . . . defined by battlefield dominance through precision strike [and] targeting capabilities, supported by highly-networked command and control, reconnaissance and surveillance."[109] The lesson learned by leaders in Beijing was the need for A2/AD capabilities to "deter, delay or deny an advanced enemy from entering the theatre of operations in Asia."[110]

A 2018 US report assessed Chinese naval modernization as focused on developing capabilities for a war with Taiwan, defending China's claims in the South and East China Sea, including its claimed 200-mile exclusive economic zone (EEZ) around disputed islands, defending trading routes (especially for oil from the Middle East), "displacing American influence in the Western Pacific," and asserting China's status as a regional and global great power.[111] To support these goals, the report noted, "China wants its military to be capable of acting as an [A2/AD] force that can deter U.S. intervention in a conflict in China's near-seas region over Taiwan or some other issue, or failing that, delay the arrival or reduce the effectiveness of intervening U.S. forces."[112] Additional tasks might include maritime security, anti-piracy, noncombatant evacuation, humanitarian assistance, and disaster response.[113]

China's naval evolution thus came to be dominated by the drive for two complementary sets of capabilities: one suite of tools to emulate the United States' global role and another to counter US operations in China's sphere of influence. The first required a modern surface, subsurface, and aviation capability. China's surface warfare fleet began to expand and improve in the late 1990s with the purchase of four Sovremenny-class destroyers from Russia, which sparked significant concern in the United States when they began to enter service in the mid-2000s.[114] Over the next decade, the PLAN upgraded these ships and introduced several new classes of frigates and destroyers, developing the largest shipbuilding industry in the world along the way.[115] Underwater, the PLAN again began with Russian types in the form of twelve non-nuclear-powered Kilo-class submarines, then added a series of increasingly sophisticated, Chinese-designed diesel-electric subs, while developing a class of nuclear-powered ballistic missile submarines (SSBNs).[116] As of 2020, according to the US Office of Naval Intelligence, the PLAN submarine fleet would be around seventy-four boats, of which eleven would be nuclear-powered, up from two (neither of which was nuclear) at the time of the Third Taiwan Strait Crisis.[117]

Thus, from a slow start in the 1990s, when China seriously lagged behind both the United States and the Soviet Union in naval power, the country leapfrogged into the modern era, eclipsing Russia and rivaling America. The need to modernize by acquiring advanced technologies was a key driver for industrial and technological espionage—as well as efforts to woo Chinese scientists working at US sites such as Los Alamos National Laboratory back to China—and for the forced technology transfer that has made Chinese firms notorious with Western partners.[118] The typical approach was to acquire a Soviet starter platform, upgrade it while learning how to operate it, then integrate Chinese designs with technologies acquired (legally or otherwise) or reverse-engineered from Western, especially American, sources. Focusing first on quality, China would replicate and improve on its initial platform and then scale up.

This pattern held for naval aviation, where China initially acquired a Soviet-era *Admiral Kuznetsov*–class aircraft carrier, renamed *Liaoning* in PLAN service. Purchased in a rusty, half-completed state from a near-bankrupt shipyard in post-Soviet Ukraine in 1998, the *Liaoning* was commissioned in September 2012, marking a milestone in Chinese history as the country's first-ever aircraft carrier.[119] China brought in Ukrainian personnel as advisers and technicians, built a skilled Chinese workforce around them, and acquired or copied US and other technologies to improve the original design.[120] Since then, the PLAN has been going through the demanding process of learning to operate its J-15 aircraft from the carrier's deck while building two more aircraft carriers, each thought to be larger than the *Liaoning* and equipped with catapult launch systems, a considerable advance over *Liaoning*'s ski jump; at least one of these is believed to be a fully indigenous design.[121] Following the pattern just mentioned, China's first carrier is a starter platform with limited capacity for fleet air defense.[122] By contrast, subsequent ships represent a true carrier aviation capability, and the advanced type under construction will form the basis for a mature PLAN power projection platform, aiming at a fleet of four to six CSGs in operational service by 2030.[123]

A similar pattern holds for amphibious ships, including the *Yuzhao*-class Landing Platform Dock (LPD), a type of assault ship capable of launching over-the-horizon amphibious assaults using Russian-made *Zubr*-class armored assault hovercraft and helicopters, the development of a new type of helicopter assault ship (LPH), and a design for a floating sea base. Sensors—including over-the-horizon radars, electro-optical/infrared and radar satellites, and seabed sonar networks—are being built, while UAVs are under development, with China planning for up to 41,800 drones, some to be stealth systems capable of operating from ships at sea, by 2023.[124]

The second capability set (A2/AD or, as Chinese planners call it, "counter-intervention operations") consisted of "anti-ship and other precision ballistic missiles, longer-range air defenses both land-based and sea-based, and longer-range surface-, subsurface- and air-launched cruise missiles" with anti-shipping and land-attack roles.[125] Starting in the late 2000s, the PLARF acquired multiple-launch rocket systems (MLRS) of very long range, including the A-100 (firing ten 300mm course-correcting rockets in a single salvo, with a 400-mile range) and the SR-5 (firing twelve 220mm or forty 122mm guided rockets out to 600 miles).[126] These are easily capable of striking Taiwan, which is less than 100 miles from the mainland, while ranging well beyond the island to threaten, and thereby delay or deter, incoming reinforcements. The MLRS therefore provides exactly the capability that China would have needed in order to prevent the United States from reinforcing Taiwan during the Third Straits Crisis in 1996—and its acquisition thus represents, in effect, a direct adaptation in response to that crisis.

China also mounted a major industrial and technological effort to acquire long-range anti-ship systems such as the DF-21 and DF-26, so-called carrier killer ballistic missiles capable of carrying conventional or nuclear warheads more than 2,000 miles and equipped with maneuvering reentry vehicles employing radar and other sensors to allow them to strike a moving target at sea.[127] The YJ-18 anti-ship cruise missile, launched from a submarine or surface ship with a supersonic "sprint vehicle" that can close with its target at more than Mach 3, the air-launched YJ-12 anti-ship missile, which can perform supersonic evasive maneuvers to get past shipborne defenses, and a new class of hypersonic missiles complement these ballistic systems, creating a serious survival challenge for any force trying to get near the Chinese mainland or offshore islands.

And if that force launched from anywhere near Coronado, Guam, Okinawa, Saipan, or Darwin, the presence of listening posts, which as we've seen may be present in all those locations, would make a major difference to Chinese warning time. Because of space limitations, I will not examine the PLAAF or PLARF in detail here, but the same patterns of wartime coevolution since the late 1990s, focusing on quality, then quantity, and acquisition of two capability sets (those enabling China to compete globally and those counterintervention capabilities needed to deter the United States regionally), are evident in aerospace, UAVs, missile systems, stealth, cyberwarfare and cyberspace, as in the maritime and land domains.

All these capabilities have emerged in the past two decades, and all are targeted against the United States—and toward preventing any repetition of the humiliating events of 1995–96. But this is conventional A2/AD, and in some ways the nonconventional aspect has been more important. This is reflected in the Chinese commercial penetration already discussed, which creates economic incentives for countries to restrict US access, slows American responses by forcing them to launch from farther away, and thus creates a less permissive operating environment for the United States and allies like Australia and Japan. But perhaps the most significant nonconventional A2/AD effort has been China's island-building and fortification campaign in the South China Sea.

UNSINKABLE AIRCRAFT CARRIERS

The South China Sea—lying between the southeastern Chinese mainland and what strategists call the "first island chain"—contains islands, reefs, rocks, and shoals disputed by six nations (China, Taiwan, Vietnam, Brunei, Malaysia, and the Philippines).[128] The concept of a series of island chains off the Asian mainland was originally an American one, put forward by then–secretary of state John Foster Dulles in 1951 in an effort to rally Pacific nations against China's intervention in the Korean War.[129] Dulles's idea was to use the first island chain (from Japan through Taiwan to the Philippines) to contain China and Russia, preventing Communist expansion to the second chain (stretching from the archipelago that includes Iwo Jima through the Marianas to New Guinea) or the third (from the Aleutians through Hawaii to Australasia). Unsurprisingly, Chinese planners found this notion provocative, and to counter it they developed a long-term strategy—the response had to be long-term because China in the 1950s had no resources to support it.[130]

In 1974–75, the PLAN exploited South Vietnam's preoccupation at the climax of the Vietnam War to seize the Paracel Islands, in the northern section of the South China Sea. Over the next four decades until 2014, China built 730 structures in the Paracels, which it completely controls, along with a smaller number—including barracks, airstrips, and docks—in the

Spratly Islands, occupied by several nations, farther south.[131] By 2015, partially in response to the Obama administration's rebalance to Asia, China had shifted focus to the Spratlys, turning reefs, atolls, and shoals into islands by dredging up sand, coral, and other seabed material and distributing it, landfill style, to form artificial islands.[132] By 2017, China had a total of 1,652 structures in place across both archipelagos—more than three times as many as all other claimants combined.[133] Chinese forces constructed three large bases in the Spratlys—at Subi, Fiery Cross, and Mischief reefs—and built barracks, sensor suites, harbors, and airstrips across the region. In the Paracels, Woody Island was already a well-developed base by about 2015 but has since been equipped with radars and long-range air defense missiles, extending an A2/AD "bubble" over much of the region.[134]

China claims the South China Sea as part of its EEZ and has previously suggested that its island- and base-building program is mainly designed to protect life at sea, establish permanent habitation, and enforce economic interests, as part of upholding its claim to the region under international law.[135] That claim was undermined in 2016, however, when the Permanent Court of Arbitration in The Hague ruled in favor of the Philippines in its dispute with China over the Spratlys.[136] Increasingly, Beijing has acknowledged that the program is what it always appeared to be: an effort to construct a series of unsinkable aircraft carriers to dominate the disputed region and deny others access to it. The motivation is partly economic and legal (inhabited islands, capable of independently sustaining human life, can form part of an EEZ claim, whereas submerged rocks, shoals, and uninhabited reefs cannot) but also clearly military. A network of sensors, electronic warfare systems, air bases, and missile sites across the region would allow China to dominate its entire southeastern flank out to the first island chain, providing a firm base for further expansion to the second or third chains later this century while increasing its ability to pressure regional players such as the Philippines. And there is also the issue of nuclear strategy.

China's nuclear arsenal historically relied on land-based missiles, with fixed and mobile launch platforms but no significant submarine-launched systems as recently as 2010.[137] Since then, China's growing SSBN fleet has given the PLAN a submarine nuclear option, but in order to be an effective nuclear deterrent the subs have to be survivable. The United States (with its triad of land-based, airborne, and submarine-launched nuclear weapons) and Russia (with its Arctic submarine bastion discussed in the preceding chapter) can hide missile submarines at sea, giving them the ability to survive a nuclear attack and retaliate in what is known as a "second strike," and therefore deterring other nuclear powers from contemplating a first strike. Britain keeps at least one of its Faslane-based submarines continuously at sea for precisely this reason.

But US surveillance flights into the South China Sea—of which there are thousands every year—mean that even with its SSBN base at Yulin-East on Hainan island, the PLAN has been hard pressed to hide its submarines, denying China a second-strike capability.[138] An A2/AD bubble in the South China Sea, complete with missiles, patrolling ships, and aircraft, and with radars and sensors forcing the United States and others to keep their distance, could offer that capability.[139] This might not, of course, be a bad thing—a guaranteed second-strike capability could help stabilize US-China relations through mutual deterrence. But it helps explain the surge in island construction and base-building, which has closely tracked the growth of the PLAN's SSBN fleet.

Thus, since the 1990s, China—across all areas, driven by its evolving internal circumstances and shifts in the external landscape, and spurred by a series of shocks and humiliations—has undertaken a conventional modernization that directly challenges US primacy in the Pacific and increasingly lets China compete globally. This has been the most widely discussed aspect of Chinese evolution over the past quarter century. But a smaller, less prominent group has simultaneously sought to sidestep US superiority altogether, following a different, more asymmetric path.

UNRESTRICTED WARFARE

In February 1999, two PLA senior colonels—Qiao Liang of the air force and Wang Xiangsui of the ground forces—published a short book on war.[140] Written after the Third Taiwan Strait Crisis and the Asian financial crash of 1997–98 but before the Kosovo campaign, the Belgrade bombing, Y2K, the dotcom collapse, and the 9/11 attacks, *Chao Xian Zhan* (*Unrestricted Warfare*, also known as *War beyond Rules*) is a product of its time, a turn-of-the-century period piece, yet also a remarkably prescient document. Though issued by a PLA publishing house, discussed in Party newspapers, and read by Jiang Zemin and then–defense minister Chi Haotian (suggesting official approval), it was not necessarily authoritative.[141] Rather, *Unrestricted Warfare* (URW) was a product of the debate over strategy, capability, and technology that, as noted earlier, had been roiling the PLA since 1991.

The book transcended the three main schools of thought in that debate—traditionalists seeking a return to people's war, neo-traditionalists pushing for the A2/AD and power-projection capabilities just discussed, and technologists advocating a "revolution in military affairs with Chinese characteristics"—instead presenting a response to the transformative impact of the Gulf War *on war itself*.[142] As a student reading URW at the Australian command and staff college in 2001, I found that one of the book's most intriguing aspects was precisely that it indicated the existence of an active, rigorous, and somewhat public professional debate within the PLA. Far from being a "master plan to destroy America" (as its English subtitle suggested), URW actually underlined the degree to which Chinese thinking was in flux at the turn of the century.

In an interview with a Communist Party newspaper at the time, Qiao suggested that the United States had rewritten the rules of war with its 1991 victory and that "strong countries make the rules while rising ones break them and exploit loopholes [but the United States] has to observe its own rules or the whole world will not trust it."[143] The notion of a United States dominating the post–Cold War scene as the sole remaining superpower, master of the battlefield but constrained by a rules-based order of its own creation while its adversaries are not, is one key theme of URW.

But the book's most salient feature is that it dramatically broadens the definition of war beyond battlefield dominance, suggesting that war no longer means "using armed force to compel the enemy to submit to one's will" but rather "using all means, including armed force or non-armed force, military and non-military, and lethal and non-lethal means to compel the enemy to accept one's interest" and that "non-war actions may be the new factors constituting future warfare."[144] The authors write of "trans-military" and "non-military war operations" in which all aspects of society, technology, and the international system (whether directly under a protagonist's control or not) are leveraged to achieve war aims. These might include financial disruption, currency and stock market manipulation, trade wars, exploitation of humanitarian aid and foreign assistance, cyberwarfare and information warfare, narcotics trafficking, smuggling, and other criminal activities, ecological warfare (including the creation and exploitation of artificial earthquakes or tsunamis), capturing control of key technologies (or of standards for future technologies), and "lawfare," or the manipulation of rules and norms for advantage in war or as a substitute for armed conflict.

Alongside an extension of the scope of conflict, Qiao and Wang argue for a geographical expansion: they suggest that "the battlefield is everywhere" and that "all the boundaries lying between the two worlds of war and non-war, of military and non-military, will be totally destroyed . . . and even that the rules of war may need to be rewritten."[145] The goal set forth in URW is "to use all means whatsoever—means that involve the force of arms and means that do not involve the force of arms, means that involve military power and means that do not involve military power, means that entail casualties and means that do not entail casualties—to force the enemy to serve one's own interests."[146] The difference between this vision and the US view—epitomized by Cortez Cooper's comment about a new way of war, characterized by battlefield dominance through precision strike and advanced C2 and ISR—is stark. Indeed, URW elides the distinction between armed conflict (traditionally defined as organized violence among states) and competition short of war.

Qiao and Wang offer a perceptive analysis of US conventional dominance as it existed during its peak pre-Iraq period, at the turn of the century. They note that the American way of war carries key vulnerabilities, including dependence on technology, aversion to casualties, and the need for international support. Previewing the struggle against adaptive enemies after 9/11, they note that "compared to [nonstate] adversaries, professional armies are like gigantic dinosaurs which lack strength commensurate to their size in this new age. Their adversaries, then, are rodents with great powers of survival, which can use their sharp teeth to torment the better part of the world."[147] Qiao and Wang argue that US network-centric warfare may create "an electronic Maginot line that is weak because of its excessive dependence on a single technology."[148] This is prescient, given that when URW was published, the internet and GPS were still in their infancy, social media and smartphones were yet to be invented, and Western reliance on electronic "system-of-systems" and cyber-enabled infrastructure was slight compared with what it is today. One critique is worth quoting at length:

> [The] Americans' unlimited extravagance in war has already become an addiction ... even if the American generals knew as soon as they began [the Gulf War] that they need not spend so much on this unrestrained battle banquet costing US$61 billion, using such an ostentatious battle style of "attacking birds with golden bullets," their over-extravagance would still not have been prevented. An American-made bomber is like a flying mountain of gold, more costly than many of its targets ... What you must know is that this is a nationality that has never been willing to pay the price of [loss of] life ... "Pursuit of zero casualties," this completely compassionate simple slogan, has actually become the principal motivating factor in creating American-style extravagant warfare. Therefore, unchecked use of stealth aircraft, precision ammunition, new tanks, and helicopters, along with long distance attack and blanket bombing [made the Gulf War] a sumptuous international fair of high technology weapons with the United States as the [sales] representative and, as a result, began the spread of the disease of American style war extravagance on a global scale.[149]

Qiao and Wang suggest that only an idiot would now seek to fight the United States in a symmetrical, force-on-force engagement on America's terms. In a darkly humorous passage they describe how US forces, dominant since the

Cold War, have "shrunk into a watching tree hung full with various types of sophisticated weapon fruits waiting alone for a muddle-headed and idiotic rabbit to come and knock into it. However, after Saddam knocked himself dizzy at the bottom of this tree, who else is there who would become the second type of this rabbit?"[150] (Ironically, of course, the next rabbit turned out to be Saddam again—though if his defeat in 2003 reminded everyone of the futility of fighting the United States on its own terms, the subsequent insurgency showed how vulnerable America was to amorphous resistance warfare.)

Rather than fighting symmetrically, then, Qiao and Wang suggest two general approaches to dealing with US dominance. The first, as we have seen, involves expanding the definition of war, drawing in nontraditional categories of conflict, leveraging aspects of the international system to constrain the United States, and thereby creating a bandwidth challenge where Washington would struggle even to perceive the entire range of Chinese activity, let alone respond coherently to it. This would imply a warfighting strategy akin to the aggregation model adopted by international terrorist groups such as Al Qaeda and discussed in Chapter 2 or the "combination of all forms of struggle" proposed by Marxist thinkers.[151] In capability terms, it would require expanding the tools available to the PLA for economic, technological, legal, and cyber and information operations while using nonmilitary networks, civil organizations, criminal networks, and allies (witting or unwitting) to create "trans-military" or "non-military" war operations. By definition, many such tools are not owned by the PLA, implying whole-of-government or internationally networked operations by national bodies (intelligence services or cabinet-level agencies) rather than PLA commanders.

As discussed in my opening remarks on conceptual envelopment, expanding the boundaries of war in this way could be considered a horizontal escalation in terms of both geography and scope and might be graphically represented as in Figure 5.1. Across the bottom of the diagram are categories of activity, loosely based on the PMESII model (political, military, economic, social, infrastructural, and informational) used in Western war colleges, but with the addition of criminal, legal, cyber, space,

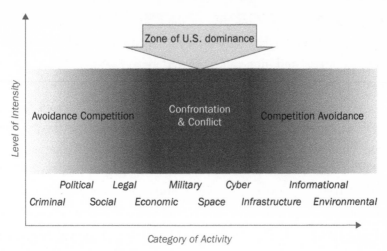

Figure 5.1. Unrestricted Warfare

and environmental categories to capture some of the other elements of URW and organized as a spectrum.[152] As can be seen, the strongest US capabilities are clustered in the center of the spectrum, from economic through military, space, and cyber capability. Thus, any Chinese attempt to escalate in this part of the spectrum would involve symmetrical confrontation and possible conflict. Outside that zone of confrontation, in the categories of social, legal, and infrastructure activity, China would be better placed to compete, given weaker American capabilities and the fact that US leaders might not consider these part of the conflict spectrum, whereas Chinese strategists applying a URW construct would. Finally, at the edges—criminal, political, and environmental warfare are examples listed by Qiao and Liang—Chinese activity would incur negligible opposition, given how far these capabilities sit outside US notions of war, creating avoidance zones that China could exploit. (We might also note that these activities "on the edge" fit the definition of liminal warfare discussed in the preceding chapter, but in a horizontal sense rather than the vertical—riding the edge of detectability and response—that we explored for Russia.)

In fact, even my broad depiction of the spectrum of activities that might be considered "warfare" under URW is considerably narrower than Qiao and Wang's. Table 5.1, adapted from their book, indicates not only how wide that spectrum might be, but how heavily it is slanted in the direction of "trans-military" and "non-military" warfare.

Two examples spring to mind: what Qiao and Wang call "drug warfare" and what they term "resources warfare." The synthetic opioid fentanyl, mass-produced in China and shipped in industrial quantities directly to the United States in powdered form (often disguised as legal pharmaceutical supplies) and to Canada and Mexico, where it is illegally trafficked into the United States, caused up to thirty thousand deaths in the United States in 2017 alone.[153] Despite agreeing in December 2018 to crack down on fentanyl production and officially declaring fentanyl a controlled substance in April 2019, China has been accused of waging a "reverse Opium War" to undermine Western societies.[154] This is almost certainly an exaggeration—there is no evidence of Chinese government sponsorship of fentanyl smuggling. Rather, lax enforcement, poor regulation, and individual corruption within Chinese law enforcement seem mostly to blame.[155] But URW creates a conceptual framework within which sponsorship of (or deliberately turning a blind eye to) drug exports to weaken an adversary and

Table 5.1 Military, Transmilitary and Nonmilitary Methods of Unrestricted Warfare

Military	Trans-military	Non-military
Atomic warfare	Diplomatic warfare	Financial warfare
Conventional warfare	Network warfare	Trade warfare
Biochemical warfare	Intelligence warfare	Resources warfare
Space warfare	Psychological warfare	Ecological warfare
Tactical warfare	Guerrilla warfare	Economic aid warfare
Electronic warfare	Terrorist warfare	Regulatory warfare
	Virtual warfare (deterrence)	Smuggling warfare
		Drug warfare
		Sanction warfare
		Media warfare
		Ideological warfare

Adapted from Qiao Liang and Wang Xiangsui, *Unrestricted Warfare*, 146.

divert enemy efforts into law enforcement and internal health crises can be considered forms of "non-military war operation."

Likewise, with "resources warfare." When the Zimbabwean leader Robert Mugabe was overthrown in mid-November 2017, initial reports suggested the ruling ZANU-PF party had engineered his ouster due to anger (mostly that of independence war veterans who have dominated Zimbabwe since the 1980s) over the ninety-three-year-old's plan to transfer power to his fifty-year-old wife, Grace, who had taken no part in the independence struggle.[156] But it soon emerged that Constantino Chiwenga, head of the Zimbabwean Defence Forces (ZDF), had visited China immediately prior to the coup, met with China's defense minister and members of the Central Military Commission, and was allegedly given the go-ahead to overthrow Mugabe—an allegation Beijing has strongly denied.[157]

I happened to be in South Africa just after the coup and spent three days with Zimbabwean democracy activists, who told a different story. According to them, the military moved on Mugabe because he was nationalizing mining ventures co-owned by the ZDF and Chinese PLA-owned companies.[158] Zimbabwe's intelligence service (the Central Intelligence Organization, CIO) and the Zimbabwean police also held large stakes in joint mining ventures with Chinese state-owned enterprises under threat from Mugabe's moves.[159] Along with diamond and gold mining, ZDF involvement in platinum and rare-earth mining has been acknowledged by the Zimbabwean government, and Russian and Chinese firms with military links have formed joint ventures with military-backed enterprises in Zimbabwe, and elsewhere in Africa, in a drive to control resources in the continent.[160]

By 2017, China not only accounted for the overwhelming majority of production of rare earths (essential components for smartphones, GPS devices, and other modern electronics) but held more than 80 percent of the world's rare-earth refining capability, giving it control over a critical twenty-first-century technology resource.[161] Beginning in 2015, Mugabe had nationalized a series of PLA-ZDF joint mining ventures, threatening both military income and Chinese control. Within weeks of the coup, Zimbabwe's new president (former ZDF commander, defense minister, and CIO chief Emerson Mnangagwa) reversed the nationalization of Chinese mines. By 2018, PLA-backed Chinese companies and Russian defense industry firms were back in previously nationalized mining areas, and in March 2019, Zimbabwe announced that Anjin Investments—a Chinese state-owned firm with links to the PLA—would return to a disputed diamond mining district in partnership with Matt Bronze, the ZDF's investment arm.[162] A month later, Zimbabwe signed a $4 billion agreement with Russia for a jointly owned platinum mine.[163]

Again, there is ambiguity here, or at least difficulty of attribution. This could all simply be a result of internal politics in the tottering ZANU-PF gerontocracy in Zimbabwe, combined with corruption among members of the military and intelligence services as well as commercial penetration by Chinese enterprises that just happen to have PLA links. Similarly, General Chiwenga's meetings in Beijing, from which he returned to Zimbabwe and immediately launched the coup, might have had nothing to do with Mugabe's plans to strip the ZDF and PLA of key resources, as China claims. But URW would consider actions to control such global resources, including covert support for coups in order to secure them, "trans-military" or "non-military" operations within an overall warfighting strategy.

The notion of opponents sidestepping US conventional dominance and exploiting around the edges, depicted here and implied in the categories of "non-military" or "trans-military" war operations, is both a rather trivial observation and an old one—as long ago as 2005–2006, the US *National Defense Strategy* and the *Quadrennial Defense Review* examined this kind of avoidance behavior in detail.[164] But in fact, what we have seen from China over the past two decades since URW was published is *not* actually avoidance but rather a combination strategy.[165] Chinese conventional military modernization—the advanced programs discussed in the preceding section—challenges the United States directly in its sweet spot, forcing American planners to keep developing conventional concepts and capabilities, and encouraging the United States to keep sinking money into costly weapons and high-end platforms to support an exquisitely expensive warfighting style. China's acquisition of carrier strike groups, fifth-generation fighter aircraft, and stealth drones, for example, encourages the United States to keep spending on such capabilities—even as the decisive action may be taking place elsewhere, in a domain that we do not consider to be warfare, through the manipulation of technology transfer, the leveraging of cyberwarfare by civilian actors, control of key mineral resources, or the purchase of strategic real estate. Simultaneously, out on the fringes, China has made swift and significant advances in fields (such as 5G mobile telecommunications, cyberoperations, nanotechnology, artificial intelligence, robotics, human performance enhancement, quantum computing, genomics and biotech, political warfare, and financial manipulation) that lie outside the ken of Western warfighters and thus invoke limited direct military competition. Our tunnel vision on terrorism after 9/11 also helped: as Qiao and Wang put it, "When a military [puts] excessive focus on dealing with a certain specified type of enemy this can possibly result in their being attacked and defeated by another enemy outside of their field of vision."[166]

Widening the definition of war involves *addition* and *combination*—bringing into play the maximum range of categories of conflict and combining them in novel ways to pose integrated challenges that an adversary may neither understand nor have the capacity to counter. Qiao and Wang suggest that "any of the above types of methods of operation can be combined with another . . . to form a completely new method of operation."[167] This combination strategy—encouraging the United States to double down on conventional capacity while simultaneously developing alternative, asymmetric options—reflects the second approach that Qiao and Wang recommend for dealing with US dominance.

In a section titled "The Side-Principal Rule," they describe through historical examples an approach to warfighting that encourages a superior adversary to expend its strength in a series of frontal efforts before responding with a decisive blow that comes from an unexpected direction, takes an unexpected form, or applies elements that an enemy has not considered. The defensive but frontal aspect (the principal) does not deliver victory but rather absorbs an enemy's strength before the decisive but indirect blow (the side element) defeats the now-weakened enemy. They argue that "the side-principal rule is opposed to all forms of parallel placement, balance

[and] symmetry [but] instead, advocates using the sword to cut the side."[168] Again, this may seem like simply a restatement of the "asymmetric warfare" or "indirect approach" familiar to any Western strategist, but Qiao and Wang see it operating at a much higher level than military strategy.

Rather, in their formulation, all military means of any kind whatsoever (conventional or otherwise) can be considered the defensive or absorptive element, whereas the decisive element consists of the novel and organic combination of "non-military" means. "It is becoming obsolete to automatically consider military action the dominant means and the other means supporting means in war . . . As the arena of war has expanded, encompassing the political, economic, diplomatic, cultural, and psychological spheres, in addition to the land, sea, air, space, and electronics spheres, the interactions among all factors have made it difficult for the military sphere to serve as the automatic dominant sphere in every war. War will be conducted in non-war spheres. [We must] be ready to carry out a war which, affecting all areas of life of the countries involved, may be conducted in a sphere not dominated by military actions . . . the war will be fought and won in a war beyond the battlefield."[169]

THE FLIP SIDE OF CONCEPTUAL ENVELOPMENT

If URW represents one aspect of conceptual envelopment—where an adversary may be engaging in actions it considers warlike, while we remain oblivious—then the flip side of the same phenomenon is that an adversary may be interpreting our behavior as warfare, while we consider it mere peacetime competition. Two sides may so misunderstand each other's concept of war that they end up fighting one another by accident.

We saw in the preceding chapter that the Gerasimov doctrine, which on the surface looks like a clever and devious approach to fighting the United States, may in reality represent a Russian interpretation of how the United States itself operates. That is, rather than a blueprint for offensive asymmetric approaches to undermine US power, the "doctrine" (not actually a doctrine, as noted) may be a defensive Russian attempt to understand the threat Moscow faces from us. In developing their capabilities for liminal warfare, as we have seen, Russian strategists may believe they are reacting to a preexisting asymmetric offensive on the part of the West. In seeking to undermine the 2016 US elections, they may have thought they were retaliating for 2012 and 1996 while neutralizing potential similar future threats from Washington. Something similar is at play in China's case, as a quick survey of what happened to URW (and its authors) after 1999 indicates.

It has been two decades since *Unrestricted Warfare* was published, and while at the time it was hard to determine the concept's degree of official endorsement—whether its authors were in the mainstream of Chinese thought, heretical outliers, representatives of a rising or falling faction in the PLA debate, or simply free thinkers—looking back now, at a distance of twenty years, it is possible to see URW in action. In 2003, China officially adopted a "Three Warfares" doctrine based on URW, creating capabilities for "psychological warfare, public opinion warfare, and legal warfare ("lawfare").[170] That same year, Beijing launched "Go Abroad," a "sophisticated neo-mercantilist offensive involving strategic investments abroad; meanwhile the PLA organized its first units for cyber warfare, and the magnitude of the so-called 'Titan Rain' offensive by Chinese hackers raised the question of the degree of involvement of the Chinese government itself."[171] By 2008, the US State Department had concluded that a "three-pronged non-kinetic war was already underway."[172] By 2009, the United States had decided to create a new Cyber Command, prompted by "mounting concerns about Chinese financial warfare and cyber-warfare capabilities."[173] And as we've seen, by 2017 China was being accused of fentanyl smuggling and of supporting the Zimbabwe coup in order to retain control over key resources, both of which actions (if indeed they were state-sponsored) would fit within URW's definitions of "non-military" and "trans-military" operations. In other words, far from being an isolated or purely theoretical work of speculation, it seems at least arguable that URW has been put into practice. The careers of Qiao and Wang after 1999 also suggest that their ideas were far from heretical.

Wang Xiangsui became a professor at Beihang University, one of China's top research universities, with a focus on science, technology, engineering, and mathematics, and highly regarded projects in aviation, spacecraft, robotics, and computer science. Qiao Liang retired as a major general of the PLAAF, having served as deputy director of the creative department of the Chinese Air Force, as well as deputy secretary general of the Council for National Security Policy Studies (a well-regarded defense think tank), and having authored five works of futuristic military fiction. As of 2015, he was on the staff of the University of Defense, China's war college, in charge of curriculum design for the education of the PLA's next generation of senior officers.[174]

In a speech to a class of elite PLA war college students at the Defense University that July, Qiao surveyed the United States' history of global primacy since the Second World War, noting that it rested in part on America's establishing "three world systems: a political system, the United Nations; a trading system, the GATT (which then became the WTO); and a monetary and financial system, the Bretton Woods system."[175] He argued that the United States achieved dominance through these rule-based systems, but then proved willing to break its own rules when they proved inconvenient (e.g., abandoning the gold standard in 1971).

Qiao went on to emphasize America's deliberate manipulation of its own currency as a means to maintain global dominance, identifying a cyclical sixteen-year pattern of a weak versus strong US dollar exchange rate engineered by the US government. He surveyed the deliberate US provocation of financial crises in Latin America (1979) and East Asia (1997) in order to control other countries' economic growth and the US decision to start wars in Iraq and Afghanistan in order to maintain control over dollar-denominated oil trading. He mentioned the financier George Soros, echoing several passages in *Unrestricted Warfare* that describe Soros as a "financial terrorist," highlighting him as one tool of the US method of manipulating others to preserve its financial imperialism.[176] He explained how the United States sponsored the 2012 "Occupy Central" movement in Hong Kong, precisely timing that uprising to coincide with the Federal Reserve Bank's phased reduction in its quantitative easing program. He went on to explain to his senior PLA audience the way in which the United States deliberately undermined Ukraine, covertly sponsoring a color revolution there with the goal of attacking the EU in order to worsen the

European investment environment, how Washington started the war in Kosovo to undermine the newly introduced euro as a potential rival currency to the US. dollar, provoked the 2012 Sino-Japanese Senkaku Islands dispute, and manipulated Filipino opposition to China in the South China Sea in order to weaken the Chinese RMB as a challenger to the dollar.[177] In other words, however brilliant his insight as a strategist, Qiao's understanding of the United States as of 2015 is, not to put too fine a point on it, completely loopy.

Not only is he deeply conspiratorial, prone to ascribing agency to things most Americans (perhaps excluding Michael Moore, Noam Chomsky, and Oliver Stone) would consider acts of random incompetence rather than deliberate malice, but his description of US motivation is one that virtually no Washington decision-maker would recognize. Beyond the basic error of treating the United States as a single, rational (let alone competent) actor, Qiao either misreads American intentions almost completely, or—what amounts to the same thing—presents a picture of the United States that bears little or no resemblance to America's understanding of itself. In this sense, the scariest thing about the rise of URW in the PLA's repertoire may not be that Chinese strategists understand our vulnerabilities better than we do, but rather that none of us has a clue about what goes on in each other's heads. This, then, is the flip side of conceptual envelopment: China's approach to warfare may now not only be so broad as to present a bandwidth challenge for the United States and other Western countries; it may also be based on a fundamentally flawed understanding of US capabilities, competence, and intent.

This, of course, raises another obvious question: Would Chinese decision-makers recognize our understanding of them? Would they recognize the sophisticated combination strategy outlined here, integrating conventional military modernization with unrestricted warfare, that Western analysts perceive? Were actions such as the acquisition of ports at Hambantota, Djibouti, and Darwin, the attempt to buy the Hotel Del, cyberespionage and forced technology transfer, the purchase of *Liaoning* and the "Three Warfares," cornering the rare-earth market, and conniving with fentanyl smugglers all carefully considered elements of an integrated strategy, or were they just a string of random events that only look planned to observers already primed to see them that way?

How unitary an actor is China, anyway? Is its strategy a conscious effort to sidestep US superiority, an unconscious adaptive response to the external fitness landscape, or just an illusion—an apparent pattern, existing only in the eyes of Western observers, that Chinese strategists would not recognize in themselves, just as we would not recognize their perception of us? As the next and final chapter will illustrate, the danger of miscalculation, of talking ourselves into war with adversaries—or of strategists misinterpreting each other's actions and thereby provoking an escalatory security dilemma that ends in the war of the century—is just one of many disturbing implications of an environment in which the dragons are back but have learned to fight like snakes and in which unquestioned US conventional warfighting dominance is very much a thing of the past.

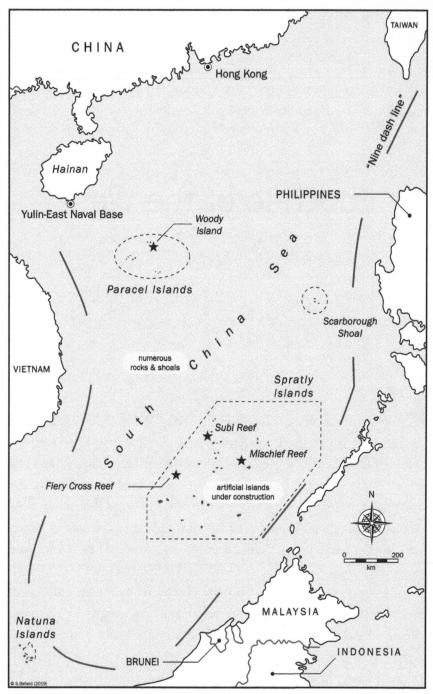

Map 6 The South China Sea

Ebb Tide of the West

Historians of the American Civil War still debate exactly when and where the Confederacy peaked. According to one school of thought, it was at 2:30 p.m. on the sultry afternoon of 3 July 1863 at a place called The Angle, a bend in the stone wall roughly one-third of the way down the Union defensive line south of Gettysburg, Pennsylvania. As Pickett's Charge foundered on the rifle fire and hasty defenses of Union forces on Cemetery Ridge, Confederate brigadier-general Lewis Armistead reached The Angle, leapt the wall with the leading troops of his Virginian brigade, put his hand on the still-hot barrel of a Union cannon, and was immediately shot down, just inside the federal line.[1] Standing on Little Round Top, the hill that overlooks the battlefield from the south, you get a clear view of what later came to be called the "High Tide of the Confederacy."[2] The spot where Armistead fell, it turned out, was the farthest reached by any Confederate assault at Gettysburg, which itself turned out to be the farthest into federal territory of any southern offensive during the war.[3] At the time, of course, nobody knew that; only in retrospect did it become clear that, for the South, it was all going to be downhill from there.

In war, we call these moments "culminating points"—when the tide turns, an advancing side's energy starts to ebb and its adversaries begin (imperceptibly at first) to push back.[4] Future historians may decide that the high tide of the West, the culminating point for our post–Cold War military supremacy, came at 5:30 a.m. local time on 20 March 2003 at the Dora Farms complex on the southern outskirts of Baghdad. At that moment the United States launched a "decapitation strike"—a preemptive attempt, in the final moments before the Iraq War, to kill Saddam Hussein and his sons Uday and Qusay. It failed.

As the strike went in, at 1:30 p.m. Australian Eastern Daylight Time, I was driving too fast in a rented car, running late for my flight from Melbourne back to Army Headquarters in Canberra. We all knew war was imminent—it had not yet been declared, but my colleagues and I had been aware of the planning for months and we knew (though our government had yet to acknowledge) that Australian special forces had crossed the Iraqi-Jordanian border almost twenty-four hours before. By now, as the final minutes of the coalition ultimatum ticked down, the Australians were already well inside Iraq's western desert, moving fast in the dark, about to fight one of the first ground engagements of the war. At 2:15 p.m. Melbourne time, over the car radio, came President Bush's voice announcing the start of the conflict. I pulled over in the middle of nowhere and sat by the road in the warm afternoon light, listening to the first hours of live coverage. I stayed as the sun began to sink in the west, and missed my plane.

Looking back, it seems clear that Dora was the culminating point for Western military power in its conventional, post–Cold War form. It marked the peak of the high-tech, intelligence-led, precision-strike model of battlefield dominance and of the related notion that battlefield dominance equaled success in war. That way of war, which the United States had pioneered in 1991 and which everyone else, allies and enemies, had been forced to reckon with ever since, began to decline from this point on.

Tactically, the strike was a masterpiece. Two F-117 stealth ground-attack aircraft from the US Air Force's Eighth Fighter Squadron, piloted by Major Mark Hoehn and Lieutenant Colonel Dave Toomey, penetrated some of the heaviest air defenses on the planet, completely undetected. They were supported by a pair of US Navy EA-6B electronic attack aircraft and two US Air Force F-16 fighters; a KC-135 Stratotanker refueled them in midair on their way to the target.[5] At 5:30 a.m. Baghdad time, Hoehn and Toomey released four of the newly developed GPS-guided 2,000-pound "bunker-buster" bombs, known as EGBU-27s, designed to penetrate hardened structures like the bunker believed to hold Saddam and his sons at Dora. The two pilots and their expensive aircraft (each with an average unit cost of 111.2 million US dollars) made it back unscathed to their base at al-Udeid, Qatar.[6] The first anyone knew of the strike was when four enormous explosions, reported by the BBC at 5:33 a.m., split the air.

The US Air Force pulled the entire strike package together in less than five hours, at no notice, in response to a pop-up target—the opportunity to kill Saddam and his sons—which in the view of analysts at CIA headquarters and decision-makers in the White House might have averted the entire war.[7] Instead of pursuing the original plan of hitting the entire Iraqi senior leadership (the coalition's "deck of cards"), decision-makers directed the air force to knock out just Saddam and his blood relatives in a single, surgical, precision strike using brand-new technology. Simultaneously with the airstrike, US Navy surface ships and submarines in the Red Sea and Arabian Gulf launched forty Tomahawk cruise missiles at the same site.[8]

This kind of battlefield excellence—demonstrating an exquisite degree of precision, highly specialized for an extremely narrow range of tasks—is the hallmark of the Western way of war as practiced since 1991. But it was tactical excellence in the service of flawed intelligence, with an ill-considered strategy and no viable exit plan. It was also enormously expensive: the "flying mountain of gold" described by Qiao Liang and Wang Xiangsui in *Unrestricted Warfare*.

Saddam and his sons were not at Dora. It turned out that a SIGINT analyst had misunderstood an intercepted conversation, and Saddam hadn't visited the place since 1995.[9] The bombs and cruise missiles missed the palace, one falling entirely outside the compound, and the bunker busters proved unnecessary, since—as ground troops discovered a few weeks later when they reached the site—the bunker where Saddam and his sons were supposedly hiding turned out not even to exist.[10] All that expensive firepower did hit something, though: a subsequent study by the International Committee of the Red Cross found that the strike killed one civilian and wounded fourteen, including nine women and a child, but no Iraqi leaders, let alone members of Saddam's inner circle.[11] Not for the first or last time, the execution was impressive but the thinking behind it was flawed.

Even more flawed was the strategic assessment that killing Saddam could render the war unnecessary—as if Saddam *was* Iraq, as if the Ba'ath Party was not the single most effective nationwide institution in the country, able to rally guerrillas and resistance cells in every Iraqi city (as indeed it did, just a few months later). This was as unrealistic as imagining that once their dictator was dead, Iraqis would shake off Saddam's enchantment and welcome the coalition like Munchkins celebrating the demise of the Wicked Witch of the East in *The Wizard of Oz*.

The beginning of the end for the post–Cold War world—the long decade of unchallenged Western military supremacy, the superb warfighting capability that had spooked the Chinese, humiliated the Russians, scared the North Koreans, and given the Iranians pause—can be dated to Dora. This strike on the outskirts of Baghdad was thus the bookend to the 1991 "highway of death": just as Desert Storm showed everyone the West's strengths, Dora and the invasion and occupation of Iraq that followed showed everybody its weaknesses. The vulnerability of precision systems to inaccurate intelligence, their dependence on data and connectivity, and their irrelevance against an amorphous, cell-based enemy who blended into the physical and human terrain of a society and culture we barely understood became increasingly obvious as the war dragged on. We could, more or less (give or take a near miss or two and a few unfortunate civilian casualties), put a bomb through any window we chose; figuring out who was behind that window, what the broader effect would be, or how to translate bomb blasts into strategic outcomes was a different matter. To reiterate

Israeli intelligence chief Avraham Shalom's comment in Chapter 2, "It was point-specific: there was no strategy, only tactics."[12]

EBB TIDE OF THE WESTERN WAY OF WAR

Since then, the Western way of war has been on the wane, even though—as at Gettysburg—the ebb tide became evident only in retrospect. Pinned in Iraq, unable to spare the resources to stop Afghanistan from sliding into chaos, we lacked the cognitive bandwidth to deal with issues beyond the immediate; to borrow a term used by aircrew like those who flew the Dora mission, we were "task-saturated."[13] While decision-makers tried valiantly to lift their eyes from the day-to-day struggle in Iraq and Afghanistan, in order to contain North Korean nuclearization, counter Russian resurgence, or compete with Chinese expansionism, we were locked on the Middle East, unable to extricate ourselves. In military parlance, we had become "fixed"—bogged down—while others maneuvered around us.

The "snakes," the nonstate adversaries we fought in the war on terrorism, engaged in what I described in Chapters 2 and 3 as a form of wartime co-evolution, evolving in direct response to our adaptation, just as we adapted to theirs, so that over time we increasingly came to resemble each other. Enemies who failed to adapt were destroyed, while those who developed certain key characteristics (or luckily had them already, as pre-adaptations) survived. Those characteristics proliferated through face-to-face contact, via social learning within human networks, and virtually, through data sharing via the dramatically increased electronic connectivity now available to everyone on the planet. Guerrilla groups and terrorist networks fissioned and merged, newer networks reflecting both the conscious lessons learned by their predecessors and the unconscious effects of blind natural selection. We began to see speciation, with different kinds of nonstate enemies emerging in distinct niches in a combat ecosystem.

At the same time, our own actions bred a better class of enemy through artificial selection, and those who survived were better able to handle the periodic population crashes that accompanied predator effects—triggered by troop surges in Iraq and Afghanistan or created by actual predators: the

MQ-1 "Predator" drones (and later MQ-9 Reapers) that we employed to strike targets in Pakistan, Yemen, Somalia, and elsewhere. Those who survived this cycle of repeated near-death experiences became tougher, smarter, stealthier, and much more lethal over time: survival of the fittest in action. They also started increasingly to look like us, with ISIS fielding special forces, drones, engineers, and eventually tanks and artillery.

The ways in which this process of coevolution affected us were no less dramatic. We oriented ourselves to the main threat, continuously improving our capability for precision strikes, drone warfare, counterinsurgency, special operations raids, and a host of other tools and techniques. As the threat evolved, so did we—each side taking its evolutionary cues from the other in an adaptive two-part dance. This was absolutely necessary to deal with dangerous adversaries in the moment, and it made us operationally better, of course. But each innovation brought a corresponding improvement in the enemy, in a tit-for-tat evolutionary arms race that seemed never-ending (and increasingly costly) even as other challenges proliferated. And the better we adapted to the nonstate enemy, the more specialized and focused we became, making ourselves less fit for other adversaries, even as state-based threats multiplied.

Those state adversaries, the "dragons" not directly involved in the war on terrorism, were able to sit back, watch, and innovate in a more conscious manner, initially following what I described in Chapters 1 and 2, following Stephen Rosen's framework, as a peacetime pattern of concept-led innovation. But they too switched into wartime mode when they began to treat us as a "pacing threat," matching their development to our capabilities and weaknesses. In Russia's case, as explained in Chapter 4, the shift to a war footing began around 2011 and was fully in place by 2014. The New Look reforms, prompted by perceived poor performance in Chechnya and Georgia, helped modernize Russia's military and created the basis for subsequent success in Crimea, Ukraine, and Syria. Simultaneously, liminal warfare—involving patriotic hackers, militias, the political warfare "firehose of falsehood," *coup de main* operations optimized for speed, surprise, ambiguity, and political leverage—evolved from a blend of old Soviet ideas, newer notions like reflexive control, and emerging technologies such as social media. Massive improvements in air defense, tactical nuclear weapons, and missile technology helped Russia develop A2/AD bubbles in critical regions like the Baltic, Ukraine, and Syria. And the world's second-largest thermonuclear arsenal provided the ultimate deterrent umbrella.

China, for its part, moved on multiple fronts simultaneously. The country's industrialization, urbanization, and economic development—averaging 9.55 percent annual GDP growth rate from 1989 to 2018—dramatically increased its market clout, and Chinese leaders took conscious steps to convert this into political and military influence.[14] As discussed in Chapter 5, the 1991 Gulf War convinced Chinese leaders that they needed to catch up in conventional terms, and the Chinese military has most certainly done so, modernizing its air and space capabilities, building a blue-water navy almost from scratch, and investing in the professionalization and "informationalization" (to use the Chinese term) of the People's Liberation Army. Today the PLA—with advanced ground, air, naval, space, cyber, and rocket forces—is second only to the US military in size and capability (though it lacks combat experience, for the moment).[15] An extremely capable set of A2/AD systems—including the construction of unsinkable aircraft carriers in the South China Sea—is helping China dominate sea space out to the first island chain. Advanced long-range missile systems such as the DF-26 Anti-Ship Ballistic Missile now arguably give China the ability to kill a US carrier strike group on the move, at sea, anywhere west of Guam or north of New Guinea.[16] Thus, in military terms, China is not rising; it has risen. And its return as a maritime power with global reach—for the first time since the mid-fifteenth century—is transformative.

Since June 1999, after what Beijing considered the outrage of the Belgrade embassy bombing, China too has been in wartime adaptation mode, treating the United States as a pacing threat, developing capabilities specifically to counter and compete with America. *Unrestricted Warfare*—with its principles of addition and combination, and the conceptual broadening of conflict into "nonmilitary war operations" discussed in Chapter 5—appeared at this time, seeking to overwhelm us with multiple small challenges across the widest possible range of categories and geographies, taking advantage of our narrow and expensive way of warfare by breaching its boundaries. Beijing's formal adoption of the "Three Warfares" doctrine four years later gave this approach official approval. It has been fully implemented since, through China's strategic real estate acquisitions, technology harvesting, industrial-scale cyberwarfare, attempts to control future technologies such as 5G mobile telecommunications, "lawfare," space warfare, organized crime linkages, and espionage and influence operations in the West.

Because their situations (and hence their starting positions in a dynamic adaptive landscape) are different, China and Russia have taken distinctly different evolutionary paths, and today the threats they pose differ also. The danger from China is one of conceptual envelopment, a horizontal expansion of warfare to the point where we may not realize we are in a conflict until it is too late or may end up fighting each other though neither side necessarily wants war. The risk from Russia is that of vertical signature manipulation, of subliminal shaping and liminal maneuver, followed by a sudden strike so ambiguous that we may still not be sure it is really happening, even in the moment. The danger is that we may be "decisively shaped," so that before the first tank rolls we have already lost. If China's approach is a mindset shift, Russia's reflects a time shift, moving decisive action back in time to defeat us before our superior battlefield capabilities can become relevant. But despite these differences, two key similarities are worth noting.

First, neither China nor Russia is pursuing a purely conventional or a solely nonconventional path; rather, each is following both simultaneously. That means we can't simply stop building ships or buying tanks and aircraft and go fully asymmetric instead. If we did that, we would soon be outclassed conventionally, making war both more dangerous and more likely. On the other hand, if we focus just on conventional capacity, betting on a model of battlefield dominance that is already waning, we open ourselves to what Qiao Liang and Wang Xiangsui called the "side-principal rule": exhausting ourselves against adversaries who deliberately encourage us to overcommit in our traditional areas of strength (and our conceptual comfort zone) while simultaneously preparing an unconventional sidestroke from an unexpected direction.

If the first similarity seems scary, the second is scarier: it is the possibility that none of our leaders actually understand each other at all. At the end of Chapter 5, I quoted a speech by Qiao Liang which suggests that, despite the conceptual genius he demonstrates in *Unrestricted Warfare*, he has a disturbingly distorted perception of Western motivations and methods— arguing that Washington started the war in Kosovo to undermine the euro, that George Soros is a financial terrorist, and that the United States consciously manipulates its economy and currency on a regular sixteen-year cycle in order to trigger economic crises as a way of controlling its geopolitical rivals. The easiest riposte to Qiao's argument, of course, is that even if the US government wanted to do this, it simply lacks the competence to coordinate it (as a friend in the CIA put it years ago, discussing this kind of conspiracy theory: "If. Fucking. Only").

Yet this is the identical argument you hear from Russians responding to American media derangement since the election of Donald Trump. Reading the Moscow media or listening to what Russians tell each other about "Russiagate," it's clear that many are mystified by the paranoia and hostility suddenly directed their way and baffled by the idea that their government could be considered competent enough to pull off the plots alleged against it or that Putin and his cronies have anywhere near the control to do so.[17] Valeriy Gerasimov, supposed author of the eponymous doctrine, seems to have thought he was describing our way of war, not Russia's, and Russian planners tend to ascribe the same evil genius to us that some Westerners believe of them. In other words, it's entirely possible that none of us actually know what we're doing, that far from having cunningly executed master plans we are all reacting instinctively, often incompetently, in the moment—stumbling around in a fog, bumping into things without really understanding each other. This mutual incomprehension is a recipe for miscalculation, and nuclear miscalculation at that.

Owing to space limitations, I have not included specific chapters on North Korea and Iran, though as I explained earlier, each of these "little dragons" exhibits characteristics similar to those of the larger ones. North Korea's skill in coaxing concessions out of global powers on all sides while continuously furthering its nuclear weapons program has helped it build not only an atomic arsenal but, in all probability, an ICBM that can now deliver a thermonuclear or boosted atomic warhead anywhere in the continental United States.[18] The stakes for war on the Korean Peninsula are thus higher than ever, even as Kim Jong-un consolidates power internally and reaps the benefits—in prestige and credibility—of his completed ICBM program and his series of summits with Presidents Trump, Xi, and Putin. Like Moscow and Beijing, Pyongyang pursues its goals through both conventional and nonconventional means—nuclear weapons, advanced conventional artillery and non-nuclear rockets, and massed military capabilities, on the one hand, and cyberwarfare (North Korea has been called a "cyber-superpower"), state-sponsored drug trafficking and other organized crime, and espionage and influence operations, on the other.[19]

At the other end of Asia, the Islamic Republic of Iran is today the biggest beneficiary of the Iraq War and the Arab Spring, with unprecedented influence in Iraq and a powerful position in Syria since its successful bailout of Bashar al-Assad in 2015–17. Iran—with Russia and Hezbollah—now shapes events in Damascus, with de facto control of a corridor from the Iranian border with Afghanistan all the way to the Israeli frontier at the Golan Heights. Though its weapons program seems to have slowed since the 2015 nuclear deal, Iran retains atomic ambitions and a full nuclear fuel cycle, is actively acquiring A2/AD and missile systems from Russia, and is exploiting the lifting of export and travel restrictions to strengthen its regional reach.[20] At the same time, Iran (like North Korea) can call on Russia and China for support in international forums or in economic or military terms. The dragons, big and little, are not monolithic—but they do collaborate.

The West, as I have used the term here, is not a monolithic entity either, and arguably never was. Rather, it is a loose collection of countries with shared history, values, culture, and interests but dramatically differing strategic circumstances. Thus, the policies of Australia, Canada, Germany, and the United Kingdom toward Iran, China, and Russia, for example, are all different from those of the United States. Likewise, each has its own security needs and budgetary constraints, and allies have had to adapt to the uniquely dominant American way of war over the past quarter century as much as adversaries.

For some, the goal has been to keep up with US capability in key areas only—for Australia these include fifth-generation fighter aircraft, top-tier special forces, amphibious helicopter assault ships capable of doubling as midsized aircraft carriers, a growing submarine fleet, and world-class SIGINT. The new Australian Space Agency, the creation of the Australian Cyber Command, and moves to improve ballistic missile defense show Canberra's increasing concern about space, cyber, and missile threats.[21] In the United Kingdom, the purchase of two new full-size aircraft carriers has become central to national defense and important for post-Brexit national prestige. With its own budgetary and personnel limitations, Britain keeps up in terms of quality across a wider range of areas but compromises on quantity, a necessary choice given the enormous share of defense spending that will be consumed by the carriers.

For others—Germany springs to mind, but many NATO nations are in the same boat—the ability to rely on US strategic deterrence to offset a lack of domestic defense spending has enabled them to focus on other areas such as international assistance or to devote industrial resources to civilian manufacturing, while maintaining large defense export industries. And a third group of countries, including those in the Baltic and Scandinavia, along with Japan, now find themselves on the frontline, living inside the Russian or Chinese A2/AD bubble (or both, in Japan's case) and subject to the kinds of frontier incursions and covert disruptions described for Norway in Chapter 4. These countries are doing what they can (including defensive guerrilla warfare) to deter malign activity, build resilience, and make themselves harder targets for a potential aggressor. Yet they are also continually looking over their shoulders at a fractious America whose patience and commitment seem to be wearing thin, even as its military dominance is declining.

DECLINE OF THE WEST?

There has been much talk in recent years about the decline of the West. Fareed Zakaria has written, in generally favorable terms, of a "post-American world" where the very success of the West's global agenda of economic up-lift and political liberalization has, by definition, enabled the rise of others and thus the relative decline of the United States and its allies.[22] He starts his book with the hopeful assertion that this is "not about the decline of America but rather about the rise of everyone else," a sentiment that al-ready sounded overly optimistic in 2008 but is even less convincing after the global financial crisis, Libya, Syria, Crimea, ISIS, the European migra-tion crisis, the 2016 election, Brexit, and "Russiagate."[23]

According to Jonah Goldberg, whose book was published after all those things had happened, we face the "suicide of the West," in which a rebirth of tribalism, populism, nationalism, and identity politics is de-stroying American democracy.[24] Zakaria and Goldberg come from dif-ferent frequency bands on the political spectrum, and while neither is focused mainly on military matters, both tend to link what happens in the United States with the fate of a broader West, and both understand Western military decline as tied to a general trend. They differ most on the matter of inevitability. Goldberg begins his concluding chapter by quoting the late columnist Charles Krauthammer, arguing that "decline is a choice."[25] By contrast, Zakaria prefaces his introduction with a quote from the British historian Arnold Toynbee, arguing that "growth takes place whenever a challenge evokes a successful response that, in turn, evokes a further and different challenge" and that this process might repeat itself indefinitely, even though "a majority of civilizations have failed, as a historical fact."[26]

One of Toynbee's major influences was the German philosopher of his-tory Oswald Spengler, whose best-known book—*The Decline of the West*—was published in two volumes in 1918 and 1923. Spengler was highly influential in the first half of the twentieth century, with his notion that civilizations were super-organisms that followed a life cycle through stages of birth, growth, flourishing, decline, and death and his prediction that Western civilization was declining and would reach a state of crisis around the year 2000.[27] His ideas reflect, in part, the collapse of civilizational confi-dence on all sides at the end of the Great War—the same image of organic decay appears, for example, in the Anglo-American poet Ezra Pound's 1920 lament that during the war "there died a myriad, and of the best, among them, for an old bitch gone in the teeth, for a botched civilization."[28]

More broadly, Spengler drew on a long intellectual tradition of social cycle theory, treating civilizations as his unit of analysis and using biological systems as analogies for social change. That tradition runs back through Herbert Spencer (who coined the phrase "survival of the fittest" in 1864) to Edward Gibbon's *History of the Decline and Fall of the Roman Empire* (published between 1776 and 1789 during the American and French Revolutions), to Ibn Khaldûn's *Muqaddimah* of 1377, to the organic theories of society and state advanced by Plato in *The Republic* and Aristotle in *Politics*.[29] Following Toynbee, many modern writers invoke the notion of a civilizational life cycle—Carroll Quigley's *The Evolution of Civilizations*, Paul Kennedy's *The Rise and Fall of the Great Powers*, Niall Ferguson's *Empire*, and Samuel Huntington's *Clash of Civilizations* are just a few of many examples—frequently enough to suggest that the idea of inevitable decline is intuitively persuasive.[30]

Whether or not Western decline is inevitable in geopolitical or world-historical terms, it seems clear that the utility of the current Western military model as a set of techniques and technologies is fading. The propensity to lose effectiveness over time is probably inherent in any successful military system. As I suggested in Chapter 2, the more successful any particular method, the greater the selection pressure it imposes on adversaries and therefore the faster they adapt in response. The model of battlefield dominance that the United States pioneered in 1991 transformed the environment for everyone else, allies and adversaries alike; that model peaked between about 1998 and 2003, and it has been eroding ever since, as others have figured out how to fight us.

STRATEGIC RESPONSES

It seems possible—though by no means certain—that actions we take now in response to that erosion can either accelerate or delay the decline and can steer it toward a hard crash or alternatively achieve a soft landing. It might even be possible to pioneer a new military model, thereby reshaping a dynamic fitness landscape for our adversaries once again. As we consider how to respond, there are essentially three courses of action open to us at the strategic level. We might refer to these as "doubling down," "embracing the suck," and "going Byzantine."

Doubling Down

A strategy of doubling down would start from a philosophical position that rejects the inevitability of Western decline. It would argue (against Toynbee, Spengler, Ferguson, Kennedy, and the rest) that there is no inherent reason why US dominance should not last forever, and it would be committed to spending and doing whatever it might take to preserve that primacy. This strategy would regard America's role as guarantor of the post–Cold War order—the set of political, economic, and security institutions that defined the "international community" of the 1990s—as both beneficial and essential for the international system. This, indeed, has been the consensus among elites in the United States since the end of the Cold War.

In this view, since the United States props up a generally beneficent global order, what is good for America is, by definition, good for the world and for every other country. It follows that whoever opposes the United States is deeply misguided (at best) or an enemy of the international community and that America's unique role in protecting and preserving that community gives it the unique right to do whatever is needed in response (even, perhaps especially, to do things that would be unacceptable for any other power). Thus, America need not be formally constrained by global rules, since as the creator and sustainer of the Western-led world order it can always be relied on to act in the best interests of the entire system.

If this recipe for liberal interventionism sounds outrageously naive now, it's worth remembering that to many policymakers these ideas seemed self-evidently true in the 1990s. Indeed, they were so axiomatic that they shaped a generation of foreign policy, media, and national security elites in Washington, on both sides of the political aisle. The formula was most succinctly stated by Secretary of State Madeleine Albright, who told the television host Matt Lauer in February 1998, "If we have to use force, it is because we are America. We are the indispensable nation. We stand tall. We see further into the future."[31] These ideas were not unique to Albright or to Democrats, nor did they end with the 1990s: rather, they ran like a crimson thread throughout the Reagan and Clinton administrations, both Bush presidencies, and that of Barack Obama (we will come to President Trump in a moment).

Unapologetic American exceptionalism of the Albright variety is harder to sustain when you can no longer count on a military model that delivers guaranteed overmatch against all likely opponents—especially when those opponents have watched you conspicuously fail to "see further into the future" or "stand tall" in places like Iraq, Afghanistan, Syria, Libya, and Ukraine. As I suggested earlier, since the moment the Dora strike failed and Saddam's weapons of mass destruction turned out to be as ephemeral as his imaginary bunker, the credibility of that military model (and of its originator) has been ebbing away.

As a result, there are two key problems with a strategy of doubling down on American conventional dominance. Even if it were feasible to fund the perpetual capability upgrades needed to preserve American primacy, the first problem is the one we have explored in this book—that of adaptive responses from evolving state and nonstate enemies. If our adversaries have figured out how to invalidate our conventional model, then we are past the point of diminishing marginal returns. The more we spend on conventional capabilities, the less advantage our expenditure buys: DF-26 carrier-killer missiles are cheaper, are faster to build, and have longer range than the strike radius of carrier-based aircraft. As the strategist T. X. Hammes points out, if our principal naval platforms are already range-obsolete, building more of them will not help.[32] In that circumstance, far from preventing decline, doubling down might merely hasten it by expending our strength more rapidly.

The Third Offset Strategy proposed by the Pentagon during the second term of the Obama administration and one of a suite of such "offset strategies" mentioned in Chapter 1—the idea that advanced technologies (such as autonomous systems, artificial intelligence, human-machine teaming, and "network-enabled, cyber-hardened weapons") could offset a loss of conventional battlefield dominance—recognized this problem.[33] The third offset strategy sought tools to restore the effectiveness of the American way of battle, but without questioning its conventional boundaries. As such, it too was a doubling down—retaining the strategic concept while replacing high-tech with different tech—and was more a technological innovation policy than a new strategy. In any case, the strategy ended with the Obama administration and (since rivals like China are already equal to or ahead of the United States in many of the same technologies, and in others, such as genomics, human performance enhancement, quantum computing, and military biotechnology) would probably have bought only limited time.[34]

The other problem is simpler but starker: whatever the consensus within the Washington beltway, the electoral evidence of 2016 strongly suggests that the American people are no longer willing to carry the cost of their government's claim to be the indispensable nation and guarantor of the international system, let alone to do and pay what would be needed to preserve that position. With the national debt at $22 trillion and counting, and rising troubles at home, the need for the United States to maintain eight hundred overseas military bases in eighty countries seems, to put it mildly, not immediately obvious to the average American citizen.[35] After nearly thirty years of the post–Cold War order, of conflicts in Iraq, Afghanistan, Libya, Syria, and elsewhere, the failure of "experts" and institutions during and after the 2008 financial crisis, and the refusal of elites to even acknowledge the problem, people no longer seem willing to bear the burden of primacy, even if losing it would undoubtedly suck.

Embracing the Suck

In military slang, "embracing the suck" means making your peace with something unpleasant but unavoidable, accepting its inevitability, then doing your best to mitigate its worst aspects. In this context, a strategy of embracing the suck would start from a theory of reality opposite to that of doubling down. It would accept that all empires eventually decline, so to the extent that the post–Cold War order is a form of American-led Western imperium, this too will pass. Instead of exhausting scarce resources and public patience in pursuit of perpetual primacy, this strategy would attempt to manage our inevitable decline, engage in sensible retrenchment, and seek a soft landing.

President Obama appeared to have come into office with some version of a retrenchment strategy in mind: his notions of "leading from behind," the rebalance to Asia, withdrawing from Iraq and Afghanistan, reaching an accommodation with Iran and Russia, and leaving a light footprint (drones, intelligence, and special forces) in combating terrorism made the most sense in this context.[36] That strategy has been criticized as "declinism"—the idea that if we are going to lose anyway, we should just get it over with—but this is unfair to President Obama.[37] The fact that it did not work in practice was not necessarily the fault of the strategy itself, though the precipitate withdrawal from Iraq, half measures in Afghanistan, failed intervention in Libya, and equally failed nonintervention in Syria certainly did not help.

Beyond any errors of execution, President Obama's strategy was mugged by reality, or maybe just ahead of its time. The Arab Spring upended the Middle East just as America withdrew from Iraq; the resulting rise of ISIS forced reengagement despite the president's ardent desire to leave; the Syrian war demanded responses from America and Europe that neither was prepared to provide; Russia's seizure of Crimea and intervention in Syria surprised the White House; and the administration's focus on the Iran deal, the Asia rebalance, and the Russia reset left limited bandwidth for other issues. And domestic issues—the worst financial crisis since the Great Depression and contentious health reforms—crowded out foreign affairs in the administration's crucial early years.

President Obama's strategy of managed decline (or of deliberate disengagement from imperial overstretch, to put it more positively) was arguably also sandbagged by his own administration. Hillary Clinton as secretary of state was firmly in the Albright tradition of robust liberal interventionism, as was her successor, John Kerry; the military team tasked with designing the Afghan surge brought the president a plan to win the war, when he had asked for a plan to leave; diplomats dealing with Libya and Syria continually agitated for more robust responses, with one ambassador dying on the job and another retiring early in protest.[38] More broadly, the entire foreign policy and national security establishment, across the executive and legislative branches, had grown up in the era of post–Cold War American primacy, and the assumption of US exceptionalism and indispensability was so deeply ingrained that it was hard to shake. Like President Trump, whose supporters have inveighed against a supposed "deep state" conspiracy to undermine the policies of a democratically elected president, President Obama arguably also experienced resistance from his cabinet and from the permanent US bureaucracy.

Paradoxically, it may take a Trump to execute the Obama strategy. Precisely because the current president comes from so far outside the liberal interventionist tradition, because his administration has been boycotted and undermined by the same national security establishment, because his populist instinct is to play to the American people's loss of patience with the burden of empire, and because (to put this in the kindest possible way) he seems unbothered by the traditional niceties that beltway elites—including, or perhaps especially, the news media—expect from a president, Trump has the freedom to step back from a quarter century of overstretch.

His approach to the Middle East amounts to a version of a traditional offshore balancing strategy, outsourcing actions to local allies such as Israel and Saudi Arabia, preventing any single rival (Iran, China, or Russia) from dominating the region, disengaging from large-footprint or long-duration military operations, and ending the post-9/11 wars of occupation.[39] Likewise, in Europe, the president's policy on NATO involves replacing an unconditional security guarantee to every alliance member (under Article V of the North Atlantic Treaty) with a conditional commitment to defend European countries only when doing so directly furthers America's interests, not automatically as a matter of course. Again, however Trump-skeptical the advocates of offshore balancing—principally, the strategists John Mearsheimer and Stephen Walt—may be, this approach can be seen as a version of that strategy.[40]

President Trump's attitude to NATO has triggered howls of outrage from the policy establishment. But on its face, it is a perfectly rational response to the problem of a NATO alliance now so big (and so threatening to Russia) that an unconditional security guarantee risks dragging nuclear powers into general war through a local crisis, in a twenty-first-century re-play of the Kaiser's "blank check" to Austria-Hungary in July 1914.[41] The president's mixed messages on Article V—reluctantly supporting it when pressed, while informally setting limits to its applicability—send clear sig-nals to NATO nations to avoid risky behavior on the alliance's frontier. This helps mitigate the moral hazard of free-riding inherent in an unconditional guarantee—the unequal burden-sharing that American presidents of both parties have complained about for decades (even while treating the guar-antee that encourages such free-riding as an article of faith). The NATO secretary-general Jens Stoltenberg, in 2018, credited the new approach with increasing defense spending across the alliance, which, he argued, helps deter Russian adventurism.[42] The articulation of limits on Article V may also help reassure Russia, whose perception of NATO encroachment is, as we have seen, a key source of confrontation.

Despite its rhetoric, the Trump administration's practical actions toward Russia—arming Ukraine, abrogating the Intermediate-Range Nuclear Forces Treaty in retaliation for Russian breaches, developing new mis-sile systems, strengthening ballistic missile defense, and ramping up the European Deterrence Initiative, all while saying friendly things about Vladimir Putin—show a similar combination of practical robustness and rhetorical de-escalation. Thus, if anyone could successfully embrace the suck, it might be the current president. But there are nevertheless two key problems with this approach. One is specific to the current US administra-tion, the other inherent in the strategy itself.

As noted, President Trump's Russia policy is actually more forceful in many ways than his predecessor's. But whatever the reality, the "Russiagate" collusion allegations have tainted Trump. Some of the president's behavior, such as his pro-Russian tweets and his bizarrely submissive demeanor to-ward President Putin at their Helsinki summit in June 2018, makes strategic sense as part of rhetorical de-escalation, but it hardly helps him shake the equally bizarre conspiracy theories accusing him of being a Manchurian Candidate.[43] It is also not obvious that the current administration, however sound the president's instincts might be, has the coherence or competence to put them into practice. More important, domestic political pressure to be tough on Russia locks the administration into a confrontational stance, making it harder to act on the realization that Moscow and Washington actually have considerable common interests. Notably, the rise of China (which Trump clearly considers the critical geopolitical, economic, and security challenge for the United States in this century) is at least as much a threat to Russia's geopolitical position as it is to America's. Likewise, Islamic State threatened Russia at least as directly as it threatened the United States, so that selective cooperation on shared interests might make sense even against a backdrop of broader competition. But media hysterics and partisan rancor make that outcome politically impossible while President Trump remains in office. (Ironically, this suggests that if Russiagate did originate in a Russian liminal warfare operation, as discussed in Chapter 4, it backfired spectacularly.)

The other problem is more basic and relates to the fact that a strategy of accepting and managing a loss of primacy implies transition to a successor. That successor could be a great power, a concert of powers, a supranational entity, or some form of meta-national system. (Decline with no successor is also theoretically possible but practically unlikely, since the very reason for Western decline is that challengers and would-be successors have already arisen.) To be acceptable to the West, a successor would need to be strong and not unfriendly: that is, it would have to be capable enough to carry the burden of preserving a stable global system while having values and interests close enough to our own that, even after a transfer of leadership, Western countries and values could prosper in a post-Western world order. This sounds unlikely in the abstract, but it has actually happened before—recently when Great Britain, exhausted after the world wars, passed the baton to the United States between 1947 and 1956, then went on to recover and prosper, and in classical antiquity when ancient Rome conquered the Greek city-states in the second century BC, then absorbed and propagated Hellenic civilization while giving Greece the longest period of peace and prosperity it had ever experienced (albeit after a violent transition as it brought the Greek states under Roman hegemony).

The problem, of course, is that it's not clear such a successor exists, at least not yet. Supranational institutions are too weak, too dependent on US hard power, or too lacking in legitimacy to serve as successors to the current system. Likewise, neither the authoritarian, revisionist government of Russia nor the Communist, expansionist government of China shares our values and interests to the point where Westerners would trust them as successors. Arguably, the Chinese people are closer to the West than their rulers, given their strong preference for democratized technology, commerce, and trade and constant calls for human rights and democratic freedoms. We should also remember that the People's Republic is not the sole source of Chinese culture—Hong Kong, Singapore, Taiwan, and millions of overseas Chinese in communities predating the Communist Party by decades are equally legitimate in civilizational, if not geopolitical terms. Still, values aside, neither Russia nor China is currently strong enough—and Russia likely never will be—to sustain the burden of sole global leadership.

For its part, India has an interest in competing with China, and the world's largest democracy shares many values with Western countries. But for all its economic growth and military modernization, India is likely to focus on its own development in the near future. A multipolar post-Western order, with the West as just one grouping alongside Russia, China, and India, is thus a potential outcome—one that Russian foreign minister Sergei Lavrov, among others, has advocated.[44] In this context, India's boycott of China's Belt and Road Initiative (in contrast to Pakistan's eager acceptance of it) gives Western countries significant common interest with India and could help create shared strategic goals over the long term. A multipolar order of this kind could result in a stable (or unstable) competitive balance of power or in some variant of a concert of powers where rivals selectively cooperate to preserve stability, perhaps through supranational institutions like a modified UN. In any case, it would spell the end of the global environment as it has existed since the Cold War.

A variant of this might see the United States ceding leadership, or perhaps just shedding certain responsibilities, to others in the current Western alliance. This could involve NATO countries or individual allies like Britain,

Australia, Japan, Colombia, the UAE, and South Korea taking much more active and self-reliant regional roles while America steps back (perhaps temporarily) to focus on resilience and recovery at home. President Obama tried this under the rubric of "leading from behind," but at least in the case of European and Middle Eastern allies, it proved ineffective due to lack of military capacity and political will, along with the well-founded belief that America was not really serious about stepping back.[45] But in the event of true US disengagement—which would reshape the evolutionary landscape for allies overnight—we could expect rapid adaptation.

Going Byzantine

This leaves a final strategic option—playing for time, influencing the environment to shape our adversaries' next cycle of evolution in directions favorable to us, and adopting military methods that optimize long-term affordability and sustainability rather than short-term battlefield dominance. I have called this the Byzantine option in reference to the eastern Roman Empire, which is known to us as Byzantium but "was never anything but Roman to its rulers and their subjects" and survived more than a millennium, from the partition of the Roman Empire in January 395, through the fall of Rome in September 476, until the Ottoman conquest of Constantinople on 29 May 1453.[46]

This strategy, too, would start from the philosophical position that all civilizations, certainly all empires and great powers, eventually decline. But it would be informed by what we have seen in this book: namely that during the quarter century of Western battlefield dominance since 1991, our own military model has shaped the evolutionary landscape for all other actors. Changing that model might therefore reshape the environment, and so influence adversaries' next cycle of adaptation in ways that favor our long-term interest. By "long-term interest" here, I do not mean the perpetuation of US primacy in its current form (which, by definition, this strategy assumes to be impossible). Rather, I mean setting conditions to preserve peace and prosperity, to "assure the survival and the success of liberty," even in a world that the West no longer dominates militarily.[47] This is in some ways a soft-landing strategy, but one which recognizes that, since no viable or acceptable successor currently exists, our best bet is to play for time and encourage one to emerge.

We might do that in much the same way the Byzantines did, by adopting some of their methods. These included developing new military models (in part by selectively copying Byzantium's enemies); broadening the conception of successful strategy beyond battlefield dominance; consciously optimizing for long-duration sustainability; focusing on financial and societal resilience; maintaining a selective edge in certain key technologies; keeping enemies distracted with internal challenges; and turning adversaries against each other. This was, in effect, a drawn-out, centuries-long strategic delaying action—albeit one that incorporated periodic offensive phases.

The western Romans had succumbed to a flood of barbarian immigrants and hordes of sword-wielding Goths and Vandals arriving from the north in huge numbers, by land, on foot. For their eastern cousins in Constantinople, the threat was much more diverse: fast-moving horse archers, sometimes in enormous numbers (the Huns, Avars, and other steppe nomads) or accompanied by infantry and armored lancers (the Persians and Saracens) or siege cannon (the Ottomans), approaching across a wide arc from the Eurasian steppe and Black Sea coast in the north and northeast through the eastern and southeastern Mediterranean, by land, river, and sea.[48] Later in its history, Byzantium also faced threats from farther west in the form of the Normans, the Frankish kingdoms, the Fourth Crusade, and the militant merchant republics of Venice, Pisa, and Genoa.[49]

Dealing with this diversity of enemies along an extended imperial frontier, the Byzantines developed unique fighting forces that combined armored horse archers with lancers, specialized heavy and light cavalry, fast-moving light infantry, and agile amphibious forces, selectively borrowing ideas and technologies from their enemies.[50] They maintained an edge in key technologies, often with a defensive bent, such as fortification, siege warfare, and the fearsome incendiary weapon known as Greek Fire.[51] They created relatively efficient taxation systems and civil service structures to support mobile, highly trained professional forces that almost never fought alone, instead serving as the hard core for a swarm of auxiliaries, allies,

mercenaries, surrogates, and partners, and they maintained small but capable expeditionary strike forces as quick-reaction reserves.[52]

The Byzantines also evolved a strategy of defensive guerrilla warfare,
"in which enemy forces were allowed to penetrate the borderlands before being cut off from their bases and harried and worried until they
broke up or were forced to return to their own lands."[53] Byzantine forces
denied frontiers using "scorched earth" tactics and encouraged resilience
in endangered regions through home guards, surveillance and reporting
networks, and a system of mountain fortresses that became refuges during
enemy incursions.[54] Byzantine emperors did launch offensive expeditions,
but these usually had limited goals—for example, to preempt, disrupt, or
punish enemy attacks.[55]

The eastern Roman Empire did not define success solely by battlefield
dominance and the exaction of tribute. Rather, it broadened its notion of
war beyond the military to a model of flexible statecraft that included diplomacy, capable (if informal) intelligence services, and the soft power of religious authority, which the Byzantines weaponized to align allies and divide
adversaries. The goal was not to win every engagement, let alone to defeat
every enemy, but rather to preserve strength for the long haul. Emperors
were not above paying tribute (euphemistically known as "subsidies")
to deter attackers, partnering with enemies in times of weakness (as in
the peace treaty with Persia in 562 that blocked the Huns—an enemy
common to both the Persians and Byzantines—from vulnerable provinces) or sponsoring rebellions in their enemies' heartlands (as in Sicily
during the legendary Sicilian Vespers in 1282, part of a broader Byzantine
effort to deter a French-Italian invasion).[56] By the time Byzantium fell, its
thousand-year survival—and the fact that it seeded the Italian Renaissance,
which transformed Europe in the decades after the Ottoman conquest of
Constantinople—arguably made it one of the most successful great powers
in history.[57] In the next and final section I will examine ways in which we
might follow similar approaches; for now, though, we should note that as
for the other courses of action, there are objections to going Byzantine.

One is that it might already be too late. Byzantium was not founded when
Rome was on its last legs, but 150 years earlier when the empire was at its

greatest geographical extent, albeit already suffering strains. The Roman military model—as dominant, in its day, as post-1991 US methods—was still going strong when the emperor Constantine I, in AD 330, selected the Greek town of Byzantion as his eastern capital, 146 years before the fall of Rome to the barbarians. Today we see not only a waning of Western military dominance (which I have argued began in 2003) but also collapsing international credibility through failures in Iraq, the rise of ISIS, chaos in Libya, Syria, and Yemen, and a combination of bluster and ineffectiveness on Iran, North Korea, and Venezuela. We have also seen a loss of domestic credibility by governments, through the global financial crisis (2008) and subsequent unrest (from 2011 onward), loss of societal cohesion in Europe and the United States, "boomerang effects" from terrorism abroad, and collapse of confidence in institutions and elites. This loss of confidence was readily apparent in the European currency crisis (2009–16), mass migration and the backlash against it (from 2015, including a run of related terrorist attacks), the Brexit debacle (since 2016), and the rise of "illiberal democracy" in European and Asian countries (from 2016). President Trump's election and the associated hysteria and political polarization are symptoms, not causes, of this string of breakdowns—though it (and he) have undeniably exacerbated those breakdowns' effects—suggesting that future Western leaders will start from an even weaker position.

On balance, I think, this objection is real but overstated. True enough, the West has suffered a series of setbacks since high tide, and the evidence of ebbing influence is around us not just militarily but in political, social, and economic terms. But we are far from collapse: by the time Byzantium was founded, the Roman Empire had already been divided, reunited, governed in four parts, then partitioned again. Major defeats had rocked the empire's eastern and western zones. Nothing as severe as this has yet afflicted the West—though arguably it could be around the corner if we fail to adapt.

Another objection is that we may not have the political will (or may lack sufficiently capable leaders and institutions) to pull off a complicated— one might almost say Byzantine—strategy of this kind. This may well be true: as we saw in previous chapters, Western leaders since the Cold War have played a strong hand very poorly at times, and as just noted, economic and political stresses are appearing in many Western societies. Likewise, elected political leaders in democracies are not famous for their competence in managing complex situations over long time frames. But this problem is not unique to a Byzantine strategy: it applies to all the courses of action outlined here, not just this one.

A final objection is that the military leverage available to Western countries may no longer be sufficient to shape the landscape in which adversaries evolve. If our military model has already eroded to the point that it has now been rendered irrelevant by our enemies' adaptation, then changing that model would likely have little impact on their subsequent evolution. Likewise, factors outside our control, such as the connectivity explosion, the democratization of lethality, emerging technologies, and climate change (which is extending military competition into unprecedented regions of the Arctic, for example) may influence others' evolution more than our actions.[58] This is a more serious objection, and dealing with it will depend on developing a new military model.

A NEW MODEL

That new model would start with selective learning from the enemy, since many of the technologies and tactics adopted by our adversaries are also open to us. I absolutely do not advocate the brutality, fanaticism, corruption, or authoritarianism of these adversaries, by the way—I merely note that many of their methods are neither good nor bad in themselves. Western democracies could adopt or modify some of them without compromising our values and ethics or destroying the things that make our societies worth fighting for.

Russian notions of decisive shaping, escalating to de-escalate, creating political leverage through limited-objective *coup de main* operations, using military means to achieve political objectives and vice versa, and emphasizing creative ambiguity rather than fully covert activity would make sense for the West. Russian advances in hypersonic missiles, electromagnetic pulse weapons, thermobaric (heat-and-blast) munitions, and other specialized systems are also worth studying—and, ironically, are things Russia likely lacks the resources to exploit fully, whereas we could. China's expanded conception of warfare, mobilizing multiple dimensions of national power well outside the traditional military-owned domains, is something that Western countries already do, in theory, but which could benefit from better conceptualization and organization. The PLA's anti-ship ballistic missile technology, like its creative approach to ballistic missile defense, could be worth studying for countries like Australia, Japan, and the Scandinavian and Baltic states that are now inside, or on the edge of, adversary A2/AD bubbles themselves.

Our terrorist enemies, whose brutal behavior we rightly abhor, have nevertheless pioneered technologies (such as tele-operated weapons and improvised precision fire control systems for artillery and mortars) and tactics (such as the use of small, stealthy, multipurpose autonomous battlegroups that move and fight in an agile, dispersed combat swarm) that we could copy. These could be significantly enhanced by the insertion of certain high-tech tools currently being developed by Western militaries; these adversaries' networked, swarming urban tactics also offer many lessons. The recruitment of patriotic cyber militias by Russia, China, Iran, North Korea, and others is equally open to us (though in our case these would be defensive "cyber home guards")—and in fact the Baltic states are leading the way on this. Estonia's Cyber-Defense Unit, part of the Estonian Defense League (Eesti Kaitseliit)—a volunteer national defense association that acts as an extended adjunct to Estonia's defense forces—is one potential model here.[59]

Another area in which the Baltic states are leading the way is defensive guerrilla warfare. This too resembles elements of the Russian approach, but it applies them (in line with a Baltic and Scandinavian tradition going back more than a century) for defensive purposes. Like the Byzantine guerrilla defense noted earlier, this is designed to deter invaders by making clear the costs and difficulties that would confront them. Should deterrence fail, the same methods prevent invaders from sustaining their presence at acceptable cost. And when an attacker has a choice of routes, a guerrilla defense may help to channel the attack into approaches or methods that are easier to counter. Local defense associations (as in Finland, Latvia, and Estonia), combined with mobile response forces, supported by specialist reservists trained and equipped for modern guerrilla warfare in their home districts and backed by capable ISR and community information networks, can help create societal resilience and serve as a sustainable, lower-cost military model.[60]

While not strictly a case of learning from enemies, this is an example of learning from countries—Finland, Scandinavia, and the Baltic states— that adapted by copying their own primary adversaries, the Soviets, in an environment where they lacked the military dominance we have taken for granted since 1991. These techniques also offer a way of building common purpose within society and linking remote or minority communities in frontier areas (such as the Arctic frontier discussed in Chapter 4) to a broader national identity. Countries like Australia and Canada, each—like Scandinavia—with enormous, underpopulated, economically vital but strategically vulnerable northern regions, have historically had their own irregular defense units (Australia's Regional Force Surveillance Units and the Canadian Rangers) and could usefully consider how these might look in a future operating environment.[61] Partnering with private industry— especially providers of essential services and utilities such as fuel, electricity, food, water, and connectivity—to reduce risk to critical infrastructure and increase survivability against both natural and adversary-driven hazards is a key aspect of defensive resilience, which NATO leaders have described as the first line of defense and is also an approach several of our enemies (notably, China, Russia, and Iran) have adopted, albeit in very different ways.[62]

Another way we might selectively copy our enemies' adaptations would be to use the connectivity and remote engagement capabilities that allow terrorists to radicalize individuals in our own societies (discussed in Chapter 3) to reach out and mobilize friendly individuals and groups ourselves. There is no technical limitation (though there are legal and policy restraints) on the ability of unconventional warfare organizations within Western militaries to exploit exactly the same kinds of connectivity that allowed, say, Anwar al-Awlaki to mobilize individuals in Canada, Britain, and the United States, as a means of mobilizing friendly networks in otherwise denied environments. Techniques like leaderless resistance, remotely organized guerrilla operations, ad hoc self-organizing cells, and singletons or "solo-cells" are all as open to us as to our adversaries, though of course Western countries would put them to different purposes.

Beyond selectively copying our enemies, we could consider selectively targeting their vulnerabilities. For example, Russia and China are far more sensitive to casualties than they might superficially appear to be. Russia's use of "little green men," patriotic volunteers, and private military companies in Ukraine, Syria, Venezuela, and elsewhere exposes Moscow to risks when these poorly controlled para-state actors commit atrocities (as in the shooting down of Malaysian Airlines MH17 in 2014). Conversely, the Kremlin's reluctance to acknowledge such groups can create significant backlash when they suffer casualties—as happened to the Wagner Group, a private military company owned by a close confidant of President Putin. Wagner may have lost up to 218 employees, who were killed during a battle with American-backed Kurdish forces in Syria in early 2018, in part because Russia was unwilling to acknowledge their presence and therefore unable to call off US air strikes, despite a deconfliction hotline designed for just that purpose.[63] Likewise, the one-child policy has made China's PLA an army of only sons.[64] By 2006, only-children made up "more than half of the force, up from just 20 percent a decade earlier, giving China the largest-ever military with a majority of only-children."[65] Even since the cancellation of the policy in 2016, China's birth rate has continued to fall and shows no signs of returning to replacement rate, causing Chinese researchers to observe that aging, rather than overpopulation, is China's main demographic challenge.[66] Chinese parents' completely understandable reluctance to lose their "little emperors" in anything less than a major national emergency imposes significant limits on what China can do with its forces and on how many casualties it can tolerate.[67] Over time, an aging population may discourage military adventurism—though the male youth bulge generated by the one-child policy may also portend greater propensity for involvement in war, at least until that demographic bulge passes through the Chinese population pyramid.[68] In any case, despite Qiao Liang's criticisms in *Unrestricted Warfare*, China may therefore be becoming as casualty-averse as the United States—and indeed, unwillingness to accept mass casualties in conventional conflict may be an internal or subconscious driver for the kinds of "non-military war operations" advocated by Qiao and Wang.

Likewise, China's extensive strategic real estate acquisitions, discussed in Chapter 5, can be seen as aggressive attempts to penetrate and co-opt our economies, but they also represent a series of hostages that China has given the West. If our governments were to nationalize these Chinese-owned facilities or seize their assets in times of crisis, this could cost Chinese state-owned enterprises billions. Chinese strikes against Western cities could also be costly for Chinese companies, imposing limits on Beijing. To be sure, China could exploit its presence in, say, the port of Rotterdam to disrupt the container terminal there, but since that port's largest container operator (COSCO) is a Chinese state-owned enterprise, this would be an expensive "own goal." It's possible to overstate the effect of interdependence in deterring conflict—wars among economically interdependent countries are not actually particularly rare—but the extent of Chinese commercial exposure to the West creates a larger attack surface, increasing China's vulnerability in the event of war and raising its exposure to sanctions short of conflict.[69]

Finally, much has been made of China's increasingly sophisticated surveillance state, its ability to ingest and process vast amounts of personal and behavioral data about Chinese citizens inside and outside the country, as well as the government's use of facial recognition, social credit scores, and mandatory smartphone apps to keep extensive tabs on its people's every move. If this is true, then China has very helpfully created a portal into its own internal conditions that (one might speculate) every Western SIGINT agency and foreign intelligence service could hypothetically be seeking to hack and exploit.

We could summarize these elements of a new military model as getting out of our defensive crouch—ceasing to regard hybrid operations as abnormal or problematic activities outside the bounds of acceptable practice in war and instead diving into them as a new, potentially very advantageous operating environment ripe for exploitation. I am reminded of Australia's leading jungle warfare expert, Brigadier "Ted" Serong, who observed on arriving in Vietnam in 1962 that "conventional soldiers think of the jungle as being full of lurking enemies. Under our system, we will do the lurking."[70] In this sense, the future is hybrid and gray: focusing solely on *counter*-hybrid operations would be a mistake, while actively exploiting them could form part of a new-model approach.

Another element in a new model would be broadening our conception of successful strategy beyond battlefield dominance. As we have seen, the Western way of war is really a way of battle—an operational style—rather than a strategic system.[71] Repeatedly since the Cold War, our armed forces have defeated enemies on the battlefield, only for our governments to fail to translate those battlefield successes into advantageous, enduring strategic outcomes. Broadening our approach would mean creating new capabilities within civilian agencies (or repurposing military capabilities developed for tasks like counterinsurgency) to enable that translation.

Civil-military officials—whom we might call envoys—appropriately trained and prepared, able to meld intelligence, diplomatic, economic, in-formational, and military tools into a single local strategy, empowered and supported from home capitals, and able to draw on specialized funds and niche capabilities, would be essential in this strategic system. Developing them would require a mindset shift among many (if not all) Western dip-lomatic services, as well as the military. But if correctly constructed, such a system could generate integrated teams able to shift seamlessly between military-led operations during crisis and war and civilian-led activities during competition short of conflict.

One reason this has not happened in the past is that aid agencies, in-telligence services, and diplomatic organizations are generally very small, and they have repeatedly been swamped by gigantic military formations with overwhelmingly enormous personnel and equipment assets. During my time in Iraq in 2006 and 2007, for example, US Mission Baghdad had around thirty-two hundred staff members, of whom almost three thousand (including twelve hundred civilians) worked on military-related coun-terterrorism and counterinsurgency operations, leaving less than 50 ac-tual diplomats in-country. In many operations since the end of the Cold War, our forces have thus been unbalanced and lopsided, with the military crowding out civilian capabilities, leaving soldiers feeling put upon as they pick up the slack for tiny civilian agencies, while the civilians feel their expertise and local knowledge are undervalued.

Adopting a Byzantine-style policy, emphasizing small-footprint operations optimized for low cost and long duration, would mean that, rather than deploying the maximum available military forces and then expecting civilian agencies to scale up to match, we would deploy balanced missions with an appropriate civilian-military mix for the mission, which of necessity would imply far smaller forward-deployed military forces, tailored down to meet the civilian element rather than vice versa. Historical examples (Oman in the 1970s, El Salvador in the 1980s, Afghanistan in 2001, and Syria in 2015–18) show that light-footprint missions with a strong civilian component can achieve results out of proportion to their size. Even if they do not achieve such outcomes, limiting the forward footprint can significantly reduce costs in terms of money and lives, letting operations continue much longer before they become too expensive (or too politically controversial) to sustain.

Now—lest anyone misunderstand this as an argument for continuing the "forever wars" that I have criticized throughout this book—I should be clear that this is absolutely not a call for continued wars of occupation in distant places, like the operations we launched after 9/11. As discussed earlier, militant liberal internationalism and the associated Western interventionism have turned out extraordinarily badly since the 1990s, and even if they had not, the model of military dominance that underpinned them has lost much of its effectiveness since 2003. Rather, this is an argument for including more civilian, and potentially far less military, capability as part of a policy of persistent forward presence in order to head conflicts off at the source, detect threats ahead of time, contain costs, and thus increase long-term civilizational sustainability. Combined with electronic connectivity to create forms of "virtual persistent presence," this could potentially mean that even when our forces do have to deploy, they need never again go in "blind."

The sustainability benefits could indeed be significant. As one example, combat deaths among American forces during the entire anti-ISIS campaign in Syria between 2015 and the end of 2018 totaled only two people. Another four were killed in early 2019, bringing US combat deaths incurred in return for the total territorial destruction of ISIS in Syria (completed in April 2019) to only six.[72] While any loss of life is heartbreaking—and of course many thousands of our local partners and millions of civilians have been tragically killed, wounded, or put to flight in the fight against ISIS—such a low US military death toll has kept the conflict largely off the front pages of Western newspapers, increasing its political sustainability. In the words of a colleague working on Syria in 2016, "You can go long, or you can go large, but you can't do both." A Byzantine strategy—and the military model to support it—would be optimized for the former. But it would not call for a return to forever wars; rather, in line with the offshore balancing strategy I discussed earlier, we would avoid conflicts unless they directly affected our interests and focus instead on withholding and building up our military strength rather than expending it in a series of far-flung wars of choice.

Two final aspects of such a strategy are worth noting: the need to maintain a selective edge in certain key technologies and the need to give enemies internal challenges to distract them or turn them into mutual adversaries. Selective technologies for a strategy of long-term sustainability would optimize not for technological excellence per se, but for maximum technological leverage per unit cost. This principle would suggest a larger number of small, relatively cheap, multipurpose platforms rather than a small number of "flying mountains of gold" or their land and maritime equivalents. Airborne platforms—both piloted aircraft and UAVs—would be critical for a long-term, light-footprint strategy, but they would need to be carefully designed (and creatively financed) for economic sustainability. The same would be true at sea: submarines, SEALs, and a large number of anti-ship ballistic missiles might make more sense than a few very expensive aircraft carriers, for example. A very large number of advanced, portable anti-armor weapons might make more sense than a few expensive tanks. Ballistic missile defense and A2/AD systems might be more sensible than offensive missiles, as well as cheaper, for most Western countries. And certain high-technology inserts—artificial intelligence being the obvious example—might make more sense as onboard narrow systems than as ambitious "general AI" for most applications.

Getting both financial and human costs under control in this way would help position us to give the enemy a bandwidth problem—including potential internal challenges that would soak up lots of cost, attention, and effort, and might therefore delay or divert an adversary from operations directed against us. This is not the place to canvass options of that kind, but it might hypothetically make sense to think through how such operations would work in a Byzantine strategy.

THE LONG TWILIGHT STRUGGLE

Would the model just described work, and could we execute it? If by "work" we mean reversing the declining effectiveness of the current Western military model or preserving American preeminence forever, then the answer is clearly no. As I have outlined in this book, the Woolseyan security environment as it existed from the end of the Cold War until about 2003 is no more. From 2003 to 2013 we persisted with a Woolseyan security model in a post-Woolseyan environment and paid the price in lost influence, imperial overstretch, and cascading chaos. From 2013 onward, the rise of state competitors—the return of the dragons—made it clear that our adversaries have learned how to fight us, increasingly invalidating the much-vaunted superiority of our post–Cold War battlefield dominance. At the same time, the resurgence of enemies like ISIS, who learned to fight like states (even as states like Russia adopted techniques from nonstate actors), showed how both categories of enemy had learned from each other even as they adapted to us.

Creating a new, more viable military model will not, in itself, fix the West's problems. As our quick survey of strategic options has shown, there are serious political, fiscal, and social objections to any course of action we might choose. On balance, I think a Byzantine strategy offers the best chance of success—if by success we mean achieving sufficient strategic delay to allow an acceptable successor order to emerge. But no military solution can remedy the civilizational and cultural strains that underpin our loss of primacy, nor (in a democracy) should soldiers seek to solve problems that are rightly the province of politicians and their bosses, the people who elect them. Rather, the imperative for military thinkers in this new environment is to break out of our conceptual comfort zone, consider the consequences of the past quarter century of Western dominance and its effects on our adaptive enemies, and develop viable options that might help our societies evolve and survive for the long twilight struggle ahead.

Epilogue

A Better Peace?

*N*orfolk, Virginia, 9 April 2019

James Woolsey was fifty-one in February 1993 when he gave the testimony with which I began this account; he was seventy-two when we first met to discuss my early research for this book. Today, as I interview him at a NATO conference, he is seventy-seven years old, sharp as a tack, and as outspoken and future-focused as ever.

As CIA director, Woolsey had a famously distant relationship with President Clinton, allegedly never meeting the president one-on-one and quipping, "Remember the guy who crashed his plane onto the White House lawn? That was me trying to get an appointment to see President Clinton."[1] He ended up taking the fall for a Russian penetration of CIA that had begun almost a decade earlier: Aldrich Ames, a counterintelligence officer, betrayed a dozen American agents to the KGB, causing "catastrophic and unprecedented loss of Soviet intelligence sources."[2] Though Ames had been spying since 1985, CIA had been pursuing an unsuccessful mole hunt since 1989, and the joint investigation that uncovered Ames was initiated under Woolsey in March 1993, he was blamed by Congress and resigned in December 1994.[3] By then, the Soviet Union was long gone: Woolsey's career, ironically, was cut short in one of the final aftershocks of the Cold War, by the same dragon whose death he had declared in February 1993.

Thus, it was from outside government that Woolsey watched the unfolding of the security environment he had predicted: escalation in Bosnia, war in Kosovo, NATO expansion, chaos in the former Soviet Union, civil wars in Africa and narcoterrorism in Latin America, nuclear proliferation, the rise of transnational terrorism, and repeated clashes with Iraq through the 1990s. In general, looking back, we can say that he called things correctly: the issues he identified as critical for post–Cold War security turned out to be the right ones, and they played out pretty much exactly as he had predicted. He did make his share of errors, most notably on Iraq: in 1998, he was one of the signatories of a letter advocating the overthrow of Saddam Hussein, and on the morning after 9/11, speaking on CNN, Woolsey was one of the first to blame Iraq for the attacks (along with the 1993 World Trade Center and, initially, the 1995 Oklahoma City bombing) and to call for war against Saddam.[4] In this, of course, he was not just mistaken; he was also a contributor to the media and congressional echo chamber of that period, which ultimately led to the Iraq War. This in turn hastened the decline of US military power, bringing an end to the post–Cold War security environment of US conventional dominance that Woolsey had so ably analyzed ten years earlier.

Where Woolsey differed from others, however, was in his willingness to recognize flaws in US intelligence on Iraqi weapons of mass destruction, reflect on the implications, and quickly perceive the perils of becoming bogged down in Iraq—particularly given US dependence, until the fracking and natural gas revolutions of the past decade, on imported foreign oil. He was one of the first to make the national security case against fossil fuels, arguing for a shift to renewable energy and distributed electricity generation as a means of alleviating American strategic vulnerability to oil shocks and of reducing the global impact of instability in the Middle East.[5] As an investor, he put his money where his mouth was, into solar power and alternative energy. He later focused on securing the electrical grid against cyberattack, on critical infrastructure protection, and on "hardening" systems against electromagnetic pulse weapons and natural hazards such as solar storms (known as "space weather") that can knock out an electrical grid just as surely as an enemy attack.[6]

In Woolsey's view, the rise of China, the return of Russia, and the emergence of North Korea and Iran as regional risks are important challenges—China most of all. But domestic political polarization, the collapse of confidence in national institutions, and the rise of authoritarian populism give him even more concern. Likewise, modern dependence on systems such as smartphones, satellites, and GPS that can easily be disrupted, as well as vulnerabilities to climate change, pandemic disease, economic disruption, and electrical grid failure, occupy his mind as much as military enemies.

Hardening and redundancy are components of what we now call "resilience," and today Woolsey focuses as much on the internal sources of strength that make societies and cities capable of withstanding and responding to shocks and stresses as he does on external threats. And one of the most important aspects of resilience is adaptation—both in the moment, when societies have to unlock adaptive resources quickly to deal with natural or human-caused disasters, and between shocks, when learning from disruptions and evolving new tools and methods to reduce future fragility are key capabilities.

We have spent much of this book exploring how state and nonstate adversaries evolve and how they have adapted to the Western way of war in the quarter century since the end of the Cold War. The eroding effectiveness of Western military methods during that period emerges clearly through the case studies of Al Qaeda, Hezbollah, Russia, China, Iran, and North Korea. But there is one final point to mention, one that Woolsey's recent emphasis on resilience makes clear—the need to understand what militaries and military systems are *for*.

J. F. C. Fuller—the irascible, controversial, brilliant British infantry officer, pioneer of tank warfare on the western front, and military theorist of
the twentieth century—wrote in 1926 that the object of war is not victory,
but a better peace. Echoing Clausewitz, Fuller argued that "it is only as a
means, and not as an end, that [military success] is of value," for the goal
in war is to enforce or safeguard "a policy the aim of which is to maintain
national liberty and prosperity. From this we may deduce [that] a military
victory is not in itself equivalent to success in war."[7] We might put this another way: when a military method becomes an end in itself, when victory
on the battlefield becomes its sole rationale, and when it ceases to support
the national need for liberty and prosperity, that military method is unsustainable, and it has to change.

Despite what soldiers (or the public) might think, the purpose of
Western military methods is not to achieve an unbroken string of battlefield victories. Nor is it to preserve Western primacy, which itself is also
only a means to the end of securing the liberty and prosperity of nations
that ascribe to what we might loosely call the tenets of Western civilization.
These include human rights and the rule of law; respect for the dignity and
property of the individual; freedom of speech and belief; rationalism, innovation, and scientific discovery; and forms of government that are respon-
sive to the will and interests of the citizen. Military systems, in societies that
embody these principles, are always dangerous, and they become positively
pernicious when they begin to undermine the very liberty and prosperity
they were instituted to defend.

We are not there yet. But the erosion of Western military effectiveness
since the Cold War is not of merely military importance. Rather, that
ineffectiveness—our repeated failure to convert battlefield victory into
strategic success or to translate that success into a better peace—is a key
reason for the seemingly endless string of continuous, inconclusive wars
that have sapped our energy while our rivals prospered, tied us down while
new threats gathered, and contributed to internal unrest across the world.
In evolutionary terms, not only is our existing military model ineffective,
it is maladaptive—that is, our approach is now so ill-suited to the environment that it is actively harming us.

I have sketched several options for dealing with this challenge. In essence, my recommendation is for a return to offshore balancing, disengaging from permanent wars of occupation, ceasing any attempt to dominate rivals or spread democracy by force, and focusing instead on preserving and defending our long-term viability. Rather than dominating potential adversaries, our objectives can and should be much more modest: to prevent them from dominating us, to do so at an acceptable and sustainable long-term cost, and to avoid any action that harms the prosperity and civilizational values that make our societies worth living in.

Disengaging from wars of occupation, which—to be fair to both President Obama and President Trump—we are well on the way to doing, will create an opportunity for us to focus on societal resilience and, most important, on domestic political reconciliation at home, while maintaining pressure on adversaries using light-footprint methods (including the Byzantine strategy discussed in the preceding chapter) abroad. Ultimately, such an approach might even shake up the adaptive landscape, directing adversaries into evolutionary pathways that favor our survival and success.

But reforms of this kind can work only if elected leaders and citizens in Western societies use the breathing space thus created to do the hard work of reconciling, recognizing where we went wrong in the quarter century after the Cold War, and determining a way forward that our methods can sustain and our peoples can support. That kind of societal adaptation, more than mere military modernization, will be critical if we are to find a better peace.

ACKNOWLEDGMENTS

So many people contributed to this book, and in so many ways, that it's even harder than usual to know where to begin in acknowledging their help. Let me start, though, with James Woolsey—one of the busiest people I have ever met—who very generously granted me two long interviews several years apart, sharing significant details without ever asking to review, or seeking to influence, what I wrote. My great friend Nadia Schadlow introduced me to Woolsey and set up our initial meeting; far more important, her excellent book *War and the Art of Governance: Consolidating Combat Success into Political Victory* (Georgetown University Press, 2017) shaped my view of the relationship between battlefield dominance and long-term success in war.

David Betz of King's College London, who rejoices in the title of Professor of War in the Modern World (and lives up to it with gusto), gave me an immensely helpful suggestion—that I should examine the work of the late Rafe Sagarin on ecosystems in crisis as a way of understanding military adaptation—and offered insight into frontier fortifications as a way of analyzing military systems. Also at King's, Sir Lawrence Freedman generously shared his views on Cold War and post–Cold War strategy during several panel discussions and conversations. His recent book, *Ukraine and the Art of Strategy* (Oxford University Press, 2019), came out too late to influence my Russia chapter, but I avidly checked it once it did appear, to discover what I had gotten wrong!

Hew Strachan, one of the world's authorities on the First World War and the founding head of the Changing Character of War program at Oxford University, has very kindly helped me formulate my thoughts on military adaptation for more than a decade. His ideas on military adaptation on the western front in 1914–18 and social learning within the British and Commonwealth armies are reflected throughout this book. He also pointed me toward some critical developments in naval warfare and in the Arctic.

Professor Strachan's Oxford colleague Dr. Rob Johnson offered useful comments on frontier warfare in British India and put me onto his namesake, Professor Dominic D. P. Johnson of St Antony's College, Oxford, whose work on the application of natural selection to irregular and asymmetric warfare profoundly influenced my chapters on nonstate actors. Martin Van Creveld, during several conversations in Denmark in 2018, gave me a number of ideas about the applicability of these ideas to states, as well as the evolution of Israeli defense thinking.

Justin Bronk and Igor Sutyagin's work on Russian ground force modernization, along with Jack Watling and Peter Quentin's writings on Russian political and information warfare—as well as Linda Robinson's broader work on modern political warfare—were hugely helpful. Keir Giles, during several informal conversations, reshaped my understanding of Russian motivations and very helpfully published an outstanding book on the subject just as I was finalizing my Russia chapter, allowing me to quote him extensively. Lieutenant General Ben Hodges, when serving as commanding general of the United States Army Europe, helped me understand Russian hybrid tactics on NATO's frontiers (and inside the alliance) and the thinking behind major Russian exercises in 2017. His analysis, published in 2018 after his retirement, of Poland's Suwałki Corridor—the forty-mile gap between the heavily armed Russian enclave of Kaliningrad and the border of Belarus, the modern equivalent of the Cold War's Fulda Gap—is invaluable for anyone trying to understand the new threat in central Europe. Ben's successor, my old friend from Afghan days, Lieutenant General Chris Cavoli, gave me some hugely useful comments while I was working on the Russia chapter.

On China, John Owens—one of my oldest friends and a China and Korea watcher of note—gave me some important ideas on the Tiananmen Square incident, the impact of the modernization of the People's Liberation Army on China's outlook, North Korean attitudes toward China and Russia, and the formation of the People's Armed Police. Professor Conrad Crane of the United States Army War College pointed me toward the impact of the one-child policy (and the proliferation of only-children within the PLA) on Chinese thinking. My former PhD supervisor, Professor Carlyle Thayer of the University of New South Wales, shared several analytical pieces on China's relationship with Vietnam and on the 1979 Sino-Vietnamese War. He also—as my undergraduate politics tutor, way back in 1987—first awakened me to the interlocking security challenges of the South China Sea, a region where his predictions have, unfortunately, proved all too accurate.

In Africa, Jonathan Oppenheimer, through his Brenthurst Foundation, generously sponsored the fieldwork in East Africa and Somaliland that let me observe China's expansion in those regions and offered extraordinarily helpful perceptions on regional resilience and economic development. Dr. Greg Mills—who leads the Brenthurst Foundation, whom I first met in Djibouti, and whose work on Africa, Latin America, and Afghanistan has made him a leading authority on how states and cities succeed and fail—helped me understand the geopolitics of resource extraction, the workings of several African states, the nature of societal resilience, and the history of key regions in Africa. His patience and willingness to tolerate stupid questions and intermittent communications still astound me.

My editors, David McBride at Oxford University Press and Michael Dwyer at Hurst & Co., were, if anything, even more tolerant of delays and zigzags as this book took shape. The ISIS irruption in Iraq and Syria in 2014, after I had already been working on this book for more than a year, forced me to set it aside and instead write a completely different one, *Blood Year*, which soaked up a lot of effort in 2015–16 and delayed this book for so long that I am sure none of us really expected it to ever be finished. Their characteristically helpful and gentle criticisms on various drafts of this manuscript helped tighten my prose and question my assumptions. Also at Oxford, Sarah Russo has become an expert, over the past decade, in the fine art of hunting me down and making me reply to emails from weird places—a skill I hope she'll need far less in her new adventures. Henry Rosenbloom at Scribe Books was endlessly patient as I worked on the manuscript, though he would have been entirely justified in getting frustrated at my dalliance with another Melbourne-based publisher on *Blood Year*. I hope the result turns out to be worth the wait!

I would not recommend that anyone write a book, especially a fieldwork-driven book of this kind, while simultaneously trying to run a company. I was extraordinarily lucky in that regard: the team at Caerus Associates provided extremely valuable analysis on the evolution of ISIS and developments in Iraq, Syria, and Libya, which shaped Chapters 2 and 3. My partners at Cordillera—Alex Case, Roman Ortiz, and Gordon Pendleton—proved absolutely reliable even when I disappeared for long periods to write or do field research. Without the complete trust and mutual respect in our small team this would have been impossible, and they have my eternal gratitude. Roman's work on Europe and in Southeast Asia, Gordon's on urbanization, resilience, and regional issues in several locations central to this book, and suggestions by Jim Wetzel, Graham Fairclough, and Alex Case on the liminal warfare model proved extremely helpful.

A number of institutions—foremost among them the New America Future of War Program in Washington, DC, along with Arizona State University's School of Politics and Global Studies, the School of Humanities and Social Sciences at the University of New South Wales in Canberra, and the Royal United Services Institution in London—provided funding, access to research materials, mentoring, or collegial support as I struggled to get this book back on track after the ISIS detour. Peter Bergen, Daniel Rothenberg, and Jeff Kubiak, in particular, have been endlessly tolerant and supremely helpful.

Several of those who helped me the most—analysts in Norway, security police in Finland, a government official in Somaliland, two officers of the British Royal Marines, one current and two former CIA officers, an expert on Chinese organized crime, a Russian security analyst, and troops of the Sør-Varanger garrison on the Norwegian-Russian border—provided extraordinary insights (and in some cases wonderful hospitality), yet cannot be thanked by name. I hope they will accept my gratitude nonetheless. As ever, any errors, omissions, or misstatements are mine entirely.

As always, and with relief that this is finally finished, all my love and respect go to my wife, Dr. Janine Davidson, who scrupulously refrained from criticizing the many parts of this book where she knows the underlying material far better than I do. My parents, John and Anne Kilcullen, gave me several key insights into the historical and cultural aspects of the book, while also generously making me welcome even as I acted like a hermit while finishing it, as did my siblings and their wonderful families. Finally, to my son, Harry, with much love—and many thanks for helping me figure out Chinese pronunciation and orthography—this book, and our future, are dedicated.

Chapter 1

1. This account is based partly on Woolsey's published testimony and partly on the author's email correspondence with Woolsey in 2014 and 2015, and on interviews with Woolsey in 2015 and 2019.
2. Mark Bowden, *Black Hawk Down: A Story of Modern War* (New York: Atlantic Monthly Press, 1999).
3. United States Senate, *Hearing before the Select Committee on Intelligence of the United States Senate, One Hundred Third Congress, First Session, on Nomination of R. James Woolsey to Be Director of Central Intelligence, Tuesday, February 2, and Wednesday, February 3, 1993*, 76, https://www.intelligence.senate.gov/sites/default/files/hearings/103296.pdf.
4. Madeleine Albright, *Madam Secretary: A Memoir* (New York: Harper Perennial, 2003), 182.
5. See Gary Smith and St. John Kettle, eds., *Threats without Enemies: Rethinking Australia's Security* (Canberra: Pluto Press, 1992); and Loup Francart and Jean-Jacques Patry, *Mâitriser la violence: Un Option stratégique*, 2nd ed. (Paris: Economica, 2002).
6. For two recent accounts among many in this genre, see Robert L. Grenier, *88 Days to Kandahar: A CIA Diary* (New York: Simon & Shuster, 2015); and Douglas Laux and Ralph Pezzullo, *Left of Boom: How a Young CIA Case Officer Penetrated the Taliban and Al-Qaeda* (New York: St. Martin's Press, 2016), 89ff. For CIA secret armies and CTPTs, see Julius Cavendish, "How the CIA Ran a Secret Army of 3,000 Assassins," *Independent*, 22 September 2010; and Mark Mazzetti and Dexter Filkins, "U.S. Military Seeks to Expand Raids in Pakistan," *New York Times*, 20 December 2010.
7. Ben Fenton, "Bin Laden 'Wanted to Behead the US Snake'," *Telegraph*, 8 February 2001, https://www.telegraph.co.uk/news/worldnews/middleeast/yemen/1321715/Bin-Laden-wanted-to-behead-the-US-snake.html.
8. President of the United States, *The National Security Strategy of the United States*, September 2002, https://www.state.gov/documents/organization/63562.pdf.
9. Ibid., 1–2.
10. See, e.g., Mary Habeck, *Knowing the Enemy: Jihadist Ideology and the War on Terror* (New Haven, CT: Yale University Press, 2006).

11. 107th Congress, Public Law 107-40, Joint Resolution, *Authorization for Use of Military Force*, 18 September 2001, https://www.gpo.gov/fdsys/pkg/PLAW-107publ40/pdf/PLAW-107publ40.pdf.

12. Many have used the term "forever war" to describe the post-9/11 war on terrorism, but Dexter Filkins's account is the best. See Filkins, *The Forever War: Dispatches from the War on Terror* (New York: Vintage, 2009).

13. Eric Schmitt, "Iraq-Bound Troops Confront Rumsfeld Over Lack of Armor," *New York Times*, 8 December 2004, http://www.nytimes.com/2004/12/08/international/middleeast/iraqbound-troops-confront-rumsfeld-over-lack-of.html.

14. The price of an M1A2 Abrams tank, as of 2016, was estimated at US$8.92 million. For the price of an explosively formed penetrator (EFP) in 2007, see Andrew Cockburn, "In Iraq, Anyone Can Make a Bomb," *Los Angeles Times*, 16 February 2007, http://www.latimes.com/news/la-oe-cockburn16feb16-story.html.

15. Two Afghan incidents almost a decade apart illustrate this: the downing of a Ch-47 Chinook helicopter by an RPG during the battle of Takur Ghar in March 2002 and the shootdown of Ch-47 Extortion One-Seven, with the loss of its whole crew and the Naval Special Warfare team on board, in Wardak Province on 6 August 2011. See Adam Geibel, "Operation Anaconda, Shah-i-Khot Valley, Afghanistan, 2–10 March 2002," *Military Review*, May–June 2002, 72–77; and Ed Darack, *The Final Mission of Extortion 17: Special Ops, Helicopter Support, SEAL Team Six and the Deadliest Day of the U.S. War in Afghanistan* (Washington, DC: Smithsonian Books, 2017).

16. Rudyard Kipling, "Arithmetic on the Frontier" (1886), in *Departmental Ditties and Other Verses*, http://www.kiplingsociety.co.uk/poems_arith.htm

17. Neta C. Crawford, *Costs of War: U.S. Budgetary Costs of Wars Through 2016: $4.79 Trillion and Counting* (Brown University: Watson Institute for International & Public Affairs, 2016), http://watson.brown.edu/costsofwar/files/cow/imce/papers/2016/Costs%20of%20War%20through%202016%20FINAL%20final%20v2.pdf.

18. See "Death Highway, Revisited," *Time*, 18 March 1991; and Carl Conetta, *The Wages of War: Iraqi Combatant and Noncombatant Fatalities in the 2003 Conflict*, Research Monograph 8 (Washington, DC: Project on Defense Alternatives, 20 October 2003), app. 2, sec. 5, http://www.comw.org/pda/0310rm8ap2.html#5.%20The%20Highway(s)%20of.

19. Steven A. Bourque, *Jayhawk! The VII Corps in the Persian Gulf War* (Washington, DC: United States Army Center of Military History, 2002), 323–48.

20. It may seem ahistorical to describe the Afghan insurgency as if it followed the Iraqi occupation—after all, we invaded Afghanistan eighteen months before Iraq. But the insurgency in Afghanistan did not emerge until well after the Iraq invasion, in the spring of 2004. The Quetta Shura, the Taliban group overseeing the insurgency, was not even formed until October 2003.

21. Robert Martinage, *Toward a New Offset Strategy: Exploiting U.S. Long-Term Advantages to Restore U.S. Global Power Projection Capability* (Washington, DC: Center for Strategic and Budgetary Analyses, 2014), http://csbaonline.org/uploads/documents/Offset-Strategy-Web.pdf.

22. Woolsey, interview with the author, 2 February 2015, Washington, DC.

23. Ibid.

24. "Address by the President of the Russian Federation," 18 March 2014, http://en.kremlin.ru/events/president/news/20603.

25. See Matt Potter, *Outlaws Inc.: Under the Radar and on the Black Market with the World's Most Dangerous Smugglers* (New York: Bloomsbury, 2011), 29ff.

26. Andrei Shleifer and Daniel Treisman, "A Normal Country: Russia After Communism," *Journal of Economic Perspectives* 19, no. 1 (Winter 2005): 151–74.

27. Peter Conradi, *Who Lost Russia? How the World Entered a New Cold War* (London: Oneworld, 2017), Kindle ed., locations 1390–93.

28. See Paul Beaver et al., "Race for Pristina," *Guardian*, 11 June 1999, https://www.theguardian.com/world/1999/jun/12/nicholaswatt; and BBC News, "Confrontation Over Pristina Airport," 9 March 2000, http://news.bbc.co.uk/2/hi/europe/671495.stm

29. See Alexei G. Arbatov, *The Transformation of Russian Military Doctrine: Lessons Learned from Kosovo and Chechnya*, Marshall Center Papers no. 2 (Garmisch-Partenkirchen: George C. Marshall Center for European Security Studies, 2000), 17–19.

30. Associated Press, "Putin Suggested Russia Joining NATO to Clinton," 12 June 2017, http://www.thehindu.com/news/international/in-his-interview-with-oliver-stone-vladimir-putin-suggested-russia-joining-nato-to-bill-clinton/article18965562.ece.

31. Conradi, *Who Lost Russia?*, locations 2820–21.

32. Ibid.

33. Angela Stent, *The Limits of Partnership: U.S.-Russian Relations in the Twenty-First Century* (Princeton, NJ: Princeton University Press, 2015), 62.

34. For an analysis of the pact and its successor, see Harvey Cole, "The U.S.-Russia Agreement for Peaceful Nuclear Cooperation," NTI (Nuclear Threat Initiative), 22 June 2010, http://www.nti.org/analysis/articles/us-russian-peaceful-cooperation/.

35. Craig Whitlock, "'Reset' Sought on Relations with Russia, Biden Says," *Washington Post*, 8 February 2009, http://www.washingtonpost.com/wp-dyn/content/article/2009/02/07/AR2009020700756.html.

36. Paul Richter, "Hillary Clinton Meets with Russian Foreign Minister Sergei Lavrov," *Los Angeles Times*, 7 March 2009, http://articles.latimes.com/2009/mar/07/world/fg-clinton7.

37. U.S.-Russia Bilateral Presidential Commission, "2013 Joint Report," 4, https://2009-2017.state.gov/documents/organization/219326.pdf.

38. Ibid., 33–34.

39. KKSO (командование сил специальных операций, Komandovanie sil spetsial'nalnykh operatsii), founded in 2009 as part of the second wave of Russian military modernization discussed in detail in Chapter 4, differs from traditional Russian special-purpose (Spetsnaz) organizations, which have historically been controlled by intelligence services such as the military's GRU or the civilian FSB and SVR, in that it (much like US or British Commonwealth special forces) sits directly under Army Headquarters command and performs elite military missions such as raiding, unconventional

warfare, and foreign military assistance. For joint training with the US special operations forces, see ibid. and David Majumdar, "Meet Russia's Very Own 'Delta Force,'" *National Interest*, 26 November 2018, https://nationalinterest.org/blog/buzz/meet-russias-very-own-delta-force-37147.

40. U.S.-Russia Bilateral Presidential Commission, *Fall Newsletter*, September–November 2013, 6, https://2009-2017.state.gov/documents/organization/219290.pdf.

41. Commission on Presidential Debates, Debate transcript, 22 October 2012, 6, http://www.debates.org/index.php?page=october-22-2012-the-third-obama-romney-presidential-debate.

42. Using officially announced gross domestic product as a rough indicator of economic size, China's economy in 2017 was 20.7 times larger than in 1993. See National Bureau of Statistics of China, "National Accounts: Gross Domestic Product," *National Data*, http://data.stats.gov.cn/english/.

43. Dean Cheng, "Chinese Lessons from the Gulf Wars," in Andrew Scobell, David Lai, and Roy Kamphausen (eds.), *Chinese Lessons from Other People's Wars* (Carlisle, PA: United States Army War College, 2011), 153.

44. Arthur Waldron, foreword to Richard D. Fisher, *China's Military Modernization: Building for Regional and Global Reach* (Westport, CT: Praeger Security International, 2008), Kindle ed., locations 50–55.

45. Bonnie S. Glaser and Evan S. Medeiros, "The Changing Ecology of Policy-Making in China: The Ascension and Demise of the Theory of 'Peaceful Rise,'" *China Quarterly*, no. 190 (July 2007): 291–310.

46. Gilbert Rozman, *Chinese Strategic Thought Toward Asia* (London: Palgrave Macmillan, 2010), 65.

47. For example, see Lee Branstetter and Nicholas Lardy, *China's Embrace of Globalization*, NBER Working Paper no. 12373 (Cambridge, MA: National Bureau of Economic Research, 2006), http://www.nber.org/papers/w12373.pdf.

48. Arta Khakpour, Mohammad Mehdi Khorrami, and Shouleh Vatanabadi, *Moments of Silence: Authenticity in the Cultural Expressions of the Iran-Iraq War, 1980–1988* (New York: NYU Press, 2016), 2. However, note that the authenticity of the quote is disputed.

49. Joseph Kostiner, *Conflict and Cooperation in the Gulf Region* (Wiesbaden: VS Verlag für Sozialwissenschaften, 2009), 175.

50. Ibid.

51. Ibid.

52. For a brief account of this history see Ariana Rowberry, "Sixty Years of 'Atoms for Peace' and Iran's Nuclear Program," *Brookings* (blog), Brookings Institution, 18 December 2013, https://www.brookings.edu/blog/up-front/2013/12/18/sixty-years-of-atoms-for-peace-and-irans-nuclear-program/.

53. Farhad Rezaei, "The Islamic Revolution and the Bomb: Quran Meets Realism," in *Iran's Nuclear Program: A Study in Proliferation and Rollback* (London: Palgrave Macmillan, 2017), 13–34.

54. Shahram Chubin, "Iran's Strategic Environment and Nuclear Weapons," in Geoffrey Kemp (ed.), *Iran's Nuclear Weapons Options: Issues and Analysis* (Washington, DC: Nixon Center, 2001), 19.

55. Farhad Rezaei, "Khatami's Dialogue among Civilizations and the Nuclear 'Disappearance Act,'" in *Iran's Nuclear Program: A Study in Proliferation and Rollback* (London: Palgrave Macmillan, 2017), 78–118.

56. For a summary of major incidents see David Reese, "North Korea's 'Nuclear Card,'" *Adelphi Papers*, 38, no. 323 (1998): 39–40. For two (among dozens at the same site) of the declassified Cold War intelligence reports on this activity see National Photographic Interpretation Center, *Sea Infiltration Facilities North Korea*, Photographic Intelligence Report PIR 020-70, April 1970, https://www.cia.gov/library/readingroom/docs/CIA-RDP78T05162A000100010077-6.pdf; and Central Intelligence Agency, *Terrorist Threats to the Seoul Olympics*, Intelligence Memorandum EA M 88-2049/GI M 88-2042, 1988, https://www.cia.gov/library/readingroom/document/cia-rdp90t00100r000201120001-7.

57. See Jae-Cheon Lim, *Leader Symbols and Personality Cult in North Korea: The Leader State*, Advances in Korea Studies (London: Routledge, 2015), 158–60; and Alexander V. Vorontsov, "North Korea's Military-First Policy: A Curse or a Blessing?" *Brookings*, 26 May 2006, https://www.brookings.edu/opinions/north-koreas-military-first-policy-a-curse-or-a-blessing/.

58. James R. Woolsey, "Proliferation Threats of the 1990s," testimony before US Senate Committee on Governmental Affairs, 24 February 1993, quoted in Paul Kerr, Mary Beth Nikitin, and Steven Hildreth, *Iran–North Korea–Syria Ballistic Missile and Nuclear Cooperation* (Washington, DC: Congressional Research Service, 2016), 3n, https://crsreports.congress.gov/product/pdf/R/R43480.

59. David Sanger, "Missile Is Tested by North Korea," *New York Times*, 16 June 1993, https://www.nytimes.com/1993/06/13/world/missile-is-tested-by-north-koreans.html.

60. Michael Elleman, *Iran's Ballistic Missile Capabilities: A Net Assessment* (London: International Institute for Strategic Studies, 2010), 36.

61. According to a 2015 assessment, North Korea has excellent oil and gas reserves but has never been able to develop them. See Mike Rego, "North Korea: Hydrocarbon Exploration and Potential," *GEO Expro* 12, no. 4 (September 2015): 22–27, https://assets.geoexpro.com/uploads/6b0d8623-a955-496c-a3d8-53ecb6ac488b/GEO_ExPro_v12i4.pdf.

62. Lee Jae-Bong, "US Deployment of Nuclear Weapons in 1950s South Korea & North Korea's Nuclear Development: Toward Denuclearization of the Korean Peninsula," *Asia-Pacific Journal Japan Focus* 7, no. 3 (February 2009): 1–17, https://apjjf.org/-Lee-Jae-Bong/3053/article.html.

63. See Olli Heinonen, "North Korea's Nuclear Enrichment: Capabilities and Consequences," *38 North*, 22 June 2011, https://www.38north.org/2011/06/heinonen062211/.

64. Lee, "US Deployment of Nuclear Weapons," 12.

65. Joseph Bermudez, *Jane's Defence Weekly*, 10 April 1993, 20, 22, quoted in Center for Nonproliferation Studies, "Chronology of North Korea's Missile Trade and Developments: 1980–1989," Middlebury Institute of International Studies at Monterey, http://www.nonproliferation.org/chronology-of-north-koreas-missile-trade-and-developments-1990-1991/.

66. David E. Rosenbaum, "U.S. to Pull A-Bombs from South Korea," *New York Times*, 20 October 1991, https://www.nytimes.com/1991/10/20/world/us-to-pull-a-bombs-from-south-korea.html.

67. For an additional examination of the psychology behind this, see Jacques E. C. Hymans, "North Korea's Nuclear Neurosis," *Bulletin of the Atomic Scientists* 63, no. 3 (May–June 2007): 44–74.

68. Steve Coll, "The Madman Theory of North Korea," *New Yorker*, 2 October 2017, https://www.newyorker.com/magazine/2017/10/02/the-madman-theory-of-north-korea.

69. David Albright and Christina Walrond, *North Korea's Estimated Stocks of Plutonium and Weapon-Grade Uranium* (Washington, DC: Institute for Science and International Security, August 2012), 13–21, http://isis-online.org/uploads/isis-reports/documents/dprk_fissile_material_production_16Aug2012.pdf.

70. Foreign Broadcast Information Service, "KCNA 'Detailed Report' Explains NPT Withdrawal," 22 January 2003, https://fas.org/nuke/guide/dprk/nuke/dprk012203.html.

71. See Korean Central News Agency, "DPRK FM on Its Stand to Suspend Its Participation in Six-Party Talks for Indefinite Period," 10 February 2005, https://web.archive.org/web/20090531175657/http://kcna.co.jp/item/2005/200502/news02/11.htm#1; and David Sanger, "North Koreans Say They Tested Nuclear Device," *New York Times*, 9 October 2006, https://www.nytimes.com/2006/10/09/world/asia/09korea.html.

72. See BBC News, "North Korea Nuclear Test: Hydrogen Bomb 'Missile-Ready,'" 3 September 2017, https://www.bbc.com/news/world-asia-41139445; Missile Threat, Center for Strategic and International Studies, "Hwasong-15/KN-22," https://missilethreat.csis.org/missile/hwasong-15-kn-22/; and Ruediger Frank, "Kim Jong Un's 2018 New Year's Speech: Self-Confidence After a Tough Year," *38 North*, 3 January 2018, https://www.38north.org/2018/01/rfrank010318/.

73. Frank, "Kim Jong Un's 2018 New Year's Speech."

Chapter 2

1. This incident took place well before YouTube existed, but years later someone posted it to the video-sharing site. See https://youtu.be/-vAByo1wvEg.

2. This definition is adapted from E. O. Wilson, *Sociobiology: The New Synthesis* (Cambridge, MA: Harvard University Press, 2000), 578.

3. Stephen P. Rosen, *Winning the Next War: Innovation and the Modern Military* (Ithaca, NY: Cornell University Press, 1991).

4. For a critical evaluation of these concepts, see Roman Kupriyanov and Renad Zhdanov, "The Eustress Concept: Problems and Outlooks," *World Journal of Medical Sciences* 11, no. 2 (2014): 179–85.

5. Roger A. Beaumont, *Military Elites: Special Fighting Units in the Modern World* (New York: Bobbs-Merrill, 1974).

6. Ibid., 173–74, 177–79.

7. Ibid., 179–81.

8. See T. R. Moreman, *The Army in India and the Development of Frontier Warfare, 1849–1947* (New York: Palgrave, 1998).

9. Robert Boyd and Peter J. Richerson, "Why Culture Is Common, but Cultural Evolution Is Rare," *Proceedings of the British Academy* 88 (1996): 77.

10. Esther Herrmann et al., "Humans Have Evolved Specialized Skills of Social Cognition: The Cultural Intelligence Hypothesis," *Science* 317, no. 5843 (7 September 2007): 1360–66.

11. Fiona M. Jordan et al., "Cultural Evolution of the Structure of Human Groups" in Peter J. Richerson and Morten H. Christiansen (eds.), *Cultural Evolution: Society, Technology, Language, and Religion* (Cambridge, MA: MIT Press, 2013), 101.

12. Ibid.

13. Ibid.

14. Ibid.

15. Ibid., 90.

16. R. I. M. Dunbar, "Gossip in Evolutionary Perspective," *Review of General Psychology* 8, no. 2 (2004): 100–110.

17. I use the term "institution" here in its sociological sense, meaning a complex, stable set of behaviors that include "regulative, normative, and cultural-cognitive elements that, together with associated activities and resources, provide stability and meaning to social life." See Richard Scott, *Institutions and Organizations*, 3rd ed. (Thousand Oaks, CA: Sage, 2008), 49.

18. For an example, see Stefanie Hoss, "The Roman Military Belt: A Status Symbol and Object of Fashion," in Toby F. Martin and Rosie Weetch (eds.), *Dress and Society: Contributions from Archaeology* (Oxford: Oxbow Books, 2017), 94–113.

19. For two examples from a rich literature see Xurong Kong, "Military Uniform as a Fashion During the Cultural Revolution," *Intercultural Communication Studies* 17, no. 2 (2008), https://web.uri.edu/iaics/files/24-Xurong-Kong.pdf; and Megan Cipollini, *Dressed to Kill: How Military Style Has Invaded Fashion*, https://www.1stdibs.com/blogs/the-study/military-fashion/.

20. For an excellent illustration of this debate see Steven Pinker, "The False Allure of Group Selection," *Edge*, 18 June 2012, https://www.edge.org/conversation/steven_pinker-the-false-allure-of-group-selection; and the replies by Peter J. Richerson, http://www.des.ucdavis.edu/faculty/Richerson/Comment%20on%20Pinker%20Edge%20essay.pdf, Peter Turchin, http://peterturchin.com/cliodynamica/steven-pinker-on-the-false-allure-of-group-selection/, and Andrew Gelman, http://andrewgelman.com/2012/07/12/steven-pinkers-unconvincing-debunking-of-group-selection/.

21. See General Sir Andrew Skeen, *Passing It On: Short Talks on Tribal Fighting on the North-West Frontier of India* (1932), ed. Lester Grau and Robert Baer (Fort Leavenworth, KS: Foreign Military Studies Office, 2010), 28.

22. This is a broader application of the evolutionary psychologist Donald T. Campbell's model of blind variation and selective retention (BVSR), first described in 1960 and originally applied to creative thought but subsequently expanded to other forms of human cultural evolution. For the original paper see Donald T. Campbell, "Blind Variation and Selective Retention in Creative Thought as in Other Knowledge Processes," *Psychological Review*, no. 67 (1960): 380–400. For a more recent commentary see Dean Keith Simonton, "Creativity and Discovery as Blind Variation: Campbell's (1960) BVSR Model After the Half-Century Mark," *Review of General Psychology* 15, no. 2 (2011): 158–74.

23. United Nations Security Council, *Fourth Report of the Analytical Support and Sanctions Monitoring Team Submitted Pursuant to Resolution 2082 (2012) Concerning the Taliban and Other Associated Individuals and Entities Constituting a Threat to the Peace, Stability and Security of Afghanistan*, 9 June 2014, 6, http://www.securitycouncilreport.org/atf/cf/%7B65BFCF9B-6D27-4E9C-8CD3-CF6E4FF96FF9%7D/s_2014_402.pdf.

24. For an Afghan example, see David Kilcullen, *Blood Year: The Unraveling of Western Counterterrorism* (New York: Oxford University Press, 2016), Kindle ed., locations 3289–91.

25. See Lionel Beehner, "Iraq: Insurgents' Tactics," Council on Foreign Relations, 6 May 2005, https://www.cfr.org/backgrounder/iraq-insurgents-tactics.

26. United States Army, *Human Factors Considerations of Undergrounds in Insurgencies*, Department of the Army Pamphlet no. 500-104 (Washington, DC: Headquarters, Department of the Army, 1966), 290.

27. David J. Kilcullen, *Out of the Mountains: The Coming Age of the Urban Guerrilla* (New York: Oxford University Press, 2013), 105–6.

28. Jordan et al., 89.

29. For a discussion of cell types and sizes, as well as rules of clandestine behavior in several historical underground movements, see United States Army, *Human Factors Considerations of Undergrounds in Insurgencies*, 284–86, 288.

30. R. I. M. Dunbar, "Neocortex Size as a Constraint on Group Size in Primates," *Journal of Human Evolution* 22, no. 6 (1992): 469–73.

31. Robin I. M. Dunbar and Richard Sosis, "Optimising Human Community Sizes," *Evolution and Human Behavior* 39, no. 1 (January 2018): 106.

32. Ibid. For military group size see R. I. M. Dunbar, "Constraints on the Evolution of Social Institutions and Their Implications for Information Flow," *Journal of Institutional Economics* 7, no. 3 (Evolution of Institutions; September 2011): 345–71.

33. Dominic Johnson, "Darwinian Selection in Asymmetric Warfare: The Natural Advantage of Insurgents and Terrorists," *Journal of the Washington Academy of Arts and Sciences* 95, no. 3 (Fall 2009): 89–112.

34. Rafe Sagarin, *Learning from the Octopus: How Secrets from Nature Can Help Us Fight Terrorist Attacks, Natural Disasters, and Disease* (New York: Basic Books, 2003), Kindle ed., 7–8. I am indebted to my friend Professor David Betz of the Department of War Studies at King's College, London, for pointing out Sagarin's work and its relevance to that of Dominic Johnson and others.

35. The concept of fitness landscapes is controversial; for a useful introduction see Michael Dietrich and Robert Skipper, "A Shifting Terrain: A Brief History of the Adaptive Landscape," in Erik Svensson and Ryan Calsbeek (eds.), *The Adaptive Landscape in Evolutionary Biology* (New York: Oxford University Press, 2012), 3–14.

36. David Kilcullen, "Countering Global Insurgency" (2003), in *Counterinsurgency* (New York: Oxford University Press, 2010), 205.

37. Ibid.

38. The origin of dogs is an active point of discussion in studies of human evolution; for two fairly recent discussions see Jun-Feng Pang et al., "mtDNA Data Indicate a Single Origin for Dogs South of Yangtze River, Less than 16,300 Years Ago, from Numerous Wolves," *Molecular Biology and Evolution* 26, no. 12 (1 December 2009): 2849–64; and Angela Perri, "A Wolf in Dog's Clothing: Initial Dog Domestication and Pleistocene Wolf Variation," *Journal of Archaeological Science*, no. 68 (April 2016): 1–4.

39. Charles Darwin, *The Origin of Species and the Voyage of the* Beagle (1859), introduction by Richard Dawkins (New York: Knopf, Everyman's Library, 2003), 560ff.

40. T. Ryan Gregory, "Artificial Selection and Domestication: Modern Lessons from Darwin's Enduring Analogy," *Evolution: Education and Outreach* 2, no. 1 (March 2009): 5–27.

41. Julian Davies and Dorothy Davies, "Origins and Evolution of Antibiotic Resistance," *Microbiology and Molecular Biology Reviews* 74, no. 3 (September 2010): 418, 423.

42. For a concise discussion of the application of population ecology to counterinsurgency and irregular warfare, see Dominic Johnson, *Evolutionary Models of Irregular Warfare*, research report, US Air Force Office of Scientific Research and US Office of Naval Research, 4 March 2013, www.dtic.mil/get-tr-doc/pdf?AD=ADA581874.

43. For a nonspecialist introduction to predator-prey models, see Frank Hoppensteadt, "Predator-Prey Model," *Scholarpedia* 1, no. 10 (2006): 1563, http://www.scholarpedia.org/article/Predator-prey_model.

44. See M. Beals, L. Gross, and S. Harrell, "Predator-Prey Dynamics: Lotka-Volterra," 1999, http://www.tiem.utk.edu/~gross/bioed/bealsmodules/predator-prey.html.

45. David Kilcullen, *The Accidental Guerrilla: Fighting Small Wars in the Midst of a Big One* (New York: Oxford University Press, 2009), 238–42.

46. See Laila Bokhari, *Waziristan: Impact on the Taliban Insurgency and the Stability of Pakistan* (Kjeller: Forsvarets Forskingsinstitutt [Norwegian Defence Research Establishment], 2006), FFI/RAPPORT-2006/02894, https://www.ffi.no/no/Rapporter/06-02894.pdf.

47. Ibid.

48. Mrs. Bhutto's assassination is a matter of dispute in Pakistan, with various conspiracy theories—including one that blames former Pakistani president Pervez Musharraf and others that blame the Pakistan Army for failing to protect the candidate. The most widely accepted theory, however, remains that TTP under Beitullah Mehsud was responsible for the killing.

49. United States Department of State, *Designations of Tehrik-e Taliban Pakistan and Two Senior Leaders*, 1 September 2010, https://www.state.gov/j/ct/rls/other/des/266652.htm

50. Ronen Bergman, *Rise and Kill First: The Secret History of Israel's Targeted Assassinations* (New York: Random House, 2018), Kindle ed., 539.

51. Ibid.

52. Ibid., 629–30.

53. Ibid.

54. Avraham Shalom, at 12:20–30 and 19:20–29 of Dror Moreh's film *The Gatekeepers*, Sony Pictures Classics, 2013.

55. Discussion with officers in the field, Kandahar and Asadabad, 2013. See also Lauren McNally and Marvin Weinbaum, *A Resilient Al Qaeda in Afghanistan and Pakistan* (Washington, DC: Middle East Institute, 2016), 5–6; and Catherine Putz, "Is Al Qaeda Back in Afghanistan?," *Diplomat*, 15 April 2016, https://thediplomat.com/2016/04/is-al-qaeda-back-in-afghanistan/.

56. For a description of the center see CIA, Open Source Center, https://www.cia.gov/careers/games-information/view-our-advertising/pdf/OSC%20Insert.pdf.

57. Open Source Center, GMP20110501000003 Ansar al-Mujahidin Network in Arabic, 1 May 2011, article attributed to "Shinkai al-Najdi": "Petraeus and Panetta: Sign of a New Era in Facing Al-Qa'ida," posted by "Abu-Turab al-Said," unclassified document in the author's possession.

58. Ibid., 8.

59. Ibid., 4.

60. Ibid., 7–8.

61. Williamson Murray and Barry Watts, *Military Innovation in Peacetime* (Ohio State University, Merson Center, 1995), 2–3, http://indianstrategicknowledgeonline.com/web/MIilInnovPeace.pdf.

62. Ibid.

63. For a discussion of this conceptual approach see "Social Institutions," *Stanford Encyclopedia of Philosophy*, 2007, https://plato.stanford.edu/entries/social-institutions/.

64. Rosen, *Winning the Next War*.

Chapter 3

1. For the original concept see Sewall Wright, "The Roles of Mutation, Inbreeding, Cross-Breeding and Selection in Evolution," in Donald F. Jones (ed.), *Proceedings of the Sixth International Congress of Genetics* (Austin: University of Texas, 1932; rpt. 1968), 356–66, http://www.esp.org/books/6th-congress/facsimile/contents/6th-cong-p356-wright.pdf. For a computational model employing this concept, see Stuart Kauffman and Sonke Johnsen, "Coevolution to the Edge of Chaos: Coupled Fitness Landscapes, Poised States, and Coevolutionary Avalanches," *Journal of Theoretical Biology*, no. 149 (1991): 467–505, https://www.sccs.swarthmore.edu/users/08/bblonder/phys120/docs/kauffman.pdf.

2. Barrett Steinberg and Marc Ostermeier, "Environmental Changes Bridge Evolutionary Valleys," *Science Advances* 2, no. 1 (January 2016), https://www.ncbi.nlm.nih.gov/pmc/articles/PMC4737206/pdf/1500921.pdf.

3. Kauffman and Johnsen, "Coevolution to the Edge of Chaos."

4. Globalization here means "the freer movement of goods, people, money, technology, ideas, and cultures across and within international borders [that] has prompted the emergence of a Western-dominated world culture, an interdependent world economy, and a global community of business, political, and intellectual elites." David Kilcullen, *The Accidental Guerrilla: Fighting Small Wars in the Midst of a Big One* (New York: Oxford University Press, 2009), 8.

5. Peter Grier, "April 15 1953: No US Ground Troop Has Been Killed in an Enemy Aircraft Attack Since the Korean War," in *Air Force Magazine*, June 2011, 54–57, http://www.airforcemag.com/MagazineArchive/Documents/2011/June%20 2011/0611april.pdf.

6. See Tyler Rogoway, "America's Startling Short-Range Air Defense Gap and How to Close It Fast," *Drive*, 9 August 2017, http://www.thedrive.com/the-war-zone/ 13284/americas-gaping-short-range-air-defense-gap-and-why-it-has-to-be-closed-immediately?iid=sr-link4; and Joseph Trevithick, "US Army Rushes to Add Hundreds of Stinger Missile Teams as Threat from Small Drones Evolves," *Drive*, 17 January 2018, http://www.thedrive.com/the-war-zone/17747/us-army-rushes-to-add-hundreds-of-stinger-missile-teams-as-threat-of-small-drones-evolves?iid=sr-link2.

7. William Harrell Jr., *Air Campaign Central Europe: Comparative Analysis between World War II and the Present*, Air War College Research Report ([Montgomery,] AL: Maxwell Air Force Base, 1989), 55–56, http://www.dtic.mil/dtic/tr/fulltext/ u2/a217761.pdf.

8. David Lednicer and Adrian Camp, "US Air-to-Air Losses in the Vietnam War," revised 9 June 2002, http://myplace.frontier.com/~anneled/usloss.html.

9. Adolfo J. Fernandez, *Military Space Control: An Intuitive Analysis*, Air War College Research Report ([Montgomery,] AL: Maxwell Air Force Base, 2004), 12, http:// www.dtic.mil/dtic/tr/fulltext/u2/a434364.pdf.

10. See Andrew Davies, "Western Airpower and the Strikes in Iraq," *ASPI Strategist* (blog), 2004, https://www.aspistrategist.org.au/graph-of-the-week-western-air-power-and-the-strikes-in-iraq/.

11. Benjamin Lambeth, *Air Power against Terror: America's Conduct of Operation Enduring Freedom* (Santa Monica, CA: RAND Corporation, 2005), 247n2.

12. Ibid.

13. Missy Ryan and Loveday Morris, "When Air Power Works, and When It Doesn't: A Snapshot of U.S. Operations against the Islamic State," *Washington Post*, 20 December 2016, https://www.washingtonpost.com/news/checkpoint/wp/2016/12/20/ when-air-power-works-and-when-it-doesnt/?utm_term=.f561982e04c7.

14. This is not intended to offer a fine-grained analysis, simply a comparative heuristic measure. The calculation is based on average number of strike sorties per day divided by land area of each theater, giving strikes per day per square kilometer.

15. Eyal Weizmann, *Hollow Land: Israel's Architecture of Occupation* (London: Verso, 2007), 185–86.

16. For a late–Cold War view of this, see Lauren G. Mullenore, *The Future of the Joint Air Attack Team in the AirLand Battle*, Air War College Research Report ([Montgomery,] AL: Maxwell Air Force Base, 1989), http://www.dtic.mil/dtic/ tr/fulltext/u2/a217470.pdf.

17. See Mike Benitez, "How Afghanistan Distorted Close Air Support and Why It Matters," *War on the Rocks*, 29 June 2016, https://warontherocks.com/2016/06/how-afghanistan-distorted-close-air-support-and-why-it-matters/.

18. Alexander A. Pikayev, "A Few Speculations on Russia's Deterrence Policy," in Ian Kenyon and John Simpson (eds.), *Deterrence and the New Global Security Environment* (London: Routledge, 2013), 101–2.

19. The author attended Australia's Royal Military College during 1985–88, at the height of late–Cold War tensions in Europe, and watched many such training films.

20. See Tom Clancy, *Red Storm Rising* (London: Penguin, 1986); and John Rouch, *Hard Target*, book 4 of *The Zone* (London: Zebra Books, 1980), and subsequent books in the series. For the public's reaction to Edward Hume's 1983 film *The Day After*, see Hank Steuver, "Yes, 'The Day After' Really Was the Profound TV Moment 'The Americans' Makes It Out to Be," *Washington Post*, 11 May 2016.

21. William R. Hittinger, *Rules of Engagement as a Force Multiplier* (Quantico, VA: Command and Staff College, 2000), 28–29, http://smallwarsjournal.com/documents/hittinger.pdf.

22. Ibid.

23. See, e.g., Department of Defense, *Conduct of the Persian Gulf War: Final Report to Congress* (Washington, DC: DOD, 1992), 130–33, http://www.dtic.mil/dtic/tr/fulltext/u2/a249270.pdf.

24. Colin H. Kahl, "How We Fight," *Foreign Affairs*, November–December 2006, 1, 4.

25. Ibid., 5–6.

26. Ibid., 8.

27. See Loch K. Johnson, "The Aspin-Brown Intelligence Inquiry: Behind the Closed Doors of a Blue Ribbon Commission," *Studies in Intelligence* 48, no. 3 (Spring 2004), https://www.cia.gov/library/center-for-the-study-of-intelligence/csi-publications/csi-studies/studies/vol48no3/article01.html.

28. United States Government, *Report of the Commission on the Roles and Capabilities of the United States Intelligence Community*, 1996, chap. 2, https://fas.org/irp/offdocs/int006.html.

29. Ira Sager, "Before iPhone and Android Came Simon, the First Smartphone," *Bloomberg Business*, 29 June 2012, https://www.bloomberg.com/news/articles/2012-06-29/before-iphone-and-android-came-simon-the-first-smartphone.

30. Matthew M. Aid, "The Time of Troubles: The U.S. National Security Agency in the 21st Century," in Roger Z. George and Robert D. Kline (eds.), *Intelligence and the National Security Strategist: Enduring Issues and Challenges* (Oxford: Rowman & Littlefield, 2006), 192.

31. Ibid., 194.

32. Julian Sanchez, "What the Ashcroft 'Hospital Showdown' on NSA Spying Was All About," 29 July 2013, *Ars Technica*, July 2013, https://arstechnica.com/tech-policy/2013/07/what-the-ashcroft-hospital-showdown-on-nsa-spying-was-all-about/.

33. Michael T. Flynn, Matt Pottinger, and Paul D. Batchelor, *Fixing Intel: A Blueprint for Making Intelligence Relevant in Afghanistan* (Washington, DC: Center for a New American Security, 2010), 8.

34. Hannan Gefen, "Espionage in the Cyber Era," *Israel Defence*, 2 February 2014, http://www.israeldefense.co.il/en/content/espionage-cyber-era.

35. "Meet the CIA's Venture Capitalist," *Bloomberg Businessweek*, 9 May 2005, http://www.businessweek.com/stories/2005-05-09/meet-the-cias-venture-capitalist.

36. Google Blog, "Google Earth Downloaded More Than One Billion Times," 5 October 2011, https://maps.googleblog.com/2011/10/google-earth-downloaded-more-than-one.html.

37. European Global Navigation Satellite System Agency, *GNSS Market Report: Issue 5* (Luxembourg: European Union, 2017), 5.

38. Scott Pace et al., *The Global Positioning System: Assessing National Policies* (Santa Monica, CA: RAND Corporation, 1995), 246.

39. US Government, "Selective Availability," GPS.gov, https://www.gps.gov/systems/gps/modernization/sa/.

40. See https://www.gps.gov.

41. David Hambling, *Swarm Troopers: How Small Drones Will Conquer the World* (New York: Archangel Ink, 2015), 4.

42. See Liz Sly, "Who Is Attacking Russia's Bases in Syria? A New Mystery Emerges in the War," *Washington Post*, 10 January 2018, https://www.washingtonpost.com/world/who-is-attacking-russias-main-base-in-syria-a-new-mystery-emerges-in-the-war/2018/01/09/4fdaea70-f48d-11e7-9af7-a50bc3300042_story.html?utm_term=.82074807908e.

43. National Academies of Sciences, Engineering and Medicine, *Counter-Unmanned Aircraft System (CUAS) Capability for Battalion-and-Below Operations: Abbreviated Version of a Restricted Report* (Washington, DC: National Academies Press, 2018), 1.

44. Ibid.

45. Peter Bergen and Paul Cruickshank, "Revisiting the Early Al Qaeda: An Updated Account of Its Formative Years," *Studies in Conflict and Terrorism* 35, no. 1 (2012): 1–36.

46. See Fawaz Gerges, "The World According to ISIS," *Foreign Policy Journal*, 18 March 2016, https://www.foreignpolicyjournal.com/2016/03/18/the-world-according-to-isis/#_edn19.

47. Bill Roggio, "Shabaab Leader Recounts al Qaeda's Role in Somalia in the 1990s," *Long War Journal*, 31 December 2011.

48. Anne Stenersen, "Thirty Years After Its Foundation—Where Is al-Qaida Going?," *Perspectives on Terrorism* 11, no. 6 (December 2017): 5–16.

49. Sayyid Qutb, *Milestones* (1964) (New Delhi: Islamic Book Service, 2006).

50. For one example see Dale C. Eikmeier, "Qutbism: An Ideology of Islamic-Fascism," *Parameters*, Spring 2007, 85–98.

51. Vladimir Lenin, *What Is to Be Done?* (1902), trans. Tim Delaney, Marxists Internet Archive, 56, 97, https://www.marxists.org/archive/lenin/works/download/what-itd.pdf.

52. "US Informant Tells Court bin Laden Ordered Attacks," *Irish Times*, 7 February 2001, https://www.irishtimes.com/news/us-informant-tells-court-bin-laden-ordered-attacks-1.373817.

53. Assaf Moghadam, *Top-Down and Bottom-Up Innovation in Terrorism: The Case of the 9/11 Attacks*, ICT Working Papers Series no. 18 (Herzliya, Israel: International Institute for Counterterrorism, 2013), 16.

54. Stimson Study Group on Counterterrorism Spending, *Protecting America While Promoting Efficiencies and Accountability* (Washington, DC: Stimson Center, 2018), 5.

55. Peter Bergen, "The Account of How We Nearly Caught Osama bin Laden in 2001," *New Republic*, 29 December 2009, https://newrepublic.com/article/72086/the-battle-tora-bora.

56. Moghadam, *Top-Down and Bottom-Up Innovation.*

57. Bergen, "How We Nearly Caught Osama bin Laden."

58. United States Senate, Committee on Foreign Relations, *Tora Bora Revisited: How We Failed to Get Bin Laden and Why It Matters Today* (Washington, DC: US Government Printing Office, 2009).

59. A modified version of parts of the following section was published in David Kilcullen, *Blood Year: The Unraveling of Western Counterterrorism* (New York: Oxford University Press, 2016), Kindle ed., locations 2226ff.

60. For a discussion of the urban siege aspect of the Mumbai attacks see David Kilcullen, *Out of the Mountains: The Coming Age of the Urban Guerrilla* (London: Hurst; Oxford: Oxford University Press, 2013), 52–66.

61. David J. Goodman, "American Who Waged 'Media Jihad' Is Said to Be Killed in Awlaki Strike," *New York Times*, 30 September 2011, https://thelede.blogs.nytimes.com/2011/09/30/american-who-waged-media-jihad-is-said-to-be-killed-in-awlaki-strike/.

62. Louis Beam, "Leaderless Resistance" in *Seditionist*, issue 12, February 1992, http://www.louisbeam.com/leaderless.htm.

63. Louise Kelly and Christopher Booth, "Catastrophic Success," in *Dictionary of Strategy: Strategic Management, A–Z* (Thousand Oaks, CA: Sage, 2004), 20.

64. A portion of this section was previously published as "Al Qa'ida's Not Done with Us Yet," *Weekend Australian*, 10 August 2018.

65. Mary Anne Weaver, "The Short, Violent Life of Abu Musab al-Zarqawi," *Atlantic*, July–August 2006, https://www.theatlantic.com/magazine/archive/2006/07/the-short-violent-life-of-abu-musab-al-zarqawi/304983/.

66. For a discussion of Saddam's strategic miscalculations see Stephen Hosmer, *Why the Iraqi Resistance to the Coalition Invasion Was So Weak* (Santa Monica, CA: RAND, 2007), 15–26.

67. Charles Winslow, *Lebanon: War and Politics in a Fragmented Society* (London: Routledge, 1996).

68. Edna Bonacich, "A Theory of Middleman Minorities," *American Sociological Review* 38, no. 5 (October 1973): 583–94. See also Walter P. Zenner, "Arabic-Speaking Immigrants in North America as Middleman Minorities," *Ethnic and Racial Studies* 5, no. 4 (October 1982): 457–77; and Mara Leichtman, "The Legacy of Transnational Lives: Beyond the First Generation of Lebanese in Senegal," *Ethnic and Racial Studies* 25, no. 4 (October 2005): 663–86.

69. Shana Marshall, "Hizbollah: 1982–2009," in United States Army Special Operations Command, *Casebook on Insurgency and Revolutionary Warfare*, vol. 2: *1962–2009* (Fort Bragg, NC: USASOC, 2012), 529.

70. See Janet Klein, *The Margins of Empire: Kurdish Militias in the Ottoman Tribal Zone* (Stanford, CA: Stanford University Press, 2011); and Ussama Makdisi, *The Culture of Sectarianism: Community, History, and Violence in Nineteenth-Century Ottoman Lebanon* (Berkeley: University of California Press, 2000).

71. Ahmad Nizar Hamzeh, "Clientalism, Lebanon: Roots and Trends," *Middle Eastern Studies* 37, no. 3 (July 2001): 167–78.

72. Augustus R. Norton, *Hezbollah: A Short History*, 3rd ed., Princeton Studies in Muslim Politics (Princeton, NJ: Princeton University Press, 2018), 22.

73. Amal Saad-Ghorayeb, *Hizbullah: Politics and Religion* (Sterling, VA: Pluto Press), 11, quoted in Marshall, "Hizbollah: 1982–2009," 539n.

74. For an account of Iranian support for the founding and development of Hezbollah see Nicholas Blanford, *Hezbollah's Evolution: From Lebanese Militia to Regional Player* (Washington, DC: Middle East Institute, 2017), https://www.mei.edu/sites/default/files/publications/PP4_Blanford_Hezbollah.pdf.

75. Marshall, "Hizbollah: 1982–2009," 541n.

76. Hamzeh, "Clientalism, Lebanon," 102.

77. Ibid., 544–45.

78. Ibid.

79. Kilcullen, *Out of the Mountains*, 142–44.

80. For a timeline of Hezbollah attacks see United States Army, Training and Doctrine Command G2 ACE Threats Integration, "Threat Tactics Report: Hizballah," APAN, 2017, 12, https://community.apan.org/wg/tradoc-g2/ace-threats-integration/m/documents/211605.

81. For descriptions of the bombing and its aftermath see David Martin and John Walcott, *Best-Laid Plans: The Inside Story of America's War against Terrorism* (New York: Harper & Row, 1988); and Timothy Geraghty, *Peacekeepers at War: Beirut, 1983—The Marine Commander Tells His Story* (Washington, DC: Potomac Books, 2009).

82. Hala Jaber, *Hezbollah: Born with a Vengeance* (New York: Columbia University Press, 1997), 82.

83. Robert C. McFarlane, "From Beirut to 9/11," *New York Times*, 23 October 2008, https://www.nytimes.com/2008/10/23/opinion/23mcfarlane.html?_r=1&oref=slogin.

84. Marshall, "Hizbollah: 1982–2009," 550–51.

85. Jaber, *Hezbollah: Born with a Vengeance*, 28.

86. Joshua Gleis and Benedetta Berti, *Hezbollah and Hamas: A Comparative Study* (Baltimore: Johns Hopkins University Press, 2012), 64ff.

87. Ibid.

88. Hamzeh, "Clientalism, Lebanon," 112.

89. Norton, *Hezbollah: A Short History*, 102.

90. Marshall, "Hizbollah: 1982–2009," 548–50.

91. Nicholas Blanford, "The Quandary of an SLA Amnesty," *Daily Star*, 16 August 2005, quoted in Marshall, "Hizbollah: 1982–2009," and http://www.dailystar.com.lb/Opinion/Commentary/2005/Aug-16/95688-the-quandary-of-an-sla-amnesty.ashx.

92. Iver Gabrielsen, "Hezbollah's Strategy and Tactics in the Security Zone from 1985 to 2000," *Small Wars Journal*, no. 35, n.d., http://smallwarsjournal.com/jrnl/art/hezbollahs-strategy-and-tactics-in-the-security-zone-from-1985-to-2000.

93. Ibid.

94. Marshall, "Hizbollah: 1982–2009," 551–52.

95. Ibid.

96. For a detailed analysis of this conflict see Andrew Exum, *Hizballah at War: A Military Assessment*, Policy Focus no. 63 (Washington, DC: Washington Institute for Near East Policy, December 2006).

97. Kilcullen, *Out of the Mountains*, 142–44.

98. See Andrew Chadwick, "The 2006 Lebanon War: A Short History, Part II," *Small Wars Journal*, 12 September 2012, http://smallwarsjournal.com/jrnl/art/the-2006-lebanon-war-a-short-history-part-ii.

99. Bassem Mroue, "Hezbollah Chief Says Group Is Fighting in Syria," Associated Press, 25 May 2013, https://news.yahoo.com/hezbollah-chief-says-group-fighting-syria-162721809.html.

100. Kilcullen, *Blood Year*, locations 1387–88, 2990–3001.

101. Colin Clarke and Chad Serena, "Hezbollah Is Winning the War in Syria," *National Interest*, 29 January 2017, https://nationalinterest.org/feature/hezbollah-winning-the-war-syria-19229.

102. Blanford, *Hezbollah's Evolution*, 1. See also Mona Alami, "Hezbollah's Role in Syria Evolving as Assad Nears Victory," *al-Monitor*, 17 August 2018, https://www.al-monitor.com/pulse/originals/2018/08/syria-assad-victory-lebanon-hezbollah-iran-russia.html; and Laila Bassam and Tom Perry, "Hezbollah Emerges a Winner from Mideast Turmoil, Alarming Foes," Reuters, 30 November 2017, https://www.reuters.com/article/us-mideast-crisis-hezbollah/hezbollah-emerges-a-winner-from-mideast-turmoil-alarming-foes-idUSKBN1DU10C.

103. See Mona Alami, "Hezbollah Enters Drone Age with Bombing Raids in Syria," *Middle East Eye*, 20 March 2017, https://www.middleeasteye.net/news/analysis-hezbollah-enters-new-war-use-armed-drones-syria-11412100. See also Blanford, *Hezbollah's Evolution*, and Blanford, "Hezbollah Unveils Its Military Might in Syria," *Arab Weekly*, 20 November 2016, https://thearabweekly.com/hezbollah-unveils-its-military-might-syria.

104. Christopher Kozak, *"An Army in All Corners": Assad's Campaign Strategy in Syria*, Middle East Security Report no. 26 (Washington, DC: Institute for the Study of War, April 2015), 15–16.

Chapter 4

1. Unless otherwise noted, the direct observations reported in this chapter took place during periods of fieldwork in Norway in May 2015 and September–October 2016, Finland in September 2017, and Denmark in November–December 2018.

2. For espionage incidents see Rick Noack, "All over Europe, Russian Spies Are Getting Busted," *Washington Post*, 24 September 2018, https://www.washingtonpost.com/world/2018/09/24/its-not-great-time-be-russian-spy-europe/; and for an alleged Norwegian spying operation in Russia see Reid Standish, "A New Cold Front in Russia's Information War," *Foreign Policy*, 3 October 2018, https://foreignpolicy.com/2018/10/03/the-new-cold-front-in-russias-information-war-nato-norway/. For Norwegian moves to bolster border forces see Thomas Nilsen, "Norway Creates New Army Unit on Border to Russia," *Barents Observer*, 17 June 2016, https://thebarentsobserver.com/en/security/2016/06/norway-creates-new-army-unit-border-russia; and Bård Wormdal and Julie Kristin Karlsen Groset, "Frykter at deler av Finnmark kan bli okkupert av Russland," NRK Finnmark, 27 July 2017, https://www.nrk.no/finnmark/frykter-at-deler-av-finnmark-kan-bli-okkupert-av-russland-1.13574906. For Marine deployments to northern Norway see Reuters, "Hundreds of U.S. Marines Land in Norway, Irking Russia," 16 January 2017, https://www.reuters.com/article/US-norway-usa-military-idUSKBN1501CD.

3. David Shlapak and Michael Johnson, *Reinforcing Deterrence on NATO's Eastern Flank: Wargaming the Defense of the Baltics* (Santa Monica, CA: RAND Corporation, 2016), 1, https://www.rand.org/pubs/research_reports/RR1253.html.

4. Bjørn Thomassen, "The Uses and Meanings of Liminality," *International Political Anthropology* 2, no. 1 (2009): 5–28.

5. See, e.g., United States Special Operations Command, *White Paper: The Gray Zone* (2015), https://info.publicintelligence.net/USSOCOM-GrayZones.pdf.

6. For brief overviews of Norwegian partisan groups in northern Norway see Kåre Wahl, "Partisanene Sibblund Og Søderstrøm," 2002, http://nkpmn.org/Historiesidene/okkupasjonstida/WahlPartisan.html; and "Partisanen und Spione in Nord-Norwegen," http://www.71nord.de/NoNoPartisanen.html.

7. Thomas Alkärr, "Partisanene i Finnmark," NRK news, 10 December 2008, https://www.nrk.no/arkiv/artikkel/partisanene-i-finnmark-1.6346141.

8. Discussion with troops on patrol near Grense Jakobselv, Norway, 17 September 2016.

9. Interview with defense intelligence personnel, Oslo, 20 September 2016.

10. Liudmila Sorokina, *Managing Stereotypes About Russians in Northern Norway Through the Barents Regional Youth Programme* (master's thesis in peace and conflict transformation, University of Tromsø, 2012), 56–59. See also Geir Hønneland, *Borderland Russians: Identity, Narrative, and International Relations* (London: Palgrave MacMillan, 2010), 65ff.; Professor Geir Hønneland, *Borderland Russians: Identity, Narrative and International Relations*, Palgrave Studies in International Relations (London: Palgrave Macmillan,2010), Kindle ed.

11. Discussion with commander of Norwegian border troops, Kirkenes, 14 September 2016.

12. For comparative alcohol prices as of July 2017, see https://www.globalalcoholprices.com/alcohol_prices/; for comparative gasoline prices as of December 2018, see https://www.globalpetrolprices.com/gasoline_prices/. The most common passenger car in Norway, the BMW 2 Series, has a fuel tank capacity of 13.7 gallons.

13. Charles Maynes, "Refugees Choose Russia's Arctic as a Backdoor to Europe," *Voice of America News*, 31 October 2015, https://www.voanews.com/a/middle-eastern-refugees-choose-russia-arctic-to-europe/3030949.html.

14. Nick Gutteridge, "Fortress Europe: Now Baltic Countries Start Work on Huge Fence to Keep Out Migrant Influx," *Express*, 9 March 2016, https://www.express.co.uk/news/world/650923/EU-migrant-crisis-Baltic-Estonia-Latvia-Lithuania-Russia-fence-refugees-Greece-Turkey.

15. Adam Taylor, "Finland Blocks Refugees from Cycling across Russian Border into Lapland," *Washington Post*, 28 December 2015, https://www.washingtonpost.com/news/worldviews/wp/2015/12/28/finland-blocks-refugees-from-cycling-across-russian-border-into-lapland/?utm_term=.16a07f89b8cb.

16. Øysteyn Bogen, "Norway: Exploiting the Balancing Acts," in Alina Polyakova, Flemming Splidsboel Hansen, Robert van der Noordaa, Øystein Bogen, and Henrik Sundbom, *The Kremlin's Trojan Horses 3.0* (Washington, DC: Atlantic Council, 2018), 17.

17. Interview with Finnish *Supo* officer, Helsinki, September 2016. See also Øystein Bogen, *Russlands hemmelige krig mot Vesten* (Oslo: Kagge, 2018).

18. Bogen, "Norway: Exploiting the Balancing Acts."

19. See Sean Gallagher, "How Russia's 'Influence Operations' Targeted the Midterms (and How They Still Do)," *Ars Technica*, 22 October 2018, https://arstechnica.com/tech-policy/2018/10/how-russias-influence-operations-targeted-the-midterms-and-how-they-still-do/; and DFRLab, "#TrollTracker: Favorite Russian Troll Farm Sources," *Medium*, 20 October 2018, https://medium.com/dfrlab/trolltracker-favorite-russian-troll-farm-sources-48dc00cdeff. See also Anton Shekhovtsov, *Russian Interference and Where to Find It* (Warsaw: European Platform for Democratic Elections, 2019), https://www.epde.org/en/news/details/new-epde-publication-russian-interference-and-where-to-find-it.html?file=files/EPDE/RESSOURCES/2019%20Publications/EPDE_bookA5_RusInterf_EN_D02.pdf.

20. For one of several examples see United States Department of Justice *United States of America v. Internet Research Agency et al.*, grand jury indictment in the United States District Court for the District of Columbia, filed 16 February 2018, https://www.justice.gov/file/1035477/download.

21. For GRU hacking and dumping operations, see Special Counsel Robert S. Mueller III, *Report on the Investigation into Russian Interference in the 2016 Presidential Election* (Washington, DC: Department of Justice, 2019), 36–51, https://www.justice.gov/storage/report.pdf. For redactions relating to Trump campaign interactions with GRU see 51–56.

22. Office of the Director of National Intelligence, "Assessing Russian Activities and Intentions in Recent US Elections, Intelligence Community Assessment" (2017), ii, https://www.dni.gov/files/documents/ICA_2017_01.pdf.

23. Ibid., 13.

24. Luke Harding and Alec Luhn, "Putin Says Russian Role in Election Hacking 'Theoretically Possible,'" *Guardian*, 1 June 2017, https://www.theguardian.com/world/2017/jun/01/putin-says-russian-role-in-election-hacking-theoretically-possible.

25. Mueller, *Report*, 36–51; see also Federal Bureau of Investigation, *U.S. v. Elena Alekseevna Khusyaynova*, criminal complaint released 28 September 2018, https://www.justice.gov/opa/press-release/file/1102316/download; and Robert S. Mueller, *U.S. v. Viktor Borisovich Netyksho, et al.*, indictment dated 13 July 2018, https://en.wikisource.org/wiki/U.S._v._Viktor_Borisovich_Netyksho,_et_al.

26. Michael Schwirtz and Jose Bautista, "Poisoned Russian Ex-Spy Is Said to Have Worked with Spanish Intelligence," *New York Times*, 6 September 2018, https://www.nytimes.com/2018/09/06/world/europe/skripal-poison-russia-spy-spain.html.

27. Britain's Secret Intelligence Service (SIS) called Russian denial of the MH-17 shootdown an "outright falsehood" and concluded that "we know beyond any reasonable doubt that the Russian military supplied and subsequently recovered the missile launcher." See Intelligence and Security Committee of Parliament, *Annual Report, 2016–17*, https://assets.publishing.service.gov.uk/government/uploads/system/uploads/attachment_data/file/727949/ISC-Annual-Report-2016-17.pdf.

28. Svetlana Savranskaya and Tom Blanton, *NATO Expansion: What Gorbachev Heard—Declassified Documents Show Security Assurances against NATO Expansion to Soviet Leaders from Baker, Bush, Genscher, Kohl, Gates, Mitterrand, Thatcher, Hurd, Major, and Woerner*, Briefing Book no. 613 (Washington, DC: George Washington University National Security Archive, 12 December 2017), https://nsarchive.gwu.edu/briefing-book/russia-programs/2017-12-12/nato-expansion-what-gorbachev-heard-western-leaders-early#_edn1.

29. Ibid.

30. For an official Russian perspective see RT News, "25 Years On: Failed Coup That Ended the Soviet Union," 19 August 2016, part 1, https://www.rt.com/news/356469-ussr-coup-1991-gorbachev/, and part 2, https://www.rt.com/news/356579-ussr-coup-august-yeltsin/.

31. Savranskaya and Blanton, *NATO Expansion: What Gorbachev Heard*.

32. Svetlana Savranskaya and Tom Blanton, *NATO Expansion: What Yeltsin Heard—Russian President Led to Believe Partnership for Peace Was Alternative to Expanded NATO*, Briefing Book no. 621 (Washington, DC: George Washington University National Security Archive, 16 March 2018), https://nsarchive.gwu.edu/briefing-book/russia-programs/2018-03-16/nato-expansion-what-yeltsin-heard.

33. Central Intelligence Agency, "Reorganization of Soviet Ground Forces in East Germany," intelligence assessment, August 1983, declassified 18 June 2012, www.cia.gov/library/readingroom/docs/1983-08-01b.pdf.

34. For assessments of Sachs's role see Janine B. Wedel, "The Harvard Boys Do Russia," *Nation*, 14 May 1998, https://www.thenation.com/article/harvard-boys-do-russia/; and Peter Passell, "Dr. Jeffrey Sachs, Shock Therapist," *New York Times*, 27 June 1993. For Sachs's own interpretation see Jeffrey Sachs, "What I Did in Russia," 14 March 2012, http://jeffsachs.org/2012/03/what-i-did-in-russia/; and for Bill Browder's account of the corrupt fire sale of Russian government assets see Bill Browder, *Red Notice: A True Story of High Finance, Murder, and One Man's Fight for Justice* (New York: Simon & Schuster, 2015), 59–70.

35. Figures from Markar Melkonian, "US Meddling in 1996 Russian Elections in Support of Boris Yeltsin," *Global Research*, 11 November 2017, https://www.globalresearch.ca/us-meddling-in-1996-russian-elections-in-support-of-boris-yeltsin/5568288.

36. Ben Mezrich, *Once Upon a Time in Russia: The Rise of the Oligarchs* (New York: Atria, 2015), Kindle ed., locations 1337–41. See also "Oleg Deripaska and the Russian Aluminium Wars," *European CEO*, 24 January 2012, https://www.europeanceo.com/profiles/oleg-deripaska-and-the-russian-aluminium-wars/, and Zita Whalley, "Yekaterinburg's Mafia Gang Warfare of the 1990s," *Culture Trip*, 16 October 2017, https://theculturetrip.com/europe/russia/articles/yekaterinburgs-mafia-gang-warfare-of-the-1990s/.

37. Barry Newman, "A Cold Shoulder for Cold-War Vets," *Wall Street Journal*, 12 November 2012, https://www.wsj.com/articles/SB10001424052970203846804578103272647950486.

38. David Satter, "Boris Yeltsin," Hudson Institute, 24 April 2007, https://www.hudson.org/research/4893-boris-yeltsin.

39. Browder, *Red Notice*, 87.

40. Ibid.

41. Peter Beinart, "The U.S. Needs to Face Up to Its Long History of Election Meddling," *Atlantic*, 22 July 2018, https://www.theatlantic.com/ideas/archive/2018/07/the-us-has-a-long-history-of-election-meddling/565538/.

42. Eleanor Randolph, "Americans Claim Role in Yeltsin Win: Consultants Say They Spent Months in Moscow Secretly Devising U.S.-Style Strategy," *Los Angeles Times*, 9 July 1996, http://articles.latimes.com/1996-07-09/news/mn-22423_1_boris-yeltsin.

43. For an analysis dismissive of recent Russian efforts see Douglas Murray, "Snowplow Politics," *National Review*, 10 January 2019; for a contrary view see Rick Noack, "Everything We Know About Russian Election Meddling in Europe," *Washington Post*, 10 January 2018.

44. Mikhail Barabanov, "Hard Lessons Learned: Russian Military Reform up to the Georgian Conflict," in Colby Howard and Ruslan Pukhov (eds.), *Brothers Armed: Military Aspects of the Crisis in Ukraine* (Moscow: Center for Analysis of Strategies and Technologies, East View Press, 2014), Kindle ed., locations 1716–45.

45. Defense Intelligence Agency, *Russia Military Power: Building a Military to Support Great Power Aspirations* (Washington, DC: DIA, 2017), http://www.dia.mil/Portals/27/Documents/News/Military%20Power%20Publications/Russia%20Military%20Power%20Report%202017.pdf?ver=2017-06-28-144235-937.

46. Dale Herspring, "Russian Nuclear and Conventional Weapons: The Broken Relationship," in Stephen J. Blank (ed.), *Russian Nuclear Weapons: Past, Present and Future* (Carlisle, PA: United States Army War College, 2011), 5–6.

47. Barabanov, "Hard Lessons Learned," location 1848.

48. Olga Oliker, *Russia's Chechen Wars, 1994–2000: Lessons for Urban Combat* (Santa Monica, CA: RAND Corporation, 2001), 13–14.

49. For details of this dispute and its impact on the formation of the Ukrainian navy see "Ukrainian Naval History," https://www.globalsecurity.org/military/world/ukraine/vms-hist.htm.

50. Los Angeles Times, "Only 5 States Now Favor Combined Armed Forces, Ukraine Seeks Fleet, Creation of Own Army," *Baltimore Sun*, 5 January 1992, https://www.baltimoresun.com/news/bs-xpm-1992-01-05-1992005013-story.html.

51. Matt Potter, *Outlaws Inc.: Under the Radar and on the Black Market with the World's Most Dangerous Smugglers* (London: Bloomsbury, 2011), 28–29.

52. Ibid.

53. For the Belgrade embassy bombing, see Kyle Mizokami, "In 1999, America Destroyed China's Embassy in Belgrade (and Many Chinese Think It Was On Purpose)," *National Interest*, 21 January 2017, https://nationalinterest.org/blog/the-buzz/1999-america-destroyed-chinas-embassy-belgrade-many-chinese-19124; and for the involvement of MPRI in the Krajina (and the subsequent lawsuit against it) see Courthouse News Service, "U.S. Mercenaries Accused of Abetting Genocide," 18 August 2010, https://www.courthousenews.com/u-s-mercenaries-accused-of-abetting-genocide/.

54. See Charles K. Bartles, "Getting Gerasimov Right," *Military Review*, January–February 2016, 32, https://usacac.army.mil/CAC2/MilitaryReview/Archives/English/MilitaryReview_20160228_art009.pdf.

55. BBC News, *Timeline: NATO*, 21 February 2012, http://news.bbc.co.uk/1/hi/world/europe/country_profiles/1543000.stm.

56. Ibid.

57. Ministry of Foreign Affairs of the Republic of Latvia, "Baltic States' Peacekeeping Battalion to Mark 7th Anniversary," 24 March 2004, https://www.mfa.gov.lv/en/news/latest-news/newsletters/1114-baltic-states-peacekeeping-battalion-to-mark-7th-anniversary-bns. See also T. D. Møller, "BALTBAT: Lessons Learned and the Way Ahead," *Baltic Defence Review*, no. 3 (2000): 38–42, http://www.bdcol.ee/files/docs/bdreview/04bdr100.pdf.

58. BBC News, *Timeline: NATO*.

59. I am indebted to my friend (and perceptive longtime Russia watcher) Dimitri Klimenko for this framing.

60. George Kennan, *The Chargé in the Soviet Union (Kennan) to the Secretary of State*, 861.00/2-2246: telegram, Moscow, 22 February 1946 (the "long telegram"), https://nsarchive2.gwu.edu/coldwar/documents/episode-1/kennan.htm.

61. Keir Giles, *Moscow Rules*, Chatham House Insights Series (New York: Brookings Institution Press, 2019), Kindle ed., location 26.

62. Ibid., location 36.

63. Alexander Dugin, *Last War of the World-Island: The Geopolitics of Contemporary Russia* (London: Arktos, 2015), Kindle ed., location 161ff.

64. See Catherine A. Fitzpatrick, "Is Colonel Strelkov Making a Comeback or Has He Been Tamed?" *Interpreter*, 2 September 2014, http://www.interpretermag.com/is-colonel-strelkov-making-a-comeback-or-has-he-been-tamed/, and "Главарем диверсантів на Сході України виявився спецназівець із Росії—СБУ" [Leader of saboteurs in eastern Ukraine was Spetsnaz agent from Russia—SBU], TSN Network, 15 April 2014, https://tsn.ua/politika/glavarem-diversantiv-na-shodi-ukrayini-viyavivsya-specnazivec-iz-rosiyi-sbu-345381.html.

65. See Fitzpatrick, "Colonel Strelkov".

66. See Marlene Laruelle, *The "Russian World": Russia's Soft Power and Geopolitical Imagination* (Washington, DC: Center on Global Interests, 2015), http://globalinterests.org/wp-content/uploads/2015/05/FINAL-CGI_Russian-World_Marlene-Laruelle.pdf.

67. For commentary on this concept see Giles, *Moscow Rules*, 26.

68. Igor Zevelev, "The Russian World in Moscow's Strategy," Center for Strategic & International Studies, 22 August 2016, https://www.csis.org/analysis/russian-world-moscows-strategy.

69. Otto Büsch, *Das 19. Jahrhundert und Große Themen der Geschichte Preußens* (*Handbuch Der Preussischen Geschichte*) (Berlin: de Gruyter, 1992), 26–57.

70. Edward M. Spiers, *The Late Victorian Army, 1868–1902* (New York: Manchester University Press, 1992), 23ff., 272–73.

71. Heinz Guderian, *Achtung—Panzer! The Development of Tank Warfare* (1937), trans. Christopher Duffy (London: Cassell, 1999), Kindle ed., locations 868ff.

72. Ibid., esp. locations 4166ff.

73. David Dexter, *The New Guinea Offensives* (*Australia in the War of 1939–45*) (Canberra: Australian War Memorial, 1961), 228–29, 242.

74. Michael Bottoms, "SOF History: Tragedy of Desert One Creates the Four Tribes of U.S. Special Operations Command," *NewsRep*, 15 January 2016, https://thenewsrep.com/46167/sof-history-tragedy-of-desert-one-creates-the-four-tribes-of-u-s-special-operations-command/.

75. Dominic Johnson, "Darwinian Selection in Asymmetric Warfare: The Natural Advantage of Insurgents and Terrorists," *Journal of the Washington Academy of Arts and Sciences* 95, no. 3 (2009): 89–112, at 89.

76. Ibid.

77. Barabanov, "Hard Lessons Learned," location 1768.

78. For an account of this evolution see Oliker, *Russia's Chechen Wars*.

79. I am grateful for this insight to Keir Giles of the Royal Institute of International Affairs.

80. See Robert Moore, *A Time to Die: The Untold Story of the Kursk Tragedy* (New York: Three Rivers Press, 2004).

81. Herspring, "Russian Nuclear and Conventional Weapons," 3.

82. Central Intelligence Agency, *Evidence of Russian Development of New Subkiloton Nuclear Warheads* [*redacted*], Intelligence Memorandum, declassified 2005, https://www.cia.gov/library/readingroom/docs/DOC_0001260463.pdf.

83. See Mark B. Schneider, "Escalate to De-Escalate," *Proceedings*, vol. 143/2/1,368, February 2017, https://www.usni.org/magazines/proceedings/2017-02/escalate-de-escalate.

84. For examples of this see Sam Heller, "Russia Is in Charge in Syria: How Moscow Took Control of the Battlefield and Negotiating Table," *War on the Rocks*, 28 June 2016, https://warontherocks.com/2016/06/russia-is-in-charge-in-syria-how-moscow-took-control-of-the-battlefield-and-negotiating-table/; and Mathieu Boulègue, "Five Things to Know About the Zapad-17 Military Exercise," Chatham House, 25 September 2017, https://www.chathamhouse.org/expert/comment/five-things-know-about-zapad-2017-military-exercise.

85. Defense Intelligence Agency, *Global Nuclear Landscape, 2018*, open source intelligence assessment (Washington, DC: DIA, 2018), 10.

86. See, e.g., Jay Ross, "Time to Terminate Escalate to De-Escalate: It's Escalation Control," *War on the Rocks*, 24 April 2018, https://warontherocks.com/2018/04/time-to-terminate-escalate-to-de-escalateits-escalation-control/.

87. Ibid.

88. See Lyle J. Goldstein, "What Russia's Vostok-18 Exercise with China Means," *National Interest*, 5 September 2018, https://nationalinterest.org/feature/what-russias-vostok-18-exercise-china-means-30577; and Minnie Chan, "Vostok 2018 War Games: China's Chance to Learn Russia's Military Lessons from Syria," *South China Morning Post*, 29 August 2018, https://www.scmp.com/news/china/diplomacy-defence/article/2161909/vostok-2018-war-games-chinas-chance-learn-russias.

89. See Georgii Samoilovich Isserson, *The Evolution of Operational Art* (1936), trans. Bruce W. Menning (Fort Leavenworth, KS: United States Army Combat Analysis Center, 2013), 80–81, 99–102.

90. Ibid., 99–102.

91. For two among many examples see Andrew Roth, "Putin Threatens Arms Race If US Dumps Nuclear Treaty," *Guardian*, 5 December 2018, https://www.theguardian.com/world/2018/dec/05/putin-threatens-arms-race-if-us-dumps-nuclear-treaty; and Adam Withnall, "Russia Threatens Denmark with Nuclear Weapons if It Tries to Join Nato Defence Shield," *Independent*, 22 March 2015, https://www.independent.co.uk/news/world/europe/russia-threatens-denm . . . uclear-weapons-if-it-tries-to-join-nato-defence-shield-10125529.html.

92. Central Intelligence Agency, *Foreign Missile Developments and the Ballistic Missile Threat Through 2015: Unclassified Summary of a National Intelligence Estimate* (December 2001), 3, https://www.dni.gov/files/documents/missilethreat_2001.pdf.

93. See Shaan Shaikh, "Russia Conducts Second Sarmat ICBM Test Launch," Missile Threat, Center for Strategic and International Studies, 30 March 2018, last modified 15 June 2018, https://missilethreat.csis.org/russia-conducts-second-sarmat-icbm-test-launch/; and Missile Defense Project, "Russia Test Fires Topol ICBM," Missile Threat, Center for Strategic and International Studies, 2 January 2018, last modified 15 June 2018, https://missilethreat.csis.org/russia-test-fires-topol-icbm/.

94. For a video released by the Russian Ministry of Defense on the weapons, see https://youtu.be/LY99w6Xu4XU. For the capabilities of Status-6 (designated *Kanyon* by US intelligence) see Kyle Mizokami, "Pentagon Document Confirms Existence of Russian Doomsday Torpedo," *Popular Mechanics*, 16 January 2018, https://www.popularmechanics.com/military/weapons/a15227656/pentagon-document-confirms-existence-of-russian-doomsday-torpedo/.

95. For an account of the Transcaucasian conflict of the 1920s and the incorporation of Georgia into the USSR see Jonathan D. Smele, *The "Russian" Civil Wars, 1916–1926* (London: Hurst, 2015), 145–48.

96. Transparency International Georgia, *Georgia's Oil and Gas Potential: Georgia as a Traditional Transit Country for Azeri Energy Resources* (2008), https://www.transparency.ge/sites/default/files/Oil%20and%20Gas%20Potential%20of%20Georgia_ENG.pdf.

97. Zevelev, "The Russian World in Moscow's Strategy."

98. Giles, *Moscow Rules*, 75–76.

99. S. Neil MacFarlane, "Frozen Conflicts in the Former Soviet Union: The Case of Georgia/South Ossetia," *OSCE Yearbook, 2008*, Organisation for Security and Co-operation in Europe, 23.

100. Luke Harding, "WikiLeaks Cables Claim Russia Armed Georgian Separatists," *Guardian*, 1 December 2010, https://www.theguardian.com/world/2010/dec/01/wikileaks-cables-russia-georgian-separatists.

101. For a critique of this position see Olga Oliker, "Kosovo and South Ossetia More Different Than Similar," *RANDBlog*, 25 August 2008, https://www.rand.org/blog/2008/08/kosovo-and-south-ossetia-more-different-than-similar.html.

102. Harding, "WikiLeaks Cables."

103. Sputnik News, "Georgians Back NATO Membership in Referendum," 11 January 2008, https://sptnkne.ws/dqfq.

104. Michael Evans, "Vladimir Putin Tells Summit He Wants Security and Friendship," *Times*, 5 April 2008, http://www.timesonline.co.uk/tol/news/world/article3681609.ece.

105. Vyacheslav Tseluiko, "Georgian Army Reform Under Saakashvili Prior to the 2008 Five Day War," Ruslan Pukhov (ed.), *The Tanks of August* (Moscow: Centre for Analysis of Strategies and Technologies, 2010), 17.

106. Harding, "WikiLeaks Cables."

107. Anton Lavrov, "Timeline of Russian-Georgian Hostilities in 2008," in Pukhov, *The Tanks of August*, 41–43.

108. For an estimate of troop numbers see Carolina Vendil Pallin and Fredrik Westerlund, "Russia's War in Georgia: Lessons and Consequences," *Small Wars & Insurgencies* 20, no. 2 (2009): 400.

109. See Lavrov, "Timeline of Russian-Georgian Hostilities"; and Ariel Cohen, James Carafano, and Lajos F. Szaszdi, "Russian Forces in the Georgian War: Preliminary Assessment and Recommendations," *Report Europe*, 20 August 2008, Heritage Foundation, https://www.heritage.org/europe/report/russian-forces-the-georgian-war-preliminary-assessment-and-recommendations.

110. For an analysis of the 2007 Estonia attacks see R. Ottis, "Analysis of the 2007 Cyber Attacks against Estonia from the Information Warfare Perspective," in *Proceedings of the 7th European Conference on Information Warfare and Security, Plymouth, 2008* (Reading: Academic, 2008), 163–68.

111. Sarah P. White, *Understanding Cyberwarfare: Lessons from the Russian-Georgian War, 2008* (West Point, NY: Modern Warfare Institute, 2018), 1, 7.

112. John Markoff, "Before the Gunfire, Cyberattacks," *New York Times*, 12 August 2008, https://www.nytimes.com/2008/08/13/technology/13cyber.html.

113. Ibid.

114. Markoff, "Before the Gunfire."

115. White, *Understanding Cyberwarfare*.

116. Jeffrey Carr, "Faith-Based Attribution," *Medium*, 10 July 2016, https://medium.com/@jeffreyscarr/faith-based-attribution-30f4a658eabc.

117. Thom Shanker, "Russians Melded Old-School Blitz with Modern Military Tactics," *New York Times*, 16 August 2008, https://www.nytimes.com/2008/08/17/world/europe/17military.html.
118. Cohen et al., "Russian Forces in the Georgian War."
119. Vladimir Isachenkov, "War Reveals Russia's Military Might and Weakness," Associated Press, 18 August 2008, http://www.aviation.com/technology/080818-russia-georgia-air-war.html.
120. Ibid.
121. Pallin and Westerlund, "Russia's War in Georgia," 400.
122. Nikita Petrov, "Russian Army's Weaknesses Exposed During War in Georgia," *Sputnik News*, 9 September 2008, https://sputniknews.com/analysis/200809091166657490/.
123. Cohen et al., "Russian Forces in the Georgian War."
124. Pallin and Westerlund, "Russia's War in Georgia," 404.
125. Ibid., 401.
126. Ibid.
127. White, *Understanding Cyberwarfare*, 7.
128. I am indebted to Keir Giles for these details.
129. Mikhail Barabanov, "Changing the Force and Moving Forward After Georgia," in Howard and Pukhov, *Brothers Armed*, locations 2031–40.
130. Ibid., location 2047.
131. Ibid., locations 2085–95.
132. Ibid.
133. Portions of the following section appear in David Kilcullen, "The Evolution of Unconventional Warfare," *Scandinavian Journal of Military Studies* 2, no. 1 (June 2019) 61–71.
134. See Amos C. Fox, *Hybrid Warfare: The 21st-Century Russian Way of War* (Fort Leavenworth, KS: School of Advanced Military Studies, 2017), https://apps.dtic.mil/dtic/tr/fulltext/u2/1038987.pdf; Christopher Chivvis, *Understanding Russian Hybrid Warfare and What Can Be Done About It* (Santa Monica, CA: RAND Corporation, 2017), https://www.rand.org/pubs/testimonies/CT468.html; and Michael Kofman and Matthew Rojansky, *A Closer Look at Russia's "Hybrid War"* (Washington, DC: Wilson Center, 2015), https://www.wilsoncenter.org/sites/default/files/7-KENNAN%20CABLE-ROJANSKY%20KOFMAN.pdf.
135. See Alina Polyakova, *Weapons of the Weak: Russia and AI-Driven Asymmetric Warfare* (Washington, DC: Brookings Institution, 2018), https://www.brookings.edu/research/weapons-of-the-weak-russia-and-ai-driven-asymmetric-warfare/.
136. See Peter Pomerantsev, "How Putin Is Reinventing Warfare," *Foreign Policy*, 5 May 2014, http://www.foreignpolicy.com/articles/2014/05/05/how_putin_is_reinventing_warfare; and Mark Galleotti, "The 'Gerasimov Doctrine' and Russian Non-Linear War," *In Moscow's Shadows*, 6 July 2014, https://inmoscowsshadows.wordpress.com/2014/07/06/the-gerasimov-doctrine-and-russian-non-linear-war/.
137. United States Army, Asymmetric Warfare Group, *Russian New Generation Warfare Handbook* (2017), https://publicintelligence.net/awg-russian-new-warfare-handbook/.

138. United States Special Operations Command, *Gray Zone*.

139. Bartles, "Getting Gerasimov Right," 30–38.

140. See David G. Perkins, "Multi-Domain Battle: The Advent of Twenty-First-Century War," *Military Review*, November–December 2017, 8–13, https://www.armyupress. army.mil/Portals/7/military-review/Archives/English/Multi-Domain-Battle-The-Advent-of-Twenty-First-Century-War.pdf?ver=2017-10-26-160929-763.

141. Author's personal observation and discussion with intelligence personnel in Iraq, February 2006 and February–July 2007, and in Afghanistan, March 2008–December 2013.

142. For a detailed discussion of failure-to-fire ratios from World War II to Vietnam see Russell W. Glenn, *Reading Athena's Dance Card: Men against Fire in Vietnam* (Annapolis, MD: Naval Institute Press, 2000). For average ratios of deployed, combat-role, and combat-participant troops since 1917 see John J. McGrath, *The Other End of the Spear: The Tooth-to-Tail Ratio (T3R) in Modern Military Operations* (Fort Leavenworth, KS: Combat Studies Institute Press, 2007), 65, 73–75.

143. For a slightly different take on this see Julian Sanchez, "Russia Wanted Trump to Win. And It Wanted to Get Caught," *New York Times*, 17 February 2018, https:// www.nytimes.com/2018/02/17/opinion/russia-interference-elections-trump. html?searchResultPosition=4.

144. Christopher Paul and Miriam Matthews, *The Russian "Firehose of Falsehood" Propaganda Model: Why It Might Work and Options to Counter It* (Santa Monica, CA: RAND Corporation, 2016), 1, https://www.rand.org/pubs/perspectives/PE198.html.

145. Ibid.

146. Timothy L. Thomas, "Russia's Reflexive Control Theory and the Military," *Journal of Slavic Military Studies* 17 (2004): 237–56, quoted in Mark Mateski, "Russia, Reflexive Control, and the Subtle Art of Red Teaming," *Red Team Journal*, 13 October 2016, http://redteamjournal.com/2016/10/reflexive-control/.

147. Mateski, "Russia, Reflexive Control, and the Subtle Art of Red Teaming."

148. Thomas, "Russia's Reflexive Control Theory," 248–49, quoted in Mateski, "Russia, Reflexive Control, and the Subtle Art of Red Teaming."

149. For examples of Russian reflexive control theory from the 1990s, see S. A. Komov, "About Methods and Forms of Conducting Information Warfare," *Military Thought*, July–August 1997, 18–22; and N. I. Turko and S. A. Modestov, "Refleksivnoe upravlenie razvitiem strategicheskikh sil gosudarstva kak mekhanizm sovremennoy geopolitiki (Reflexive Control in the Development of Strategic Forces of States as a Mechanism of Modern Geopolitics)," report at the "Systems Analysis on the Threshold of the 21st Century: Theory and Practice" conference, Moscow, February 1996, 366, both referenced in Thomas, "Russia's Reflexive Control Theory."

150. Office of the Director of National Intelligence, "Assessing Russian Activities."

151. For further discussions of reflexive control see Thomas, "Russia's Reflexive Control Theory"; Mateski, "Russia, Reflexive Control, and the Subtle Art of Red Teaming"; and Diane Chotikul, *The Soviet Theory of Reflexive Control in Historical and Psychocultural Perspective: A Preliminary Study*, technical report (Monterey, CA: Naval Postgraduate School, 1986), https://apps.dtic.mil/dtic/tr/fulltext/u2/a170613.pdf.

152. Paul and Matthews, *The Russian "Firehose of Falsehood" Propaganda Model*.

153. Ibid., 1–3.

154. Orwell's reference in *Nineteen Eighty-Four* to the constantly changing enemy ("Oceania was at war with Eastasia. Oceania had always been at war with Eastasia"), though fictional, was based on his experience of Soviet propaganda in the Spanish Civil War. George Orwell, *Nineteen Eighty-Four* (New York: Houghton Mifflin Harcourt, 1949), 172. See also Arthur Koestler, *Darkness at Noon*, trans. Daphne Hardy (New York: Scribner, 1941), 242–44.

155. For a discussion of Gerasimov's role and its relation to the General Staff function see Bartles, "Getting Gerasimov Right," 30–31.

156. Valeriy Gerasimov, "Ценность Науки В Предвидении: Новые Вызовы Требуют Переосмысления Форм И Способов Ведения Боевых Действий [The value of science in foresight: New challenges require rethinking forms and methods of conducting military actions]," *Военно-Промышленный Курьер* [Military-industrial courier], no. 8 (476) (27 February–5 March 2013): 1–3, https://vpk-news.ru/sites/default/files/pdf/VPK_08_476.pdf.

157. Mark Galeotti, "The 'Gerasimov Doctrine' and Russian Non-Linear War," *In Moscow's Shadows*, 6 July 2014, https://inmoscowsshadows.wordpress.com/2014/07/06/the-gerasimov-doctrine-and-russian-non-linear-war/.

158. Mark Galeotti, "I'm Sorry for Creating the 'Gerasimov Doctrine,'" *Foreign Policy*, 5 March 2018, https://foreignpolicy.com/2018/03/05/im-sorry-for-creating-the-gerasimov-doctrine/.

159. Anthony Cordesman of the Center for Strategic and International Studies attended the conference and published detailed notes (including screenshots of Gerasimov's slides). See Anthony H. Cordesman, *Russia and the "Color Revolution": A Russian Military View of a World Destabilized by the US and the West* (Full Report) (Washington, DC: Center for Strategic and International Studies, 2014), https://csis-prod.s3.amazonaws.com/s3fs-public/legacy_files/files/publication/140529_Russia_Color_Revolution_Full.pdf.

160. Gerasimov, "The value of science in foresight," 2.

161. Bartles, "Getting Gerasimov Right," 34.

162. Gerasimov, "The value of science in foresight," 3, diagram at right. For a translation see Bartles, "Getting Gerasimov Right," 36.

163. Ibid.

164. Ibid.

165. Ibid.

166. "Transcript of the Third Presidential Debate," *New York Times*, 22 October 2012, https://www.nytimes.com/2012/10/22/us/politics/transcript-of-the-third-presidential-debate-in-boca-raton-fla.html.

167. Gerasimov, "The value of science in foresight."

168. Ibid., 3, diagram at left. For a translation see Bartles, "Getting Gerasimov Right," 35.

Chapter 5

1. See "Chinese Government Takes Over Troubled Insurance Giant Anbang," *Guardian*, 2 February 2018, https://www.theguardian.com/world/2018/feb/23/chinese-government-anbang-insurance-giant.

2. See Nectar Gan, "Chinese Princeling and Anbang 'Adviser' Chen Xiaolu Dies at 71," *South China Morning Post*, 1 March 2018, https://www.scmp.com/news/china/policies-politics/article/2135337/chinese-princeling-and-anbang-adviser-chen-xiaolu-dies; and Lucy Hornby, "Chen Xiaolu, 1946–2018: Princeling Who Atoned for Cultural Revolution," *Financial Times*, 1 March 2018.

3. Arash Massoudi and James Fontanella-Khan, "China's Anbang Agrees $6.5bn Hotel Deal with Blackstone," *Financial Times*, 13 March 2016.

4. See Royal Navy, *Her Majesty's Naval Base Clyde*, https://www.royalnavy.mod.uk/our-organisation/where-we-are/naval-base/clyde.

5. See Graeme, "Chinese Investor Buys Rosslea Hall Hotel in Rhu," *Hotel News Scotland*, 20 April 2018, https://www.hotelnews.scot/archive/2018/april/chinese-investor-buys-rosslea-hall-hotel.

6. For the relevant company filing history see Companies House, United Kingdom, Filing History, https://beta.companieshouse.gov.uk/company/11152727/filing-history.

7. Ibid.

8. For the composition of CFIUS see https://www.treasury.gov/resource-center/international/foreign-investment/Pages/cfius-members.aspx.

9. Hui-yong Yu and David McLaughlin, "Blackstone Ends Plan to Sell Landmark Hotel to China's Anbang After U.S. Opposition," *Bloomberg News*, 21 October 2016, https://www.bloomberg.com/news/articles/2016-10-21/blackstone-said-to-end-anbang-deal-for-hotel-near-u-s-navy-base.

10. For an account of the air battles around Darwin see Anthony Cooper, *Darwin Spitfires: The Real Battle for Australia* (Sydney: University of New South Wales Press, 2011).

11. Seth Robson, "Australia-Bound Battalion Will Boost Marines' Darwin Presence to 2,500," *Stars and Stripes*, 26 April 2019, https://www.stripes.com/news/pacific/australia-bound-battalion-will-boost-marines-darwin-presence-to-2-500-1.578356

12. Wayne Shields, "Defence White Paper: NT Economy Set for Massive Boost on the Back of Spending to Match Asia's Growing Military Presence," ABC News (Australia), 24 February 2016, https://www.abc.net.au/news/2016-02-25/nt-economy-set-for-massive-boost-on-back-of-defence-spending/7199816.

13. Lisa Murray, "Chinese State-Owned Newspaper Confirms Landbridge's Military Ties," *Australian Financial Review*, 17 November 2015, https://www.afr.com/news/world/chinese-stateowned-newspaper-confirms-landbridges-military-ties-20151117-gl0i2v. See also Geoff Wade, "Landbridge and the Port of Darwin: A Postscript," 11 November 2015, *ASPI Strategist*, https://www.aspistrategist.org.au/landbridge-and-the-port-of-darwin-a-postscript/.

14. Xiaobing Li, *A History of the Modern Chinese Army* (Lexington, KY: University Press of Kentucky, 2007), 292.

15. Geoff Wade, "Landbridge, Darwin and the PRC," *ASPI Strategist*, 9 November 2015, https://www.aspistrategist.org.au/landbridge-darwin-and-the-prc/.

16. See "Greece Sells Largest Port Piraeus to Chinese Company," RT News, 8 April 2016, https://www.rt.com/business/338949-greece-china-port-sale/.

17. Janne Suokas, "Chinese Investors Cancel Plans for Massive Deep-Water Port in Sweden," *GB Times*, 31 January 2018, https://gbtimes.com/chinese-investors-cancel-plans-for-massive-deep-water-port-in-sweden.

18. See World Shipping Council, "Top 50 World Container Ports," 2016, http://www.worldshipping.org/about-the-industry/global-trade/top-50-world-container-ports.

19. Jojje Olsson, "China's Bid to Build Scandinavia's Largest Port in Sweden Raises Security Concerns," *Taiwan Sentinel*, 22 December 2017, https://sentinel.tw/china-port-scandinavia-security/; and Suokas, "Chinese Investors Cancel Plans."

20. Chris Giles, "Ethiopia Is Now Africa's Fastest Growing Economy," CNN News, 24 April 2018, at https://www.cnn.com/2018/04/24/africa/africa-largest-economy/index.html.

21. For a few examples see Istvan Tarrosy and Zoltán Vörös, "China and Ethiopia, Part 2: The Addis Ababa–Djibouti Railway," *Diplomat*, 22 February 2018, https://thediplomat.com/2018/02/china-and-ethiopia-part-2-the-addis-ababa-djibouti-railway/; Jenni Marsh, "Skyscrapers, Trains and Roads: How Addis Ababa Came to Look Like a Chinese City," CNN, 3 September 2018, at https://edition.cnn.com/style/article/addis-ababa-china-construction-style/index.html; and *China Daily*, "Chinese-Funded Airport Project in Ethiopia to Be Completed Next January," 29 June 2017, http://www.chinadaily.com.cn/world/2017-06/29/content_29932267.htm.

22. Sébastien Le Belzic, "China's Exim Bank: Africa's Largest Financier Looks For an Even Bigger Role," *Africa Report*, 25 October 2012, https://www.theafricareport.com/6472/chinas-exim-bank-africas-largest-financier-looks-for-an-even-bigger-role/.

23. Andrew Jacobs and Jane Perlez, "U.S. Wary of Its New Neighbor in Djibouti: A Chinese Naval Base," *New York Times*, 25 February 2017, https://www.nytimes.com/2017/02/25/world/africa/us-djibouti-chinese-naval-base.html. For trade figures as of 2014 see Alfredo Burlando, Anca D. Cristea, and Logan M. Lee, "The Trade Consequences of Maritime Insecurity: Evidence from Somali Piracy," *Review of International Economics* 23, no. 3 (August 2015): 525–57.

24. See "Dubai, Chinese Firm Battle in Hong Kong for Djibouti Ports," *Hiraan*, 13 February 2019, https://www.hiiraan.com/news4/2019/Feb/162263/dubai_chinese_firm_battle_in_hong_kong_for_djibouti_ports.aspx.

25. COSCO Shipping, "COSCO Shipping Delegates Attended the Opening Ceremony and Thematic Sessions of the Belt and Road Forum for International Cooperation," 17 May 2017, http://en.coscoshipping.com/art/2017/5/15/art_6923_58594.html.

26. Taddeo Bambwale, "China to Expand Peacekeeping Role in Africa," *New Vision* (Uganda), 25 August 2016, https://www.newvision.co.ug/new_vision/news/1433624/china-expand-peacekeeping-role-africa. Note that of the twenty-five hundred peacekeepers referred to in this article, approximately four hundred are in Lebanon, while the rest are in Africa.

27. Matthew Campbell, "A Chinese Casino Has Conquered a Piece of America," *Bloomberg Businessweek*, 15 February 2018, https://www.bloomberg.com/news/features/2018-02-15/a-chinese-company-has-conquered-a-piece-of-america.

28. Sputnik News International, "Okinawan Separatists Might Get 'Chinese Protectorate' Instead of Independence," 13 January 2017, https://sputniknews. com/asia/201701131049568056-okinawa-independence-china/.

29. See Kathrin Hille and Mure Dickie, "Japan's Claim to Okinawa Disputed by Influential Chinese Commentators," *Washington Post*, 23 July 2012; and Mitsuru Obe, "Japan Presses China on Vessels Sailing Near Disputed Islands," *Wall Street Journal*, 24 August 2016.

30. See Ankit Panda, "Sri Lanka Formally Hands Over Hambantota Port to Chinese Firms on 99-Year Lease," *Diplomat*, 11 December 2017, https://thediplomat.com/ 2017/12/sri-lanka-formally-hands-over-hambantota-port-to-chinese-firms-on-99-year-lease/; Maria Abi-Habib, "How China Got Sri Lanka to Cough Up a Port," *New York Times*, 25 June 2018, https://www.nytimes.com/2018/06/25/world/ asia/china-sri-lanka-port.html; and Kai Schultz, "Sri Lanka, Struggling with Debt, Hands a Major Port to China," *New York Times*, 12 December 2017, https://www. nytimes.com/2017/12/12/world/asia/sri-lanka-china-port.html?module=inline.

31. The notion of an "escalation ladder" originated with Cold War nuclear strategists such as Herman Kahn, and by the late 1970s the idea of "horizontal escalation" was being used to explain Soviet behavior in the Persian Gulf. More recent analyses add the category of "political escalation." For a Cold War–era analysis see US Joint Chiefs of Staff, *Horizontal Escalation as a Response to Soviet Aggression in the Persian Gulf*, 3 October 1980, https://www.archives.gov/files/declassification/ iscap/pdf/2010-073-doc1.pdf; and for a more recent example see Forrest Morgan, Karl P. Mueller, Evan S. Medeiros, Kevin L. Pollpeter, and Roger Cliff, *Dangerous Thresholds: Managing Escalation in the 21st Century* (Santa Monica, CA: RAND Corporation, 2008), 18–25.

32. For impacts of a Sino-American conflict see David C. Gompert, Astrid Stuth Cevallos, and Cristina L. Garafola, *War with China: Thinking Through the Unthinkable* (Santa Monica, CA: RAND Corporation, 2016); and for US-China debt see Kimberley Amadeo, "US Debt to China, How Much It Is, Reasons Why, and What If China Sells: Why China Is America's Biggest Banker," *Balance*, 25 February 2019, https://www.thebalance.com/ u-s-debt-to-china-how-much-does-it-own-3306355.

33. For the support China provided to Iran during the Iran-Iraq War see Scott W. Harold and Alireza Nader, *China and Iran: Economic, Political, and Military Relations* (Santa Monica, CA: RAND Corporation, 2012), 6–8.

34. For the Sino-Vietnamese War see Edward C. O'Dowd, *Chinese Strategy in the Third Indochina War: The Last Maoist War* (London: Routledge, 2007). For the Yalu River battle see Bruce Elleman, *Modern Chinese Warfare: 1795–1989* (London: Routledge, 2005), 103–4.

35. Xiaobang Li, "Chinese Intentions and the 1954–55 Offshore Islands Crisis," in Lori Lyn Bogle (ed.), *The Cold War*, vol. 3: *Hot Wars of the Cold War* (New York: Routledge, 2001), 125–28.

36. Xuan Loc Duan, "27 Days of Hell: When China and Vietnam Went to War," *National Interest*, 26 February 2017, https://nationalinterest.org/blog/the-buzz/ 27-days-hell-when-china-vietnam-went-war-19596.

37. Andrew Scobell, David Lai, and Roy Kamphausen, eds., *Chinese Lessons from Other People's Wars* (Carlisle, PA: United States Army War College, Strategic Studies Institute, November 2011).

38. See Cormac O'Gráda, "Great Leap, Great Famine: A Review Essay," *Population and Development Review* 39, no. 2 (June 2013): 333–60; and Jung Chang and Jon Halliday, *Mao: The Unknown Story* (London: Jonathan Cape, 2005), 569. See also James David Banker, "The Children of the Revolution," *Quillette*, 18 December 2018, https://quillette.com/2018/12/18/the-children-of-the-revolution/.

39. Communist Party of China, "Resolution on Certain Questions in the History of Our Party Since the Founding of the People's Republic of China, Adopted by the Sixth Plenary Session of the Eleventh Central Committee of the Communist Party of China on June 27, 1981," in *Resolution on CPC History (1949–81)* (Beijing: Foreign Languages Press, 1981), 32

40. See Robert F. Dernberger, "The Drive for Economic Modernization and Growth: Performance and Trends," in Michael Ying-Mao Kau and Susan H. Marsh (eds.), *China in the Era of Deng Xiaoping: A Decade of Reform* (London: Taylor & Francis, 1993), 155–215.

41. Michael Dillon, *Deng Xiaoping: The Man Who Made Modern China* (London: I. B. Tauris, 2014), 127.

42. Yang Kuisong, "Reconsidering the Campaign to Suppress Counterrevolutionaries," *China Quarterly* 193 (March 2008): 102–21.

43. Zhiyue Bo, "A Period of Hope in Cross-Strait Relations: 1979–1992," *Chinese Law and Government* 35, no. 3 (May–June 2002):. 6.

44. Xiaobing Li, *A History of the Modern Chinese Army*, 359.

45. June Teufel Dreyer, "Reorganizing and Modernizing the Chinese Military," in Kau and Marsh, *China in the Era of Deng Xiaoping*, 334.

46. Ibid.

47. Ibid.

48. Ibid.

49. Jason H. Rosenstrauch, *Operational Art in the Sino-Vietnamese War* (Fort Leavenworth, KS: United States Army Command and General Staff College, School of Advanced Military Studies, 2014), 27–28.

50. Carlyle Thayer, *Background Brief: China-Vietnam Border War, 1979–2014*, (Canberra: Thayer Consultancy, 2014), https://www.scribd.com/document/208108717/Thayer-China-Vietnam-Border-War-1979-2014, 2.

51. Howard French, "Was the War Pointless? China Shows How to Bury It," *New York Times*, 1 March 2005, https://www.nytimes.com/2005/03/01/world/asia/was-the-war-pointless-china-shows-how-to-bury-it.html; see also Edward C. O'Dowd and John F. Corbett Jr., "The 1979 Chinese Campaign in Vietnam: Lessons Learned," in Laurie Burkitt, Andrew Scobell, and Larry M. Wortzel (eds.), *The Lessons of History: The Chinese People's Liberation Army at 75* (Carlisle, PA: United States Army War College Strategic Studies Institute, 2003), 353–54.

52. Timothy R. Heath, "China's Untested Military Could Be a Force—or a Flop," *Foreign Policy*, 27 November 2018, https://foreignpolicy.com/2018/11/27/chinas-untested-military-could-be-a-force-or-a-flop/.

53. Xiaobing Li, *A History of the Modern Chinese Army*, 252.

54. Ibid., 253.

55. Thayer, *Background Brief*.

56. For a survey of PLA documents on the war see Edward C. O'Dowd, "People's Liberation Army Documents on the Sino-Vietnamese Conflict, 1979, Part 1," *Chinese Law & Government* 42, no. 5 (2009): 3–10.

57. Xiaobing Li, *A History of the Modern Chinese Army*, 255.

58. John Pike, "Chinese Invasion of Vietnam, February 1979," n.d., https://www.globalsecurity.org/military/world/war/prc-vietnam.htm.

59. Ibid.

60. Xiaobing Li, *A History of the Modern Chinese Army*, 254.

61. Pike, "Chinese Invasion of Vietnam."

62. Ibid.

63. Xiaobing Li, *A History of the Modern Chinese Army*, 255.

64. Nguyen Minh Quang, "The Bitter Legacy of the 1979 China-Vietnam War," *Diplomat*, 23 February 2017, https://thediplomat.com/2017/02/the-bitter-legacy-of-the-1979-china-vietnam-war/.

65. O'Dowd and Corbett, "The 1979 Chinese Campaign in Vietnam," 353–54.

66. Ibid., 356–57.

67. Ibid.

68. Ibid., 366.

69. Ibid., 360–62.

70. Ibid., 357–60.

71. Ibid., 366–67.

72. Xiaobing Li, *A History of the Modern Chinese Army*, 289.

73. For a prescient analysis of these stresses, preceding Tiananmen by five years, see David Mason, "China's Four Modernizations: Blueprint for Development or Prelude to Turmoil?," *Asian Affairs: An American Review* 11, no. 3 (Fall 1984): 47–70.

74. See Kris Cheng, "Declassified: Chinese Official Said at Least 10,000 Civilians Died in 1989 Tiananmen Massacre, Documents Show," *Hong Kong Free Press*, 21 December 2017, https://www.hongkongfp.com/2017/12/21/declassified-chinese-official-said-least-10000-civilians-died-1989-tiananmen-massacre-documents-show/.

75. I am grateful to John Owens for this insight.

76. Li, *A History of the Modern Chinese Army*, 272–33.

77. Ibid., 278–79.

78. For contrasting perspectives on the "responsibility to protect" see Global Centre for the Responsibility to Protect, "The Responsibility to Protect: A Background Briefing," 2015, http://www.globalr2p.org/media/files/r2p-backgrounder.pdf; and Eric A. Heinze, "Humanitarian Intervention, the Responsibility to Protect, and Confused Legitimacy," *Human Rights & Human Welfare* 11 (2011): 17–32, https://www.du.edu/korbel/hrhw/volumes/2011/heinze-2011.pdf.

79. For example, all NATO nations have signed and ratified the North Atlantic Treaty, Article 1 of which commits them to "settle any international dispute in which they may be involved by peaceful means in such a manner that international peace and security and justice are not endangered, and to refrain in their international relations

from the threat or use of force in any manner inconsistent with the purposes of the United Nations." See North Atlantic Treaty, 4 April 1949, https://www.nato.int/cps/en/natohq/official_texts_17120.htm.

80. See Eric Schmitt, "Crisis in the Balkans: Human Error; Wrong Address of Embassy in Databases," *New York Times*, 10 May 1999, https://www.nytimes.com/1999/05/10/world/crisis-in-the-balkans-human-error-wrong-address-of-embassy-in-databases.html?pagewanted=all.

81. For a translation of Chinese Politburo members' immediate reactions see *Chinese Law and Government* 35, no. 1 (January–February 2002): 73–99.

82. Ibid.; see also George Tenet, "DCI Statement on the Belgrade Chinese Embassy Bombing," testimony before the House Permanent Select Committee on Intelligence, Central Intelligence Agency, https://www.cia.gov/news-information/speeches-testimony/1999/dci_speech_072299.html.

83. Tenet, "DCI Statement on the Belgrade Chinese Embassy Bombing."

84. See Thomas R. Pickering, "Oral Presentation of the Chinese Government Regarding the Accidental Bombing of the P.R.C. Embassy in Belgrade," 1999, United States Department of State, https://www.state.gov/documents/organization/6524.doc.

85. BBC News, "Nato Hits Chinese Embassy," 8 May 1999, http://news.bbc.co.uk/2/hi/europe/338424.stm. See also Peter Hays Gries, "Tears of Rage: Chinese Nationalist Reactions to the Belgrade Embassy Bombing," *China Journal*, no. 46 (July 2001): 25–43.

86. See Kerry Dumbaugh, *Chinese Embassy Bombing in Belgrade: Compensation Issues* (Washington, DC: Congressional Research Service Report for Congress, 2011), 3, https://www.everycrsreport.com/files/20000412_RS20547_7627e6d52e8e75fcf9d6ec7b29b15f00c96011f2.pdf.

87. John Sweeney, Jens Holsoe, and Ed Vulliamy, "Nato Bombed Chinese Deliberately," *Guardian*, 17 October 1999, https://www.theguardian.com/world/1999/oct/17/balkans.

88. De Leon Petta Gomes da Costa, *Organized Crime and the Nation-State: Geopolitics and National Sovereignty* (London: Routledge, 2018), 60. See also Peter Lee, "How It All Began: The Belgrade Embassy Bombing," *China Matters*, 24 May 2015, https://chinamatters.blogspot.com/2015/05/how-it-all-began-belgrade-embassy.html.

89. Gries, "Tears of Rage," 25.

90. Ibid.

91. Ibid., 26.

92. For a US account of this incident see Shirley A. Kan et al., *China-U.S. Aircraft Collision Incident of April 2001: Assessments and Policy Implications*, CRS Report for Congress, updated 10 October 2001 (Washington, DC: Congressional Research Service, 2001), https://fas.org/sgp/crs/row/RL30946.pdf; for an alternative perspective see Chi Wang, *Obama's Challenge to China: The Pivot to Asia* (London: Routledge, 2016), 20–21.

93. Scott W. Harold, *Defeat, Not Merely Compete: China's View of Its Military Aerospace Goals and Requirements in Relation to the United States* (Santa Monica, CA: RAND Corporation, 2018), 12.

94. See Justin Raward, "Julian Corbett and Maritime versus Continental Strategy," *Sabretache* 50, no. 1 (March 2009): 45–50; and Joel Wuthnow, "Asian Security without the United States? Examining China's Security Strategy in Maritime and Continental Asia," *Asian Security* 14, no. 3 (2018): 230–45.

95. Wuthnow, "Asian Security without the United States?"

96. Alexander Dugin, *Last War of the World-Island: The Geopolitics of Contemporary Russia* (London: Arktos, 2015), Kindle ed., location 627.

97. For an account of Zheng He (Cheng Ho) see Edward L. Dreyer, *Zheng He: China and the Oceans in the Early Ming Dynasty, 1405–1433* (New York: Pearson Longman, 2007).

98. Li Kangying, *The Ming Maritime Trade Policy in Transition, 1368 to 1567* (Wiesbaden: Harrassowitz, 2010), 3–5.

99. For example, Qing naval forces fought the British Royal Navy during the Opium Wars and mounted coastal blockades and engaged in riverine operations throughout the nineteenth century. See Steven Tsang, *A Modern History of Hong Kong* (London: I. B. Tauris, 2007), 3–13; and Richard N. J. Wright, *The Chinese Steam Navy, 1862–1945* (Newport, RI: Naval Institute Press, 2000).

100. See Jack A. Goldstone, "The Rise of the West—or Not? A Revision to Socioeconomic History," *Sociological Theory* 18, no. 2 (July 2000): 175–94; and Ronald C. Po, *The Blue Frontier: Maritime Vision and Power in the Qing Empire*, Cambridge Oceanic Histories (Cambridge: Cambridge University Press, 2018).

101. See Sarabjeet Singh Parmar and Saloni Salil, "China and India: Maritime Commonalities and Divergences," *Journal of Defence Studies* 5, no 3 (July 2011): 144–50.

102. Dean Cheng, *Sea Power and the Chinese State: China's Maritime Ambitions* (Washington, DC: Heritage Foundation, 2011), 2–3, https://thf_media.s3.amazonaws.com/2011/pdf/bg2576.pdf. See also State Oceanic Administration, Ocean Development Strategy Research Study Group, *China's Ocean Development Report* (Beijing: Maritime Publishing House, 2010), 227, quoted in ibid.

103. Mark A. Ryan, David M. Finkelstein, and Michael A. McDevitt, eds., *Chinese Warfighting: The PLA Experience since 1949* (London: Routledge, 2015), Kindle ed., 11.

104. State Council Information Office of the People's Republic of China, "China's Military Strategy," May 2015, http://eng.mod.gov.cn/DefenseNews/2015-05/26/content_4586748.htm.

105. Ronald O'Rourke, *China Naval Modernization: Implications for U.S. Navy Capabilities—Background and Issues for Congress* (Washington, DC: Congressional Research Service, 1 August 2018), 2, https://fas.org/sgp/crs/row/RL33153.pdf.

106. Ibid.

107. Bruce Elleman, *Taiwan Straits: Crisis in Asia and the Role of the U.S. Navy* (New York: Rowman & Littlefield, 2014), 130.

108. See J. Michael Cole, "The Third Taiwan Strait Crisis: The Forgotten Showdown Between China and America," *National Interest*, 10 March 2017, https://nationalinterest.org/feature/the-third-taiwan-strait-crisis-the-forgotten-showdown-19742.

109. Ibid.

110. Ibid.

111. O'Rourke, *China Naval Modernization*.

112. Ibid.

113. Ibid.

114. Patrick Devenny, "PLAN Procurement of Sovremenny-Class Destroyers: Developments and Repercussions," *RUSI Chinese* 2, no. 8 (23 May 2005), https://rusi.org/publication/plan-procurement-sovremenny-class-destroyers-developments-and-repercussions.

115. O'Rourke, *China Naval Modernization*, 4–5, 32.

116. Ibid., 10–18.

117. Ibid., 18, 17 (table 1).

118. Stephen Chen, "America's Hidden Role in Chinese Weapons Research: Many Scientists Have Returned to China After Working at Los Alamos and Other Top US Laboratories," *South China Morning Post*, 29 March 2017, https://www.scmp.com/news/china/diplomacy-defence/article/2082738/americas-hidden-role-chinese-weapons-research.

119. For an intriguing series on the acquisition of the Liaoning see Minnie Chan, "Mission Impossible: How One Man Bought China Its First Aircraft Carrier," *South China Post*, 18 January 2015, https://www.scmp.com/news/china/article/1681710/sea-trials-how-one-man-bought-china-its-aircraft-carrier; "The Inside Story of the Liaoning: How Xu Zengping Sealed Deal for China's First Aircraft Carrier," *South China Morning Post*, 19 January 2015, https://www.scmp.com/news/china/article/1681755/how-xu-zengping-became-middleman-chinas-deal-buy-liaoning; and "Mission Impossible II: The Battle to Get China's Aircraft Carrier Home," *South China Morning Post*, 20 January 2015, https://www.scmp.com/news/china/article/1682731/mission-impossible-ii-battle-get-chinas-aircraft-carrier-home.

120. Dave Majumdar, "Everything You Need to Know About China's New Aircraft Carrier," *National Interest*, 10 September 2018, https://nationalinterest.org/blog/buzz/everything-you-need-know-about-chinas-new-aircraft-carrier-30992.

121. Ibid.

122. O'Rourke, *China Naval Modernization*, 112.

123. Majumdar, "Everything You Need to Know."

124. O'Rourke, *China Naval Modernization*, 44–47; see also David Axe, "China's Navy Has Big Plans for Its Future Aircraft Carriers: Think Drones and Electromagnetic Catapults," *National Interest*, 7 January 2019, https://nationalinterest.org/blog/buzz/chinas-navy-has-big-plans-its-future-aircraft-carriers-40832.

125. Ibid.

126. For the A-100, see "A100: Multiple Launch Rocket System," http://www.military-today.com/artillery/a100.htm. For the SR-5 see "SR-5: Multiple Launch Rocket System," http://www.military-today.com/artillery/sr5.htm.

127. For DF-26 see http://www.military-today.com/missiles/df_26.htm; for DF-21D see http://www.military-today.com/missiles/df_21d.htm; and for the possible air-launched DF-21 see Tyler Rogoway, "Is This China's DF-21D Air-Launched Anti-Ship Ballistic-Missile-Toting Bomber?," *War Zone*, http://www.thedrive.com/the-war-zone/13511/is-this-chinas-df-21d-air-launched-anti-ship-ballistic-missile-toting-bomber.

128. Jin Wu, Simon Scarr, and Weiyi Cai, "Concrete and Coral: Tracking Expansion in the South China Sea," *Reuters*, 24 May 2018, https://fingfx.thomsonreuters.com/

gfx/rngs/CHINA-SOUTHCHINASEA-BUILDING/010070760H9/index.
html.

129. Hiroyuki Umetsu, "Communist China's Entry into the Korean Hostilities and a U.S. Proposal for a Collective Security Arrangement in the Pacific Offshore Island Chain," *Journal of Northeast Asian Studies* 15, no. 2 (1996): 98–118.

130. Toshi Yoshihara, "China's Vision of Its Seascape: The First Island Chain and Chinese Seapower," *Asian Politics & Policy* 4, no. 3 (July 2012): 293–314.

131. Jin et al., "Concrete and Coral."

132. For Chinese responses to the "pivot" see Michael D. Swaine, "Chinese Leadership and Elite Responses to the U.S. Pacific Pivot," *China Leadership Monitor*, no. 38 (2015): 11, https://carnegieendowment.org/files/CLM38MS.pdf.

133. Jin et al., "Concrete and Coral"; see also Manuel Mogatu, "Exclusive: Philippines Reinforcing Rusting Ship on Spratly Reef Outpost: Sources," *Reuters World News*, 13 July 2015, https://www.reuters.com/article/us-southchinasea-philippines-shoal-exclu-idUSKCN0PN2HN20150714.

134. Mogatu, "Philippines Reinforcing".

135. O'Rourke, *China Naval Modernization*, 106–7.

136. See Permanent Court of Arbitration, "The South China Sea Arbitration (*The Republic of Philippines v. The People's Republic of China*)," case information, https://pca-cpa.org/en/cases/7/.

137. Gregory Kulacki, *China's Nuclear Arsenal: Status and Evolution* (Washington, DC: Union of Concerned Scientists, 2010), https://www.ucsusa.org/sites/default/files/legacy/assets/documents/nwgs/UCS-Chinese-nuclear-modernization.pdf.

138. Kyle Mizokami, "This Is the Real Reason China Is Deploying Nuclear Missile Subs," *The Week*, 1 June 2016, https://theweek.com/articles/626869/real-reason-china-deploying-nuclear-missile-subs. See also Damen Cook, "A Closer Look at China's Critical South China Sea Submarine Base: A Deeper Look at Yulin-East, China's Burgeoning Submarine Bastion in the South China Sea," *The Diplomat*, 18 March 2017, https://thediplomat.com/2017/03/a-closer-look-at-chinas-critical-south-china-sea-submarine-base/.

139. See Mathieu Duchâtel and Eugenia Kazakova, "Tensions in the South China Sea: The Nuclear Dimension," SIPRI (Stockholm International Peace Research Institute), 27 August 2015, https://www.sipri.org/commentary/essay/2015/tensions-south-china-sea-nuclear-dimension.

140. Qiao Liang and Wang Xiangsui, *Unrestricted Warfare*, trans. Foreign Broadcast Information Service (FBIS) (Beijing: PLA Literature and Arts Publishing House, February 1999, https://www.oodaloop.com/documents/unrestricted.pdf.

141. Dean Cheng, "Unrestricted Warfare: Review Essay II," *Small Wars and Insurgencies* 11, no. 1 (March 2000): 122–23.

142. For a cogent account of the book's place in the Chinese debate see Tony Corn, "Peaceful Rise Through Unrestricted Warfare: Grand Strategy with Chinese Characteristics," *Small Wars Journal* (2010), https://smallwarsjournal.com/blog/journal/docs-temp/449-corn.pdf.

143. Ibid., 2.

144. Ibid., 6–7.

145. Ibid., 12.

146. Ibid., 55–56.

147. Ibid., 48.

148. Ibid., 87.

149. Ibid., 93–94.

150. Ibid., 127.

151. See David E. Spencer and Hugo Acha Melgar, "Bolivia, a New Model Insurgency for the 21st Century: From Mao Back to Lenin," *Small Wars & Insurgencies* 28, no. 3 (2017): 629–60.

152. For a critique of the PMESII construct see Brian M. Ducote, *Challenging the Application of PMESII-PT in a Complex Environment* (Fort Leavenworth, KS: School of Advanced Military Studies, United States Army Command and General Staff College, 2010), https://apps.dtic.mil/dtic/tr/fulltext/u2/a523040.pdf.

153. United States Drug Enforcement Administration, *National Drug Threat Assessment* (Washington, DC: DEA, 2018), 21–37.

154. Greg R. Lawson, "The Fentanyl Crisis Is a Reverse Opium War," *National Interest*, 26 December 2017, https://nationalinterest.org/feature/the-fentanyl-crisis-reverse-opium-war-23812.

155. Sean O'Connor, *Fentanyl: China's Deadly Export to the United States*, staff report (Washington, DC: U.S.-China Economic and Security Review Commission), 7, https://www.uscc.gov/sites/default/files/Research/USCC%20Staff%20Report_Fentanyl-China's%20Deadly%20Export%20to%20the%20United%20States020117.pdf. See also Liana Rosen and Susan Lawrence, *Illicit Fentanyl, China's Role, and U.S. Foreign Policy Options* (Washington, DC: Congressional Research Service, 2018), https://fas.org/sgp/crs/row/IF10890.pdf.

156. Tom Phillips, "China Rejects Claims It Had Hand in Efforts to Oust Robert Mugabe," *Guardian*, 21 November 2017, https://www.theguardian.com/world/2017/nov/21/china-rejects-claims-it-had-hand-in-efforts-to-oust-robert-mugabe; and see Ben Westcott and Steve George, "The Chinese Connection to the Zimbabwe 'Coup,'" CNN, 17 November 2017, https://www.cnn.com/2017/11/17/africa/china-zimbabwe-mugabe-diplomacy/index.html.

157. Ibid.

158. Interview with CL, BB, and CZ at Tswalu Kalahari, South Africa, 1 December 2017, and remarks by BB at Tswalu, 3 December 2017.

159. Mukasiri Sibanda, "Zimbabwe: Questions as Chinese Resurface on Anjin's Marange Diamond Claims," *All Africa*, 23 April 2018, https://allafrica.com/stories/201804240627.html.

160. See Cecilia Jamasmie, "Zimbabwe Confirms Army Ownership of Diamond Mine," *Mining*, 19 June 2012, http://www.mining.com/zimbabwean-government-confirms-army-ownership-of-diamond-mine/; and Linda Mujuru, "Chinese-Owned Mining Companies Bring Work and Hazards to Zimbabwe," *Global Press Journal*, 6 April 2018, https://globalpressjournal.com/africa/zimbabwe/chinese-owned-mining-companies-bring-work-hazards-zimbabwe/ .

161. Nabeel Mancheri, Lalitha Sundaresan, and S. Chandrashekar, *Dominating the World: China and the Rare Earth Industry* (Bangalore: National Institute of

Advanced Studies, April 2013), http://investorintel.com/wp-content/uploads/
2014/01/China-rare-earth-strategyin-wHighlights-.pdf. See also Interagency Task
Force, *Assessing and Strengthening the Manufacturing and Defense Industrial Base
and Supply Chain Resiliency of the United States* (Washington, DC: Department
of Defense, September 2018), 27–28, 134, https://media.defense.gov/2018/
Oct/05/2002048904/-1/-1/1/ASSESSING-AND-STRENGTHENING-
THE-MANUFACTURING-AND%20DEFENSE-INDUSTRIAL-BASE-
AND-SUPPLY-CHAIN-RESILIENCY.PDF; and Valentina Ruiz Leotaud,
"Rare Earths: Battling China's Monopoly After Molycorp's Demise?," *Mining*, 10
September 2016, http://www.mining.com/rare-earths-battling-chinas-monopoly-
after-molycorps-debacle/.

162. Andrew Mambondiyani, "Chinese Company to Return to Zimbabwe's
Controversial Marange Diamond Fields," *Epoch Times*, 7 March 2019, https://www.
theepochtimes.com/chinese-company-to-return-to-zimbabwes-controversial-
marange-diamond-fields_2814988.html.

163. Felix Njini, "Zimbabwe, Russia Sign \$4 Billion Platinum Mine Deal," *Bloomberg
News*, 10 April 2019, https://www.bloomberg.com/news/articles/2019-04-10/
zimbabwe-russia-finalize-deal-for-4-billion-platinum-mine.

164. See United States Department of Defense, *The National Defense Strategy of the
United States of America* (Washington, DC: DOD, 2005), 2–3, http://archive.
defense.gov/news/Mar2005/d20050318nds1.pdf; and United States Department
of Defense, *Quadrennial Defense Review Report* (Washington, DC: DOD, 2006), 3,
19–20, http://archive.defense.gov/pubs/pdfs/QDR20060203.pdf.

165. Spencer and Melgar, "Bolivia, a New Model Insurgency."

166. Qiao and Wang, *Unrestricted Warfare*, 144.

167. Ibid., 146.

168. Ibid., 164.

169. Ibid., 168–69, 179.

170. Sangkuk Lee, "China's 'Three Warfares': Origins, Applications, and Organizations,"
Journal of Strategic Studies 37, no. 2 (2014): 198–221.

171. Corn, "Peaceful Rise Through Unrestricted Warfare," 8–9.

172. Ibid.

173. Ibid.

174. Francesco Sisci, preface to Qiao Liang, "One Belt, One Road," speech delivered
at University of Defense, China, 17 July 2015, http://www.limesonline.com/en/
one-belt-one-road?refresh_ce.

175. Qiao, "One Belt, One Road."

176. For references to Soros in URW see Qiao and Wang, *Unrestricted Warfare*, 48, 52–
53, 60, 116.

177. Qiao, "One Belt, One Road."

Chapter 6

1. See "It's Again a Tented Field: Sickles and Longstreet at Gettysburg," *New York
Times*, 1 July 1888, https://timesmachine.nytimes.com/timesmachine/1888/
07/01/106327211.pdf; Carl Smith and Adam Hook, *High Tide of the Confederacy:*

Gettysburg, 1863, Campaign Series no. 52 (London: Osprey, 1998); and U.S. Historical Marker Database, *High Water Mark*, https://www.hmdb.org/marker. asp?marker=16160.

2. Smith and Hook, *High Tide of the Confederacy*.
3. James D. Coomler, *Clausewitz's Concept of the Culminating Point and Its Application in the Gettysburg Campaign of 1863* (Carlisle, PA: United States Army War College, 1993), https://apps.dtic.mil/dtic/tr/fulltext/u2/a264855.pdf.
4. Ibid.
5. Adam J. Herbert, "The Baghdad Strikes," *Air Force Magazine*, July 2003, 46–50, http://www.airforcemag.com/MagazineArchive/Documents/2003/July%20 2003/0703strikes.pdf.
6. Mark Kinkade, "The First Shot," *Airman: Magazine of America's Air Force*, July 2003, http://www.af.mil/news/airman/0703/air.html, and https://web.archive.org/ web/20080517050321/http://www.af.mil/news/airman/0703/air.html. The cost quoted for the F-117 is average unit cost; see David Aronstein and Albert Piccirillo, *HAVE BLUE and the F-117A* (Reston, VA: American Institute of Aeronautics and Astronautics, 1997), 267.
7. See "Decapitation Attempt Was Worth a Try, George," *Sydney Morning Herald*, 22 March 2003, https://www.smh.com.au/world/middle-east/decapitation-attempt-was-worth-a-try-george-20030322-gdgh06.html; and David Martin, "Ex-CIA Officer on the Strike That Could Have Averted Iraq War," CBS News, 19 March 2013, https://www.cbsnews.com/news/ex-cia-officer-on-the-strike-that-could-have-averted-iraq-war/.
8. Michael Gordon and Bernard Trainor, "Iraqi Leader, in Frantic Flight, Evaded U.S. Strikes," *New York Times*, 12 March 2006, https://www.nytimes.com/2006/03/ 12/world/middleeast/iraqi-leader-in-frantic-flight-eluded-us-strikes.html.
9. Ibid.; see also Douglas Jehl and Eric Schmitt, "The Struggle for Iraq: Intelligence; Errors Are Seen in Early Attacks on Iraqi Leaders," *New York Times*, 13 June 2004, https://www.nytimes.com/2004/06/13/world/struggle-for-iraq-intelligence-errors-are-seen-early-attacks-iraqi-leaders.html.
10. Joel Roberts, "At Saddam's Bombed Palace," CBS News, 28 May 2003, https:// www.cbsnews.com/news/at-saddams-bombed-palace/; see also Jehl and Schmitt, "The Struggle for Iraq."
11. "Decapitation Attempt Was Worth a Try, George."
12. Avraham Shalom, at 12:20–30 and 19:20–29 of Dror Moreh's film *The Gatekeepers*, Sony Pictures Classics, 2013.
13. United States Navy, *CNATRA P-912 Low Altitude Training*, Flight Training Instruction, Department of the Navy, Chief of Naval Air Training, 2018, 1–5.
14. For Chinese historic GDP figures, see "China GDP Annual Growth Rate," *Trading Economics*, https://tradingeconomics.com/china/gdp-growth-annual.
15. For a discussion of recent Chinese military complaints about lack of combat experience, see Minnie Chan, "China's Army Infiltrated by 'Peace Disease' After Years without a War, Says Its Official Newspaper," *South China Morning Post*, 3 July 2018, https://www.scmp.com/news/china/diplomacy-defence/article/2153579/ chinas-army-infiltrated-peace-disease-after-years; and Philip Wen, "What Is China's

'Peace Disease'? (And Why Australia Should Care)," *Sydney Morning Herald*, 2 September 2015, https://www.smh.com.au/world/what-is-chinas-peace-disease-and-why-australia-should-care-20150902-gjd3as.html.

16. Jordan Wilson, *China's Expanding Ability to Conduct Conventional Missile Strikes on Guam*, Staff Research Report (Washington, DC: U.S. China Economic and Security Review Commission, 2016), https://www.uscc.gov/sites/default/files/Research/Staff%20Report_China's%20Expanding%20Ability%20to%20Conduct%20Conventional%20Missile%20Strikes%20on%20Guam.pdf.

17. See, e.g., "We Told You So: Russian Officials React to Mueller Report on Collusion," *Moscow Times*, 25 March 2019, https://www.themoscowtimes.com/2019/03/25/we-told-you-so-russian-officials-react-to-mueller-report-on-collusion-a64939; and Leonid Bershidsky, "The U.S. Needs a Post-Mueller Reality Check: The Conspiracy Narrative Wasn't Borne Out. Now Americans Should Dismiss the Idea of a Russian 'Hybrid War,'" *Moscow Times*, 31 March 2019, https://www.themoscowtimes.com/2019/03/31/the-us-needs-a-post-mueller-reality-check-a65027.

18. See Missile Threat, Center for Strategic and International Studies, "Hwasong-15 (KN-22)," https://missilethreat.csis.org/missile/hwasong-15-kn-22/.

19. Colin Clark, "'North Korea Is a Cyber Super Power': Former ROK Commander," *Breaking Defense*, 23 May 2018, https://breakingdefense.com/2018/05/north-korea-is-a-cyber-super-power-former-rok-commander/.

20. Tasnim News (Tehran), "Iran among 8 Countries with Full Nuclear Fuel Cycle: Ex-Negotiator," 11 February 2019, https://www.tasnimnews.com/en/news/2019/02/11/1944690/iran-among-8-countries-with-full-nuclear-fuel-cycle-ex-negotiator.

21. David Wroe, "Australia Gets into the Missile Defence Game as Rogue Threat Rises," *Sydney Morning Herald*, 7 October 2017, https://www.smh.com.au/politics/federal/australia-gets-into-the-missile-defence-game-as-rogue-threat-rises-20171006-gyw298.html.

22. Fareed Zakaria, *The Post-American World, and the Rise of the Rest; Release 2.0* (New York: Penguin, 2011).

23. Ibid., 1.

24. Jonah Goldberg, *Suicide of the West: How the Rebirth of Tribalism, Populism, Nationalism, and Identity Politics Is Destroying American Democracy* (New York: Crown Forum, 2018).

25. Ibid., 331.

26. Zakaria, *The Post-American World*, xiv.

27. See Oswald Spengler, *The Decline of the West* (New York: Oxford University Press, 1991).

28. Ezra Pound, *Hugh Selwyn Mauberley*, vv. 1–8.

29. See Herbert Spencer, *The Principles of Biology* (1864), rev. ed., vol. 1 (New York: D. Appleton & Company, 1904), 530n; Edward Gibbon, *The History of the Decline and Fall of the Roman Empire*, 6 vols. (London: J. M. Dent & Sons, 1776–89, 1954); Ibn Khaldûn, *The Muqaddimah: An Introduction to History* (1377), trans. Franz Rosenthal (Princeton, NJ: Princeton University Press, 1967); Aristotle, *Politics*, trans. Ernest Baker (Oxford: Oxford University Press, 1998); and Plato, *The Republic*, trans. Desmond Lee (London: Penguin Classics, 2007).

30. See Carroll Quigley, *The Evolution of Civilizations: An Introduction to Historical Analysis*, 2nd ed. (New York: Liberty Fund, 1979); Paul Kennedy, *The Rise and Fall of the Great Powers: Economic Change and Military Conflict from 1500 to 2000* (New York: Vintage Books, 1987); Niall Ferguson, *Empire: The Rise and Demise of the British World Order and the Lessons for Global Power* (New York: Basic Books, 2003); and Samuel P. Huntington, *The Clash of Civilizations and the Remaking of World Order* (New York: Simon & Schuster, 1996).

31. Bob Herbert, "In America; War Games," *New York Times*, 22 February 1998, https://www.nytimes.com/1998/02/22/opinion/in-america-war-games.html.

32. T. X. Hammes, personal communication, Copenhagen, December 2018.

33. See Robert Work, "The Third U.S. Offset Strategy and Its Implications for Partners and Allies," speech delivered by Deputy Secretary of Defense Bob Work, 28 January 2015, https://dod.defense.gov/News/Speeches/Speech-View/Article/606641/the-third-us-offset-strategy-and-its-implications-for-partners-and-allies/; for an overview of key technology focus areas see Katie Lange, "3rd Offset Strategy 101: What It Is, What the Tech Focuses Are," DOD Live, 30 March 2016, http://www.dodlive.mil/2016/03/30/3rd-offset-strategy-101-what-it-is-what-the-tech-focuses-are/.

34. For an unclassified insight into Chinese military biotech see U.S.-China Economic Security Review Commission, *Annual Report*, 2018, 507–8, https://www.uscc.gov/sites/default/files/Annual_Report/Chapters/Chapter%204%2C%20Section%201%20-%20China%27s%20Pursuit%20of%20Dominance%20in%20Computing%2C%20Robotics%2C%20and%20Biotechnology.pdf.

35. Yoram Hazony and Ofir Haivry, "Why America Needs New Alliances," *Wall Street Journal*, 5 April 2019, https://www.wsj.com/articles/why-america-needs-new-alliances-11554503421?mod=hp_opin_pos3.

36. See Jeffrey Goldberg, "The Obama Doctrine," *Atlantic*, April 2016, https://www.theatlantic.com/magazine/archive/2016/04/the-obama-doctrine/471525/.

37. Andrew Moran, "Barack Obama and the Return of 'Declinism': Rebalancing American Foreign Policy in an Era of Multipolarity," in Edward Ashbee and John Dumbrell (eds.), *The Obama Presidency and the Politics of Change* (London: Palgrave Macmillan, 2016), 265–87.

38. For Afghan planning see Bob Woodward, *Obama's Wars* (New York: Simon & Schuster, 2011), 330–31. The ambassador to Libya, J. Christopher Stephens, was killed in a forward diplomatic outpost in Benghazi in September 2012; the ambassador for the Syrian opposition, Robert Ford, resigned in 2014. See PBS News, "Former U.S. Ambassador Says He Could 'No Longer Defend' Obama Administration's Syria Policy," 3 June 2014, https://www.pbs.org/newshour/show/former-ambassador-discusses-mistakes-u-s-policy-syria.

39. For a description of offshore balancing by two Trump-skeptical strategists, see John J. Mearsheimer and Stephen M. Walt, "The Case for Offshore Balancing: A Superior U.S. Grand Strategy," *Foreign Affairs*, July–August 2016, 70–83, https://mearsheimer.uchicago.edu/pdfs/Offshore%20Balancing.pdf.

40. See Stephen M. Walt, "The Tragedy of Trump's Foreign Policy," *Foreign Policy*, 5 March 2019, https://foreignpolicy.com/2019/03/05/the-tragedy-of-trumps-foreign-policy/.

41. For an account of this see Christopher Clark, *The Sleepwalkers: How Europe Went to War in 1914* (London: HarperCollins, 2013), 414–15.

42. David Wemer, "NATO's Stoltenberg Credits Trump as Allies Increase Defense Spending," *Atlantic Council*, 11 July 2018, https://www.atlanticcouncil.org/blogs/new-atlanticist/stoltenberg-nato-engages.

43. See Nick Miller, "In Helsinki, Trump Shows His Weakness for Putin to the World," *Sydney Morning Herald*, 17 July 2018, https://www.smh.com.au/world/europe/in-helsinki-trump-proves-his-weakness-for-putin-to-the-world-20180717-p4zrv7.html.

44. See Sputnik News, "Lavrov: World Is Clearly Entering the Post-Western Era," *Sputnik International*, 09.03.2017, https://sputniknews.com/world/201703091051409715-lavrov-post-western-world/.

45. Goldberg, "The Obama Doctrine."

46. Edward Luttwak, *The Grand Strategy of the Byzantine Empire* (Cambridge, MA: Harvard University Press, 2009), Kindle ed., locations 1, 12. See also John Haldon, *Byzantium at War: AD 560–1453* (London: Routledge, 2003), 8.

47. "Inaugural Address of John F. Kennedy," 20 January 1961, Avalon Project of Yale Law School, https://web.archive.org/web/20070514235348/http://www.yale.edu/lawweb/avalon/presiden/inaug/kennedy.htm.

48. Luttwak, *The Grand Strategy of the Byzantine Empire*.

49. Haldon, *Byzantium at War*, 8, 29–35.

50. Savvas Kyriakidis, *Warfare in Late Byzantium, 1204–1453* (Leiden: Brill, 2011), 138–56.

51. For Byzantine fortifications and siege warfare see Leif Inge Ree Petersen, *Siege Warfare and Military Organization in the Successor States (400–800 AD): Byzantium, the West and Islam* (Leiden: Brill, 2013), 256–98; and Kyriakidis, *Warfare in Late Byzantium*, 157–220. For Greek fire, see John Pryor and Elizabeth M. Jeffreys, *The Age of the ΔΡΟΜΩΝ: The Byzantine Navy ca. 500–1204* (Leiden: Brill, 2006), 621–28.

52. For an overview see Michael J. Decker, *The Byzantine Art of War* (Yardley, PA: Westholme, 2013), 213–32, 1–41.

53. Haldon, *Byzantium at War*, 14.

54. Ibid.

55. Ibid.

56. Luttwak, *The Grand Strategy of the Byzantine Empire*, 5, 36, 85, 106.

57. Steven Runciman, *The Fall of Constantinople, 1453* (Cambridge: Cambridge University Press, 1965), xi.

58. For Russia's Arctic strategy and its relation to climate change see Pavel Devyatkin, "Russia's Arctic Strategy," four-part series at the Arctic Institute, Center for Circumpolar Studies, 6–27 February 2018, https://www.thearcticinstitute.org/russias-arctic-strategy-aimed-conflict-cooperation-part-one/, https://www.thearcticinstitute.org/russias-arctic-military-and-security-part-two/, https://www.thearcticinstitute.org/russias-arctic-strategy-energy-extraction-part-three/, and https://www.thearcticinstitute.org/russias-arctic-strategy-maritime-shipping-part-iv/.

59. For an examination of the applicability of this model see Monica Ruiz, "Is Estonia's Approach to Cyber-Defense Feasible in the United States?," *War on the Rocks*, 9 January 2018, https://warontherocks.com/2018/01/estonias-approach-cyber-defense-feasible-united-states/.

60. See James K. Wither, "'Modern Guerrillas' and the Defense of the Baltic States," *Small Wars Journal*, January 2018, https://smallwarsjournal.com/jrnl/art/modern-guerrillas-and-defense-baltic-states.

61. Australia's Regional Force Surveillance Units and the Canadian Rangers have proved effective in defense terms as well as in linking indigenous communities to national networks and identity. See Aaron Waddell, "Indigenous Pride, National Security and the Regional Force Surveillance Units," *Australian Defence Force Journal*, no. 202 (July 2017): 27–36, http://www.defence.gov.au/adc/adfj/Documents/issue_202/Waddell_July_2017.pdf; and Canadian Armed Forces, *Canadian Rangers*, http://army-armee.forces.gc.ca/en/canadian-rangers/index.page.

62. See Wolf-Dieter Roepke and Hasit Thankey, "Resilience: The First Line of Defense," *NATO Review*, 27 February 2019, https://www.nato.int/docu/review/2019/Also-in-2019/resilience-the-first-line-of-defence/EN/index.htm.

63. See Alec Luhn, "Russian Mercenary Boss Spoke with Kremlin Before Attacking US Forces in Syria, Intel Claims," *Telegraph*, 23 February 2018, https://www.telegraph.co.uk/news/2018/02/23/russian-mercenary-boss-spoke-kremlin-attacking-us-forces-syria/; and France 24, "The Business of War: Russian Mercenaries in Syria," 23 February 2018, https://www.france24.com/en/20180223-russia-fighters-syria-exclusive-interview-mercenary-wagner.

64. I am indebted to Professor Conrad Crane of the US Army War College for this insight.

65. Drew Thompson, "Think Again: China's Military," *Foreign Policy*, 11 February 2010, https://foreignpolicy.com/2010/02/11/think-again-chinas-military/.

66. See Scott Neuman and Rob Schmitz, "Despite the End of China's One-Child Policy, Births Are Still Lagging," NPR News, 16 July 2018, https://www.npr.org/2018/07/16/629361870/despite-the-end-of-chinas-one-child-policy-births-are-still-lagging; and "Patriotism May Hold Key to China Births Challenge," *South China Morning Post*, 19 June 2018, https://www.scmp.com/comment/insight-opinion/article/2151359/patriotism-may-hold-key-china-births-challenge.

67. For a discussion of the behavioral effects of the one-child policy see L. Cameron, N. Erkal, L. Gangadharan, and X. Meng, "Little Emperors: Behavioral Impacts of China's One-Child Policy," *Science* 339, no. 6122 (22 February 2013): 953–57.

68. For the theory that countries with aging populations are less likely to engage in conflict see Mark L. Haas, "A Geriatric Peace? The Future of U.S. Power in a World of Aging Populations," *International Security* 32, no. 1 (Summer 2007): 112–47, https://www.belfercenter.org/sites/default/files/legacy/files/is3201_pp112-147.pdf. For the alternative theory that a male demographic youth bulge may predispose a nation to engage in international conflict see Valerie Hudson and Andrea den Boer, "A Surplus of Men, A Deficit of Peace: Security and Sex Ratios in Asia's Largest States," *International Security* 26, no. 4 (July 2002): 5–38.

69. Thomas Friedman's "golden arches" and "Dell" theories of conflict prevention— suggesting that integration into the global economy prevents conflict among states—turned out to have little or no predictive value. The related democratic and capitalist peace theories (suggesting that trade-interdependent capitalist democracies are less likely to fight each other) have also been criticized on empirical grounds. See Thomas Schwartz and Kiron Skinner, "The Myth of the Democratic Peace," *Orbis* 46, no. 1 (2002): 159–72; and Michael Mousseau, "Coming to Terms with the Capitalist Peace," *International Interactions* 36, no. 2 (2010): 185–92.

70. Anne Blair, " 'Get Me Ten Years': Australia's Ted Serong in Vietnam, 1962–75," symposium paper, Texas Tech Vietnam Center and Archive, https://www.vietnam. ttu.edu/events/1996_Symposium/96papers/tenyears.php.

71. For a detailed examination of the distinction see Antulio J. Echevarria, *An American Way of War or Way of Battle?* (Carlisle, PA: United States Army War College, 2004), https://apps.dtic.mil/dtic/tr/fulltext/u2/a426321.pdf.

72. Eric Schmitt, Ben Hubbard, and Rukmini Callimachi, "ISIS Attack in Syria Kills 4 Americans, Raising New Worries About Troop Withdrawal," *New York Times*, 16 January 2019, https://www.nytimes.com/2019/01/16/world/middleeast/isis-attack-syria-troops.html.

Epilogue

1. Woolsey claims that others began making the joke shortly after the incident in question, which occurred on 12 September 1994, and he began using it himself shortly thereafter. Woolsey, interview with author, Norfolk, VA, 9 April 2019.

2. United States Department of Justice, Office of the Inspector General, "A Review of the FBI's Performance in Uncovering the Espionage Activities of Aldrich Hazen Ames (April, 1997)," https://oig.justice.gov/special/9704.htm.

3. United States Senate, Select Committee on Intelligence, *An Assessment of the Aldrich H. Ames Espionage Case and Its Implications for U.S. Intelligence* (Washington, DC: US Government Printing Office), 40, 41, 50–52, https://www.intelligence. senate.gov/sites/default/files/publications/10390.pdf.

4. See CNN, "America Under Attack: Former CIA Director Asserts Iraq May Be Behind Terrorist Attacks," transcripts, *CNN Live This Morning*, 12 September 2001, http://transcripts.cnn.com/TRANSCRIPTS/0109/12/ltm.13.html; and Micah Morrison, "The Iraq Connection," *Wall Street Journal*, 5 September 2002, https:// www.wsj.com/articles/SB1031184073773956835.

5. See World Future Society, "Interview with R. James Woolsey," *Futurist*, July–August 2007, https://web.archive.org/web/20070626213353/http://www.wfs.org/ futintervja07.htm.

6. See R. James Woolsey and Peter Vincent Pry, "Obama Team Fails to Protect the Grid," *National Review*, 6 November 2015, https://www.nationalreview.com/ 2015/11/national-space-weather-action-plan-inadequate-r-james-woolsey/.

7. J. F. C. Fuller, *The Foundations of the Science of War* (London: Hutchinson & Co., 1926), 77.

INDEX

For the benefit of digital users, indexed terms that span two pages (e.g., 52–53) may, on occasion, appear on only one of those pages.

Abkhazia, 141–43, 144, 146–47, 160
Abrams tanks, 16–17
Academy of Military Sciences, China, 182–83
active measures, 143–44, 149–50
Addis Ababa, Ethiopia, 173–74
Admiral Kuznetsov–class aircraft carriers, 196
Afghanistan, 3, 60–61
　Islamic State in, 4
　al-Qaeda in, 63, 85, 86–87
　Soviet War (1979–89), 19–20, 98
　US-led War (2001–14), *see* Afghanistan War
Afghanistan War (2001–14), 12, 13, 19–20,
　　161–62, 188, 232–33, 247
　air campaign, 70–71
　asymmetry of cost, 16–17
　Battle of Tora Bora (2001), 55, 86–87
　guerrilla band sizes, 46–47
　predation models and, 60
　rules of engagement, 74
　surveillance, 77
　Zarqawi and, 92–93
African Union, 173
African US embassy bombings (1998), 85
Agreed Framework (1994) 34–35
air supremacy, 68–72
Alakurtti, Murmansk, 117
Albright, Madeleine, 12, 15–16,
　　229–30, 232–33
Aleppo, Syria, 96, 109–10, 154–55
Aleutian Islands, 198
Alta, Finnmark, 118
Amal, 101–2, 103, 106, 111
American Civil War (1861–5), 216–17
Anbang Group, 168–69, 170, 176–77

Android, 63–64, 78
Anjin Investments, 207–8
Ansar al-Mujahidin, 60–62
anti-access and area denial (A2/AD) systems,
　　241–42, 248
　China, 27–28, 193, 194–95, 196–97,
　　198–99, 200, 201, 222, 226
　Iran, 225
　Russia, 117, 221–22, 226
anti-ship systems, 197, 241–42
antibiotic-resistant bacteria, 54, 59
Arab Socialism, 98
Arab Spring (2011–12), 2–3, 94, 161–62,
　　225, 232
Arab-Israeli Wars
　1948: 98, 101
　1956: 98
　1967: 98
　1973: 98
Arctic region, 115–19, 120–22, 125–26, 160,
　　164, 191, 199–200, 241, 243
Argentina, 99–100, 106
Aristotle, 228
'Arithmetic on the Frontier' (Kipling) 17
Armenia, 2
Armistead, Lewis, 216–17
arms trafficking, 21
artificial intelligence, 208–9, 230–31, 248
artificial selection 53–60
Asian financial crisis (1997–8), 200–1, 212–13
Aspin-Brown inquiry (1994), 75
al-Assad, Bashar, 2, 3, 94, 96, 109–10, 225
al-Assad, Hafez, 110
asymmetry of cost' 16–17

Atoms for Peace program, 30
attribution threshold, 153–54
attribution, 124, 145–46, 208
Australia, 11–12, 36, 38–39, 40–41, 44–45, 86–87, 225–26, 236–37
  Battle of Tora Bora (2001), 55
  cellular telephone networks in, 75–76
  Darwin port sale (2015), 170–72, 213–14
  East Timor, interventions in (1999–2000, 2006–13), 11–12, 170–71
  Islamic State and, 98
  Lebanese diaspora in, 99–100
  liminal warfare and, 151–52
  Operation Papua New Guinea Assist (2007), 170–71
  al-Qaeda and, 92–93
  Regional Force Surveillance Units, 243
  Second World War (1939–45), 135–36, 170–71
  Space Agency, 226
Austria, 123
Austria-Hungary (1867–1918), 133–34, 233–34
Authorization for the Use of Military Force (2001), 16
Avdiivka offensive (2017), 154–55, 156–57, 159
al-Awlaki, Anwar, 90, 92–93, 243–44
'Axis of Evil' speech (2002), 34–35
Azerbaijan, 2

Ba'ath Party, 219
al-Baghdadi, Abubakr, 94–95, 96, 98
Baker, James, 126
Bali bombings (2002, 2005), 92–93
Baltic Battalion (BALTBAT), 133
Bangladesh, 98
Barabanov, Mikhail, 130–31
Barak, Ehud, 102
Bartles, Charles, 161–62
battalion tactical groups (BTGs), 136–37, 140–41, 144
al-Battar, 62
Battle of 73 Easting (1991) 19
Battle of Fallujah (2004), 49
Battle of Mogadishu (1993), 12, 75, 84
Battle of Mosul (2016), 49
Battle of Raqqa (2017), 49
Battle of the Paracel Islands (1974), 177, 192, 198–99

Battle of the Yalu River (1894), 177
Battle of Tora Bora (2001), 55, 86–87
Battle of Yijiangshan (1955), 177, 192
Beaumont, Roger, 41–42, 50
Beheshti, Mohammed, 30
Beihang University, 211–12
Beirut, Lebanon, 73–74, 100, 102, 103–4
  Barracks bombing (1983), 104
Beitullah Mehsud, 55–56
Beiyang Fleet, 177
Belarus, 132
Belgrade, Serbia, 132–33, 185–88, 193, 222
Belleau Wood, USS, 193–94
Belt and Road initiative, 172, 173–75, 236
Beqaa Valley, Lebanon, 100, 102, 103–4
Bergman, Ronen, 57–58
Beria, Lavrentiy, 141
Berlin Wall, 33–34, 126–27
Berlusconi, Silvio, 22
Best Sunshine International, 174
Bhutto, Benazir, 55–56
Biden, Joseph, 22–23
Bin Laden, Osama, 14–15, 63, 84, 87–88, 92
  Battle of Tora Bora (2001), 86
  'cutting the head of the snake', 13, 85
  death (2011), 87, 94
biotechnology, 230–31
Black Hawk Down (Bowden), 10
Black Sea Fleet, 131–32, 144
BlackBerry, 63–64
Blair, Anthony 'Tony', 22, 31
blind variation and selective retention (BVSR) 46, 51
Blitzkrieg, 135–36
Blood Year (Kilcullen), 4
Borneo Confrontation (1963–6), 40–41
Bosnia, 11–12, 132–33
Bowden, Mark, 10
Brazil, 99–100
Bretton Woods system, 212
Brexit, 5, 123, 226–27, 239–40
British India (1858–1947), 42–44, 46, 52
Browder, William 'Bill', 128–30
Brunei, 198
Bucharest, Romania, 143
Buk-4M anti-aircraft missiles, 125
Bulgaria, 128, 133
Bush, George Herbert Walker, 229–30
Bush, George Walker, 22, 24, 34–35, 78–79, 188, 217, 229–30

Bushehr, Iran, 30
Byzantine Empire (395–1453), 228–29,
    237–41, 247–50

Cambodia, 11–12, 179–80
Camp Chapman Khost, 56
Camp Lemonnier, Djibouti, 173–74
Canada, 99–100, 206–7, 225–26, 243
Carl Vinson, USS, 167–68
Carr, Jeffrey, 145–46
Carrier Strike Groups (CSGs), 167–68, 193,
    196, 208–9
Carter, James 'Jimmy', 9–10
Catalonia, 5, 123
catastrophic success, 91–93, 94–95
caveats, 72–73
Central Intelligence Agency (CIA), 9–10, 12–13,
    20–21, 56
  al-Awlaki/Khan assassination (2011), 90
  Belgrade Chinese embassy bombing
    (1999), 186–87
  conspiracy theories and, 224
  Group of Soviet Forces Germany, assessment
    of, 128
  Keyhole Viewer, 78
  Open Source Center (OSC), 60–61
  Russian nuclear program, assessments of,
    138, 139–40
century of humiliation (1839–1949), 190
Chao Xian Zhan (Qiao and Wang), 200–14,
    218, 222–24, 244–45
Chechen Wars
  First (1994–6), 131–32, 136–37,
    140–41, 221–22
  Second (1999–2009), 136–37, 140–41,
    146–48, 221–22
Chen Xiaolu, 168–69, 176–78
Chen Yi, 168–69
Chengdu, Sichuan, 187
Chi Haotian, 200–1
China, People's Republic of, 3, 5–6, 18, 24–28,
    36, 167–214, 222–24
  Academy of Military Sciences, 182–83
  Belgrade embassy bombing (1999), 132–33,
    185–88, 193, 222
  Cambodia, relations with, 179–80, 189
  Communist Party, 24, 171, 177–79, 188, 201
  conceptual envelopment, 175–76, 204–5,
    210, 213, 223
  construction companies, 173

continental power, 188–93
Cultural Revolution (1966–76), 44–45,
    177–80, 182–83
cyberwarfare, 27–28, 197, 200, 201–3, 204–5,
    208–9, 211

Djibouti naval base, 173–74, 213–14
  economic reforms (1978–2012), 168–69,
    177–78, 184–85, 190–92
  exclusive economic zone (EEZ),
    194–95, 198–99
  Exim Bank, 173
  famine (1959–61), 177–78
  fentanyl production, 206–7, 211, 213–14
  Four Modernizations, 179
  Gang of Four, 177–78, 182–83
  Go Abroad, 211
  Great Leap Forward (1958–62), 177–79
  Gulf War (1990–91), influence of, 25, 26,
    176–77, 183, 193, 201, 203–4, 222
  Hainan Island incident (2001), 188, 193–94
  Hong Kong, return of (1997), 27
  hotels, investment in, 168–70, 176–77
  India, relations with, 24–25, 189, 236
  Iran, relations with, 189
  Islamic State and, 98
  Japan, relations with, 174, 177, 189
  Johnson South Reef Skirmish (1988),
    177, 192
  Korean War (1950–53), 24–25, 179–80, 198
  Liaoning, 2, 196, 213–14
  littoralization, 191–92, 193–94
  Macau, return of (1999), 27
  Mao Zedong, death of (1976), 177–78
  maritime power, 188–93
  Maritime Silk Road, 172
  Military Commission, 25
  Ministry of Public Security, 24–25
  Ministry of State Security, 24–25
  North Korea, relations with, 31–32, 189
  nuclear weapons, 27–28, 195, 197, 199–200
  One Belt, One Road, 172, 173–75, 236
  one child policy (1979–2016), 244–45
  Pakistan, relations with, 172, 189
  Paracel Islands conflict (1974), 177,
    192, 198–99
  peaceful rise, 26
  People's Armed Police, 24–25, 184–85
  People's Liberation Army (PLA), *see* People's
    Liberation Army

Djibouti naval base (*cont.*)
People's Political Consultative Conference
(CPPCC), 172–73
People's Security Bureaus, 24–25
ports, investment in, 2, 170–74, 213–14
princelings, 168–69
Russia, relations with, 139, 189, 195
South China Sea island building, 2, 5–6,
198–200, 222
Sri Lanka, relations with, 2, 174, 213–14
surveillance state, 245
Taiwan, relations with, 172–73, 177, 189,
192, 193–94, 195, 196–97, 198, 200–1
Three Warfares, 26, 211, 213–14, 222–23
Tiananmen Square massacre (1989),
24–25, 184–85
Titan Rain offensive (2003–6), 211
Ukraine, relations with, 196
unrestricted warfare, 200–14, 218,
222–24, 244–45
Vietnam War (1979), 24–25, 177, 179–82
Vostok-18 exercise (2018), 139
WTO accession (2001), 27
Zimbabwe, relations with, 207–8, 211
China Ocean Shipping Company
(COSCO), 172–74
China Merchants Port Holdings, 173–74
Chinese People's Political Consultative
Conference (CPPCC), 172–73, 245
Chinook helicopters, 16–17
Chiwenga, Constantino, 207, 208
Cho-do, North Korea, 69
Chomsky, Noam, 213
Chubin, Shahram, 30
Clancy, Thomas, 73
Clash of Civilizations (Huntington), 228
Clinton, Hillary, 22–23, 123–24,
154–55, 232–33
Clinton, William 'Bill', 9–10, 21–22, 31, 34–35,
78–79, 130, 186–87, 229–30
Cold War, 1, 3, 6, 9–10, 11–12, 17, 24, 28
air forces and, 69–70
Norway and, 116–17
nuclear weapons, 9–10, 73
Soviet Union, collapse of (1989–91), 9–10,
20–21, 25, 126–28, 133, 141–42
terrain and, 73
Cole, USS, 85
Collateral Damage Estimation Methodology
(CDEM), 74

Colombia, 2, 36, 236–37
China, relations with, 2
Fuerzas Armadas Revolucionarias de
Colombia (FARC), 14, 47–48
Partido Comunista Clandestino, 47–48
color revolutions, 161–62
Combat Darwinism, 40, 136
combined arms effect, 71–72
Committee on Foreign Investment in the
United States (CFIUS), 170
Commonwealth, 152–53
Commonwealth of Independent States, 128
Commonwealth of the Northern Mariana
Islands (CNMI), 174, 198
Communism, 84–85, 88
conceptual envelopment, 175–76, 204–5, 210,
213, 223
connectivity, 49, 63–64, 75–76, 78–82, 89
conscription, 11–12
constant combat readiness units, 136–37
Constantine I, Roman Emperor, 239–40
consumer smart systems, 49, 63–64,
75–76, 78–82
continental powers, 134–35, 188–93
contre-guerre, 12, 74
Conventional Armed Forces in Europe Treaty
(1990), 9–10
Coonawarra, HMAS, 170–71
Cooper, Cortez, 194, 202
Corbett, John, 182
Council for National Security Policy
Studies, 211–12
Counter-T Pursuit Teams (CTPTs), 12–13
counterwar, 12, 74
coup de main operations, 118, 139, 146–47,
159–60, 161, 221–22, 241–42
Crimea
Crimean War (1853–6), 133–34
Russian annexation (2014), 2, 5, 121–22,
125, 161, 221–22, 226–27, 232
Croatia, 132–33
Cuba, 2
culminating points, 217
Cultural Revolution (1966–76), 44–45,
177–80, 182–83
cyberkinetic operations, 80, 145, 151–52
cyberwarfare, 20, 63–64, 66, 75, 77–78, 125–26
attribution, 124, 145–46
China and, 27–28, 197, 200, 201–3, 204–5,
208–9, 211

cyberkinetic operations, 80, 145, 151–52
Iran and, 5–6
North Korea and, 5–6
Russia and, 2, 5, 117, 123, 145–46, 149, 154, 160
Cyprus, 11–12
Czech Republic, 133
Czechoslovakia, 128

D-30 122mm howitzer, 80
Dabiq, 62
Daraa, Syria, 110
Darwin, Charles, 53–54, 136
Darwin, Northern Territory, 170–72, 197, 213–14
Day After, The, 73
Decline of the West, The (Spengler), 227–28, 229
Defense Department, 170
dehumanization, 52
Democratic Republic of Congo, 173–74
Deng Xiaoping, 177–79, 183–85, 190–91
Desert One disaster (1980), 135–36
detection threshold, 19, 47, 119, 150, 151–54, 159–60
DF-21 and DF-26 ballistic missiles, 197, 222, 230
dialogue among civilizations, 31
disaggregated battlespace, 47
distributed command-and-control tools, 20
distributed denial-of-service (DDOS) attacks, 145
Djibouti, 173–74, 213–14
doctrine, 40–42, 62
dog breeds, 53
Donetsk People's Republic (2014–), 134
Dora Farms strike (2003), 217–20, 230
Doraleh container terminal, Djibouti, 173–74
DOTMLPFI, 62–63
doubling down, 228–31
Dreyer, June Teufel, 179
drones, 68, 69
China, 196
hobby drones, 80–81
Iran, 30–31
Islamic State and, 80–81
kamikaze drones, 80–81
Status-6 underwater drone, 139–40
Tehrik-e Taliban Pakistan and, 55–57
United States, 55–57, 220–21
drug trade, 10–11, 14, 75, 201–2, 206–7, 211, 213–14, 224–25, 252

drug warfare, 206–7, 211, 213–14
drug-resistant bacteria, 54, 59
dual containment strategy, 29
Dubai Ports World, 173–74
Dugin, Aleksander, 134–35, 190–91
dukhi, 19–20
Dulles, John Foster, 198
Dunbar, Robin, 48, 111
Duntroon, Canberra, 40–41, 45, 46

East China Sea, 194–95
East Timor, 11–12, 170–71
Eastern Ghouta nerve agent attack (2013), 3
Egypt, 98
Eisenhower, Dwight David, 30
El Salvador, 247
electromagnetic pulse (EMP) 20, 148, 241–42
elite forces, 41–42
embracing the suck, 228–29, 231–37
Empire (Ferguson), 228, 229
end of history, 187
EP-3 signals intelligence aircraft, 188
Estonia, 2, 118, 121, 128, 133, 145, 154, 160, 242–43
Ethiopia, 173–74
European Deterrence Initiative, 234
European Union
Brexit (2016–), 5, 123, 226–27, 239–40
currency crisis (2009–16), 239–40
Qiao Liang on, 212–13, 224
Euskadi Ta Askatasuna (ETA), 14
eustress, 41
Evolution of Civilizations, The (Quigley), 228
evolution, 39, 40–60, 136
artificial selection 53–60
blind variation and selective retention (BVSR) 46, 51
fitness effect, 41
fitness landscape, 51, 66–68
institutional adaptation, 60–65
methodical selection, 53–54
natural selection, 14–15, 42, 46–53, 220
predation models, 54–60
replication, 44, 46, 49–50
reproductive isolation, 48, 49, 50
selection-destruction cycle, 41–42, 50
selective pressure, *see* selective pressure
unconscious selection, 53–54
variation, 44, 46, 49–50

Exim Bank, 173
expeditionary terrorism, 88

Facebook, 63–64
faith-based attribution, 145–46
fake news, 17–18, 125, 150–51, 155
fashion 44–45
Faslane, Gare Loch, 169–70
Federal Reserve Bank, 212–13
Federally Administered Tribal Areas
     (FATA), 55–57
fentanyl, 206–7, 211, 213–14
Ferguson, Niall, 228, 229
Fiery Cross reef, Spratly Islands, 198–99
5G mobile telecommunications,
     208–9, 222–23
Finland, 75–76, 121–22, 242–43
     defensive guerrilla warfare, 242–43
Finnmark County, Norway, 115–16, 118, 121
firehose of falsehood, 156, 221–22
First Sino–Japanese War (1894–5), 177
First Taiwan Strait Crisis (1954–5), 177
First World War (1914–18), 133–34,
     135–36, 233–34
fitness effect, 41
fitness landscape, 51, 66–68, 74–75, 81, 82, 86,
     150–51, 175
five eyes, 76
Fleet Intelligence Command Pacific, 167–68
Fort Hood shooting (2009), 90
Four Modernizations, 179
Francart, Loup, 12
France
     Crimean War (1853–6), 133–34
     Foreign Legion, 173–74
     Lebanon intervention (1982–4), 101
     liminal warfare and, 154
     Mandate for Syria and Lebanon (1923–46),
          98, 100
     Russia, relations with, 123
Franks, Tommy, 87
Frederick II 'the Great', King of Prussia, 44–45
French Foreign Legion, 173–74
Frog missiles, 33–34
frozen conflicts, 142
FSB (Federal'naya sluzhba bezopasnosti
     Rossiyskoy Federatsii), 116, 117, 121–22,
     137–38, 142–43
Fuerzas Armadas Revolucionarias de Colombia
     (FARC), 14, 47–48

Gabrielsen, Iver, 107
Gaddafi, Muammar, 35–36
Galeotti, Mark, 161, 163
Gang of Four, 177–78, 182–83
Gao Jingde, 172–73
Gare Loch, Scotland, 169–70
Gates, Robert, 10
Gefen, Hannan, 77
General Agreement on Tariffs and Trade
     (GATT), 212
genomics, 208–9, 230–31
George C. Marshall Center, 23
Georgia, 2, 22, 135, 136–37, 139, 140–50, 154,
     160, 221–22
geospatial intelligence (GEOINT), 79
Gerasimov, Valeriy, 150, 161–64, 210–11, 224
Germany, 225–26
     Berlin Wall, fall of (1989), 33–34, 126–27
     Blitzkrieg, 135–36
     Democratic Republic (1949–90), 128
     federal elections (2018), 123
     First World War (1914–18), 133–34, 135–36
     George C. Marshall Center, 23
     Group of Soviet Forces Germany
          (GSFG), 128
     Kohl–Gorbachev meeting (1990), 126
     Iran, relations with, 30
     Nazi period (1933–45), 88, 120, 133–34,
          135–36, 179
     reunification (1990), 126, 128
     Russia, relations with, 22, 123
     Second World War (1939–45), 88, 120,
          133–34, 135–36, 179
     terrorism in, 36
Gerstein, Erez, 107
Gettysburg, Pennsylvania, 216–17
Ghana, 99–100
Ghouta nerve agent attack (2013), 3
Gibbon, Edward, 228
Giles, Keir, 133–34
global financial crisis (2008), 226–27, 231,
     232, 239–40
global navigation system satellite
     (GNSS), 78, 79
Global Positioning Systems (GPS), 19, 75–76,
     78–80, 186, 202–3
global war on terrorism (GWOT), 12, 14–15
Go Abroad, 211
going Byzantine, 228–29, 237–41, 247–50
Gulf War I (1990–91), 6, 18–19, 25, 26, 28–29

air campaign, 18–19, 70–71, 73
    China and, 25, 26, 176–77, 183, 193, 201,
        203–4, 222
    'highway of death', 18, 73, 219–20
    Iran and, 28, 29
Gulf War II (2003–11), 1, 2–3, 11, 12, 13,
        14–15, 18, 19–20, 161–62, 188, 193–94,
        203–4, 246–47
    Awakening (2007), 58, 61
    armored protection, lack of, 16
    asymmetry of cost, 16–17
    Battle of Fallujah (2004), 49
    Dora Farms strike (2003), 217–20, 230
    North Korea and, 35
    predation models and, 58–59
    al-Qaeda in Iraq (AQI), 93–94
    rules of engagement, 74
    Samarra bombing (2006), 93–94
    Sons of Iraq, 58, 59–60
    Surge (2007), 58, 61, 93–94
Golan Heights, 36, 108, 225
gold standard, 212
Goldberg, Jonah, 227
Goldstone, Jack, 190
Google Earth, 78, 79–80
Gorbachev, Mikhail, 126–27
Gori, Georgia, 144
Great Leap Forward (1958–62), 177–79
Great Wall of China, 189
Greece, 123
Greece, ancient, 235
Gries, Peter Hays, 187–88, 193–94
group isolation, 48, 49, 50
Group of Soviet Forces Germany (GSFG), 128
group selection, 45
GRU (*Glavnoje Razvedyvatel'noje Upravlenije*),
        120–22, 123, 125, 134, 142–43, 146–47,
        154–55, 156–57
Guam, 174, 197, 222
Guardian, 186–87
guerrilla terrorism, 88–89
Gurkhas, 42–43
Gwadar, Pakistan, 172

Hagel, Charles 'Chuck', 23
Hainan, China, 188, 193–94, 200
Haiti, 11–12
Hakimullah Mehsud, 56
Hamas, 30–31, 57
Hambantota, Sri Lanka, 174, 213–14

Hambling, David, 80–81
Hammes, Thomas X., 230
Harakat al-Mahrumin, 101, 111
Hart Senate Office Building,
        Washington, DC, 9
Hawaii, 198
Hayat Tahrir al-Sham (HTS), 83, 96–98, 112
Helsinki summit (2018), 234–35
Her Majesty's Naval Base Clyde, Gare
        Loch, 169–70
Herat, Afghanistan, 92–93
heritability of acquired characteristics, 45
Heroes of Telemark, 120
Hezbollah, 14, 30–31, 83, 96–97, 98, 99–112
    Amal, relations with, 103
    artillery, 106, 108
    Beirut barracks bombing (1983), 104
    human-wave attacks, 105, 111
    improvised explosive devices (IEDs),
        105, 107
    Iran, relations with, 14, 30–31, 102, 103, 108,
        109, 111, 225
    Israel, relations with, 30–31, 101–3, 104,
        105, 106–9, 111, 112
    kidnappings, 104, 106–7, 108
    political warfare, 106–7
    Second Intifada (2000–5), 107–8
    Shura Council, 103
    South Lebanon Army, relations with, 102–3,
        104, 105, 106–7
    suicide bombings, 104–5
    Syria, relations with, 104, 106, 108,
        109–10, 112
    video games, 108
'highway of death', 18, 73, 219–20
*History of the Decline and Fall of the Roman
        Empire* (Gibbon), 228
Hoehn, Mark, 218
Homeland Security, 170
Hong Kong, 27, 169–70, 174, 212–13, 236
horizontal escalation, 175–76
Hotel del Coronado, California, 167–68,
        176–77, 197
Hu Jintao, 185
Hua Guofeng, 177–78
human performance enhancement,
        208–9, 230–31
human-wave attacks, 105, 111, 181
Hungary, 123, 128, 133
hunter-gatherer societies, 47–48

Huntington, Samuel, 228
Hussein, Qusay, 217–20
Hussein, Saddam, 4, 19, 25, 28, 29, 35, 176–77, 203–4, 217–20, 230
Hussein, Uday, 217–20
Hwasong-15 missile, 35–36
hybrid warfare, 29–30

IBM Simon, 75–76
Ibn Khaldûn, 228
Idlib, Syria, 96
illiberal democracy, 239–40
Imperial Pacific, 174
implausible deniability, 154
improvised explosive devices (IEDs), 105, 107
Independence, USS, 193–94
India, 236
  China, relations with, 24–25, 189, 236
  British Raj (1858–1947), 42–44, 46, 52
  Islamic State and, 98
  maritime and continental characteristics, 191
  Mumbai attacks (2008), 89, 92–93
  Sino–Indian War (1962), 24–25
individual learning, 43–44
Indonesia, 87, 92–93
information warfare, 5, 122, 123, 124, 142–43, 145, 148, 156–57, 221–22
Inspire, 62, 90
Instagram, 63–64
institutional adaptation, 60–65
intelligence, surveillance, and reconnaissance (ISR), 19, 151, 153–54, 186, 242–43
interchangeability of fires and forces, 139
intercontinental ballistic missile (ICBM), 35–36
Intermediate-Range Nuclear Forces Treaty, 234
International Monetary Fund, 130
Internet Research Agency, 156–57
iPhone, 63–64, 75–76
Iran, 2, 5–6, 18, 28–31, 97, 98, 164, 224–25
  dialogue among civilizations, 31
  dual containment strategy and, 29
  Gulf War I (1990–91), 28, 29
  Hamas, relations with, 30–31
  Hezbollah, relations with, 14, 30–31, 102, 103, 108, 109, 111, 225
  hybrid warfare, 29–30, 31
  Iraq, relations with, 2–3, 59–60, 225
  Iraq War (1980–88), 25, 28, 29, 30, 176–77

Islamic Revolution (1979) 28, 30, 97, 101–2, 111
  liminal strategy, 29–30
  neoconservatives and, 30–31
  North Korea, relations with, 33, 34
  nuclear program, 2–3, 5–6, 30, 31, 36, 232
  al-Qaeda in, 86
  Quds Force, 30–31, 59–60
  reconnaissance drones, 30–31
  Revolutionary Guard, 30–31, 103
  Syria, relations with, 2–3, 110, 225
  US embassy hostage crisis (1979–81), 28, 135–36
  Venezuela, relations with, 2
  Yemen, relations with, 2–3
Iraq, 3, 58–60
  Awakening (2007), 58, 61
  Ba'ath Party, 219
  Battle of Fallujah (2004), 49
  Battle of Mosul (2016), 49
  Dora Farms strike (2003), 217–20, 230
  dual containment strategy and, 29
  Gulf War I (1990–91), *see* Gulf War I
  Gulf War II (2003–11), *see* Gulf War II
  Iran, relations with, 2–3, 59–60, 225
  Iran War (1980–88), 25, 28, 29, 30, 176–77
  Islamic State in, 7–8, 36, 59–60, 70–71, 95
  Kurdistan, 10, 59
  no-fly zones (1991–2003), 10
  nuclear program, 29, 30, 35
  Popular Mobilization Forces, 59–60, 110
  al-Qaeda in, 60–61, 88, 92–94, 98–99
  Samarra bombing (2006), 93–94
  Sons of Iraq, 58, 59–60
Irish Republican Army (IRA), 14
Islamic State, 2–3, 4, 15, 36, 88, 91, 94–96, 98–99, 226–27, 232, 247–48
  airstrikes against, 70–71
  catastrophic success, 94–95
  Dabiq, 62
  drones, use of, 80–81
  Khorasan Province (Afghanistan and Pakistan), 4, 56
  predation models and, 56, 59–60
  Rumiyah, 62
  Russia and, 234–35
  Telegram, use of, 63–64
Israel, 57–58, 98, 233
  Arab-Israeli Wars, *see* Arab-Israeli Wars
  Gulf War I (1990–91), 29

Hezbollah, relations with, 30–31, 101–3, 104, 105, 106–9, 111
'infestation' of urban terrain, 71
Lebanon War I (1982–5), 101–3, 105, 111
Lebanon War II (2006), 107–9, 112
liminal warfare and, 154
nuclear program, 30
Second Intifada (2000–5), 107–8
Shin Bet, 58
Isserson, Georgii, 163–64
Italy, 22
Iwo Jima, Japan, 198

J-15 aircraft, 196
Jabhat an-Nusrah, 94, 96
al-Jahra, Kuwait, 18–19
Japan, 7–8, 42, 128, 226, 236–37
Australia, relations with, 135–36, 170–71
China, relations with, 174, 177, 189, 190, 212–13
North Korea, relations with, 32, 33
Russia, relations with, 135
Second World War (1939–45), 135–36, 170–71
Senkaku Islands dispute, 174, 212–13
Taiwan, invasion of (1874), 190
Jaysh al-Mahdi, 101
Jaysh al-Sha'abi, 110
Jemaah Islamiyah, 92–93
Jiang Zemin, 183–85, 186, 200–1
Johnson South Reef Skirmish (1988), 177
Johnson, Dominic, 49–50, 51, 63, 136
Joint Air Attack Teams, 72
Joint Comprehensive Plan of Action (2015), 2–3
Joint Direct Attack Munition (JDAM), 186
Joint Special Operations Command (JSOC), 23
al-Jolani, Mohammed, 94, 96–97, 98–99, 112
Jordan, 92–93, 98–99
juche, 32

Kahl, Colin, 74
Kaliningrad, 128
Kavkaz exercise (2008), 144, 145
Kazakhstan, 132
Kedah, Malaysia, 172
Kelly, Justin, 39
Kennan, George, 133–34
Kennedy, Paul, 228, 229

Kenya, 85
US embassy bombing (1998), 85
Westgate Mall attack (2013), 89
Kerry, John, 10, 232–33
Keyhole Viewer, 78
Khalid Sheikh Mohammed, 87
Khamenei, Ali, 30
Khan, Mohammed Sidique, 89, 92–93
Khan, Samir ibn Zafar, 90, 92–93
Khatami, Mohammad 31
Khmer Rouge, 180, 189
Khomeini, Ruhollah, 30
Khost, Afghanistan, 56
Khrulyov, Anatoly, 147–48
Khrushchev, Nikita, 33
Kilo-class submarines, 195
Kim il Sung, 31–32, 33
Kim Jong Un, 2–3, 35–36, 224–25
Kim Jong-il, 32, 34
Kipling, Rudyard, 17
Kirkenes, Finnmark County, 121
Kissinger, Henry, 28
Klang, Malaysia, 172
Koestler, Arthur, 157
Kohl, Helmut, 126
Komov, S. A., 156
Korean War (1950–53), 24–25, 31–32, 33, 69, 179–80
Kosovo, 11–12, 21–22, 132–33, 142–43, 185–88, 212–13, 224
Kostiner, Joseph, 29
Krajina Republic (1991–5), 132–33
Krauthammer, Charles, 227
KSSO (Komandovanie sil spetsial'nalnykh operatsii), 23
Kuantan, Malaysia, 172
Kunar, Afghanistan, 60
Kurdistan, 10
Kursk disaster (2000), 137
Kutaisi, Georgia, 144
Kuwait, 18–19, 28, 70–71, 176–77
Kyushu, Japan, 174

Landing Platform Dock (LPD), 196
Lang Son, Vietnam, 180–81
Langley, Virginia, 186–87
Laos, 179–80
Lashkar e-Tayyiba, 89
Latin American debt crisis (1982), 212–13
Latvia, 118, 121, 128, 133, 242–43

Lauer, Matt, 229–30
Lavrov, Sergey, 22–23, 236
leaderless resistance, 90–91, 94, 243–44
leading from behind, 232, 236–37
League of Nations, 98, 100
Lebanon, 99–112
    Amal, 101–2, 103, 106
    Civil War (1975–90), 73–74, 101, 104, 106
    diaspora, 99–100, 106
    French Mandate (1923–46), 98, 100
    Israel War I (1982–5), 101–3, 105, 111
    Israel War II (2006), 107–9, 112
    Maronites in, 99, 100, 101–2
    Multinational Force intervention (1982–4),
        73–74, 101, 104
    National Pact (1943), 100
    Palestinians in, 101–2, 111
    al-Qaeda in, 85
    Shi'a Islam in, 14, 99, 100–4, 111
    South Lebanon Army (SLA), 102–3, 104,
        105, 106–7
legal and political constraints, 72–75
legal warfare, 26, 201–2, 222–23
Lenin, Vladimir, 84–85, 149–50
Li Peng, 184
Liaoning, 2, 196, 213–14
Liberation Army Daily, 182
Liberation Tigers of Tamil Eelam (LTTE), 2
Liberia, 173–74
Libya, 2–3, 35–36, 226–27, 232–33
    Benghazi attack (2012), 2–3
    Islamic State in, 4
    Revolution (2011), 35–36, 79, 94, 161–62
    WMD program, 35–36
light-footprint missions, 247
liminal warfare, 29–30, 119–20, 150–64, 175–76,
        204–5, 210–11, 223
    attribution threshold, 153–54
    detection threshold, 19, 47, 119, 150,
        151–54, 159–60
    information warfare, 156–57
    reaction time, 157–60
    response threshold, 153–54, 157–58
listening posts, 76, 107, 168, 169–70, 171, 197
Lithuania, 121, 128, 133
littoralization, 68, 191–92, 193–94
Litvinenko, Alexander, 125, 154
London 7/7 bombings (2005), 89, 90, 92–93
long telegram (1946), 133–34
Los Alamos National Laboratory, 195–96

Los Angeles-class submarines, 167–68
Lourdes, Cuba, 2
Luostari, Murmansk, 117
Lysekil, Sweden, 172–73

MacArthur, Douglas, 170–71
Macau, 27, 174
MacFarlane, Neil, 142
madman theory, 34
Madrid train bombing (2004), 92–93, 104
Malaysia
    Emergency (1948–60), 40–41
    Maritime Silk Road in, 172
    South China Sea dispute, 198
Malaysian Airlines Flight MH17 shootdown
        (2014), 2, 5, 125, 154, 244–45
Mali, 173–74
Mao Zedong, 168–69, 177–79, 191
Mariana Islands, 174, 198
Marine Air-Ground Task Force
        (MAGTF), 170–71
maritime powers, 134–35, 188–93
Maritime Silk Road, 172
Marshall, Shana, 105
al-Masri, Abu Hafs, 87
Matt Bronze, 207–8
Matthews, Miriam, 156, 157
McMaster, Herbert Raymond, 19
Mearsheimer, John, 233
media manipulation, 74–75, 83, 125, 155
medium-range ballistic missile (MRBM), 33
Medvedev, Dmitri, 143, 144, 148
Melaka, Malaysia, 172
methodical selection, 53–54
Mexico, 206–7
migration, manipulation of, 5, 121–22, 149–50,
        154, 160
Milestones (Qutb), 84
Military Commission, China, 25
Military Industrial Courier, 161
Milosevic, Slobodan, 21–22
mine-resistant ambush-protected vehicles
        (MRAPs), 61
Ming Empire (1368–1644), 190
Ministry of Public Security, China, 24–25
Ministry of State Security, China, 24–25
Mischief reef, Spratly Islands, 198–99
mission creep, 10
Mnangagwa, Emerson, 207–8
mobile phones, 63–64, 75–76

Mohammed Reza Pahlavi, Shah of Iran, 30
Montenegro, 5, 123
Moore, Michael, 213
Moreman, Timothy Robert, 42–44, 46
mortars, 79–80, 105, 107
Mosul, Iraq, 3–4, 49, 94
al-Moussawi, Abbas, 104, 106
movement intelligence (MOVINT), 79
MPRI, 132–33
Mueller report (2019), 123, 124, 156–57
Mugabe, Robert, 207–8
multiple-launch rocket systems
    (MLRS), 196–97
Mumbai attacks (2008), 89, 92–93
Munich Security Conference, 22–23
Muqaddimah (Ibn Khaldûn), 228
Murmansk, Russia, 115–16, 117, 121–22
Murray, Williamson, 62–63
MV-22 Osprey tiltrotors, 167–68
Myanmar, 98

Nairobi, Kenya
    US embassy bombing (1998), 85
    Westgate Mall attack (2013), 89
Nangarhar, Afghanistan, 60
nanotechnology, 208–9
Napoleonic Wars (1803–15), 133–34, 135–36
narcotics trade, 10–11, 14, 75, 201–2, 206–7,
    211, 213–14, 224–25, 252
Nasrallah, Hassan, 101–2, 106
Nasserism, 98
National Academy of Sciences, US, 81
National Defense Strategy, US, 208–9
National Security Agency, US, 76
National Security Council, US, 170
National Security Strategy, US, 13, 14, 15, 16
natural selection, 14–15, 42, 46–53, 220
Naval Air Station North Island, 167–68
Naval Amphibious Base Coronado,
    167–68, 197
Naval Special Warfare Command, 167–68
Navy SEALs, 167–68
Nazi Germany (1933–45), 88, 120, 179
negative interdependence, 187–88, 193–94
Nek Muhammad Wazir, 55–56
neoconservatives, 30–31
Nepal, 42–43
New Guinea, 170–71, 198, 222
New Look modernization program (2008–12),
    148–50, 161, 221–22

New York, United States
    September 11 attacks (2001), *see* September
        11 attacks
    Times Square bomb plot (2010), 56
New Zealand, 98
Niger, 36
Nigeria, 4
Nikel, Murmansk, 121
Nimitz, USS, 193–94
Nixon, Richard, 34
no-fly zones, 10
no-strike lists, 74
Noatum Port Holdings, 172–73
Nodong-1 missiles, 33
North Atlantic Treaty Organization
    (NATO), 10
    Article V, 233–34
    Belgrade Chinese embassy bombing (1999),
        132–33, 185–88, 193, 222
    Bosnia intervention (1992–5), 132–33
    Bucharest summit (2008), 143
    expansion, promises on (1990), 126–28, 133
    Cold War, 73, 116–17
    Georgian membership, 142–43, 146–47
    Kosovo intervention (1999), 22, 132–33,
        142–43, 185–88
    North Atlantic Cooperation Council, 133
    Partnerships for Peace program, 133
    Piraeus, bases in, 172–73
    response threshold, 153–54
    Russia, relations with 21–22, 23, 24, 116–17,
        119, 125–28, 132–34, 138–39, 142–43,
        148–49, 185–86
    Trump and, 233–34
North Korea, 2, 5–6, 17, 18, 28, 31–36,
    164, 224–25
    Agreed Framework (1994) 34–35
    China, relations with, 31–32, 189
    Demilitarized Zone (DMZ), 32, 33–34
    Iran, relations with, 33, 34
    juche, 32
    Korean War (1950–53), 24–25,
        31–32, 33, 69
    nuclear program, 5–6, 33–36, 224–25
    Pakistan, relations with, 34–35
    People's Army, 32, 33
    songun, 32
    Soviet Union, relations with, 31–32
Norway, 115–19, 120–22, 139, 149–50,
    154, 226

Nuclear Non-Proliferation Treaty
(NPT), 33–34
nuclear weapons
China, 27–28, 195, 197, 199–200
Cold War, 9–10, 73
Iran, 2–3, 5–6, 30, 31, 36, 232
Iraq, 29, 30, 35
North Korea, 5–6, 33–36, 224–25
Russian Federation, 21–22, 132,
138–40, 148–49
Nuristan, Afghanistan, 60

O'Dowd, Edward, 182
Obama, Barack, 2–4, 22–24, 90, 123–24, 163,
198–99, 229–31, 232–33, 236–37
Occupy Central movement (2012), 212–13
offset strategies, 19–20, 230–31
Okinawa, Japan, 174, 197
Oman, 247
One Belt, One Road, 172, 173–75, 236
one child policy (1979–2016), 244–45
operational preparation of the environment
(OPE), 120–21, 160–61, 163–64
Opium Wars (1839–60), 190
Ordzhonikidze, Sergo, 141
Origin of Species, The (Darwin), 53
Orthodox Christianity, 135
Orwell, George, 157
Ottoman Caliphate (1299–1924), 98,
100, 133–34
Outlaws Inc. (Potter), 21

Pacific campaign (1942–45), 170–71
pacing threats, 163, 193–94, 221–22
Pakistan
China, relations with, 172, 189
drone warfare in, 55–57, 220–21
North Korea, relations with, 34–35
al-Qaeda in, 86–88, 89, 92, 94
Tehrik-e Taliban Pakistan (TTP), 55–57
Palestine, 57–58
Palestinian Liberation Organization (PLO),
101–2, 111
Second Intifada (2000–5), 107–8
Pallin, Carolina, 148
Papua New Guinea, 170–71
Paracel Islands, 177, 192, 198–99
Paraguay, 99–100
Partido Comunista Clandestino, 47–48
Partnerships for Peace program, 133

Passing It On (Skeen), 46
Pasvikelva River, 115–16
patriotic volunteers, 124, 145, 160, 221–22,
242, 244–45
Patry, Jean-Jacques, 12
Paul, Christopher, 156, 157
Pechenga, Murmansk, 117
Pechengsky District, Murmansk, 115–16
People's Armed Police, 24–25, 184–85
People's Liberation Army (PLA), 24–26, 168–69,
171–72, 178–85
Anbang Group, relationship with, 168–69
Cultural Revolution (1966–76),
179–80, 182–83
cyberwarfare, 27–28, 197, 200, 201–3, 204–5,
208–9, 211
informationalization, 26, 222
internal repression role, 178–79,
184–85, 191
land force structure, 183, 189, 191
political warfare, 26
Shandong Landbridge Group, relationship
with, 171
Three Warfares, 26, 211, 213–14, 222–23
Tiananmen Square massacre (1989),
24–25, 184–85
Titan Rain offensive (2003–6), 211
unrestricted warfare, 200–14, 218,
222–24, 244–45
Vietnam War (1979), 24–25, 177, 179–82
People's Liberation Army Air Force (PLAAF),
179–80, 185, 197, 211–12
People's Liberation Army Navy (PLAN),
192–200
anti-ship systems, 197, 241–42
Carrier Strike Groups (CSGs), 196, 208–9
counterpiracy operations, 173–74
Djibouti naval base, 173–74
Hainan Island incident (2001),
188, 193–94
Johnson South Reef Skirmish (1988),
177, 192
Liaoning, 2, 196, 213–14
nuclear weapons, 27–28, 199–200
submarine fleet, 195, 199–200
Paracel Islands conflict (1974), 177, 192
South China Sea island building, 2, 5–6,
198–200
Taiwan Strait Crisis I (1954–5), 177, 192
Taiwan Strait Crisis II (1958), 192

Taiwan Strait Crisis III (1995–6), 193–94, 195, 196–97, 198, 200–1
People's Liberation Army Rocket Forces (PLARF), 185, 193, 196–97
People's Security Bureaus, 24–25
Permanent Court of Arbitration, 199
Peshawar, Khyber Pakhtunkhwa, 56
Petraeus, David, 60–61
Petrov, Nikita, 147–48
Philippines, 4, 5, 36, 198, 199, 212–13
Phnom Penh, Cambodia, 180
Pickering, Thomas, 186
Pike, John, 181
Piraeus, Greece, 172–73
Plato, 228
PMESII model, 204–5
Po, Ronald, 190
Point Loma, California, 167–68
Poland, 128, 133
political warfare, 26, 74–75, 83, 106, 108, 109, 125–26, 154–55, 160, 208–9, 221–22
Popular Mobilization Forces, 59–60, 110
Poti, Georgia, 144, 146–47
Potter, Matt, 21
Pound, Ezra, 228
Powell, Colin, 12
predation models, 54–60, 92
Pristina, Kosovo, 21–22
private military companies, 244–45
Prussia (1701–1918), 44–45, 135–36
psychological warfare, 26
public opinion warfare, 26
Putin, Vladimir, 3, 22, 23, 24, 125, 132–33, 136–38, 164
  Dugin, relationship with, 134–35
  Georgian War (2008), 143, 148
  Kursk disaster (2000), 137
  NATO, relations with, 22, 127, 143
  North Korea, relations with, 224–25
  nuclear diplomacy, 139–40
  Soviet collapse, views on, 21
  Trump, relationship with, 234–35
  US presidential election (2016), 123–18
  al-Qaeda, 13, 14–15, 24, 55, 83, 84–94, 98–99, 204
    African US embassy bombings (1998), 85
    Ansar al-Mujahidin, 60–62
    Bali bombings (2002, 2005), 92–93
    al-Battar, 62
    Battle of Mogadishu (1993), 12, 75, 84

catastrophic success, 91–93
decentralization, 87–88, 92
far enemy, targeting of, 85, 98
Fort Hood shooting (2009), 90
hierarchical structure, 85, 87, 91, 92
Inspire, 62, 90
in Iraq (AQI), 60–61, 88, 92–94, 98–99
leaderless resistance, 90–91, 94, 243–44
London 7/7 bombings (2005), 89, 90, 92–93
Madrid train bombing (2004), 92–93, 104
near enemy, targeting of, 85, 98
predation models and, 92, 94
as-Sahab, 62
Samarra bombing (2006), 93–94
September 11 attacks (2001), see September 11 attacks
USS Cole attack (2000), 85

Qatar, 28, 218
Qiao Liang, 200–10, 211–13, 218, 223–24, 244–45
Qing Empire (1636–1912), 177, 190
Quadrennial Defense Review, US, 208–9
quantitative easing, 212–13
quantum computing, 208–9, 230–31
Quds Force, 30–31, 59–60
Quigley, Carroll, 228
Qutb, Sayyid, 84–85

Rafsanjani, Akbar Hashemi, 30
RAND Corporation, 118
rare earths, 207–8
reaction time, 157–60
Reagan, Ronald, 229–30
reconnaissance drones, 30–31
Red Notice (Browder), 129–30
Red Storm Rising (Clancy), 73
redlines, 153–54
reflexive control, 156–57, 158–59
refugees, manipulation of, 5, 121–22, 149–50, 154, 160
remote radicalization, 89, 90
replication, 44, 46, 49–50
reproductive isolation, 48, 49, 50
resources warfare, 207–8
response threshold, 153–54, 157–58
responsibility to protect, 185–86
Rhu, Scotland, 169–70
RIA Novosti, 147–48
Riga, Latvia, 118

Rise and Fall of the Great Powers, The
   (Kennedy), 228, 229
Rise and Kill First (Bergman), 57–58
Rizhao, Shandong, 171
Robertson Barracks, Darwin, 170–71
robotics, 208–9
rocket-propelled grenades (RPGs), 16–17, 38
Roki tunnel, Ossetia, 144
Romania, 128, 133, 143
Rome, ancient, 44–45, 235, 237–41
Romney, Willard Mitt, 23–24
Rose Revolution (2003), 142
Rosen, Stephen, 40, 64, 85, 91–92,
   163, 221–22
Rosneath, Scotland, 169–70
Rosslea Hall Hotel, Rhu, 169–70
Rotterdam, Netherlands, 245
Rouch, James, 73
Royal Bank of Scotland, 170
Royal Military College, Duntroon, 40–41, 45, 46
rules of engagement, 72–73, 74
Rumiyah, 62
Rumsfeld, Donald, 16, 87
Russian Federation, 17, 18, 20–24, 36, 98,
   115–64, 221–22, 223
  active measures, 143–44
  Armenia, relations with, 2
  Avdiivka offensive (2017), 154–55,
   156–57, 159
  Azerbaijan, relations with, 2
  Baltic states, relations with, 2, 118, 121, 128,
   133, 145, 154, 160
  battalion tactical groups (BTGs), 136–37,
   140–41, 144
  Black Sea Fleet, 131–32, 144
  Chechen War I (1994–6), 131–32, 136–37,
   140–41, 221–22
  Chechen War II (1999–2009), 136–37,
   140–41, 146–48, 221–22
  China, relations with, 139, 189, 195
  constant combat readiness units, 136–37
  Crimea annexation (2014), 2, 5, 121–22,
   125, 161, 226–27, 232
  Cuba, relations with, 2
  cyberwarfare, 2, 5, 117, 123, 145–46,
   149, 154
  financial crisis (1998), 131
  FSB (*Federal'naya sluzhba bezopasnosti
   Rossiyskoy Federatsii*), 116, 117, 121–22,
   137–38, 142–43

Georgia, relations with, 2, 22, 135, 136–37,
   139, 140–50, 154, 160, 221–22
  GRU (*Glavnoje Razvedyvatel'noje
   Upravlenije*), 120–22, 123, 125, 134,
   142–43, 146–47, 154–55, 156–57
  information warfare, 5, 122, 123, 124,
   142–43, 145, 148, 156–57, 221–22
  interchangeability of fires and forces, 139
  Islamic State and, 98
  Kavkaz exercise (2008), 144, 145
  Kosovo intervention (1999),
   21–22, 185–86
  KSSO (*Komandovanie sil spetsial'nalnykh
   operatsii*), 23
  Kursk disaster (2000), 137
  liminal warfare, 29–30, 119–20, 150–64,
   175–76, 210–11, 223
  Litvinenko poisoning (2006), 125, 154
  Malaysian Airlines Flight MH17 shootdown
   (2014), 2, 5, 125, 154, 244–45
  military evolution, 128–30
  Montenegro, relations with, 5, 123
  NATO, relations with 21–22, 23, 24, 116–17,
   119, 125–28, 132–34, 138–39, 142–43,
   148–49, 185–86
  New Look modernization program (2008–12),
   148–50, 161, 221–22
  Norway, relations with, 115–19, 120–22,
   139, 149–50, 154, 226
  nuclear weapons, 21–22, 132,
   138–40, 148–49
  Orthodox Christianity, 135
  privatization of defense industry, 132, 137
  shock therapy, 20–21, 128–30
  Skripal poisoning (2018), 125, 154
  Spetsnaz, 117, 125, 134, 144
  Syria, relations with, 2, 3, 110, 136–37, 139,
   154–55, 156–57, 159, 221–22, 232
  Ukraine, relations with, *see under* Ukraine
  US elections, interference in, 123–24,
   154–55, 156–57, 159, 160, 210–11, 224,
   226–27, 234–35
  VDV (*Vozdushno-Desantnye Voyska*), 117,
   125, 144, 146–47
  Vostok-18 exercise (2018), 139
  Wagner Group, 244–45
  Zapad-17 exercise (2017), 139
  Zimbabwe, relations with, 207–8
Russian Revolution (1917), 141
Russian World, 135

Rwanda, 11–12
Ryukyu Archipelago, 174

S-400 sur air missiles, 117
Saakashvili, Mikheil, 142–44, 145
Sachs, Jeffrey, 128–29
al-Sadr, Muqtada, 101
al-Sadr, Musa, 101, 103, 111
Sagarin, Rafe, 23
as-Sahab, 62
Saif al-Adel, 84, 85, 86
Saipan, 174, 197
Salafi jihadism, 13, 14, 15
San Diego, California, 167–68
Sarkis, Elias, 101–2
Sasser, James, 187
Saudi Arabia, 2, 98, 233
    Gulf War I (1990–91), 28, 29
    al-Qaeda in, 85, 87
Schröder, Gerhard, 22
Scotland, 169–70
Scud missiles, 29, 33–34
Seahawk helicopters, 167–68
Second Intifada (2000–5), 107–8
Second Taiwan Strait Crisis (1958), 192
Second World War (1939–45), 88, 117–18,
        120, 128, 133–34, 135–36, 170–71, 179
selection-destruction cycle, 41–42, 50
selective pressure, 14–15, 39, 40, 41, 43, 48–53,
        54, 66–67, 68, 70–71, 82, 228
    China and, 178–79
    Hezbollah and, 108
    Islamic State and, 59
    Israel and, 57–58, 108
    predation models, 54
    Russia and, 136, 137, 164
    Tehrik-e Taliban Pakistan and, 56–57
Senegal, 99–100
Senkaku Islands, 174, 212–13
September 11 attacks (2001), 5–6, 13, 14–16,
        63, 85–86, 91, 188, 193–94
    Authorization for the Use of Military Force
        (2001), 16
    China and, 193–94, 202–3, 208–9
    as 'expeditionary terrorism', 88
    SIGINT and, 76
Serbia, 21–22, 132–33, 185–88
Serdyukov, Anatoly, 148
Serong, Francis Philip 'Ted', 245–46
Severomorsk, Murmansk, 117

al-Shabaab, 89, 92–93
Shalom, Avraham, 58, 219–20
Shandong Landbridge Group, 170–71
Shanghai, China, 174
shaping operations, 120–21, 160–61, 163–64
Shaposhnikov, Yevgeny, 131–32
Sheb'aa farms, 108
shemagh scarfs, 38, 44–45
Shevardnadze, Eduard, 141
Shi'a Islam
    in Iraq, 58, 59–60, 93–94, 96–97
    in Lebanon, 14, 99, 100–4, 111
Shin Bet, 58
Shinkai al-Najdi, 60–61
shock therapy, 20–21, 128–30
Short-Range Air Defense, 69
Shoygu, Sergey, 23
side-principal rule, 209–10, 223–24
Sidon, Lebanon, 109–10
Sierra Leone, 11–12
signals intelligence (SIGINT), 75–78, 105,
        218–19, 226, 245
Singapore, 236
Sino–Indian War (1962), 24–25
Sino–Japanese War (1894–5), 177
Sino–Vietnamese War (1979), 24–25,
        177, 179–82
Skeen, Andrew, 46
Skripal, Sergei, 125, 154
Skype, 77, 79
Slovakia, 133
Slovenia, 22, 133
smart systems, 49, 63–64, 75–76, 78–82
smartphones, 63–64, 75–76, 78, 79–80, 207–8
Snapchat, 63–64
Snowden, Edward, 76
social cycle theory, 228
social learning, 42–46
social media, 49, 60–61, 63–64, 68, 77–78, 154,
        155, 202–3
    Islamic State and, 4, 91
    al-Qaeda and, 60–61, 91
    remote radicalization, 89
    Russia and, 119–20, 150–51, 154,
        155, 221–22
Somalia, 10, 11–12, 36, 75, 84, 85, 220–21
Somaliland, 173
songun, 32
Sons of Iraq, 58, 59–60
Soros, George, 212–13, 224

South China Sea, 2, 5–6, 170–71, 194–95, 198–200, 212–13, 222
South Korea, 32, 33–34, 236–37
South Ossetia, 141–44, 145–47, 160
South Sudan, 173–74
Soviet Union (1922–91), 3, 4, 9–10, 97
   Afghanistan War (1979–89), 19–20, 98
   collapse of (1989–91), 9–10, 20–21, 25, 126–28, 133, 141–42
   Georgian SSR (1922–91), 141
   Great Purge (1936–8), 179
   Group of Soviet Forces Germany (GSFG), 128
   long telegram (1946), 133–34
   North Korea, relations with, 31–32, 33–34
   propaganda in, 156, 157
   reflexive control, 156
   Second World War (1939–45), 120, 128, 179
   Warsaw Pact, 69–70, 80, 126–27, 128, 133
Sovremenny class destroyers, 195
Space and Naval Warfare Systems Command, 167–68
Spain
   Basque separatism, 14
   Catalan separatism, 5, 123
   Hezbollah in, 106
   Madrid train bombing (2004), 92–93, 104
   Noatum Port Holdings, 172–73
   Russia mafia in, 125
special forces, 41–42
Special Operations Command (SOCOM), 135–36
Spencer, Herbert, 228
Spengler, Oswald, 227–28, 229
Spetsnaz, 117, 125, 134, 144
Spratly Islands, 177, 192, 198–99
Sri Lanka, 2, 98, 174, 213–14
SSBNs, 195, 199–200
Stalin, Josef, 31–32, 94, 97, 133–34, 141, 177–79
State Department, 170
Steele Dossier (2016), 123
Stellar Wind, 76
Stoltenberg, Jens, 233–34
Stone, Oliver, 213
Storskog, Norway, 118–19
Straits of Hormuz, 30–31
Straw, Jack, 22
Strelkov, Igor, 134

stress, 41–42
Subi reef, Spratly Islands, 198–99
Submarine Squadron 11, US, 167–68
Sudan, 85, 173–74
suicide bombings, 105
Suicide of the West (Goldberg), 227
surveillance, 75–78
Sweden, 99–100, 123, 172–73
Syria, 2, 3, 161–62, 226–27, 232–33
   Battle of Raqqa (2017), 49
   Ghouta nerve agent attack (2013), 3
   Google Earth, use in, 79–80
   Hayat Tahrir al-Sham (HTS), 83, 96–98, 112
   Hezbollah, relations with, 104, 106, 108, 109–10, 112
   Iran, relations with, 2–3, 110, 225
   Islamic State in, 7–8, 36, 70–71, 94, 95, 109–10, 247–48
   Jabhat an-Nusrah, 94, 96
   Jaysh al-Sha'abi, 110
   al-Qaeda in, 85
   Revolution (2011), 79, 94
   Russia, relations with, 2, 3, 110, 136–37, 139, 154–55, 156–57, 159, 221–22, 232
system of systems, 26, 202–3

T-80 tanks, 118–19
Tai Ping Rebellion (1850–71), 190
Taiwan, 172–73, 177, 189, 196–97, 236
   Chinese expedition (1875), 190
   Japanese invasion (1874), 190
   South China Sea dispute, 198
   Strait Crisis I (1954–5), 177, 192
   Strait Crisis II (1958), 192
   Strait Crisis III (1995–6), 193–94, 195, 196–97, 198, 200–1
Taliban, 46–47, 60, 86
Tallinn, Estonia, 118, 145
Tamil Tigers, *see* Liberation Tigers of Tamil Eelam
Tawakalna Division, 19
Tehrik-e Taliban Pakistan (TTP), 55–57
Telegram, 63–64
terrorism, 13–16, 36
   expeditionary terrorism, 88
   global war on terrorism (GWOT), 12, 14–15
   guerrilla terrorism, 88–89
   Iranian sponsorship of, 30–31
   National Security Strategy (2002), 13, 14, 15, 16
   Salafi jihadism, 13, 14, 15

Theodore Roosevelt, USS, 167–68
thermobaric explosives, 20, 241–42
Third Taiwan Strait Crisis (1995–6), 193–94, 195, 196–97, 198
Threads, 73
Threats without Enemies (Prins), 12
Three Warfares, 26, 211, 213–14, 222–23
three world systems, 212
Tiananmen Square massacre (1989), 24–25, 184
Tibet, 173
Tirah Valley, FATA, 55, 86
Titan Rain offensive (2003–6), 211
Toomey, Dave, 218
Tora Bora, Afghanistan, 55, 86–87
Townsville, Queensland, 172
Toynbee, Arnold, 227–28, 229
Treasury, 170
Treaty on Conventional Armed Forces in Europe (1990), 9–10
tribal hierarchies, 17–18
Tripoli, Lebanon, 109–10
Trotsky, Leon, 94, 97
Trump, Donald, 5, 59–60, 123–24, 224–25, 233–35, 239–40
Tskhinvali, South Ossetia, 143–44, 147–48
Tucker, Herbert, 69
al-Turabi, Hassan, 85
Turkey, 2
Twitter, 63–64

al-Udeid, Qatar, 218
Ukraine, 2, 5, 36
    Avdiivka offensive (2017), 154–55, 156–57, 159
    Black Sea Fleet dispute, 131–32
    China, relations with, 196
    Crimea annexed by Russia (2014), 2, 5, 121–22, 125, 161, 226–27, 232
    Malaysian Airlines Flight MH-17 shootdown (2014), 2, 5, 125, 154, 244–45
    nuclear weapons in, 132
    Revolution (2014), 212–13
    Russian invasion (2014), 2, 5, 136–37, 221–22
    smart systems, use of, 80
    United States, relations with, 212–13, 234
unconscious selection, 53–54
United Arab Emirates, 28, 173–74, 236–37
United Kingdom, 225–26, 235, 236–37

Crimean War (1853–6), 133–34
Brexit (2016–), 5, 123, 226–27, 239–40
Faslane naval base, 169–70
First World War (1914–18), 135–36
Indian Empire (1858–1947), 42–44, 46, 52
    liminal warfare and, 151–52
Litvinenko poisoning (2006), 125, 154
London 7/7 bombings (2005), 89, 90, 92–93
modernization of army (1870s), 135–36
Norway, troops in, 116–17
Opium Wars (1839–60), 190
Rosslea Hall Hotel sale (2018), 169–70
Royal Navy, 169–70
Second World War (1939–45), 120
Skripal poisoning (2018), 125, 154
tank warfare, invention of (1916), 135–36
United Nations, 34, 46–47, 101, 132–33, 187, 212, 236
United States, 2, 229–50
    Afghanistan War (2001–14), *see* Afghanistan War
    African US embassy bombings (1998), 85
    Agreed Framework (1994) 34–35
    Aspin-Brown inquiry (1994), 75
    Atoms for Peace program, 30
    Authorization for the Use of Military Force (2001), 16
    'Axis of Evil' speech (2002), 34–35
    Belgrade Chinese embassy bombing (1999), 132–33, 185–88, 193, 222
    Benghazi attack (2012), 2–3
    Camp Lemonnier, Djibouti, 173–74
    Central Intelligence Agency (CIA), *see* Central Intelligence Agency
    Civil War (1861–5), 216–17
    Committee on Foreign Investment in the United States (CFIUS), 170
    Defense Department, 170
    Desert One disaster (1980), 135–36
    Dora Farms strike (2003), 217–20, 230
    drone warfare, 55–57, 220–21
    dual containment strategy, 29
    Fort Hood shooting (2009), 90
    gold standard abandonment (1971), 212
    Gulf War I (1990–91), *see* Gulf War I
    Gulf War II (2003–11), *see* Gulf War II
    Hainan Island incident (2001), 188, 193–94
    Helsinki summit (2018), 234–35
    Homeland Security, 170

United States (*cont.*)
Iran hostage crisis (1979–81), 28, 135–36
Iran–Iraq War (1980–88), 28
Joint Comprehensive Plan of Action (2015), 2–3
Joint Special Operations Command (JSOC), 23
Korean War (1950–53), 33, 69, 198
Kosovo intervention (1999), 22, 132–33, 185–88, 212–13, 224
Lebanese diaspora in, 99–100
Lebanon intervention (1982–4), 73–74, 101, 104
long telegram (1946), 133–34
Marine Corps, 17, 116–17, 170–71, 174
midterm elections (2018), 123
Mueller report (2019), 123, 124, 156–57
National Academy of Sciences, 81
National Defense Strategy, 208–9
National Security Agency (NSA), 76
National Security Council, 170
National Security Strategy, 13, 14, 15, 16
Navy, 167–68, 170, 172–73, 174, 193
neoconservatives, 30–31
Norway, troops in, 116–17
presidential election (2016), 123–24, 154–55, 156–57, 159, 160, 210–11, 224, 226–27, 231, 234–35, 239–40
Quadrennial Defense Review, 208–9
Russian elections, interference in, 130
Second World War (1941–45), 170–71
Short-Range Air Defense, 69
Snowden leaks (2013), 76
Somalia intervention (1992–3), 10, 11–12, 75, 84
South Korea, relations with, 33, 34
Special Operations Command (SOCOM), 135–36
State Department, 170
Steele Dossier (2016), 123
Stellar Wind affair (2004), 76
system of systems, 26, 202–3
Taiwan Strait Crisis III (1995–6), 193–94, 196–97
Tehrik-e Taliban Pakistan, conflict with, 55–57
Treasury, 170
Ukraine, relations with, 212–13, 234
USS *Cole* attack (2000), 85
Vietnam War (1955–75), 9–10, 40–41, 47–48, 69–70, 73–74

University of Defense, China, 211–12
Unrestricted Warfare (Qiao and Wang), 200–14, 218, 222–24, 244–45
Upper Khyber Agency, FATA, 55
useful idiots, 149–50
USS *Cole* attack (2000), 85

Vanguard-class submarines, 169–70
variation, 44, 46, 49–50
VDV (*Vozdushno-Desantnye Voyska*), 117, 125, 144, 146–47
Vemork, Norway, 120
Venezuela, 2, 36, 239–40, 244–45
vertical escalation, 175–76
Victory Front, 94
Vietnam
American War (1955–75), 9–10, 40–41, 47–48, 69–70, 73–74, 245–46
Cambodian War (1978–89), 180–81
Chinese War (1979), 24–25, 177, 179–82
Johnson South Reef Skirmish (1988), 177
Paracel Islands conflict (1974), 177, 192, 198–99
South China Sea dispute, 177, 198
Vostok-18 exercise (2018), 139

Wagner Group, 244–45
Waldron, Arthur, 26
Walsh, William, 69
Walt, Stephen, 233
Wang Wei, 188
Wang Xiangsui, 200–10, 211–12, 218, 223, 244–45
War Beyond Rules (Qiao and Wang), 200–14, 218, 222–24, 244–45
Warsaw Pact, 69–70, 80, 126–27, 128, 133
Watts, Barry, 62–63
weapons of mass destruction (WMD), 10–11, 20, 35
Westerlund, Fredrik, 148
Westgate Mall attack (2013), 89
WhatsApp, 63–64
white supremacist groups, 90–91
Wikileaks, 76, 123, 160
Woody Island, Paracel Islands, 198–99
Woolsey, James, 9–11, 12, 18, 20–21, 24, 26, 36, 118–19, 164, 249
on failing states, 11, 132
on nonstate actors, 11, 132
on nuclear proliferation, 33
on 'snakes', 3, 10–11, 13, 32, 39, 52–53, 65, 66

World Trade Organization (WTO), 27, 212
World War I (1914–18), 133–34,
    135–36, 233–34
World War II (1939–45), 88, 117–18, 120, 128,
    133–34, 135–36, 170–71, 179
world-island, 134–35

Xi Jinping, 185, 224–25
Xu Shiyou, 181, 182

Yeltsin, Boris, 21–22, 127, 129–30, 131, 137–38
Yemen, 2–3, 36
    drone warfare in, 220–21
    al-Qaeda in, 85, 87, 90, 92–93, 94
    Revolution (2011), 94
Yongbyon, North Korea, 33
YouTube, 63–64

Yugoslavia (1918–92), 10, 21–22, 88,
    132–33, 142–43
Yulin-East, Hainan, 200
Yuzhao-class assault ship, 196

Zaidan, Mohammed Salah al-Din, 84, 85, 86
Zakaria, Fareed, 226–27
Zapad-17 exercise (2017), 139
al-Zarqawi, Abu Musab, 92–93, 98–99
al-Zawahiri, Ayman, 84, 87–88, 92
Zeebrugge, Belgium, 172–73
Zhao Ziyang, 184
Zheng He, 190
Zimbabwe, 207–8, 211
Zone novels (Rouch), 73
Zubr-class craft, 196
Zyuganov, Gennady, 130